FASHION AND EVERYDAY LIFE

FASHION AND EVERYDAY LIFE

London and New York

CHERYL BUCKLEY AND HAZEL CLARK

Bloomsbury Academic
An imprint of Bloomsbury Publishing Plc

B L O O M S B U R Y
LONDON · OXFORD · NEW YORK · NEW DELHI · SYDNEY

Bloomsbury Academic

An imprint of Bloomsbury Publishing Plc

50 Bedford Square	1385 Broadway
London	New York
WC1B 3DP	NY 10018
UK	USA

www.bloomsbury.com

BLOOMSBURY and the Diana logo are trademarks of Bloomsbury Publishing Plc

First published 2017

British Library Cataloguing-in-Publication Data

A catalogue record for this book is available from the British Library.

ISBN:	HB:	978-1-8478-8827-3
	PB:	978-1-8478-8826-6
	ePDF:	978-1-8478-8959-1
	ePub:	978-1-4742-7312-1

Library of Congress Cataloging-in-Publication Data

Buckley, Cheryl, 1956- author. | Clark, Hazel, author.
Title: Fashion and everyday life / Cheryl Buckley and Hazel Clark.
Description: London ; New York, NY : Bloomsbury Academic, an imprint of Bloomsbury Publishing, Plc, [2017] | Includes bibliographical references.
Identifiers: LCCN 2016029744| ISBN 9781847888266 (pbk.) | ISBN 9781847888273 (hardback) | ISBN 9781847889591 (ePDF) | ISBN 9781474273121 (ePub)
Subjects: LCSH: Clothing and dress–Social aspects–England–London–History–20th century. | Clothing and dress–Social aspects–New York (State)–New York–History–20th century. | Fashion–Social aspects–England–London–History–20th century. | Fashion–Social aspects–New York (State)–New York–History–20th century. | City and town life–England–London–History–20th century. | City and town life–New York (State)–New York–History–20th century.
Classification: LCC GT525 .B83 2017 | DDC 391.009421/0904–dc23
LC record available at https://lccn.loc.gov/2016029744

Cover design: Sharon Mah
Cover image © Museum of Modern Art/Licensed by SCALA/Art Resource, NY

Typeset by Integra Software Services Pvt. Ltd.
Printed and bound in Great Britain

For our parents,

June Buckley and Derrick Buckley

Christina Clark and Kenneth H Clark

CONTENTS

LIST OF FIGURES

ACKNOWLEDGEMENTS

Our sincere thanks to all those who have helped with this book, both in substantial and modest ways. These include friends and colleagues at our respective academic institutions, the University of Brighton and the University of Northumbria in the UK, and Parsons School of Design, The New School, New York, as well as colleagues who we met at conferences and through our subject networks and associations. Equally important were the numerous colleagues in museums, archives and the fashion business including Sally-Anne Huxtable, Gillian Robinson, Joanna Hashagen, Elizabeth Selby, Beatrice Behlen, M. Faye Prior and Tony Goldstein. A research fellowship from the Arts and Humanities Research Council in the UK was pivotal to the project's fruition as was the funding from the University of Brighton and Parsons School of Design for photographs. The latter also provided support to enable the valuable assistance of graduate student researchers throughout the years it took for this project to come to fruition. From MA Fashion Studies special thanks to Laura Beltran-Rubio, as well as to Erica Chapman, Lauren Downing Peters, Alessandro Esculapio, Maeve Kelly, Anya Kurennaya, Julie Mahdavi, Laura Peach, Lauren Sagadore, and also to PhD Philosophy candidate DS Mattison. We also appreciate the support, professionalism and good counsel from the team at Bloomsbury, in particular Anna Wright, Hannah Crump and Pari Thomson.

Finally thanks are due to our families: Clive, Jacob, Allan, Kate, Tom and Anna who provided a constant point of reference, sorted out technical glitches, made cups of tea, and generally helped us get to the end.

INTRODUCTION

This book aims to establish a new critical framework for the study of fashion and its history by examining its role in urban everyday life from the late nineteenth century to the early twenty-first century. In doing so, it recognizes how both 'fashion' and 'everyday life' are somewhat troubled terms: their definitions fluid and changing across the period under consideration. 'Everyday life' can refer to the experiential, and to synchronicity, as 'everyday experience is what happens in typical form today as it has done yesterday and will do tomorrow'; what constitutes everyday life also changes according to time and place.[1] The changes can be subtle and often go unnoticed, and unless they are consciously brought into view they can be overlooked or derided as being too 'ordinary'. Yet the 'ordinary' is an important component of the everyday, which must be investigated pragmatically through the vehicle of lived human experience, and through things or usable products. We propose in this book that fashion is an (increasingly) integral part of everyday life in the long twentieth century. Fashion had an impact on the everyday lives of more people as the century progressed, through improved buying power, greater availability, increased knowledge and the lower prices of goods, particularly those that clothed the human body. Fashion, as visual spectacle and material object, also offered the potential for the extraordinary to occur in the context of the everyday, thus enabling transformations in appearance and identities.

As we will demonstrate, the role of fashion in everyday life is not just determined by the 'fashion system', which evolved as a gradually more global and commodity-driven set of processes. Fashion must also be recognized as a cultural phenomenon that facilitates embodied identity, in other words, how individuals and groups of people present themselves in and for the world. Fashion parallels everyday life in creating, visually, materially and in writing 'a reality readily available for scrutiny'.[2] It is that reality which this book explores, as well as aspects of fashion that typically have been hidden or obscured. 'Hidden' in a number of ways, including what has not yet been researched, which has been overlooked as being too mundane or ordinary, as well as the less apparent aspects of fashion, including the daily work of ordinary people in its creation, production, consumption and use. Doing this facilitates a re-focusing of fashion discourse away from the well-trodden and power-laden dynamics, towards a re-evaluation of time, memory and, above all, history, and their relationships to fashion and everyday life. Emphasizing the importance of place and space provides the broader framework for the book, as well as issues of gender, race and social class. Across the long twentieth century, fashion contributed to an imaginary world, captured by still and moving image and in text, as well as in its material form as clothes worn by real people. While our focus is more on the role of fashion in the lives of women, we acknowledge the relationship of men to fashion in everyday life as being an area still in need of greater investigation and understanding (Breward; Cole; Edwards; McNeil and Karaminas). Ours is a story of fashion constructed through usable things and social relations, uncovered in two of the world's major urban centres: London and New York.

Conceptualizing fashion in everyday life

In this book, we want to consider some of the spaces and places in which fashion as everyday has been constituted in London and New York particularly with regard to the production of clothing, looks, styles, and to examine how these have also been constitutive of both as fashion cities. In revealing the complexity of fashion in the modern period, recent historians and theorists have examined fashion beyond specific designs, collections or garments, as a myriad of related cultural practices involving representation, promotion, performance and embodiment (Craik; Entwistle). Recognizing the diverse ways in which fashion intersects with everyday life, Elizabeth Wilson wrote of fashion 'as one of the most immediate and everyday cultural manifestations and one which we neglect at our peril'.[3] In such a context, fashion has been 'a technique of acculturation … and [g]iven the local character of fashion milieux, it is subject to different codes of behaviour and rules of ceremony and social position'.[4] In a similar vein, when discussing fashion practices outside such large centres as well as on their peripheral streets, Gilbert suggested that the inhabitants of provincial cities and marginal areas may be fluent in the 'Esperanto of high fashion', but that this is mixed with 'a local dialect of (often affordable) street labels and locally derived brands'.[5] Such ideas have particular worth for understanding fashion as part of everyday life in London and New York.

Space/place

In discussing the historiography of urban change, Mort and Ogborn proposed that space and place have been understood as largely constituted by, but not constitutive of, historical processes. With London as their example, they argued 'urban social historians have not viewed the geography of London as an active agent in the processes of modern historical change'.[6] Acknowledging that these accounts have offered enviable detail that has allowed a conception of 'the modern metropolis as a social totality, capable of analysis as a complex entity', recent work by cultural historians and historical geographers has taken a micro-history approach examining 'specific streets and thoroughfares, monuments, buildings, and even distinctive interiors'.[7] In these histories, London's geographies 'become the active sites for examining the competing uses, social meanings, and power relations that have structured the development of the city'.[8] In light of this, both London and New York were not simply 'World Fashion Cities' of the first order contingent upon a handful of special events, places and subjects, but also a series of historical landscapes and particular places and spaces in which fashion and its associated 'cultures' are axiomatically part of everyday lives that have been ordinary. Several historians have already begun to map the shifting geographies of London fashion in particular (Breward; Gilbert; Rappaport; Edwards; Ashmore) but, in doing this, they have mainly considered Fashion (in the upper case): major brands, iconic department stores, pre-eminent streets and designers. A similar process has yet to take place in terms of New York's fashion geographies as what has been published concentrates mostly on design (Rennolds Millbank; Arnold; Stanfill) and on specific features of clothing production (Goldstein and Greenberg; Rantisi; Moon).

Both London and New York were unquestionably 'World Cities', but there is a particularity and diversity about both cities that is perhaps distinctive. They are a different kind of fashion capital, 'not [only] the source of authoritative edicts on "the look" ... but a place where high fashion reinvigorates and renews itself, as it bumps up against the rawness of the real city'.[9] This 'rawness' draws from everyday lives that are permeated by fashion not only in the elite 'front regions' of the city 'where it was displayed, purchased and worn, but also in the "back regions" where it was made, finished and often copied'.[10] We owe to Goffman this conception of the 'front' and 'back' regions in everyday life. And while fashion or dress was not part of his 'presentation of self in everyday life', his ideas are nevertheless of value in informing our thinking.[11] While the front and back regions are characteristic of fashion's world cities, Gilbert observed the overlapping geographies of these two that 'can produce unexpected crossings and blurrings of the boundaries between different social worlds'.[12] In recognizing this, we begin to write the everyday into the fashion histories of these important cities. Also, rather than the binaries of 'high' and 'low' fashion or the 'front' and 'back' regions, by looking at the trajectories of fashion in everyday life, it is possible to explore the fault lines or intersections of ordinary fashion with ongoing lives. Perhaps due to the very nature of fashion, these ordinary narratives of fashion will 'cross' over and rub up against fashion's extraordinary cultures, particularly in the cities of London and New York.

Developing a critical framework for the study of fashion in everyday life in twentieth-century London and New York involves appraisal of the fashion system's over-emphasis on modernity by drawing on theories of everyday life.[13] In undertaking such a task, we utilize theories of everyday life so as to explore the routine elements of fashion. Integral to this is a re-consideration of the relationships between fashion and the modern world, and a re-thinking of the assumption that fashion is implicitly modern: symbolic and intrinsic to modernity. Prompted by new technologies, including the sewing machine, paper patterns, machine-made textiles, ready-to-wear systems, improved methods of distribution, dissemination and retailing, and shifting social and economic structures, fashionable dress permeated ordinary, everyday lives as never before in the period c.1900 to 2000.[14] Nonetheless, scholarship in fashion has tended to focus on the avant-garde, the extraordinary and the unusual. Indeed, within fashion's discourses, the truly 'ordinary' remains elusive. In part, this has been due to the positioning of fashion in relation to modernity by writers such as Thorstein Veblen, Charles Baudelaire and Georg Simmel;[15] as the latter put it, 'fashion increasingly sharpens our sense of the present'.[16] Indicative of modernity, it was to paraphrase Baudelaire: fashion's transitory, fugitive and contingent qualities, rather than its adaptability and longevity that attracted the interest of these early theorists of modern life. Aiming to unsettle these dominant views by understanding fashion as a manifestation of routine daily lives that remains with people over time, this book examines the ways in which the everyday use, appropriation, circulation, re-making and constant re-modelling of fashionable clothes over time by diverse social groups can be anti-modern and non-progressive; exemplify continuity and tradition; responsive to local, regional and national subtleties as well as global ones and disruptive of fashion's structures and systems as well as its visual codes and norms of consumption.

Fashion: Visual and material

Various writers and historians have touched upon aspects of fashion as part of day-to-day lives.[17] Some have reassessed fashion's multiplicity and the re-circulation of styles since the 1970s, while others have shown that one person's 'everyday' is part of another's fashion statement.[18] However, there remains a predominant interest in the fashion 'syntaxes' of the young, the novelty of the 'look', and the currency of the latest style – whether re-cycled, second-hand, revivalist, or new – without doubt an important part of what constitutes fashion; there still remains a vast swathe of fashionable dressing outside of these categories. This fashion – 'design in the lower case' – to quote Judy Attfield, comprises the ordinary and mundane practices of wearing that draws items from the personal wardrobe in a routine manner.[19] Accumulated over time, such fashion can encapsulate at least one lifetime particularly as clothes are handed down, recycled or re-modelled.[20] Writing about fashion as part of her study of celebrity, Pamela Church Gibson observed that it has been characterized by 'the two ends of the spectrum: high fashion on the one hand, street style and youth culture at their most confrontational on the other'.[21] In contrast, the ordinary is in the 'hinterlands beyond scholarship', where 'cheap, ubiquitous clothes which lack artistic merit of any kind are consigned … to the landfills'.[22] Significant here is Church Gibson's observation that particularly during the late twentieth and early twenty-first centuries the impact of celebrity culture had repercussions for what is meant by fashion; and the converse of this, for what constitutes the ordinary. But glamour and celebrity were not late twentieth-century inventions. As music hall stars, dancers and actresses dazzled on the stage and in the dance-halls, seduced us in the movies and intrigued us with their public personas and private lives from the late nineteenth century through the twentieth century, ordinary men and women interacted with these images of celebrity to a lesser or greater degree. At the same time, the fashion system (manufacturers, designers, journalists, retailers, magazines) played an important part in capturing and commercializing this. As Entwistle has noted, 'Different situations impose different ways of dressing, sometimes by imposing "rules" or codes of dress or sometimes simply through conventions that most people adhere to most of the time'.[23] Those conventions reference and also alter over time and in space, as social and cultural changes occur.

Gender/race/class and body

Considerations of gender, class and race are central to the study of fashion and everyday life, and take particular prominence in our period. The long twentieth century was a time of social struggle, which can be bracketed in many ways, for instance by women seeking human rights at the end of the late nineteenth century and by transgender people doing the same in the early twenty-first century. In between substantial social and cultural shifts occurred which challenged the location of power and created new narratives of gender, race, identity, sexuality, national identity, age and generation. Singly and together they impacted 'style-fashion-dress', an articulation coined by fashion scholar Carol Tulloch and highlighted by Kaiser in her discussion of fashion and cultural studies.[24] Kaiser also advocates an 'intersectional' approach to scholarship that recognizes that subject positions of race, class and gender are not independent in the lived experience of individuals or in the way that they choose to dress, style and fashion themselves.[25] We acknowledge and respect the particular and overlapping subjectivities, which were especially evident in the urban centres of London and New York, and we highlight them throughout the text at the historical moments when social change was taking place, such as the American civil rights movement, second-wave feminism and gay and lesbian rights in the 1960s. We do, nevertheless, focus our attention more on the everyday lives of women more than men, in London and New York during our period. In doing so, we also recognise the growing body of research and publications, which is expanding our knowledge, and understanding of menswear and the fashioning of masculinity.[26] Such developments also underpin Elizabeth Wilson's reminder that contemporary interest in fashion is consistent with the postmodern shift from an emphasis on knowledge to one on being, 'from knowledge to experience, from theory to practice, from mind to body'.[27]

The body must be acknowledged properly in the study of fashion and in particular in its everyday existence and experience. As Kaiser has stated succinctly, 'Fashion matters in everyday life; it becomes embodied'.[28] Joanne Entwistle noted how 'Understanding dress in everyday life requires understanding not just of how the body is represented within the fashion system and its discourses on dress, but also how the body is experienced and lived and the role dress plays in the presentation of the body/self'.[29] Entwistle's work has drawn on, among others, Foucault, Merleau-Ponty and Bourdieu. While not without criticism, such work highlights issues that are significant to fashion in everyday life. Foucault's *Discipline and Punish* (1977) charts the growth of surveillance, as well as different ways of disciplining the body, through actions or materials. Influenced by Merleau-Ponty's phenomenology, the importance is highlighted by the experience of the body, which is typically clothed and likely fashioned in the course of its day-to-day existence. Bourdieu assists with the conceptual framework for understanding fashion and dress as a situated practice for the body seen as a container of the self.[30] Entwistle too draws upon the work of Goffman, and highlights our own concern with location, being that, 'the spaces of the street, the office, the shopping mall, operate with different rules and determine how we present ourselves and how we react with others'.[31] Thus in everyday life in the extended twentieth-century London and New York, the body was not just dressed, but fashioned, in time and space.

The conceptual framework of this book then derives from ideas developed within fashion studies, and also draws upon the theories of everyday life articulated by social theorists and reinterpreted by subsequent writers. In the former category are Michel de Certeau, Henri Lefebvre and Walter Benjamin, while Ben Highmore, Barry Sandywell and Michael Sheringham have offered useful insights into the application of such ideas in a variety of domains.[32] Alongside this, in attempting to 'write the real', the book draws on the work of social, cultural and feminist historians such as E. P. Thompson, Sally Alexander and Carol Steedman, who have grappled with the everyday experiences, actions and habits of ordinary people.[33] Both Benjamin and Lefebvre were drawn to fashion as they explored the ordinary, mundane aspects of life, while De Certeau in studying the everyday exposed the 'instruments of analysis' that underpin specific disciplines.

Everyday life theories and fashion

In *Critique of Everyday Life*, Henri Lefebvre argued that everyday life is 'defined by "what is left over" after all distinct, superior, specialized, structured activities have been singled out for analysis'.[34] Fashion – as typically studied through the fashion system – has comprised the 'distinct, superior, specialized, and structured'. It is not 'what is left over'; rather it 'refers to regular (conventionally bi-annual) stylistic innovation, and a production system that is geared to making and distributing clothes'.[35] Nonetheless, everyday clothes as routinely worn by people in the West in the twentieth century reveal an ongoing engagement with fashion on a scale from extraordinary through to ordinary; indeed 'where the ordinary is exemplified by commonplace phenomena that are taken for granted and unnoticed, the extraordinary marks the disturbing eruption of the rare and the highly valued. Like other forms of *extravagant* experience, the extraordinary exceeds the limits and boundaries of ordinariness'.[36] While the extraordinariness of 'high fashion' has been clearly visible, 'ordinary' fashion has been resolutely invisible. Yet visual sources that depict people going about their daily routines show how they have interpreted fashion's cycles even if these were not always the latest nor articulated as a coherent 'look'. Such fashion was heterogeneous and represented a bringing together of familiar garments accumulated in closets and wardrobes over time. To these might be added something modern: a new coat or the latest hat, but most often they would remain ensembles of clothes acquired during a number of years. Arguably this complex relationship between everyday fashion and modernity was sharpened after 1970 by the impact of post-structuralist and post-modern discourses particularly the reassessment of modernism's progressive, technological agenda. Some theorists argued that the ordinary was representative of tradition; in effect, these were the mundane practices that 'predate the differentiated idioms of modernity'.[37] In this context, the ordinary was indicative of a pre-modern world, whereas in contrast, the extraordinary was what characterized modernity, representing the ordinary punctuated by 'the "effervescence" of social orders rendered fluid and mobile'.[38] Importantly, these terms, 'ordinary' and 'everyday', have different meanings that are usefully exposed when thinking of fashion. An item of clothing may have once been extraordinary or part of an ensemble that was extraordinary, but over time, regular use, or a changed context, it has become ordinary, or routine. Indeed, it might be argued that changes in fashion render the extraordinary, ordinary. In contrast, fashion that is everyday is embedded and undistinguishable: part of an ongoing repetition and routine that was never extraordinary. Instead it was resolutely and always ordinary in character. Nevertheless, writers have remained entranced by fashion that is extraordinary due to its technical and visual innovation, seasonal change, and its pivotal role in capturing the zeitgeist: 'of its time'.[39] Coupled with a zealous commitment to fashion's spectacular, though frequently transitory qualities, many writers cannot conceive of fashion as part of the everyday. Without ignoring these fundamental qualities of fashion and its historically close relationship to the wealthier sections of society (via one-off luxury items, couture and designer fashion), this book proposes that fashion can be ordinary as well as extraordinary, and it can be indicative of the everyday.

A central problematic of the everyday, the relationship between the latest styles, on the one hand, and tradition, on the other, is nevertheless intrinsic to it, as Sheringham argued: 'what sets the tone is without doubt the newest, but only where it emerges in the medium of the oldest, the longest past, the most ingrained'.[40] Observing that typically 'the everyday' is antithetical to the modern in that 'everyday experience is what happens in typical form today as it has done yesterday and will do tomorrow', some theorists of the everyday have proposed that in the first part of the twentieth century, there was a conjunction of modernity and everydayness around the notion of consumption.[41] Responding to this, Highmore proposed the notion of 'everyday modernity': 'Everyday life registers the process of modernization as an incessant accumulation of debris: modernity produces obsolescence as part of its continual demand for the new (the latest version becomes last year's model with increasing frequency)'.[42] From the beginning of the nineteenth century, with seasonal regularity, fashion complied with this regime; but typically these cyclical acquisitions were discarded only by those with the wealth or cultural capital to do so. Inspired in part by Baudelaire's observations about the crowd, Walter Benjamin saw the modern city as a place for 'increased accumulation and intensified sensation'.[43] This understanding of increased acquisition as a key feature of 'everyday modernity' is crucial for this discussion as the capacity to consume fashion grew exponentially as the twentieth century progressed. It is only in the last twenty years that the price accessibility of fashionable clothes in the West (the likes of Primark in Britain and Forever 21 in the United States) has enabled those on low incomes to regularly and routinely consume and discard clothing. Nevertheless, commonality, mass-experience and accelerated consumption developed as the twentieth century progressed, and fashion has played a key part in this: consider for example female mass magazine readership in the 1920s and 1930s, Hollywood cinema in the 1930s, men's magazines in the 1980s and 1990s, and internet shopping in the 2000s.[44] Equally, Benjamin's interest in sensation and the haptic experiences of the modern city pinpoints an 'everyday modernity' shaped by 'feel' and 'touch' as well as sight. Indeed if touch and feel were as much indicative of everyday modernity as seeing, consider the experience of wearing rayon (artificial everywoman's silk) in 1930s' London and New York.[45] In some ways, therefore, at the intersection of modernity and the everyday, mass-culture contributed to both the ordinariness and the extraordinariness of fashion.

In tracing fashion in everyday life, it may seem – as Highmore has argued – that what is everyday might be perceived to be obvious, readily exposed by searching out alternative sources (diaries, letters, and photographs, rather than, for example, Government papers).[46] In fact, it can be stubbornly invisible, difficult to interpret and as Lefebvre observed, 'The *unrecognised,* that is, the everyday, still has some surprises in store for us'.[47] One, in particular, is that it is hard to know: 'either way, you somehow have missed it because the everyday passes by, passes through'.[48] The ordinary escapes notice because it fails to stand out; here again fashion provides an exemplar. The clothes worn by most people going about their daily lives have been typically a synthesis of new and old, bold and mundane. This perception that the everyday is hard to locate, difficult to know and outside of traditional fields of knowledge demands an alternative approach when dealing with a subject such as fashion so as to sidestep fashion's 'distinct, superior, specialized, structured activities'.[49] By looking beyond fashion's familiar terrain – the catwalk, the magazine, the boutique, the department store, the designer – a complementary fashion trajectory can be traced over the last hundred or so years. Indeed, we argue that fashion was embedded and contingent in the practices of people's daily lives, and it was located in some familiar spaces such as the street, although not only the major thoroughfares of the modern city but also its margins and back streets. It took shape in some intimate places: the wardrobe or the sewing box as well as in the rituals and commonplace social interactions of weddings, going out on the town or to the dance.

While Gilbert has noted the symbolic ordering of cities such as Paris, New York and London by the fashion system, and the conjunction of designer names, famous brands and specific districts to create the identity of fashion's world cities, he also pointed to the city as a place of 'local taste constellations' based around fashion, music, dance and clubs, but also family and work activities and events.[50] It is in these other city spaces – interstitial and peripheral to the city's traditional fashion centres – that fashion in everyday life can be observed. These places were not only for the young; indeed one of the book's aims is to question the generational, market-driven myth of fashion.

In *The Practice of Everyday Life,* Michel de Certeau proposed everyday life as a set of practices that, although established, offer the potential for creativity. As well as 'making do' with this everyday culture, people have also been 'making with' it: transforming and inventing by appropriating and re-deploying; as he put it, 'Creativity is the act of reusing and recombining heterogeneous materials'.[51] Characteristic of self-fashioning and re-fashioning, this articulation of the everyday also recognizes the possibility of reinvention and resistance as the fashion system is refused, re-cycled and re-defined from within the realm of the everyday. At various points in the twentieth century, women re-cut and re-made existing clothes for a variety of purposes including fashionability. Some groups of people – teenagers being an obvious example – refused fashion *per se* to create their own 'identities' in opposition to an increasingly homogeneous consumer marketplace, while in parallel the fashion system appropriated and re-defined the ordinary as extraordinary with the annexing of sub-cultural street styles. This dialectical relationship between the past and the present was observed by Benjamin: 'Each time, what sets the tone is without doubt the newest, but only where it emerges in the medium of the oldest, the longest past, and the most ingrained. This spectacle, the unique self-construction of the newest in the medium of what has been, makes for the true dialectical theatre of fashion'.[52]

Two cities: London and New York

Making, selling and wearing fashionable clothes has been a vital constituent of London and New York's self-styling from the nineteenth through the twentieth centuries. As discourse, materiality and embodiment, fashion has been intrinsic to the identities of both as centres of modern metropolitan life and as the resort of the wealthy, but it has also been part of the everyday lives of their inhabitants. Fashion was flexible in its production and organization, heterogeneous as a commodity, and both cities functioned as a 'factory' and as a shop window.[53] In London and New York, the 'factory' was complex and diverse. It comprised the early tailoring trade that was dominated by skilled men; the ready-made clothing businesses established and run by immigrants and semi-skilled female outworkers in their homes and small workshops in the East End of London and the Lower East Side of Manhattan; and the up-market tailors, dress-makers and couturiers of London's West End and Manhattan's midtown. Dependent upon market and quality, fashion was also sold on London and New York's finest streets. In London's centre: Piccadilly, Regent St, Grosvenor Square and Bond St, and in its emergent suburbs: Bayswater, Kensington and Ealing, as well as in the small workshops, retail outlets and street markets in the predominantly working-class districts of Shoreditch, Spitalfields and Whitechapel. Fashion's developing geography can also be traced on New York's streets – from the street vendors on Hester Street on the Lower East Side to the department stores and specialist shops on Broadway, then up to the Ladies Mile, and finally to the grand retail edifices on Fifth Avenue. Fashion traversed London and New York's streets as it was not only made and sold but also worn by the diverse populations. Ostensibly the domain of the wealthy, it nevertheless circulated through all spheres of society as its visual styles and material qualities were recognized, understood and deployed by the society hostess, the housewife, the man about town, the shop girl, the seamstress, the office clerk, the immigrant and the servant. Though rapid and continual change helped to constitute fashion in these modern cities, it was nevertheless implicit and ongoing in everyday lives. Allowing the individual both 'to stand out and to merge with the crowd, to lay claim to the exclusive and to follow the herd',[54] fashion as part of everyday, personal narratives was intrinsic to the complex discourses of the modern city as it constantly formed and reformed due to the shifting social formations: class, race, migration, gender, sexuality, generation and place. Focusing on London and New York in the long twentieth century, this book offers a sketch of two cities by using fashion to 'trace the interlacings of a concrete sense of everyday life'.[55] The embodied ordinariness and everydayness of fashion is what preoccupies us; neither wilfully 'unfashionable' nor obsessively 'in' fashion, but rather fashion as seen in day-to-day lives, on the street, but not only as 'street style'. Typically fashion as a discourse of the exceptional has contributed to the elision of the everyday from memory as it privileges discreet modes of representation, particular historical moments and specific geographies: high-end magazines, the fashion shoot, and established shopping routes and districts. This focus on a handful of exceptional fashionable performances, sites and celebrities (models, designers, and consumers) has eclipsed the enormity, permeability and quotidian nature of fashion in these two metropolitan centres in the twentieth century. In order to map the apparent interlacing of fashion in everyday life in London and New York, we identify some of the qualities of these two cities and try to pinpoint the reasons for their comparative fashion geographies.

London

By 1900, London was unquestionably 'the richest, largest, most populous city' that the world had ever seen; an imperial city, 'immense … vast … endless'.[56] Drawing a comparison with his home city, the New Yorker W. D. Howells wrote in 1905,

> we have as yet nothing to compare with at least a half of London's magnificence … The sky-scrapers, Brooklyn Bridge, Madison Square Garden, and some vast rocketing hotels offer themselves rather shrinkingly for the contrast with those miles of imperial and municipal architecture which in London make you forget the leagues of mean little houses, and remember the palaces, the law-courts, the great private mansions, the dignified and shapely flats, the great department stores, the immense hotels, the bridges, the monuments of every kind.[57]

It was also a city shaped by its Empire and its economic prosperity, attracting immigration from former colonies and internal migration from Britain's regions. These latter migrants coming from across Britain, but particularly the south and east, were typically young and in search of work. They were supplemented by

Irish migrants from the 1840s and 1850s, by Eastern European Jews from the 1880s escaping persecution, by West Indians from the 1950s, and Indian and Pakistanis from Britain's former Empire in the 1960s, and Eastern European migrants from the 1990s. These groups settled in different districts of the city: Irish migrants in Holborn, Camden Town, Camberwell; Jewish immigrants in Whitechapel, Spitalfields; West Indian, Pakistani and Indian immigrants in Brixton, Haringey and Southall; and Eastern Europeans in the prosperous towns and cities of the south east.

In late Victorian London, two-thirds of the labour force worked in the service industries (distribution, exchange, banking, insurance, the professions and domestic service), and the remaining third worked in manufacturing: 'it was still wide in range, mainly handicraft in its structure, and for the most part based on small workshops and much domestic outwork; but large firms were important in such fields as printing, shipbuilding, or brewing'.[58] While half of London's female labour force worked in domestic service,[59] by the mid-1850s the East End districts of Stepney, Whitechapel, St. Georges-in-the-East and Bethnal Green employed half of the tailoresses in England and Wales.[60] During the first half of the twentieth century, the manufacturing jobs that had developed in inner London still remained; in the City, south of the river Thames, around the docks and in the East End. Typically poorly paid, casual or home workers, working-class women and Jewish immigrants from Russia and Eastern Europe worked in the East End garment trade. Some skilled Jews worked in West End tailoring often in small workshops producing high-quality suits and related goods that contributed to the reputation of London's West End. In the 1920s, for example, 66 per cent of businesses on Soho's Berwick St were owned by Jewish immigrants; these made hats and underwear, and sold materials and trimmings and furs.[61] Shifting over time, London's 'front and back regions' approximated with the West End and the East End at the start of the twentieth century. Arguing that this division originated in the separation of the court and its suburbs and the position of the ancient port of London below London Bridge, White commented: 'it was the Victorians who built the separation into a mystic divide between good and evil, civilisation and savagery. In between these two extremes was an infinity variegated identification of class or function with neighbourhoods, the distinctions so finely nuanced as to be almost invisible to the naked eye but real enough to Londoners all the same'.[62] By the end of twentieth century, the spatial geographies of fashion and everyday life in London had been repositioned several times, catapulted by wartime bombing, slum clearance, suburbanization, modernization and gentrification. With 'bourgeois frontiersmen' moving in to Chelsea and Hampstead from the 1920s, Pimlico and Marylebone after 1945, Camden, Paddington, Battersea, Lambeth, Camberwell and Islington from the 1960s and 1970s by the first years of the new twenty-first century, even the old East End was being rehabilitated: Shoreditch, Hoxton, Whitechapel, Spitalfields.[63]

In these areas and in the re-commercialized street markets – Portobello Road, Camden, Petticoat Lane, Brick Lane and Spitalfields – the dialectics of fashion and everyday life were repeatedly rehearsed. Street markets were particularly illustrative of this: in London, for example, Leather Lane, Berwick, Rye Lane, Watney Street, Portobello Road, Hoxton, and the Caledonian Market. At these 'women who are dressed by Hartnell and Schiaparelli have owned to buying their stockings in Berwick Market',[64] or similarly from the push cart vendors on Hester, Rivington and Orchard Street on Manhattan's Lower East Side in the early twentieth century. In New York and in London, these were also part of a distinctive 'Jewish economy [that] linked the Jewish tailors, the shopkeepers, the wholesalers, and the peddlers to each other'.[65]

New York

In New York too, the spatial geographies of fashion and the relationships of these to the patterns of everyday life were being transformed. Fashion made the city just as much as the city made fashion. From its origins, European Jewish immigrants on the Lower East Side of Manhattan in the nineteenth century played a pivotal role. Through the gradual move up the island to the midtown garment district during the first half of the twentieth century, the production of garments has been a mainstay of the city. But not only production; fashion information was generated from the midtown locations of fashion media giants such as Condé Nast, publishers of influential magazines including *Vogue* and *Vanity Fair*, and latterly the trade journal *Women's Wear Daily (WWD)*. For most of our period midtown was a major centre of fashion retailing in New York, where first department stores and later brand 'flagships' provide sources of fashion information, as well as items for consumption. In New York, fashion authority was not only construed through the channels of the fashion system, it was also generated within neighbourhoods, from the dress practices of communities and as elements of cultural practices and performances. Connections between fashion and music have been integral to the city's culture, from the fashionable clubs and speakeasies of Harlem during the 1920s and 1930s to Hip Hop in the 1980s. Fashion has also been performed on the streets, from the dress of the 'Matinee Girls' at the beginning of the twentieth century, through the gay marches of the 1970s, and the Hipsters of the twenty-first century. Fashion has been and continues to be closely associated with the performance of identity in this major city comprising a vast diversity of individuals, generations, cultures, ethnicities and races.

New York was also a city of immigrants, which developed substantially at the beginning of our period and continued to do so throughout the twentieth century and into the twenty-first century, a growth coupled with the city's rapid modernization. Immigrants, first from Eastern Europe, then Italy and Ireland, plying different trades and holding diverse belief systems and religions, Judaism and

Catholicism especially, came together and lived in close quarters. All negotiated, some willingly, others not, the complex task of 'becoming American'. Dress and fashion figured significantly in the process of acculturation and assimilation, confirming the way that individuals and groups of people present themselves externally and identifying them in time and place. The production, consumption and appearance of fashionable clothes play important roles in New York during the long twentieth century for function, show and as part of the imaginary of the burgeoning modern city. As immigrants occupied increasingly more of Manhattan and the outer boroughs, they both assimilated into American culture 'while establishing neighbourhoods and communities often based on race and ethnicity'.[66] Distinguishing themselves with their clothing choices, which often developed into hybridized forms such as the Zoot suit, West Indian immigrants moved to Harlem in large numbers in the 1920s,[67] while Italians became a political force in 1930s, when Jews were also coming to seek refuge from Nazi Germany. After the Second World War, Puerto Ricans formed the majority of a growing population from Latin America. In 1980, immigrants made up 24 per cent of the city's population, most having settled there after 1965. Many were employed in factories that formerly employed native-born workers, even after the decline of manufacturing in the 1970s. 'Dominicans and Chinese opened small factories or became sub-contractors in the garment industry, and as more labour was needed, shops and homework became common'.[68] Sweatshops returned in the 1970s and 1980s in areas such as Chinatown, which employed a large undocumented labour force, whose number declined drastically after 11 September 2001.[69]

Fashion: History and methods

If fashion is 'a kind of contemporary Esperanto, immediately accessible across social and geographical boundaries',[70] and also 'a technique of acculturation – a means by which individuals and groups learn to be visually at home with themselves in their culture', it both accelerated and proliferated during the twentieth century as various social groups (shaped by race, class, gender, age and geography) perpetually utilized and re-utilized fashion's past and present languages in their everyday lives.[71] Equally fashion can be both the 'overarching structure' that articulates an aesthetic or 'look' and an 'accumulation of particularity'.[72] By this, we mean that fashion as a practice of everyday life involves the acquisition of single garments that add to a wardrobe and help to reconfigure it, but at the same time, it can mean the purchase of a complete outfit that encapsulates 'a look'. Attempting to define fashion, Breward wrote:

> It is a bounded thing, fixed and experienced in space – an amalgamation of seams and textiles, an interface between the body and its environment. It is a

practice, a fulcrum for the display of taste and status, a site for the production and consumption of objects and beliefs; *and it is an event, both spectacular and routine, cyclical in its adherence to the natural and commercial seasons, innovatory in its bursts of avant-gardism, and sequential in its guise as a palimpsest of memories and traditions.*[73] (Our emphasis.)

In recognizing the routine as well as the spectacular, Breward also points to fashion as a site for the accumulated layers and traces of preceding looks. This is vital, as on close inspection, certain fashions have had a particular resilience and resistance over time; certain garments, shapes, fabrics and styles persist and are re-circulated and re-framed within different contexts. This can be unintentional: representing 'the unmanaged construction of the past in the present'.[74] But at the same time, in creating a 'look', fashion provided a means to 'go from one configuration of daily existence to another'.[75] This configuration can be and has been a subversive act that defines agency, it can be avowedly 'fashionable', 'of the time' and constructing 'a look' that refuses the everyday and it can be an 'accidental heterology' where the past coalesces with the present and strongly connects to the everyday.

Significantly, the study of fashion as part of routine, mundane life remains uneven; to be examined largely when the ordinary impinges upon the extraordinary, a good example is when fashion from the 'street' – influenced by popular cultures – impacts on designer-led fashion. In contrast, by probing fashion's multi-layered complexities, this book helps to unearth the 'never quite heard' or 'inner speech' of identity and everyday life that de Certeau tried to describe in *The Practice of Everyday Life*.[76] Indeed by examining fashion as a practice of everyday life, the networks of power and the repetitive practices that permeate fashion's broader discourses are thrown into sharp relief. In the final chapter of *The Practice of Everyday Life Vol 2,* de Certeau wrote: 'We know poorly the types of operations at stake in ordinary practices, their registers and their combinations, because our instruments of analysis, modelling and formalization were constructed for other objects and with other aims'.[77] Due to the proliferation of production, distribution, marketing and retailing, particularly after 1900 (initially in the West, but later globally), the impact of fashion on people's lives has been difficult for historians to ignore. Mass-production and mass-consumption meant that an array of goods – including clothes – were more visible, as a result of being made in factories, sold in retail stores, promoted and advertised in magazines, newspapers, at the cinema, on TV and the internet and worn by people on the street. In response, histories of fashion have been produced by writers from different but adjacent fields adding to the richness and complexity of discussion. By drawing on this work and that of key theorists, we aim to develop a robust critical framework that allows an interrogation of such ideas. Equally by deploying appropriate research methods, we can begin to explore fashion in everyday life.

Historical focus and theoretical priorities are interdependent with research methods. To study the ordinary, mundane practices of fashion requires a different set of procedures or methods than those that provide a 'single, superior point of view'.[78] Raphael Samuel described history as 'a social form of knowledge … the ensemble of activities and practices in which ideas of history are embedded or a dialectic of past-present relations rehearsed'.[79] This is exemplified by fashion. What people wore constituted an ongoing practice that rehearsed, among many things, the complexities of modernity and tradition, progress and stasis. One method that allows a focused discussion of these practices is the case study. Writing on histories of everyday life, John Brewer outlined two approaches: 'prospect history' so named because it looks down from above and surveys a broad scene, and 'refuge history', which is 'close-up and on the small scale'.[80] Those adopting this latter method look at 'place' not 'space'; they emphasize 'interiority and intimacy rather than surface and distance'.[81] In proposing histories that are focused and small-scale, and by critically examining historical meta-narratives, particularly those that privilege modernity and modernization, Brewer's ideas illuminate our study. Rejecting the prerogative of modernization that depends upon 'a single, linear progressive model of time against which all societies are measured', he draws on the work of social historians and micro-historians who have proposed that 'inexorable modernisation' has been univocal both in its exclusion of different voices and in its failure to recognize the contradictions and conflicts of modernization.[82] Such ideas have a bearing on this study by providing the theoretical and methodological tools that allow the reconceptualization of fashion's relationship to modernization; in particular, to question the assumption that the drive of modernity was progressive, consistent and pervasive. In so far as much of this design – in 'the lower case' – has remained 'hidden' in the domestic and private spheres, there is a parallel here with the work of feminist historians such as Sally Alexander and Sheila Rowbotham who mapped that which was 'hidden from history'.[83]

The methodological challenge then is to find the means to research those things, people and ideas that have remained unobserved, to locate and interpret the intimate, rather than to take a 'prospect' approach that delineates the surface and distance of fashion. The case study offers one such method that allows a consideration of fashion's everyday practices that can include dressing-up for one-off celebrations as well as routine activities. These reveal the way that fashion articulates particular moments in people's lives, representing life transitions – entering adulthood and marriage, for example, or highlighting corporate or professional affiliations, or familial responsibilities. Such events and celebrations have their own particular cultural codes, temporal and generational variations, which simultaneously cut across and acknowledge fashion. In a similar way, focusing on 'going out' allows us to examine the regular occasions that people participate in: going out clubbing, to the dance or to the cinema.

Fashion is powerfully visual: at its core is the desire to see and be seen, which has provided the means to lift people from the ordinary and everyday paradoxically via commonplace activities.

Using a case-study approach to explore the specific *practices* of fashion at key historical moments, we are keen to discern how people *practised* fashion; in effect how they performed socially constructed identities via fashion. Material culture and designed things such as clothes have often represented episodes and stages in individual lives. Explaining how 'gendered objects' can clarify one's thoughts (in this case about memory and bereavement), the design historian Pat Kirkham described how one particular black velvet coat, bought second-hand by her mother in the 1940s, was 'redolent of memories so powerful of the gutsy ways in which one woman negotiated enjoying life to the full, being glamorous, working in a factory, being a mother, holding to socialist and feminist principles and strong personal ethics, that wearing it almost makes her "real" and almost makes me her'.[84] Ilene Beckerman's *Love, Loss and What I Wore* attempted something similar, but in a popular format as she described different stages in her own and her family's life through particular ensembles of clothing.[85] Why are some things held onto and others thrown away, and how has a contemporary concern for sustainability impacted on personal wardrobes, on the preservation, repair and methods for the eventual disposal of items of clothing? By asking such questions we can remind ourselves that 'the past, like the present, is the result of negotiated *versions* of what happened, why it happened, with what consequence'.[86]

The sources of this study are visual, literary and material including everyday dress (collected by museum curators); family photographs that allow the archaeological excavation of aspects of everyday life within the family; documentary photographs that depict everyday life in the city (giving insights into the performance of everyday life within the public sphere); fashion and non-fashion specific journals, print media and fiction. Our study draws its methods from different disciplines (design history, social history, visual culture, urban studies and gender studies), but proposes a micro-history approach, based on archival investigation and visual and textual analysis.[87]

Archival research remains a valuable method for this study, but our interest is in archives that are less visible and informal as well as those already established. Utilizing archival sources that are more ephemeral – magazines, newspapers, catalogues and advertisements, film footage and photographic archives – we explore local libraries, archives and study centres in London and New York's districts and boroughs as well as those in their metropolitan cores. It is in these that we locate the stuff of everyday life, as museum curators and archivists have collected and acquired objects and photographs that speak to the particularities of place. Alert to 'memory's shadows – those sleeping images which spring to life unbidden, and serve as ghostly sentinels of our thought', Raphael Samuel proposed that historians take care to recognize the 'visual' which provides 'subliminal points of reference, our unspoken points of reference' particularly photographs and ephemeral graphic material.[88] As fashion and design historians, the visual and material is part of our stock in trade, but perhaps we have sustained a hierarchy of images and things that are held in the public domain, rather than those to be found in the routine places of everyday lives? In response to this, one of our research methods is the use of photographs of everyday life in the city. These proliferated particularly from the turn of the nineteenth century onwards with the growth of street photographers, the production of post-cards, and the greater availability of cheap cameras. Latterly personal glimpses of our teenage children captured by iPhone and posted on Facebook prompt some understanding of young men and women's ongoing engagement with fashion at the level of the everyday. The artifice of these self-images exposes the power of a specific 'look' or preferred way of being seen at a particular historical moment especially in the image-saturated domain of fashion. Drawing attention to the use of photographs as research tools, various writers have pointed to how photographs work in particular ways: in this study, they orchestrate space and place in the cities of London and New York, not only in the streets but also at home.[89] Many of the photographs that we have used actively 'produce' the city: reiterating particular sites, capturing specific streets, shops and markets, highlighting key landmark sites and buildings, and celebrating distinctive views and activities. Not only do they 'work' in a variety of ways, but they also do so for specific purposes. Mainly they depict people at leisure or posing in a 'staged' work context; few capture a whole workforce or those actively engaged in work. While some are posed, others record a passing moment as people walk, sit, talk or gaze in and around the city. Others, particularly those using social media (Instagram, Snapchat), will capture a moment – with friends, at an event, getting ready to go out. The representation of fashion and dress in these differs too, depending on the purpose of the photograph and who took it – amateur snap, professional street photograph, art photograph, official or semi-official document/record of an event, or a WhatsApp or iPhone photo. Indeed it is important to remember that the meaning of these photographs is complex with no singular understanding, but rather they are contingent upon time, place and viewer – including our own viewing. Nevertheless, these photographs have proved essential to our study as they offer a set of images of fashion and fashionable dressing worn in and about both cities that provide a counterpoint – in effect a different set of representations – to the fashion shoots, the high-end magazine spreads, and the runway shows. They enable us to explicate and document the diverse practices of fashion in everyday life as they allow us to glimpse the ordinary.

One of the outcomes of researching fashion in everyday life is to become keenly aware of the paucity of the ordinary not just in fashion's historical discourses but also in museum collections. The dress collection at Gunnersbury Park Museum,

'The local history museum for Hounslow and Ealing', suburban West London, is unusual in that it includes clothes made from paper patterns, garments that have been altered and changed over time (captured by a mainly hand-written card index system), and collections of dresses from local donors that span the years. Here the acquisition of the various collections aids our understanding of specific items of clothing. Often, however, curatorial and museological strategies militate against the representation of fashion as a practice of everyday life. There are several reasons for this: garments are often presented in relation to their place in the chronology of styles or they are part of the oeuvre of a particular maker, designer or producer. Within such a regime and as a result of applying these 'instruments of analysis', the everyday lacks significance. But at the intersection of the personal and the social, we would argue that fashion is and has been both 'things with attitude' and 'design in the lower case'.[90] Over time and subsumed into the everyday, both categories of fashion can 'evade notice' and/or not always do 'as they are told'.[91] They exist in a dialectical relationship to fashion's rules, often consciously so, sometimes in response to straightforward practical necessities or circumstances, but nevertheless providing the material stuff of self-identification within routine, ordinary lives. Indeed central to these arguments, fashion's 'ordinariness becomes a generic index of hitherto un-investigated processes through which people make sense of their lives given the material and cultural resources available to them'.[92] As a material and culture artefact, fashion has been instrumental in defining the self – whether consciously or unconsciously. In this discussion, our aim has been to question key assumptions about the nature of fashion, its relationship to modernity, and its presumption of change. By focusing on a number of theoretical, historiographical and methodological themes, we have begun to articulate the critical foundation for this study that traces the ways in which fashion has been integral to the practices of everyday life.

Fashion and Everyday Life is roughly chronological with a number of themes threading through; these come in and out of focus from the late nineteenth century to the early twenty-first century, the period of our study. They include: the complex processes of production and consumption, the multiple constructions of image and identity, the rapidly changing media and communication systems, and the endless displays of the body. Alongside these are several broader narratives and ongoing preoccupations that have been persistent in our period including modernity and post-modernity, tradition and continuity, and representation and performance. Cutting across and through these are social formations and cultural representations of gender and sexuality, class, race and national identity, generation and age. Intersecting with each other and with fashion and appearance, there is no single narrative, only a set of choices of where to focus, how to signal continuity and disjuncture, and how to explicate some of the overlapping layers and underlying strata. Our aim is to offer an insight into how these were played out at particular historical moments, but we make no claim to comprehensiveness. Instead we propose a selected number of case studies and historical 'instances' that allow us to explore the themes that appear to us to have been persistent. Thus in Chapter 1, 'London and New York: Clothing the City', we look at the development of both London and New York from the late Victorian period in order to map the production of clothing especially its urban geographies and its diversity (high fashion, tailoring, ready-made, and home sewn). At the same time, we outline the rapidly growing populations of these two world cities during a period of huge political, economic and social change. Not only are we interested in the processes of clothing production, but also we see the selling of these as intrinsic to everyday life. Thus those involved in making clothes were also wearing them as they went about their daily routines through and across the cities. 'Street Walking', Chapter 2, brings modernity into focus. Coupling this with consumption practices, we consider the ways in which London and New York 'produced' shoppers and shopping for a range of new products. Displaying, selecting, buying and wearing fashionable clothes in addition to performing a range of identities were centre stage in these two fashion cities. On the cusp of the new twentieth century, the desire to connect with fashion was an 'intimation of modernity' for disparate groups: the working class as well as the middle classes, incomers and immigrants to and from Britain and the USA. Expanded transport and suburbs, new shopping streets, combined with the visual spectacle of fashion and fashionable looks via magazines and the theatre ensured that fashionable items were not only more widely available, but they were increasingly integrated into the everyday lives of these cities' inhabitants. In Chapter 3, 'Dreams to Reality', we focus on fashion's relationships with specific forms of popular culture: magazines, cinema and dance. We argue that as fashion intersected with these mass-cultures, it offered a vital space in which identities were re-configured. In such a context, everyday life engaged with modernity routinely: looking, picturing, performing and fashioning via the cinema, magazines and dancing. This heterogeneous everydayness was constituted by multiple identities: masculine and feminine, black and white, working class and middle class, old and young; fashion played an increasingly important role in delineating this. In inter-war London and New York, fashion – nuanced and contingent in character – articulated the complexities of urban lives that while anchored to the past, still looked forward to a better world. This theme of performing identities comes to the fore again in Chapter 4 'Dressing Up'. Here we consider how with gender and class roles disrupted by war, dressing – 'up' or 'down' – both during and after 1945 took on distinct meanings. How did uniforms and uniformity impact on everyday life, and what strategies emerged to counter a perception that standardization ruled? Also as both Britain and America's place in the world changed irrevocably, social and cultural attitudes and values adapted too. While young people appeared to lack discipline (apparent in their dress), it appeared that social and cultural norms had been disrupted as African American and Afro-Caribbean cultures were increasingly part of everyday life in both London and New York. Informality seemed pervasive too. While the New Look that marked the final swansong of the didacticism of Paris as fashion centre might be seen to have triumphed (in that the nipped-in waist and full skirt silhouette persisted through the 1950s), the fashion business changed irrevocably as it diversified and adapted for emergent markets notably the young.

Fashion's potency developed apace in the twentieth century, and London and New York accommodated and led this. As important metropolitan centres, they had structures in place that could support the proliferation of fashion media and communication, education and exhibition, business and commerce. They had growing populations that could sustain fashion's rapidly expanding mass-markets, but they also allowed space for the critical questioning of fashion's relentless drive for innovation that was a by-product of modernity. While focusing on the ongoing assimilation of fashion into everyday life that cut across generation, sex, gender, class and race, 'Dressing Down', Chapter 5 considers how fashion became a tool for dissent by offering an accessible, pliable language with which to dissociate oneself from the mainstream. Fashion's rules were there to be broken: not only codes that governed fashion style (coordination, colour, shape and materials), but perhaps more fundamentally the inexorable commitment to what was new, to the latest look. This seemed less vital as some individuals and groups of people refused modernity and all that went with it. Some of fashion's established codes and traditional mores were resilient especially around the fault-lines of generation; and at this intersection, as we will see, a range of manufacturers and companies continued to operate with some success. By the early 1970s, Britain and America's Fordist and Imperialist models were failing and discredited, although politically the last two decades of the twentieth century marked a last ditch attempt to re-stamp authority (in the Falklands for Britain and in Iraq for the United States). While both London and New York experienced urban decline, an emerging post-industrial economy led to booms that brought regeneration that also affected the fashion geographies of both. In Chapter 6, 'Going Out', we look at the part that fashion played in the realignment and reconfiguration of these two premier fashion cities. Celebrated, promoted and advertised, both cities were a magnet for those keen to reinvent themselves, but they were also home to a huge population who utilized fashion as they carried on with their daily lives. Understanding fashion, seeing it, buying it and wearing it was one of the regular routines of life as clothing became cheap and ubiquitous, and as it also infiltrated sport, leisure and outdoor wear. At the same time, fashion also reasserted its capacity to be extraordinary and exceptional particularly as it centred on the club scene in both cities. Performing the city or 'Showing Off' is a theme of Chapter 7 as we note somewhat paradoxically that as the internet and social media dominate in the early 2000s, a sense of place that is embodied in the idea of a distinctive fashion city became embedded in the popular imagination. In such a context, it was possible to actively deploy or subconsciously reference ordinary and extraordinary forms of dress that allowed one to create a sense of identity either alone or with others. Ironically, such performance implied individualism at a point when fashion's quotidian qualities were evident wherever you were in the world. With this focus on two fashion cities, London and New York, and through their parallel development in the long twentieth century, *Fashion and Everyday Life* provides an insight into how fashion and fashioning became embedded in day-to-day life, and in doing so develops the way that we define the theory and practice of fashion.

Notes

1   Barry Sandywell, 'The Myth of Everyday Life: Toward a Heterology of the Ordinary', *Cultural Studies* 18, no. 2/3 (2004): 163.

2   Paraphrased from Ben Highmore, *The Everyday Life Reader* (London & New York: Routledge, 2002), 1.

3   Juliet Ash and Elizabeth Wilson (eds), *Chic Thrills* (Oakland: University of California Press, 1992).

4   Jennifer Craik, *The Face of Fashion: Cultural Studies in Fashion* (London: Routledge, 2004), 10.

5   David Gilbert, 'Urban Outfitting: The City and the Spaces of Fashion Culture', in *Fashion Cultures: Theories, Explorations and Analysis*, ed. Stella Bruzzi and Pamela Church Gibson (London: Routledge, 2001), 12.

6   Frank Mort and Miles Ogborn, 'Transforming Metropolitan London, 1750–1960', *The Journal of British Studies* 43 (2004): 1–14.

7   David R. Green, 'Distance to Work in Victorian London: A Case Study of Henry Poole, Bespoke Tailors', *Business History* 30, no. 2 (1988): 179; Mort and Ogborn, 'Transforming Metropolitan London', 4.

8   Mort and Ogborn, 'Transforming Metropolitan London, 1750–1960', 4

9   Gilbert, 'Urban Outfitting', 13.

10   Ibid., 16.

11   Erving Goffman, *The Presentation of Self in Everyday Life* (London: Penguin, 1971).

12   Gilbert, 'Urban Outfitting', 16.

13   This book develops from earlier work by both authors such as Cheryl Buckley and Hilary Fawcett, *Fashioning the Feminine: Representation and Women's Fashion from the Fin de Siècle to the Present* (London: I.B.Tauris, 2002); Cheryl Buckley, 'On the Margins: Theorising the History and Significance of Making and Designing Clothes at Home', *Journal Of Design History* 11, no. 2 (1998): 157–171; Eugenia Paulicelli and Hazel Clark (eds), *The Fabric of Cultures: Fashion, Identity, and Globalization* (London: Routledge, 2009); Hazel Clark, 'Slow + Fashion – an Oxymoron – or a

Promise for the Future …?' *Fashion Theory: The Journal of Dress, Body and Culture* 12, no. 4 (2008), 427–46.

14 See Ben Fine and Ellen Leopold, *The World of Consumption* (London & New York, Routledge, 1993), chapters 9–11, for a very useful discussion of the economics and manufacture of the fashion system.

15 For example: Thorstein B. Veblen, *The Theory of the Leisure Class* (New York: Macmillan, 1899); George Simmel, 'Fashion', *International Quarterly* 10 (1904): 130–155 and *On Individuality and Social Forms: Selected Writings*, ed. Donald N. Levine (Chicago: University of Chicago Press, 1971); Charles Baudelaire, *Baudelaire: Selected Writings on Art and Artists*, trans. P.S.Charvet (Cambridge: Cambridge University Press, 1972).

16 Georg Simmel, *La tragédie de la culture* (Paris: Rivages, 1988), quoted in Michael Sheringham, *Everyday Life: Theories and Practices from Surrealism to the Present* (Oxford: Oxford University Press, 2006), 181.

17 Barbara Burman Baines, *Fashion Revivals from the Elizabethan Age to the Present Day* (London: Batsford, 1981); Barbara Burman (ed.), *The Culture of Sewing: Gender, Consumption and Home Dressmaking* (Oxford and New York: Berg, 1999); Elizabeth Wilson and Lou Taylor, *Through the Looking Glass: A History of Dress from 1860 to the Present Day* (London: BBC, 1989); Christopher Breward, *The Culture of Fashion* (Manchester: Manchester University Press, 1995); Christopher Breward, *Fashioning London: Clothing and the Modern Metropolis* (Oxford and New York: Berg, 2004); Joanne Eicher (ed.), *Encyclopedia of World Dress and Fashion* (New York: Oxford University Press, 2010); Margaret Maynard, *Dress and Globalisation*, (Manchester: Manchester University Press, 2004); Carol Tulloch (ed.), *Black Style* (London: V&A Publications, 1995); Dick Hebdige, *Subculture: The Meaning of Style* (London: Methuen, 1979); Raphael Samuel, *Theatres of Memory* (London and New York: Verso, 1994); Frank Mort, 'Boy's Own? Masculinity, Style and Popular Culture', in *Male Order: Unwrapping Masculinity*, ed. Rowena Chapman and Jonathan Rutherford (London: Lawrence & Wishart, 1988); John Harvey, *Men in Black* (London: Reaktion, 1995).

18 See Angela McRobbie, *Zoot Suits and Second-Hand Dresses: An Anthology of Fashion and Music* (London: Macmillan, 1989); Caroline Evans and Minna Thornton, *Women and Fashion: A New Look* (London and New York: Quartet Books, 1989), particularly chapters 2, 3 and 4.

19 Judy Attfield, *Wild Things: The Material Culture of Everyday Life* (Oxford and New York: Berg, 2000), 6.

20 McRobbie, *Zoot Suits and Second-Hand Dresses*; Alexandra Palmer and Hazel Clark (eds), *Old Clothes New Looks: Second Hand Fashion* (Oxford and New York: Berg, 2005).

21 Pamela Church Gibson, *Fashion and Celebrity Culture* (London: Berg, 2012), 18.

22 Ibid., 18.

23 Joanne Entwistle, *The Fashioned Body* (Cambridge, MA: Polity Press, 2000), 49.

24 Susan Kaiser, *Fashion and Cultural Studies* (London and New York: Berg, 2012).

25 Ibid., 35.

26 Harvey, *Men in Black*; Tim Edwards, *Men in the Mirror: Men's Fashion, Masculinity,* *and Consumer Society* (London: Cassell, 1997); Tim Edwards, *Cultures of Masculinity* (London: Routledge, 2006); Christopher Breward, *The Hidden Consumer: Masculinities, Fashion and City Life* (Manchester: Manchester University Press, 1999); Shaun Cole, *Now We Don Our Gay Apparel: Gay Men's Dress in the Twentieth Century* (Oxford: Berg, 2000); Peter McNeil and Vicki Karaminas (eds), *The Men's Fashion Reader* (Berg: London and New York, 2009).

27 Roy Boyne, 'The Art of the Body in the Discourse of Postmodernity', *Theory, Culture and Society: Special issue on Postmodernism* 5, no. 2/3 (1988): 527, quoted by Elizabeth Wilson, 'Fashion and The Postmodern Body', in *Chic Thrills: A Fashion Reader*, ed. Juliet Ash and Elizabeth Wilson (London: Pandora Press, 1992), 14.

28 Kaiser, *Fashion and Cultural Studies*, 7.

29 Joanne Entwistle, 'Fashion and the Fleshy Body: Dress as Embodied Practice', *Fashion Theory: The Journal of Dress, Body and Culture* 4, no. 3 (2000): 344.

30 Entwistle, *The Fashioned Body*, 74.

31 Ibid., 33.

32 Ben Highmore, *Everyday Life and Cultural Theory: An Introduction* (Abingdon and New York: Routledge, 2002); Michael Sheringham, *Everyday Life*; Barry Sandywell, 'The Myth of Everyday Life'.

33 Edward P. Thompson, *The Making of the English Working Class* (London: Pelican, 1963); Sally Alexander, *Becoming A Woman* (London: Virago, 1994); Carolyn Steedman, *Landscape for a Good Woman: Two Women's Lives* (London: Virago, 1986).

34 Quoted by Gregory J. Seigworth and Michael E. Gardiner, 'Rethinking Everyday Life', *Cultural Studies* 18, no. 2 (2004): 147.

35 Joanne Entwistle, *The Aesthetic Economy of Fashion: Markets and Values in Clothing and Modelling* (Oxford and New York: Berg, 2009), 9.

36 Sandywell, 'The Myth of Everyday Life', 162.

37 Ibid.

38 Ibid.

39 A good example of this is the relatively recent Jane Farrell-Beck and Jean Parsons, *20th-Century Dress in the United States* (New York: Fairchild, 2007).

40 Sheringham, *Everyday Life*, 182.

41 Sandywell, 'The Myth of Everyday Life', 163.

42 Highmore, *Everyday Life and Cultural Theory,* 61.

43 We note the gendered nature of this particular urban modernity that ignores the domestic arena of home and fore-grounded the public space of the city. Ibid., 61.

44 Sandywell, 'The Myth of Everyday Life', 165.

45 Highmore, *Everyday Life and Cultural Theory,* 26.

46 Highmore, *The Everyday Life Reader*, 1.

47 Henri Lefebvre, 'Toward a Leftist Cultural Politics: Remarks Occasioned by the Centenary of Marx's Death', in *Marxism and the Interpretation of Culture*, ed. Cary Nelson and Lawrence Grossberg (London: Macmillan, 1988), 78.

48 Seigworth and Gardiner, 'Rethinking Everyday Life', 140.

49　Ibid., 147.

50　Christopher Breward and David Gilbert (eds), *Fashion's World Cities* (Oxford & New York: Berg, 2006); Gilbert, 'Urban Outfitting'.

51　Gilbert, 'Urban Outfitting', 12.

52　Walter Benjamin, *The Arcades Project* (Cambridge, MA: Harvard University Press, 2002), 64.

53　Christopher Breward, Edwina Ehrman and Caroline Evans (eds), *The London Look: Fashion from Street to Catwalk* (New Haven: Yale University Press, 2004), 49.

54　Elizabeth Wilson, *Adorned in Dreams: Fashion and Modernity* (London: Virago, 1985).

55　Michel de Certeau, Luce Giard and Pierre Mayol, *The Practice of Everyday Life*, Vol. 2 (Minneapolis and London: University of Minnesota Press, 1998), p. 3

56　Jerry White, *London in the 20th Century* (London: Random House, 2008), xiii; 4.

57　White, *London in the 20th Century*, 11.

58　Francis Sheppard, *London: A History* (Oxford: Oxford University Press, 1998), 292.

59　Ibid.

60　Andrew Godley, 'Immigrant Entrepreneurs and the Emergence of London's East End as an Industrial District', *London Journal* 21 (1998), 38.

61　Available online http://www.20thcenturylondon.org.uk/jews-west-end (accessed October 2012).

62　White, *London in the 20th Century,* 56.

63　Ibid., 63–65.

64　Mary Benedetta, *The Street Markets of London* (London: John Miles Ltd, 1936).

65　'Diner', in Goldstein and Greenberd (eds), *A Perfect Fit*, 32.

66　Kenneth T. Jackson (ed.), *The Encyclopedia of New York City*, 2nd edn (New Haven and London: Yale University Press), 641.

67　Ibid.

68　Ibid, 643.

69　Ibid., 494.

70　Breward, *The Culture of Fashion*, 229.

71　Craik, *The Face of Fashion*, 10.

72　Highmore, *The Everyday Life Reader*, 5.

73　Breward*, Fashioning London,* 11.

74　Highmore, *The Everyday Life Reader*, 2.

75　Sheringham*, Everyday Life*, 180.

76　Highmore, *The Everyday Life Reader*, 13.

77　de Certeau et al., *The Practice of Everyday Life*, 256.

78　John Brewer, 'Microhistory and the Histories of Everyday Life', *Cultural and Social History* 7, no. 1 (2010): 89.

79　Samuel, *Theatres of Memory*, 8.

80　Brewer, 'Microhistory and the Histories of Everyday Life', 89.

81   Ibid.

82   Ibid., 93. He cites in particular Carlo Ginzburg and Giovanni Levi writing about Italy as well as Carolyn Steedman in Britain, page 90.

83   Sally Alexander, *Becoming A Woman*; Sheila Rowbotham, *Hidden From History* (London: Pluto Press, 1973).

84   Pat Kirkham (ed.), *The Gendered Object* (Manchester: Manchester University Press, 1996), xiii–xiv.

85   Ilene Beckerman, *Love, Loss and What I Wore* (Chapel Hill, NC: Algonquin Books, 1995).

86   Liz Stanley, *The Auto/Biographical I: The Theory and Practice of Feminist Auto/ Biography* (Manchester: Manchester University Press, 1992), 7.

87   Brewer, 'Microhistory and the Histories of Everyday Life', 87–109.

88   Samuel, *Theatres of Memory,* 27.

89   See Joan M. Swartz and James Ryan (eds), *Picturing Place* (London: I.B. Tauris, 2002); Gillian Rose, *Doing Family Photography: The Domestic, the Public, and the Politics of Sentiment* (Farnham: Ashgate, 2010).

90   Attfield, *Wild Things*, 6.

91   Ibid.

92   Sandywell, 'The Myth of Everyday Life', 176.

1

LONDON AND NEW YORK: CLOTHING THE CITY

Introduction

London

At the end of the nineteenth century, London was the capital city of an empire that extended over a quarter of the land surface of the globe and it comprised 20 per cent of the population of England and Wales.[1] Fifty years later, describing Britain just prior to the Second World War, the historian Charles Mowat noted that London had seen rapid population growth in the 1920s and 1930s to peak at 8.6 million in 1939 from 6.5 million in 1899.[2] This growth from the beginning of the twentieth century was particularly in its outer suburbs, which increased by 27 per cent, while concurrently inner London had decreased by 2 per cent by 1939.[3] London's population gradually declined after 1972 to 6.8 million in 1981 but thereafter rising again to 7.56 million in 2007.[4] Whereas in the earlier part of the nineteenth century, the working class had to live near to their places of employment, as transportation across London was transformed with the development of modern systems such as the Underground, new working-class suburbs developed in Stoke Newington, Walthamstow, West Ham and Lewisham, and by '1912 workmen's tickets represented about 40 per cent of all suburban railway journeys within 6 to 8 miles of the centre of London'.[5] As an example, in the 1850s, the skilled workforce of Henry Poole, Bespoke Tailors of Savile Row lived near to work to the east of Regent Street in Soho, to the north between Oxford Street and Great Portland Street, and to the north east towards Camden. By 1890, they had moved west to Kensal Green and Shepherds Bush and south to Battersea and Brixton.[6] These well-paid artisans travelled 2.2 km to work in 1857, whereas by the 1890s they travelled an average of 4.5 km to homes in these newer suburbs. This shifting urban geography – between the West End and East End, the inner city slums and the burgeoning suburbs, the home and the workplace – signalled social and gender differentiation. In 1891, Charles

Booth had estimated that the middle class and those above represented some 17 per cent of the population; this upper echelon was increased by the arrival of leading families into London's West End for the season during the summer months, and at the turn of the century, although 'there were still only about 4,000 families which took an active part in London society, the influence of that society was nevertheless immense'.[7]

Describing the 'trades of the East London connected with Poverty' in the fourth volume of his influential social survey *Life and Labour of the People of London* of 1902, Charles Booth offered detailed descriptions of the tailoring trade in London.[8] He explained how

On the one side … we find the Jewish contractor with his highly organized staff of fixers, basters, fellers, machinists, button-hole hands, and pressers, turning out coats by the score, together with a mass of English women, unorganised and unregulated, engaged in the lower sections of the trade; whilst on the other side of the boundary we see an army of skilled English tradesmen with regulated pay and restricted hours working on the old traditional lines of one man one garment.[9]

Produced at a pivotal moment in the transformation of the clothing industry in Britain, Booth's survey identified three systems of production:

The 'Factory System', which involves the utmost use of machinery; the 'Sweating System', which by division of labour makes use of the workmanship of all qualities at varying prices; and the employment of individual artisans who themselves perform all parts of the work, may roughly be taken as representing the 'Provincial', the 'East End', and the 'West End' methods of production respectively.[10]

With the East End as his focus, he described an area of less than one square mile (the whole of Whitechapel, a small piece of Mile End, and a part of St George's-in-the-East) that housed thirty or forty thousand Jews of all nationalities and from all countries. Within this area, some 76 per cent of businesses employed fewer than ten people.[11] As Newman put it: 'The new labour force was provided by thousands of eastern European Jews driven from their homes by persecution. Most of these refugees went on to the United States, but many stayed in Britain, especially in London and in Leeds; and it was to the clothing industry that they gravitated'.[12] Examining the clothing industry in Britain from the mid-nineteenth century, historians have argued that 'as demand for cheaper ready-made clothing increased it was London based clothiers who began to organise cheap female labour, sub-divide the assembly tasks, and eventually, to introduce the early sewing-machines to speed up the manufacturing processes'.[13] By the early 1870s, this mainly female workforce laboured in early sweatshops that appeared archaic and primitive especially in light of the recent development of mechanized (based on the sewing-machine) clothing factories established outside London. Significantly, it was in this context that the decline of the sweated trades of London was anticipated, however by the beginning of the twentieth century, the East End garment trade was successful and highly efficient, but not as a result of following the new principles of factory organization. Rather,

> with a growing aggregate demand employers could be reasonably confident that enough work would come their way even if it was not to their own designs... Workers needed to be skilled enough to be able to assemble a wide array of garment styles. Employers needed to concentrate on finding market-niches where the firm's speciality would give some guarantee of future income free from the uncertainty of sub-contracted orders. Combined together this resulted in an increasingly high-skilled workforce concentrated in the East End and a proliferation of small firms specialising in one or more of the minutiae tasks in the assembly-process.[14]

In the East End 'slop trade', cheap ready-made clothes were made based on flexible labour divisions as complex skilled methods of production were broken down into simple elements: 'Different pairs of hands cut, sewed, buttonholed, ironed and packed'.[15] It was the skill level and diversity of specialized practices that gave 'the East End clothing industry its collective advantage over all other regions and which differentiated the industry there from that organised in large firms with unskilled operatives in Leeds and other provincial centres'.[16] The downside of this was that 'wages and conditions [were] screwed down to starvation and slum levels' but casual labour was in abundance as 'wives and children [were] chained to the district near to their husbands' or fathers' place of work, and constrained to slave for a pittance to supplement the family budget; and by the ceaseless stream of poor unskilled migrants from Ireland and the continent as well as from England, also ready to work at anything available'.[17] Discussing the clothing practices of immigrants in London's East End in the 1890s, Breward commented,

> the real clothing practices of immigrants (as producers and consumers of dress) were perhaps more humdrum. Economic and social necessities frequently demanded that the vulnerable foreigner adapt to local circumstances, and historians of immigration have shown how incoming communities gradually adopted practices of public assimilation in order to 'fit' while reserving the memories and customs of the old country for the private world of home.[18]

The capacity to buy such everyday garments that allowed one to fit in – particularly for wear outside the home – was vital. Photographs of tailor's shops from the Jewish Museum in London show men and women dressed in clothes that clearly comply to 'fashion's rules': men wearing formal stiff-collared shirts and waistcoats, the women wearing high-neck blouses with lace, pin-tucks and leg of mutton sleeves over sharply tailored skirts (Figure 1.1).

With the high price of land and subsequent high rents, large factories in the centre of London were uneconomic, but this abundance of labour suited 'sweating' whereby production was fragmented among home workers. Thriving in this context was Elias Moses & Son, tailors, clothiers, hatters, hosiers and furriers. Based in the East End but with a retail outlet in the City of London, by the mid-nineteenth century, Moses employed 3,500 workers to make fashionable clothes for men, and as Ehrman wrote: 'The scale of their operation was ambitious, integrating manufacturing, wholesaling and retailing, tailoring and outfitting, and the sale of ready-made and bespoke garments'.[19] These companies produced a range of everyday fashions by their enterprise: 'the standard garments of coat, waistcoat, trousers and topcoat were available in a range of imaginatively named styles and a large choice of materials, at prices which reflected the variety of cut, fabrics and trimmings'.[20] Although they frequently supplemented their ready-to-wear trade with a bespoke service: 'Moses' bespoke clients entered his shop through a private waiting hall which gave a gloss of exclusivity to the service'.[21]

Figure 1.1 Workers in the tailoring workshop of Harris Chaimofsky, Christian St., the East End, London, c. 1910. Courtesy of Jewish Museum of London.

By 1911, London's East End and Leeds in the north of England employed one in four of tailoring workers in England and Wales. In Leeds in the mid to late Victorian period, a company such as John Barran was pioneering the introduction of new technologies such as the sewing machine as well as inventing the band-knife. It was with this increasingly technological production that Barran mass-produced low-quality boys' wear for Empire markets.[22] Although the sewing machine's principle advantage was and remains the greatly improved speed of stitching, its inability to handle fabrics sensitively meant that craft skills in handling and manipulating the cloth continued to be a necessity and as a result the clothing industry remained highly labour intensive. With Singer sewing machines representing three-quarters of the market share in Britain by the 1880s, there was, as Godley argued, 'a strong correlation between the period of most rapid gains in efficiency in the industry and the demand for improved (Singer) sewing machines'.[23] As the restructured industry in Leeds and other northern cities allowed economies of scale in production, this enabled these companies to take market share, thus putting pressure on wages in other areas, particularly in London's East End, which could not compete in economies of scale. Nevertheless, as historians have shown, these workshops were still the dominant mode of organization in the clothing trade in the late nineteenth and early twentieth centuries accounting for 56 per cent of total employment. Thus by 1935 the 'relative efficiency of small scale organisation was enhanced, and with it the place of London as the centre of Britain's clothing industry'.[24] From the late 1880s, 'the East End trade had become increasingly focused on the rapidly growing ladies' trade', and by the 1930s, it was dominant particularly in the key market sector of women's clothing.[25] Whereas prior to the 1880s, women bought their clothes in pieces to be made up by a dressmaker, men were already buying ready-made clothing. Godley cites the turn of the nineteenth into the twentieth centuries as the pivotal moment when women's wear began to be made up in advance by tailors. Citing Morris Cohen, a Russian émigré who established himself in the East End, as an example, he explained that by 1902, Cohen employed 180 people in a collection of small workshops in Stepney.[26] In fact by 1939, 50 per cent of women's and girl's tailored outerwear and 48 per cent of daywear was made in London, with a number of well-known firms established – Windsmoor and Berketex were examples. Berketex grew out of Morris Cohen's Stepney workshops and Windsmoor grew from Ellis Goldstein's Commercial Street premises.[27] Typically these women's wear firms were much smaller that men's tailoring firms due in part to a production process that had to be more responsive to the vagaries of fashion. As women's styles changed quickly, production needed to be highly responsive and thus the advance outlay of textiles, for example, was curtailed until a particular design was assured of success.

It has been remarked that 'London is to men what Paris is to women – the paradise of fashion shops'.[28] The West End was the site of traditional bespoke businesses including tailors and dressmakers who, at the turn of the nineteenth into the twentieth century, still produced beautifully made, one-off garments for all occasions for the wealthy sectors of society – both in London and in the rest of the country: 'English tastes informed much of the clothing made in London. These were dictated by the lifestyle of the upper classes who moved from town to country according to the social calendar'.[29] A member of land-owning society in the north of England, pioneer aviator Linda Morrit of Rokeby Hall near Barnard Castle bought her wedding dress and ball gowns from the couturier Lucile, who was established in 1896 on Hanover Square. Like many of Britain's social elite, Morrit frequented London during the season and bought tailored costumes, gowns, dresses and hats in London's premier fashion quarter. Situated west of Regent Street, with Piccadilly to the south, Oxford Street to the north and numerous small streets in between, this represented the heart of the West End dress-making and tailoring district.[30] Importantly this area was close by Oxford Street, which by the 1930s had become London's 'Main Street'.[31] In the first half of the twentieth century, the West End of London had a range of smart establishments that offered alternatives to Paris, including Sarah Fullerton-Montieth Young on Grosvenor Square, Reville and Rossiter on Hanover Square, Russell & Allan on Old Bond Street, Madame Ross on Grafton Street, with Victor Stiebel opening in 1932 on Bruton Street and Lachasse opening on Farm Street just off Berkeley Square in 1928.[32] An air of exoticism was discernible particularly in West End fashion businesses in 1920s due in part to an influx of Russian Jewish dressmakers and milliners recorded in the 1921 census.[33] These contributed to a discernible 'aestheticism' in English fashion in the period immediately after the end of the First World War that resulted in bold colours and a touch of the exotic that coalesced with a distinctly 'odd, eccentric and aesthetic' strand of fashion in Britain that was already evident at the end of the nineteenth century.[34]

At the same time, there was a substantial group of women dressmakers based in this area and in Knightsbridge and South Kensington who, though not part of the upper-echelon of London couturiers and court dressmakers, remained important producers of good quality women's fashions. South Kensington-based dressmakers included Thorpe on Cromwell Place and Goodwill on Alfred Place West, while in the West End they included Kate Reilly on Dover St and Isobel on Regent St. The latter also had a branch in the fashionable Yorkshire spa town of Harrogate. Her clothes, which were exported to America, were 'well-tailored, supremely wearable, totally appropriate and chic'.[35] Isobel's business was atypical as she employed over 550 staff including 400 girls, whereas the average dressmaker of this type employed between ten and thirty workers.[36] In addition to these established elite dressmakers, there was also a plethora of small dressmakers who would make up clothes for particular clients often suggesting ideas and adapting Paris models. Nevertheless, 'The glamorous setting and fanciful products of London's elite dressmaking sector, dominated by women proprietors in this period, still disguised exploitative working practices'.[37] As the various campaigns against sweated labour made clear, in the early part of the twentieth century, women in particular still worked in their own homes in poor light for long hours to produce all manner of garments including those at the top end of the fashion business. Alongside these, of course, were the department stores, many of which operated workrooms producing clothes to their own designs plus copies of Paris models. Marshall and Snelgrove on Oxford St and Harvey Nichols in Knightsbridge were examples of these.

The finest London tailors firms were also based adjacent to these West End dressmakers particularly around Savile Row, however the tailoring trade comprised a number of categories of shop.[38] Elite 'West End' establishments offered exquisitely hand-sewn garments that were dependent on the acquired craft skills of a tailoring aristocracy who worked for specific companies. In 1902, Booth wrote,

> we have in Central London the 'West End' trade, that is work done for the fashionable shops of Regent St and the neighbourhood. The general characteristic of this trade is high-class work, commanding a good price, and those who get enough of it do very well … the best 'bespoke' work, which is the kernel of the West End trade, has a limited and perhaps shrinking sphere, but the supply of first-rate workmen is as limited as the trade.[39]

In between this type of production and the sweated production described earlier were tailoring companies that – in the late nineteenth and early twentieth centuries – combined mechanized processes, particularly machine cutting and sewing machines, with a degree of bespoke tailoring. Some of this would be outsourced. The 'spectacle of the shop' occupied by these different categories of tailor revealed all: whereas Henry Poole's tailor's shop on Savile Row was 'the closest that a tailor's shop might come to impinging on the magnificence of the department store', more typical were the tailors occupying second-floor premises which combined production and fitting in the same spaces.[40] From 1883, Henry Poole, 'tailor by appointment to all the crowned heads in the world of any note', was located at 15 Savile Row in the former premises of the Savile Club.[41] As Porter argued, Gentlemen's Clubs 'helped keep London a masculine city, and St James's, with its bachelor chambers around King and Jermyn Streets, was its inner sanctum'.[42] The gendering of this particular terrain of the West End at the end of the nineteenth century as masculine meant that 'gentlemen could step out of their lodgings and visit their club, hat-maker, gun-maker, boot-maker or tailor in the course of a leisurely promenade'.[43] The clientele for these top establishments was varied with customers from the city and the provinces, from Britain's Empire and from other Western countries, but unifying them was their capacity 'to pay the high prices … charged for their top-quality garments'.[44] The wealthy Americans who frequented Henry Poole's in the early twentieth century contributed to the development of new fashion practices that represented 'direct engagement with modernity ... through the increased proportion of the wealthy who worked for a living, which led to a re-negotiation of the concept of leisure and also an increased cosmopolitanism that was informed by changes in wealth accumulation and new forms of travel'.[45] Perhaps more important for this discussion of fashion and everyday lives, by the early twentieth century, although there remained a 'lingering appeal' of English aristocratic modes of production and consumption relating to tailoring, these were in flux and were being re-constituted by a 'three-way cultural exchange' between Poole's tailors, foreign consumers and British customers.[46] Men's clothing was also bought directly from drapers and hosiers: 'these emporia of ready-made articles pushed masculine attire out from the obscurity of second-floor cutters' workrooms or the back cabinets of drapers shops and into the plate glass glare of late nineteenth-century public culture'.[47]

Significantly London's new suburbs were home to an expanding number of small tailors, clothiers, hosiers and drapers who produced not only made-to-measure but also men's ready-made suits. As the fashion trade moved 'west', 'drapers led the way'.[48] From these many of the new department stores emerged: Dickens & Jones on Regent Street from the 1890s, Peter Robinson on Oxford Street from the late nineteenth century, the Newcastle-based Fenwick on Bond Street from 1891 and Bourne and Hollingsworth. Initially established in Westbourne Grove, Bayswater, in 1894 to sell blouses and women's garments, Bourne and Hollingsworth acquired premises on Oxford St in 1902 that were altered and expanded by John Slater (1847–1924) and subsequently by his son John Slater (1885–1963) in the 1910s.[49] Further west was Whiteley's on Westbourne Grove with nineteen departments housed under one roof by 1900. As the manufacture and retailing of fashion diversified, there also remained thriving street markets where clothing could be bought and sold including Petticoat Lane in Spitalfields, Camden Market in Camden Town, Portobello Road off Ladbroke Grove, Watney Street in Whitechapel, Sclater Street in Shoreditch and Berwick St in Soho. A photograph of Petticoat Lane in the East End from 1900 shows a typical London street market –chaotic, bustling, obstructed and crowded selling food, household goods as well as old clothes. Its social heterogeneity evident: young and old; well-dressed visitors and stall-holders in work clothes; and ethnically diverse (Figure 1.2).

In contrast, Berwick St market in the West End was 'renowned for its smart and reasonably priced dress shops, provided you were not deterred by the *schleppers*',[50] who as Walkowitz puts it, 'schlepped or pulled customers into "guinea gown shops"'.[51] Berwick St market became an important fashion market particularly by the 1920s and 1930s. Its unique location in the heart of London's West End (south of Oxford St and east of Regent St) complicated Goffman's 'front and back' spatial metaphor as Jewish traders rendered the market – typically a

Figure 1.2 Petticoat Lane Market, London, 1900. London Metropolitan Archives.

'back space' – open and explicit, more front than back. They transformed it into 'a retail space for stockings and ready-made gowns purveyed to fashion-conscious working women'.[52] One of the largest London street markets was the Caledonian Road Market in Southwark, which traded every Friday with 725 stalls by 1914 and expanded to Tuesday and Friday by 1932 with 3,400 stalls.[53] The 'Cally', as the Caledonian Road Market was affectionately named, had an array of stalls; some 'was taken by the very poorest of the market people. The pitches were given over to rags, old clothes...In contrast...there were Orientals, probably Indians, who sold gaudy silk ties, kerchiefs, and shawls'.[54] Re-established as the New Caledonian Market in 1949 following the bombing of the original in the Second World War, it was, as Breward argued, heir to Camden Market as it developed along the Regent's Canal north of the huge railway terminals of Kings Cross, St Pancras and Euston.[55]

New York

Local geography conditioned the history and sensibility of the everyday experiences of the different races, classes, genders and generations living together in New York and how they presented themselves to one another. From the Lower East Side at the southern tip of Manhattan, the historical, geographical and cultural transitions in the city and its people demonstrate how fashionable clothing played a significant part of the everyday lives of New Yorkers. From the second decade of the nineteenth century until the 1920s around thirty-three million people moved to the United States from all over the world, three -quarters through the port of New York. Some continued the long, slow journey westward, but many stayed and settled in the city. Initially, Irish and German Catholics were in the greatest numbers, from the 1860s, sharing a religion that marked them out in the strongly Protestant and Anglo-Saxon city, causing inevitable conflicts of lifestyle and beliefs. From the 1840s they contributed to the garment trade, with the Germans establishing a thriving second-hand clothing trade, as well as the practice of home manufacturing.[56] Irish and Germans shared neighbourhoods and tenement accommodation. Many of the same buildings were occupied by Jewish and Italian immigrants who came to the city from around the 1880s to the end of the century. These new immigrants were much poorer generally than those who had preceded them; the mass migration of Eastern European Jews at the turn of the century, to escape the Russian pogroms, being 'epic in proportion'.[57] 'The United States lured me not merely as a land of milk and honey but also, and perhaps chiefly, as one of mystery, of fantastic experiences, of marvellous tranformations'.[58] 'The immigrant's arrival in his new home is like a second birth to him'.[59] Schreier notes how, in the late nineteenth century, the unprecedented expansion of the American ready-to-wear clothing industry signalled the transition of America from an agrarian to a capitalist economy. Clothes were more frequently purchased than made as the country moved from one of production to consumption.

The 'slop shops' of the eighteenth century, known for cheap ready-made clothes, catering in particular to the needs of sailors, were the basis for the development of a much more sophisticated range of clothing. From rather crude beginnings as a service industry for labourers' garments (slop clothes), ready-to-wear developed into a large-scale industry supplying clothing to a mass market. Street peddlers catered for the needs of poorer New Yorkers, providing daily necessities such as food, but also providing choices for the likes of household textiles or clothing (Figure 1.3). The photograph from 1898 also shows how the female customers and vendor were dressed similarly, wearing garments for protection. This includes shawls and capes, as well as an umbrella, as guard against the climate, and aprons to avoid dust and dirt on what would be one of a small number of garments in their possession. The result was a social levelling that blurred the distinctions between 'haves' and 'have nots'.[60] Building on the success of the men's ready-to-wear industry, the earliest women's ready-made garments were simple wraps and outer garments. Improvements in standardized sizing facilitated the addition of more complex garments for women. By the 1890s, this included underwear,

Figure 1.3 Peddlers, New York, 1898. Museum of the City of New York.

corsets, skirts and blouses; all items of clothing that twenty years later could be purchased ready-made.[61] The catalogues issued by department stores and mail order companies provided New York City and the country at large with a vast range of goods, including the latest fashion. In the city itself, photographs from the period show the range and diversity of clothing available. The street scene from Hester Street on the Lower East Side in 1898 (Figure 1.4) shows peddlers and street vendors selling foodstuffs in front of shops offering ready-made, men's clothes, and also textiles. The everyday clothing of the vendors and purchasers are again similar, as in Figure 1.3. We can note also how women are dressed more domestically, while men are more formally attired for the outside, in the ready-made straight-cut sack jackets, common to the period and headwear, either hats or caps, depending on their status.

The availability of fashionable clothes at affordable prices was made possible by the huge expansion of the functional ready-to-wear industry in New York. A term which supplanted 'ready made' at the end of the nineteenth century, a linguistic shift distinguishing a move of emphasis from 'produced' to 'consumed' items.[62] By the end of the nineteenth century, the everyday life of many working people in New York was impacted by fashionable garments. In its various forms, the garment industry employed substantial numbers of women, men

Figure 1.4 Street scene of peddlers and street vendors on Hester Street on the Lower East Side, Manhattan, 1898. Museum of the City of New York.

and children, in enterprises of different sizes, including those in the home. The immigrant workforce contributed to the success of the burgeoning American ready-to-wear industry, which while distinct from totally hand-made custom clothing, still required large numbers of workers.[63] Such was the growth of the industry that in 1904, New York's garment factories were cited as producing 65 per cent of all ready-made clothes in the United States.[64] German Jews who began as peddlers, many specializing in second-hand clothing, later opened retail stores and finally became the clothing manufacturers who dominated the industry around 1860 to 1890. The period from 1880 to 1920 witnessed the 'Great Migration' from Eastern and Southern Europe, with Jews, who possessed needle skills, coined 'the tailors of Europe', first from Russia and Poland, stimulating the growth in ready-made clothing industry. They were joined from 1890 and increasingly after 1900 by Italian tradesmen and their wives and female family members, most of whom were already accomplished seamstresses, who eventually came to outnumber the Jews in the New York garment trade. Nevertheless, it is the Jews who have been described as making 'the volatile women's clothing industry' their own.[65] By 1924, when the Immigration and Naturalization Act had halted the flow of immigration to the United States, many of the two million Jews who had entered the country from Russia and Poland and had settled on the Lower East Side were deploying their tailoring and needle skills. As a result, 'in the last two decades of the nineteenth century, coinciding with the influx of Jewish immigration, the garment industry grew at two or three times the rate of other businesses, and by 1890 there were over one thousand women's-wear companies'.[66] Responsible for two-thirds of nationwide sales for cloaks, suits, shirtwaisters and undergarments, New York dominated volume production of ready-to-wear clothing. These predominantly Eastern European Jews working for lower wages, longer hours and minimal profit margins began to dominate the women's clothing manufacture in New York and they drove out the large German Jewish manufacturers.[67] These 'moths of Division Street', went on to found 'the most successful apparel firms on Seventh Avenue'.[68] Different grades of fashion were already being produced at this time for different social and economic groups, with social distinction having already been established with the early nineteenth-century expansion of middle classes and continued to developed over time 'through the social uses of fashion by different classes and ethnicities'.[69] 'The Germans were the first of a long succession of groups of immigrants to establish ethnic enclaves in New York where foreign languages were spoken, different clothes were worn, and different kinds of foods were sold and served in restaurants'.[70] With the growing success of Eastern European Jews in women's clothing production, German Jews 'Known as the Giants of Broadway…went into other businesses such as department stores and wholesale textiles'.[71]

Abraham Cahan's fictional character, immigrant Russian Jew David Levinsky, an apprentice cloak maker at the Manheimer Bros. factory, provides details of the organization of clothing production on the Lower East Side in the late nineteenth century. His shop belonged not to a manufacturer, but to one of his contractors, who received from him 'bundles' of material, which his employees (tailors, machine-operators, pressers and finisher girls) made up into cloaks or jackets. It is worth noting that these were probably the first garments worn in public (as distinct from the 'private' underwear or housedresses) to be sold in any quantity ready-made.[72] Photographs by Lewis Hine of 1910 and 1912 show Jewish male and Italian female *schleppers* as part of the urban everyday of the Lower East Side as they delivered cut pieces of fabric and collected them made up. The woman captured carrying a heavy load of home-work on Lafayette Street, near Astor Place (Figure 1.5), is typical of many schleppers pictured in lower Manhattan, although of particular note due to her attire, which includes a fashionable handbag, with a functional shawl, boots and apron. She would have been moving between her home and the premises of her supplier. Cheaper goods were made entirely by 'operators'; the better grades partly by tailors, partly by operators, or wholly by tailors; but these were mostly made 'inside', that is in the manufacturer's own establishment.

Figure 1.5 Tired woman with heavy load of home-work. Lafayette St., near Astor Place, New York, 1912. Lewis Hine.

Home-work was not only taking place on the Lower East Side. A photograph taken by Lewis Hine, dated December 1911, showing Mrs. Tony Totore (or Totoro), of 428 E. 116th St. 2nd floor back, is accompanied by a caption that provides valuable insights into the conditions and earnings of home workers. Mrs Totore earned from $2.00 to $2.50 a week making lace for contractor Mrs. Rosina Schiaffo, located two blocks away at 301 E 114th St, 3rd floor. Mrs. Sohiaffo, sent her lace to a manufacturer, in midtown Manhattan, M. Weber Co., 230 E 52 St. Mrs Totore, who is pictured with her husband and two children, 4 and 7 years old, is quoted as saying, 'I rather work for a factory. They pay more'.[73] Another Hine photograph of the same date pictures Mrs Mette and her family making flowers in what is described as 'a very dirty tenement', at 302 Mott Street in lower Manhattan. Pictured is thirteen-year-old Josephine who sometimes helped outside school hours until 9pm. Once she turned 14 she would likely go to work in the embroidery factory where she had been employed the previous summer. Her younger siblings, Nicholas, aged 6, and Johnnie, aged 8, were also shown at work. Eleven-year-old Rosie was not included due to sickness, and it was assumed that the family's twenty-month-old baby, pictured playing with the flowers, would help a little before long. Altogether the family earned only 40 to 50 cents a day, but the small sum was important to them, especially as the father was a coach (or hack) driver, with irregular employment.[74]

According to Cahan, the designing, cutting and making of samples were 'inside' branches exclusively. Cahan refers to Gitelson as a skilled tailor and an 'inside' man, being mostly employed on sample making.[75] The work was hard and the day was long, from 6.00am to 9.00pm, necessitated by the seasonal nature of the trade. More lowly workers had to make their annual salary in the two short seasons of three and two months, respectively, with only the sample-makers, and high-grade tailors being kept busy throughout the year. The wages were relatively high with a good mechanic, or an operator being able to earn as much as $75 a week, for a fifteen hour day.[76] Levinsky began as a mere 'operator' making around $10 a week, half of which he was able to save for when production stopped. Levinsky was so absorbed in his skill that when, 'At last the season set in. There was not a stroke of work in the shop. I was so absorbed in my new vocation that I would pass my evenings in a cloak-makers' haunt, a café on Delancey Street, where I never tired talking sleeves, pockets, stitches, trimmings, and the like'.[77] Around 1905, Levinsky moved to his own business in new quarters on Fifth Avenue and 23rd Street (proximate to the Ladies Mile shopping area at Madison Square Park residences and the newly completed Flatiron Building). He comments how 'That locality has already become the center of the cloak-and-suit trade, being built up with new sky-scrapers, full of up-to-date cloak-factories, dress-factories, and ladies'-waist factories. The sight of the celebrated Avenue swarming with Jewish mechanics out for their lunch hour or going home after a day's work was already a daily spectacle'.[78] Many would be producing the tailor-made suits for women, which were already ubiquitous on the streets of New York by the late nineteenth century, as well as in London (Figure 1.6). Based on male garments in their fabric, cut and styling, the tailor-mades were typically produced by men as they demanded skills which dressmakers did not possess; a fact that probably also accounted for them entering the factory system at an early stage.[79]

Clothing had become cheaper by 1917, the year that Cahan's account was published. As his character Levinsky notes, 'When I learned the trade a cloak made of the cheapest satinette cost eighteen dollars. To-day nobody would wear it. One can now buy a whole suit made of all-wool material and silk-lined for fifteen dollars'.[80] He writes similarly of skirts and dress manufacture, remarking how the Russian Jew had introduced the factory-made gown, constantly perfecting it and reducing the cost of its production. As a result, a ready-made silk dress 'of the very latest style and as tasteful in its lines, color scheme, and trimming as a high-class designer can make it' could be purchased for a few dollars. He comments on how 'gifted dress-designers' were succeeding in providing a good fit, suited to the bodies and tastes of American women, rather than having to adopt the established practice of copying from French fashions. He concludes that it was the Russian Jew who not only, 'Americanized the system of providing clothes for

WOMEN'S TAILORED SUITS—Beautiful New Models ¹¹

Sizes: Bust, 32 to 44 inches.   Lengths, 37 to 43 inches.   Waist Bands, 23 to 29 inches.

69B 110
$13.75

69B 112
$14.50

69B 113
$15.00

69B III
$13.75

No. 69B110. This Model Shows Good Taste and Refinement, Combined with Splendid Tailoring; it is made of good quality serge, in black, navy blue, smoke gray, Copenhagen blue, and tan; the coat is cut in a semi-fitting, single-breasted style, fastening with bone buttons; the seams are richly trimmed with tailor-stitched moire strapping, braid, and button; notched, long-roll collar; sleeves trimmed with moire strapping, braid and button giving cuff effect; lined with fine quality satin; the skirt is a charming new model, closely side plaited all around from the box-plaited panel front; the plaits are stitched down in graduated form to a little below hips, and then fall in pretty flare; price....$13.75

No. 69B111. A Suit of Distinctive Style, adapted for the requirements of those who desire smart but simple style; made of chiffon Panama cloth, in black, navy blue, gray, tan, and Copenhagen blue; the coat is cut on graceful lines; is a single-breasted, semi-fitting model, fastening with two bone buttons; has long roll collar, trimmed with moire, braid loops, and buttons; full coat sleeves, finished with fancy shaped braid-trimmed cuffs; two pockets, also braid trimmed; lined with good quality satin; the skirt is a becoming new plated style; it is closely plaited all around from the box-plaited panel on front gore; the plaits are stitched down to a little below hips, and then fall in loose side plaits; price......$13.75

No. 69B112. A Chic London Model is pictured here, made of fine quality chiffon Panama cloth, in black, navy blue, smoke gray, reseda green, and tan; the coat is designed in a semi-fitting, single-breasted cutaway style, fastening with self-covered buttons; it is excellently tailored, and trimmed back and front with soutache braid and buttons; has long roll collar, inlaid with good quality satin; the skirt is one of the pretty new plaited models; the front gore is box and side plaited, giving broad panel effect; front and back gores laid in clusters of plaits, falling gracefully at bottom; price............................$14.50

No. 69B113. Women Who Admire Plainly Tailored Models Will Appreciate This Pretty Style, made of good quality wide wale chevron, in reseda green, navy blue, gray, black, and tan; the coat is a nobby semi-fitting, single-breasted cutaway style, fastening with three large bone buttons; long roll collar, trimmed with beautiful Persian trimming; the vents in back are trimmed with tabs of self material and buttons; cuffs and pockets button trimmed; lined with good quality satin; the skirt is a stylish new model; the front gore is laid in a double box plait, giving a broad panel effect; side and back gores are cluster side plaited; price............$15.00

Figure 1.6 'Women's Tailored Suits' Siegel Cooper catalogue, 1910, p. 11, includes, on the far right, 'A Chic London Model'. Author's Collection.

the American woman of moderate or humble means',[81] but made the average American woman 'the best-dressed in the world'.[82] Ewen has described the development of factory-made goods between 1880 and 1920, as an 'explosion', which transformed the nature and quality of life in the United States; 'New

Three Charming Frocks—New Bedell Creations

A-201
$15⁹⁸
Taffeta Silk

SIZES: Women's sizes 34 to 44 bust measurement, skirt length 37 to 42 inches; also misses' 14, 16 and 18 year sizes, skirt length 36 to 40 inches.

A-202
$11⁹⁸
Silk Poplin

A-203
$15⁰⁰
Silk Satin

A-201. This beautiful Taffeta Silk gown is fresh from the hands of our very best designers, is strictly up-to-the-moment in style and altogether lovely. The waist part is draped over an inner lining and combines silk Georgette Crêpe of matching color in the collar, sleeves and softly plaited vest. A very pretty trimming is supplied in the beautiful self-embroidery and colored beads The revers and cuffs are of the taffeta, and self-covered buttons add a pretty finish. The apron-tunic falls gracefully over a narrower underskirt and is button-trimmed. High, crushed girdle. **Colors:** black, navy blue, Belgian blue, green or taupe. Price.......... **$15.98**

We Please You or Refund Your Money

A-202. Silk Poplin is still the favorite for dressy afternoon gowns and here is a perfectly beautiful new frock developed in this favorite fabric. It has all the newest style features, chief among them a double collar of contrasting silk Georgette Crêpe edged with fold of self-material, and there are roll cuffs to match. The waist is lined, richly embroidered, and the high, crushed girdle is finished with self-covered buttons. The fashionable tunic is given a wonderfully smart side dip and is attractively button-trimmed; the narrow underskirt smartly accentuating its fulness. **Colors:** black, navy blue, green, Burgundy or Belgian blue. Price **$11.98**

A-203. This beautiful new afternoon gown is made of fine quality Silk Satin, always the favorite for the dressy frock. The model is refreshingly new in every detail and combines matching silk Georgette Crêpe in the transparent sleeves which are cuffed with self-material. Very, very new and piquantly becoming is the wide sailor collar of silk Georgette Crêpe with satin fold and a wide satin tie, softly crushed and gracefully draped. At the front a contrasting silk braided design adds a very effective trimming. The favorite over-draping tunic has just the right fulness. **Colors:** black, navy blue, Belgian blue, green or plum. Price... **$15.00**

THE BEDELL COMPANY, NEW YORK CITY

Figure 1.7 'Three Charming Frocks' Bedell catalogue of 'New York Styles' for Fall/Winter, 1918–1919. Author's Collection.

industries developed a vast array of consumer products that altered the context of everyday life'.[83] Ready-to-wear clothing was a major part of this transition, as indicated by these 'Three Charming Frocks', offered for sale at 'money-saving prices' for Fall/Winter 1918–1919 (Figure 1.7).

Immigrants in the New York garment industry were key in helping to shape the US labour movement in the early twentieth century. For many employees work was all-consuming, with a working day lasting as long as eighteen hours. Working conditions were a prime topic addressed by unions, such as the International Ladies Garment Workers' Union, formed in 1900 by Jewish immigrants who were joined later by Italian immigrants. In 1909, the union had only 2,000 members when 15,000 shirtwaist makers went on strike in more than 500 factories; a protest that lasted four months and galvanized the union movement. Contemporary photographs provide extremely valuable evidence of such historical events and what women and men were wearing to work and for everyday. Change came following the tragic Triangle Shirtwaist Fire of 1911 that caused the death of 146 female employees, and forever drew attention to the conditions of garment workers in New York City, where by 1910 c. 41 per cent of the city's population were immigrants. By this time, although daughters of immigrants continued to be employed in the garment trade, they were also working in schools, offices and department stores, jobs which allowed more autonomy and leisure time for going out and socializing with work mates, and the incumbent challenges of what to wear in public, the subject of the next chapter.[84]

By 1938, the garment business, which was the largest industry in New York City and, according to *Vogue,* larger than the steel industry, employed 200,000 workers. It had also gradually moved northwards to the east and west of Fifth Avenue around the low thirties. Aiming to stem this gradual spread towards Fifth Avenue, by the late 1930s, Seventh Avenue was established as the Garment Center Capitol with the erection of several major manufacturing buildings around 38th and 40th Streets and Seventh Avenue. As *Vogue* reporter described it, 'Here, in chromium-plated, white-carpeted, thirty story skyscrapers (rabbit-warren sweat-shops have almost disappeared), more than five thousand wholesalers make most of the nation's clothes'.[85]

'Becoming American'

A number of researchers (Ewen 1985; Peiss 1986, Schreier 1994) have drawn attention to the importance of [fashionable] clothing for immigrants to the United States. Peiss, for example, notes how, 'For newly arrived immigrants, changing one's clothes was the first step in securing a new status as an American'.[86] Immigrant daughters were quoted as 'shedding their pasts' by changing their clothes.[87] Such transitions are recorded in visual culture, in written accounts and in oral histories. As Barbara Schreier has pointed out in her extensive research on Eastern European Jewish immigrants, from Russia, Romania, Poland or Ukraine, women were particularly taxed with deciding what artefacts of everyday life, including clothing, to take to their new homeland. 'From all quarters, immigrants herald the same message – to become American women, one had to look the part'.[88] She notes that there were complex reasons for dress becoming a critical symbol of immigration. However, she draws proper attention to the 'expressive potential' and 'adaptability of dress and its ability to transcend and alter an image. Their appearance and self-image were inextricably linked, and both were in constant renewal'.[89] As Enstad has remarked, 'Fashion could be a way of making connections across ethnic boundaries, as immigrants from various backgrounds adopted similar styles, as well as a way to reinterpret a specifically Jewish or Italian identity in a new context'.[90] For instance, Japanese 'picture brides' were taken to a clothing store as soon as they landed in America, in particular to distinguish themselves from Chinese immigrants, the latter, interestingly, being 'considered inassimilable because they refused to give up their native dress'.[91]

A hand-coloured New Year's postcard produced by the Hebrew Publishing Company in 1900 (Figure 1.8), representing Jewish Americans welcoming Jewish immigrants from Russia to America, shows the difference between the heavy, coarse garments of those arriving, compared with the more refined and fashionable outfits of those already assimilated. After Ellis Island opened in 1892, it was noted that most arriving Eastern European women 'wore a kerchief as part of their native costume'.[92] Immigrant mothers brought large quantities of clothing with them, 'representing sometimes their accumulations for a dowry – heavy linen underwear, thick heavily lined waists, clumsy shoes and wide, bright skirts. A coloured scarf or shawl completes the wardrobe'. These costumes were discarded in the United States: 'Only some of the older women have the courage to appear at their factories in the garments they brought. The first year in this country frequently means much skimping and saving to get new clothes, especially among the younger women who want to "look American"'.[93] While formal programmes of 'Americanization' were introduced in order to help first-generation immigrants to assimilate, there are numerous accounts of how family members took on that role, 'Donning ready-made clothing was the most visible sign of Americanization. Greenhorns quickly learned to be ashamed of old-world clothing. Americans ridiculed them on the streets or in school, and some garment manufacturers refused to hire women dressed in "un-American" clothing. All around them, movie posters, billboards, and chromos adorned women in sumptuous fashionable garments'.[94]

Oral histories are filled with accounts of relatives 'schooling their newly arrived immigrants on the finer points of dressing'.[95] For Jewish garment worker and recent immigrant, Sophie Abrams, 'becoming American' meant a total overhaul of her wardrobe:

I was such a greenhorn, you wouldn't believe. My first day in America I went with my aunt to buy some American clothes. She bought me a shirtwaist, you know, a blouse and skirt, a blue print with red buttons and a hat I had never

Figure 1.8 'A Happy New Year' Photomechanical print postcard: offset lithograph, colour shows Jewish Americans welcoming Jews immigrating from Russia to America, c. 1900. Library of Congress.

seen. I took my old brown dress and shawl and threw them away! I know it sounds foolish, we being so poor, but I didn't care. I had enough of the old country. When I looked in the mirror, I couldn't get over it. I said, boy, Sophie, look at you now. Just like an American.[96]

Such sartorial overhauls applied not only to young women. Abraham Cahan (who himself immigrated to the United States from Lithuania in 1886) relates how his fictional hero David Levinsky was taken shopping by his benefactor Mr Even:

He then took me to store after store, buying me a suit of clothes, a hat, some underclothes, handkerchiefs (the first white handkerchiefs I ever possessed), collars, shoes, and a necktie. He spent a considerable sum on me. As we passed from block to block he kept saying, 'Now you won't look green,' or, 'That will make you look American'. At one point he added, 'Not that you are a bad-looking fellow as it is, but then one must be presentable in America'.[97]

Transformations might also have taken place before the immigrant stepped onto the island of Manhattan, as described by Henry Roth in his novel based in 1907, 'the year that was destined to bring the greatest number of immigrants'.[98] He describes a man escorting a woman from a ship as follows:

The man had evidently spent some time in America and was now bringing his wife and child over from the other side. It might have been thought that he had spent most of his time in New York, for he paid only the scantest attention to the Statue of Liberty or to the city rising from the water or to the bridges spanning the East River – or perhaps he was merely too agitated to waste much time on these wonders. His clothes were the ordinary clothes the ordinary New Yorker wore in that period – sober and dull. A black derby accentuated the sharpness and sedentary pallor of his face; a jacket, loose on his tall spare frame, buttoned up in a V close to the throat; and above the V a tightly-knotted black tie was mounted in the groove of a high starched collar. As for his wife, one guessed that she was a European more by the timid wondering look in her eyes as she gazed from her husband to the harbor, than by her clothes. For her clothes were American – a black skirt, a white shirt-waist and a black jacket. Obviously her husband had either taken the precaution of sending them to her while she was still in Europe or had brought them with him to Ellis Island where she had slipped them on before she left.[99]

Specific items of clothing took on great significance to the immigrant. David Levinsky comments that 'A whole book could be written on the influence of a starched collar and a necktie on a man who was brought up as I was'.[100] Attention to head coverings was also of particular importance for both male and female Jewish immigrants. Casting off the headscarf or the wig in favour of the hat was a frequent marker of Americanness and modernity: 'When Rose Pasternak landed at Castle Garden, her brother took her directly to a hat store: "They said in this country you don't go to work without a hat."'[101] Hairstyles are also mentioned; a young immigrant woman in 1911, who had been taken by relatives to buy new clothes, styled her hair in 'an American fashion', stating that in doing so 'I'm almost an American. I have a rat for my hair. The essential thing in America is to look stylish'.[102] The hat was ubiquitous, with its style chosen to suit the occasion. A straw boater complemented a tailored skirt and cotton shirtwaist blouse in summer, while fancier millinery was worn in the afternoon and evening.

Across the social strata and different income levels, all women, even the young, wore hats, with those of more modest means often re-trimming them to create a new look (Figure 1.9). 'When twelve-year-old Celia Adler arrived in America in 1914, she discovered that it was not enough just to wear the right kind of hat'.[103] The sailor style, the first hat she had owned, given to her as a going-away present when she left Russia, was considered old fashioned by her sister who met her and insisted it was left on the dock at Ellis Island.[104]

When worn on the streets the hat became a symbol of gender and class struggle. Enstad has noted how middle- and upper-class women critiqued their working-class counterparts' display of fashion as 'putting on airs' or 'playing the lady'.[105] For middle-class women, fashion was determined as a display of class distinction and taste, as a cultural marker that distinguished them from the working class and from women of colour. Middle-class taste required women to follow, but not to lead fashion.[106] However, the everyday context was all important, capable of providing the same hats with different meanings if worn for work, or for leisure, in front of parents, or to promenade on 14th or Essex Streets, the wearers could be distinguished as 'workers', 'Americans', 'ladies', or significantly, 'all three at once'.[107] Working-class women in particular developed a very distinct everyday relationship with hats, and other items of clothing [more in the next chapter], their knowledge as consumers, enhanced by the fact that many of them were also the makers of fashionable dress. As Schreier has noted, 'the dominant role of Jewish women in the garment industry and needle trades led to a heightened fashion-consciousness'.[108] She also draws attention to the symbolic importance of clothing traditions to Eastern European Jews, and the historical roles of such as *sheitels* (wigs) and *peyes* (side locks).

'The corset also figures prominently in the acculturation process because embracing the American ideal meant accepting a new body type'.[109] For some corporeal assimilation was not such a problem. Rose R arriving from Bialystock 'discovered her figure was in vogue'. Stylish women had 'big busts, big behinds and small waistlines. And I was just built like that'.[110] But most women arriving from Eastern Europe found they were overweight by American standards and could not mould their figures to the curvaceous Gibson Girl fashionable 'hourglass' silhouette, with full hips and bosom and a small waist, the latter only made possible by wearing a corset. While well-off women in Eastern Europe had already adopted the corset, for the poorer immigrant women from remote villages, it was deemed uniquely American.[111] Initially, for Jewish immigrants, clothes were 'the most tangible proof of assimilation' that took on an almost magical quality in their potential to transform (even though it was later realized that the cultural and social mores of assimilation were much more complex). While dress was utilized to signify being modern and urban, New York City posed particular challenges. Schreier writes of Anna, a Czech girl who had lived in Vienna, where she 'dressed up Modern', but was quite unprepared for the faster

The Season's Newest Styles in Smart Untrimmed Hats

A-542 $1.25

A-543 $2.98

A-544 $1.79

A-545 $1.98

A-546 $1.69

A-547 $1.98

A-548 $1.98

A-549 $1.48

A-550 $1.00

A-551 $2.49

A-542. New mushroom poke for misses and young women. Made of good quality Velvetta with the smartly-drooped brim faced with contrasting velvet which rolls over the edge to form a flange all around. Colors: black with cherry facing; navy with sand, or rose with Copenhagen blue; also all black. Price.... $1.25

A-543. Beautiful dress hat in a large, adorably becoming shape. The draped crown is of finest quality Silk Velvet, and the brim is of doubled silk maline, finely shirred and finished with velvet flange. Lovely silk fringe falls gracefully around the edge in fascinating picture effect. Colors: black or navy blue. May be worn without further trimming if desired. Width across about 15 inches. Price.... $2.98

A-544. This smart hat is a charming new shape with particularly becoming lines. Made of good quality Velvetta with top-crown of hatter's silk plush and tapering side-roll brim. Colors: black or navy blue. Price.... $1.79

A-545. A fetching new wide brim hat that is given a piquant semi-mushroom droop that is highly becoming. It is made of extra good quality Silk Velvet, the oval crown softly draped in very smart style. Width across about 14 inches. Colors: black, navy blue or taupe grey. Price.... $1.98

A-546. The very latest New York model and a smart mushroom hat of youthfully becoming style. Made of good quality Velvetta, with medium high crown and shirred mushroom brim. Colors: black, navy or regimental blue. Requires but very little trimming. Price.... $1.69

A-547. Becoming new wide-brim sailor of fine Silk Velvet, stylish and dressy as can be. The brim shows a new plaited drape and the edge is bound with silk grosgrain ribbon. Width across about 15¾ inches. Colors: solid black; black with rose color facing, or black with Copenhagen blue facing. Price.... $1.98

A-548. Smart new close-fitting hat of particularly stylish, universally becoming shape. Made of fine quality Silk Velvet with soft top-crown and the side prettily draped. Narrow brim a trifle higher at one side and given a stylish side roll. Colors: black, navy or purple. Very little trimming required for this smart hat. Price.... $1.98

A-549. The new Jockey model—all the rage with smart dressers. Made of good quality Velvetta with real jockey crown and mushroom poke brim, very narrow at back. Colors: black, navy, emerald green or cherry red. Price.... $1.48

A-550. The small sailor is having tremendous vogue this season, and here is one of the smartest shapes to be found. It is made of good quality Velvetta with crown of becoming height and soft, draped top. Colors: black, navy blue, tan or cherry red. This is a record-breaking bargain value at.... $1.00

A-551. Fashionable new turban, particularly becoming to matrons. It is made of fine quality Velvetta with top-crown of glossy silk hatter's plush. The turban brim is bent in French tricorne shape, has top-facing of satin and is bound with silk grosgrain ribbon. Colors: black or navy. Price.... $2.49

THE BEDELL COMPANY, NEW YORK CITY 77 We Pay All Postage Everywhere

Figure 1.9 Untrimmed hats, Bedell & Co, Spring/Summer 1918/19. Author's Collection.

pace of life in New York City.[112] While wealthy women could distinguish and frown upon cheaper copies of their ensembles, to 'America's new arrivals, the ready-to-wear offerings appeared as an emblem of democracy'.[113]

Knowing Your Place

If fashion was a key to asserting 'American' identity for newly arrived immigrants at New York's Ellis Island, donning clothes that bore some relationship to fashion also signalled class respectability and appropriate gendered behaviour for London's population. As 'Londoners came from everywhere' with a third of people living in the city born outside it, it was crucial that fashion allowed an increasingly heterogeneous population to 'fit in'.[114] While to be 'indistinguishable by their clothing' was a given for the new arrivals from eastern Europe and Ireland, as well as from Britain's regions, neutral attire so they could pass unnoticed and not attract unwelcome attention was particularly vital for the army of young women traversing the city each day for work and for leisure.[115] From the start of the twentieth century, they outnumbered young men as new Londoners and their numbers swelled through the 1920s and 1930s as young working-class women came to London to take up positions first as domestic servants and then increasingly as unskilled and semi-skilled factory workers, dress-makers, shop and office workers. While the clothing practices of immigrants were 'humdrum', as 'incoming communities gradually adopted practices of public assimilation in order to "fit" while reserving the memories and customs of the old country for the private world of home', class also marked fashion in the development of London as the 'modern metropolis'.[116] Juxtaposing the tailor's workshop and the dandy's dressing room, the gorgeous displays of Regent St and the second-hand clothing trade of Whitechapel, Breward maps out a London that is shaped by shifting class formations. These helped to shape fashion in the city along with gender and ethnicity: from the West End to the East End, but also beyond these to the rapidly expanding middle-class outer suburbs and the complex cultural geographies that marked 'Mayfair hauteur and Lambeth Bravado'.[117] Describing the fluidity of class in nineteenth-century Britain, Wilson and Taylor's observation that 'the uncertainties of class were most marked in the shifting centre', could just as easily be applied to Britain's geographical and metropolitan centre, London.[118]

In the first decade of the twenty-first century, historians have argued for the rehabilitation of '"class" as a legitimate subject of historical enquiry' in order to truly understand the nuances of social lives.[119] Turning away from 'class analysis', a number have proposed that it is in the 'low-key but pervasive "languages of class"…that one finds the most determined attempts to reconstitute social understandings'.[120] Unsurprisingly, an awareness of class has been intrinsic to fashion and dress history since the theories of Veblen and Simmel at the end of the nineteenth century. The notions that fashionable looks 'trickle down' and that 'dressing well' offered opportunity for social emulation have become embedded in our Western understandings of fashion. Indeed it is a truism that domestic servants dressed to emulate their social betters, but that also their ability to dress well expanded as fashion knowledge permeated the wider society. However the desire to conform, to merge with the crowd and to know one's place should not be understated within the context of class respectability and appropriate feminine behaviour particularly at a moment historically when these were being questioned politically, socially and culturally.

Over-layering these languages of class with those of gender, fashion was one of these 'low-key but pervasive "languages of class"', particularly when it was intrinsic to working women's everyday lives.[121] Underlining the longevity of fashion and the importance of working-class respectability, this description of the dress of a female clerical worker from 1893 points to the vital significance of being 'lady-like':

> with extreme care she had preserved an out-of-doors dress into the third summer: it did not look shabby. Her mantle was in its second year only; the original fawn colour has gone to an indeterminate grey. Her hat of brown straw was a possession forever: it underwent new trimming, at an outlay of pence, when that became unavoidable. Yet Virginia could not have been judged anything but a lady. She wore her garments as only a lady can (the position and movement of the arms has much to do with this), and had the step never to be acquired by a person of vulgar instincts.[122]

Distinctive methods of clothing manufacture and the interface between these and their selling and presentation were intrinsic to the social, cultural and economic identities of London and New York in the twentieth century. In Chapter 2, we examine the ways that specific streets and areas, as well as changing retailing practices – display and performance – ensured that fashionable dress became embedded in everyday lives in London and New York in the first decades of the twentieth century. As Walkowitz notes, not only was there a burgeoning number of middle-class shoppers who frequented London's West End, they also were joined by the large army of working women – clerical workers and service workers – whose wages, increased twofold during and after the First World War, enjoyed new levels of prosperity. The social expectations of this growing number of working-class women were raised as they took on new roles and deserted domestic service. As we will see, the 'entry of women into a new culture of fashion'[123] that gathered pace in the first few decades of the twentieth century was indicative of 'a new turn in London's modernity' that was both different and similar to New York.[124]

Notes

1 Francis Sheppard, *London: A History* (Oxford: Oxford University Press, 1998), 263; 316.

2 Charles Loch Mowat, *Britain Between the Wars, 1918–1940* (Cambridge: Cambridge University Press, 1955), 227; 'Historical Overview of London Population', *London*, available online http://www.londononline.co.uk/factfile/historical/ (accessed October 11, 2012).

3 Ibid., 227.

4 'Facts and Figures: Population', *Mayor of London. London Assembly*, available online http://www.london.gov.uk/who-runs-london/mayor/publications/society/facts-and-figures/population (accessed October 11, 2012); 'Facts and Figures: DMAG Update', *Mayor of London. London Assembly*, available online http://legacy.london.gov.uk/gla/publications/factsandfigures/DMAG-Update-14.pdf (accessed October 11, 2012).

5 Sheppard, *London: A History*, 272.

6 David R. Green, 'Distance to Work in Victorian London: A Case Study of Henry Poole, Bespoke Tailors', *Business History* 30, no. 2 (1988), 187.

7 Sheppard, *London: A History*, 304.

8 Charles Booth, *Poverty, Vol. 4: The Trades of East London Connected with Poverty, Life and Labour of the People of London, 1st series* (London and New York: Macmillan & Co. Ltd., 1902).

9 Ibid., 37.

10 Ibid., 140.

11 Ibid., 47.

12 Peter K. Newman, 'The Early London Clothing Trade', *Oxford Economic Papers* 4, no. 3 (1952), 250.

13 Andrew Godley, 'Immigrant Entrepreneurs and the Emergence of London's East End as an Industrial District', *The London Journal* 21, no. 1 (1996), 38.

14 Ibid., 43.

15 Roy Porter, *London: A Social History* (London: Penguin, 2000), 240.

16 Godley, 'Immigrant Entrepreneurs', 43.

17 Sheppard, *London: A History*, 293.

18 Christopher Breward, *Fashioning London: Clothing and the Modern Metropolis* (Oxford and New York: Berg, 2004), 59.

19 Christopher Breward, Edwina Ehrman and Caroline Evans (eds), *The London Look: Fashion from Street to Catwalk* (New Haven and London: Yale University Press with Museum of London, 2004), 33.

20 Ibid., 34.

21 Ibid., 35.

22 Andrew Godley, 'The Development of the UK Clothing Industry, 1850–1950: Output and Productivity Growth', *Business History* 37, no. 4 (1995), 56–7.

23 Ibid., 59.

24 Godley, 'Immigrant Entrepreneurs', 40.

25 Godley, 'The Development of the UK Clothing Industry', 59.

26 Godley, 'Immigrant Entrepreneurs', 42.

27 Ibid., 42. See also Anne J. Kershen, *Off the Peg: The Story of the Women's Wholesale Clothing Industry 1880 to the 1960s* (London: The Jewish Museum, 1988).

28 Breward, Erhman and Evans, *The London Look*, 79.

29 Ibid.

30 *Savista Magazine*, available online http://www.savistamagazine.com/userfiles/public/ articles_blocks/image_1/three_3704.jpg (accessed January 11, 2016).

31 Breward, Erhman and Evans, *The London Look*, 79.

32 Lou Taylor, 'The Wardrobe of Mrs Leonard Messel, 1895–1929', in *The Englishness of English Dress*, ed. C. Breward, B. Conekin and C. Cox (London: Penguin, 2002), 121–2; Finlay Muirhead, *London and its Environs* (London: Blue Book, 1918).

33 Breward, Ehrman and Evans, *The London Look* 86.

34 Taylor, 'The Wardrobe of Mrs Leonard Messel', 129; Breward, Ehrman and Evans, *The London Look*, 86–87.

35 Breward, Ehrman and Evans, *The London Look*, 81.

36 Ibid.

37 Ibid., 66.

38 Christopher Breward, *The Hidden Consumer: Masculinities, Fashion and City Life 1860–1914* (Manchester: Manchester University Press, 1999), 104.

39 Booth, *Poverty*, 138–9.

40 Breward, *The Hidden Consumer*, 108–109.

41 Fiona Anderson, 'Fashioning the Gentleman: A Study of Henry Poole and Co., Savile Row Tailors 1861-1900', *Fashion Theory: The Journal of Dress, Body & Culture* 4, no. 4 (2000): 407.

42 Porter, *London*, 342.

43 Anderson, 'Fashioning the Gentleman', 408.

44 Ibid., 409.

45 Ibid., 416.

46 Ibid., 422.

47 Breward, *The Hidden Consumer*, 109.

48 Porter, *London*, 242.

49 J. Alan Slater (comp.), *Ninety Years of Architectural Practice: Some Notes on the History of the Firm of Architects now Known as Slater & Uren from the Start of the Firm in About 1876 Until 1962 When I Retired from Active Participation* (London: R.I.B.A. Library).

50 Gerry Black, *Living Up West: Jewish Life in London's West End* (London: The London Museum of Jewish Life, 1994), 35.

51 Judith R. Walkowitz, *Nights Out: Life in Cosmopolitan London* (New Haven and London: Yale University Press, 2012), 147.

52 Ibid., 145–8.

53 Jerry White, *London in the Twentieth Century: A City and Its People* (London: Random House, 2008), 252.

54 Jane Brown, *I had a Pitch on the Stones* (London: Nicholson & Watson, 1946), 49–50.

55 Ibid. 181.

56 Kenneth T. Jackson (ed.), *The Encyclopedia of New York City*, 2nd edn (New Haven and London: Yale University Press), 493.

57 Barbara A. Schreier, *Becoming American Women: Clothing and the Jewish Immigrant Experience, 1880–1920* (Chicago: Chicago Historical Society, 1994),17.

58 Abraham Cahan, *The Rise of David Levinsky* (1917; repr., New York: Penguin, 1993 [1917]), 61.

59 Ibid., 86.

60 Schreier, *Becoming American Women*, 68.

61 Nan Enstad, *Ladies of Labor, Girls of Adventure: Working Women, Popular Culture, and Labor Politics at the Turn of the Twentieth Century* (New York: Columbia University Press, 1999).

62 Rob Schorman. *Selling Style: Clothing and Social Change at the Turn of the Century* (Philadelphia: University of Pennsylvania Press, 2003), 7.

63 Claudia B. Kidwell and Margaret C. Christman, *Suiting Everyone: The Democratization of Clothing in America* (Washington, DC: Smithsonian Institution Press, 1974), 85.

64 Schorman, *Selling Style,* 3.

65 Kidwell and Christman, *Suiting Everyone*, 87.

66 JoAnne Olian, 'From Division Street to Seventh Avenue: The Coming of Age of American Fashion', in *A Perfect Fit: The Garment Industry and American Jewry, 1860–1960*, ed. Gabriel M. Goldstein and Elizabeth E Greenberg (Lubbock: Texas Tech University Press, 2012), 114.

67 Ibid., 115.

68 Ibid., 115.

69 Enstad, *Ladies of Labor*, 18.

70 Allan Schoener, *New York: An Illustrated History of the People* (New York: W.W. Norton & Co, 1998), 85.

71 Olian, 'From Division Street to Seventh Avenue', 115.

72 Schorman *Selling Style*, 47.

73 Lewis Wickes Hine, available online www.loc.gov/pictures/item/ncl2004003321/PP/ (accessed 9 December 2015).

74 Lewis Wickes Hine, available online www.loc.gov/item/ncl2004003273/PP/ (accessed 9 December 2015).

75 Cahan, *The Rise of David Levinsky*, 151.

76 Ibid., 151–152.

77 Ibid., 157.

78 Ibid., 442.

79 Schorman, *Selling Style*, 51.

80 Cahan, *The Rise of David Levinsky*, 442.

81 Ibid., 443.

82 Ibid., 443–4.

83 Elizabeth Ewen, *Immigrant Women in the Land of Dollars: Life and Culture on the Lower east Side, 1890–1925* (New York: Monthly Review Press, 1985), 22.

84 Kathy L. Peiss, *Cheap Amusements: Working Women and Leisure in Turn-of-the-Century New York* (Philadelphia: Temple University Press, 1986), 39.

85 Ibid., 119.

86 Peiss, *Cheap Amusements*, 63.

87 Ewen, *Immigrant Women in the Land of Dollars*, 67.

88 Schreier, *Becoming American Women*, 12.

89 Ibid., 4.

90 Enstad, *Ladies of Labor*, 9.

91 Schreier, *Becoming American Women*, 5.

92 Ibid., 59.

93 Ewen, *Immigrant Women in the Land of Dollars*, 68.

94 Ibid., 25.

95 Schreier, *Becoming American Women*, 56.

96 Ewen, *Immigrant Women in the Land of Dollars*, 68.

97 Cahan, *The Rise of David Levinsky*, 101

98 Henry Roth, *Call It Sleep* (New York: Robert O. Ballou, 1934), 9.

99 Ibid., 10.

100 Cahan, *The Rise of David Levinsky*, 110.

101 Peiss, *Cheap Amusements*, 63.

102 Ewen, *Immigrant Women in the Land of Dollars*, 69.

103 Schreier, *Becoming American Women*, 61.

104 Ibid., 61–62

105 Enstad, *Ladies of Labor*, 10.

106 Ibid., 27.

107 Ibid., 10. C.f. D. W. Griffith, *The New York Hat* (1912).

108 Schreier, *Becoming American Women*, 6.

109 Ibid., 64.

110 Ibid.

111 Ibid.

112 Ibid., 11.

113 Ibid., 69.

114 White, *London in the Twentieth Century*, 91.

115 Andrew Hill, 'People Dress so Badly Nowadays: Fashion and Late Modernity', in *Fashion and Modernity*, ed. Christopher Breward and Caroline Evans (Oxford: Berg, 2005), 70.

116 Breward, *Fashioning London*, 59 and introduction.

117 Ibid., 144.

118 Elizabeth Wilson and Lou Taylor, *Through the Looking Glass: A History of Dress from 1860 to the Present Day* (London: BBC, 1989), 14.

119 Jon Lawrence, 'The British Sense of Class', *Journal of Contemporary History* 35 (2000): 307.

120 Ibid., 308.

121 Ibid.

122 Wilson and Taylor, *Through the Looking Glass*, 48.

123 Walkowitz, *Nights Out*, 157.

124 Lynda Nead, 'Response', in *Fashion and Modernity*, ed. Christopher Breward and Caroline Evans (Oxford: Berg, 2005), 123.

2
STREET WALKING

Introduction

Recognizing the old alongside the new, this chapter focuses on modernity but it does this through the lens of the everyday and within a context of emerging metropolitan identities in London and New York. By examining these two major cities that were both growing in importance as fashion centres and also pivotal spaces in the articulation of what constituted modernity, we concentrate on key shopping districts and routes, retailing strategies and practices and visual display and performance as they connected everyday life in London and New York. With a focus on women, but also recognizing that men inhabited the city in different ways too, we see these two cities as 'practised spaces' producing shoppers and consumers who 'imbued the urban center with meaning'.[1] Not only did their consumption produce new attitudes to the city, but 'other images from both the past and the present conditioned their perspective'.[2] Exploring the differing and shifting fashion geographies of London and New York at a time when both cities expanded exponentially, this chapter considers the spaces within which clothes were displayed, selected, bought and worn. On the cusp of modernity, these cities were sites for the visualization and enactment of everyday life.[3] Countering the view that modernity was driven principally by bourgeois middle-class experiences and desires, we argue that fashion was a means of bringing the working-class, immigrants and a burgeoning female workforce into this complex nuanced modern world (photography and cinema are other examples). By making, selling, buying and wearing clothes that connected with contemporary styles on a daily basis, fashion became more thoroughly embedded in the diversity of people's everyday lives.

Utilizing 'the side streets and ... the street corners, as much as the new roads and thoroughfares', we propose that fashion as a network of cultural practices created new spaces that developed 'its own system of salons, catwalks, points of sale and events', but also stepped beyond the shop windows of elite stores to join ordinary lives in suburban multiple stores, high street dress stores, home dress-making and local markets.[4] While fashion constituted 'a script for imaginatively inhabiting the past and embodying the marginal', it also provided for the humdrum of everyday existence.[5] Describing the life of an Italian immigrant in the turn-of-the century London, Breward suggests that such lives can be 'told by old clothes'.[6] Fashion then was found in the most ordinary of places; in the home, at numerous places of work, on the trolley-bus and the underground. It was intrinsic to regular religious observance and social rituals, but it was also the umbilical cord to emerging social and metropolitan identities.

Shoppers and consumers in both cities were heterogeneous and affected by diverse factors including gender and social class, race and migration, age and marital status. Highly visualized – by advertising, photography, the theatre and film – some consumer identities had become fluid and permeable by the 1930s, particularly in response to the economic and social changes that were accentuated within these centres of metropolitan life. Young women, immigrants and recently enfranchised sections of the working classes and middle classes negotiated the newness and diversity of the city, while other groups were more tentative, more inclined to recourse to established routines and follow traditional patterns. A more nuanced understanding of modernity acknowledges that those immigrants in London's East End and New York's Lower East Side, for example, who laboured to secure an economic and social toe-hold in a foreign country in the early twentieth century, were a world apart from the mythologized migrant of modernist discourse who, located at the vortex of modernity, experienced life as 'transitory, fugitive and contingent'.[7] While it has been argued that 'modernity cannot be conceived outside the context of the city, which provided an arena for the circulation of bodies and goods, the exchange of glances, and the exercise of consumerism', London and New York were cities that offered a range of possibilities to be modern.[8]

Proposing the city as a gendered space, writers and historians have helped to change our understanding of the relative geographies of these two twentieth-century cities. At the same time, research on London and New York as émigré and immigrant cities has provided another layer of complexity. This adds to our perception of London at the centre of a vast, though increasingly disquieted Empire – still an 'imperial city' – and New York, a city driven by capital and fuelled by financial prowess – avowedly meritocratic. At the turn of the century, London was being transformed, but its modernity was 'unlike that of Paris, or Berlin or New York. London was a huge, imperial metropolis, with a complex and unwieldy local government'.[9] It was becoming increasingly regulated and managed in a manner that encouraged business, consumption, entertainment and tourism as 'Edwardian London's merchants, rentiers and entrepreneurs ... pushed forward the capital's modernization'.[10] Foremost was the reconstruction of Regent St, initiated by Richard Norman Shaw, but completed by Reginald Blomfield; the re-modelling of the facade of Buckingham Palace and the building of Admiralty Arch, linked to Buckingham Palace by the new Mall designed by Aston Webb in 1901 and completed in 1913; and the huge Holborn to Strand improvement scheme designed in 1892 and overseen by LCC Improvements Committee with the connected Kingsway and Aldwych opened in 1905.[11] Characteristically this ambitious modernization of the West End that swept away 'the largest remaining intact quarter of pre-Great Fire London' was 'dressed' in Edwardian Baroque,[12] but by 1911 it meant that London had begun to look like an Imperial City with 'new processional streets, a city of new palaces of gleaming white Portland stone – palaces of banking and commerce in the West End and the City; palaces for new bureaucrats in a completed wide Whitehall'.[13] But importantly alongside these grandiose schemes, modest suburban high streets developed and grew for the local consumption of goods including fashionable clothes.

In the early twentieth century, New York was the centre of trade for the United States, continuing to serve as a gateway for the whole country to Europe and the rest of the world. While some heavy industry had migrated to less populated areas, the city retained a firm grip on credit and banking and on market-sensitive industries such as fashion and publishing. At the turn of the twentieth century, around half of the millionaires in the United States lived in Manhattan, many were self-made men, including Andrew Carnegie, John D. Rockefeller and Henry Clay Frick, who had developed businesses during the Gilded Age (1870s–c. 1896), the period of widespread economic growth and industrialization following the American Civil War. They built mansions for themselves[14] on the Upper East Side of the city along Fifth Avenue, facing the newly developed Central Park.[15] On the other side of the park, the 1870s and 1880s saw the construction of luxurious apartments for upper middle-class families, including the Dakota and Ansonia buildings. All of which contrasted markedly with the teeming tenement buildings that provided rental accommodation for poor and working-class immigrants, especially on the Lower East Side. By the turn of the twentieth century, much of Manhattan was devoted to fashion, in different ways. Almost two-thirds of all ready-to-wear clothes made in the United States were manufactured in New York.[16] As the centre of the publishing industry, the city also served as the style-setter for the whole of the country

As well as the large numbers of people employed in clothing production and promotion in both cities, many others were involved in its consumption, through employment in the burgeoning retail sector, and also as active shoppers. While upper-class women relied on their carriages to transport them to shopping and to leisure activities, working- and middle-class women were appearing on the streets of New York and London during this period. Fashionable dress marked out the classes, with unobtrusive public dress and manners being the markers of middle-class women. A photograph from the British *Daily Mirror* newspaper from c. 1905 shows middle-class women dressed in their fashionable clothes walking in Hyde Park (Figure 2.1). Looking closely, this photograph shows different generations of women with one or two smart men in attendance. Layers of lace, fur and wraps, elaborate feathered hats and puffed out and built up hair styles

Figure 2.1 Edwardian women at leisure in Hyde Park, London, 1905. Mirrorpix.

seem to reinforce Elizabeth Ewing's point that 'fashion was securely controlled by the rich and socially eminent among the upper classes and by those who had achieved wealth and the limelight of either fame or notoriety, plus the copious leisure that being in fashion demanded'.[17] While for upper-class and middle-class women whether in Edwardian Britain or Gilded Age New York, the city was both a place to move through and in certain parts, one in which to enjoy leisure, for the working classes it was also becoming a space of sociability, a refuge from crowded homes and a location for leisure; with fashion and dressing well an important part of this. By the late nineteenth century, the streets, with their advertisements, posters, billboards and not least their department store windows, were places to linger and to stare.

Shopping districts and routes

Baedecker's Guide to London of 1908 described London as 'not only the largest but one of the finest cities in the world'; but it was also a modern city with two-thirds built within the previous fifty years despite its plethora of historic streets, churches and palaces.[18] With over seven miles of shops running roughly east to west, by the end of George IV's reign in 1830, 'many of the pleasures which London had to offer was diffused throughout a substantial section of the population...Bow windows, plate glass, and bright lights were all used to exploit impulse buying, and in Oxford Street alone there were over 150 shops selling "the whim-whams and fribble-frabble of fashion."'[19] In the second half of the nineteenth century, London's shopping centre moved west from around St Paul's and Ludgate Hill in the City to Tottenham Court Road, the Strand, Piccadilly, Leicester Square, the Burlington Arcade, Oxford Street, Regent Street and New and Old Bond Streets in the West End. In part this shift aligned with those areas of London where the wealthy had their homes in Belgravia, Mayfair and Bloomsbury, but it also marked the gendering of space as the City of London became associated with masculine affairs and the late Victorian and Edwardian West End was fashioned by middle-class women as 'a shopping district, a tourist sight, an entertainment centre, and an arena for female work and politics'.[20] London's spaces and places of production were also peopled by those fleeing oppression abroad, as well as working-class men and women from Britain's regions and those born in London. These people made clothes in both the West End and East End, but they also worked in shops, as waitresses, maids and butlers; 'clerked' in offices, sold flowers, groomed and stabled, portered and worked on public transport. As Charles Booth put it: 'those who can afford it move out and those who cannot escape crowd in'.[21] Old boundaries were being blurred: 'There was a time, years ago when the East End was the East End – a land apart … But the omnibus changed all that … .'[22]

The early twentieth century witnessed a rush to the suburbs that affected both the middle and working classes: 'perhaps one man in four of the working population was by 1906 using some form of public transport between home in the inner and outer suburbs and work in the City and West End'.[23] The underground system was particularly important especially following the electrification of the Metropolitan and District line that came with the opening of Lots Road Power Station in 1905 and the subsequent opening of new deep underground lines under the centre of the city between 1902 and 1914. With six and a half million living in Greater London, the outer ring of which had expanded particularly to the east, north and south-west and with a 45.5 per cent population increase in these predominantly but not solely middle-class suburbs, London's shopping routes and thoroughfares were also changing.[24] Not only middle-class suburbs in Kensington, Bayswater, Ealing, Muswell Hill and Crouch End, but also working-class suburbs developed in Stoke Newington, Walthamstow, Tottenham and Lewisham,[25] and

> by 1900 the suburban ring extending from Ealing in the west round to Hornsey in the north, West Ham in the east, and Streatham in the south measured over 12 miles from east to west, and was the largest built-up area in the world. One-fifth of all the people of England and Wales lived within Greater London, a rapidly increasing proportion of them in the outer suburbs.[26]

What these outer and inner shopping routes offered were greater and easier opportunities to sell and advertise.

The new 'High Roads', 'High Streets' and 'Parades' provided the stage for fashion as people saw, bought, made and wore it. Not only were there impressive new and re-modelled department stores on London's premier shopping routes, there were also new multiple stores on suburban streets. Notable were the American FW Woolworth and the British Marks and Spencer stores. It was Woolworth that gained the earliest toe-hold on London's suburban high streets. Well before opening on Oxford Street, it began in Brixton in 1910, Woolwich and Harlesden in 1911, Croydon, Lewisham, Wimbledon and Peckham in 1912, Wood Green, Edgware Road, Clapham Junction, Hammersmith, Cricklewood and Kingston in 1914 with its first Oxford Street store opening in 1924. By 1912, Woolworth had 596 stores in Britain with a fixed price of 3d and 6d.[27] It was the formidable expansion of Woolworth and its reliance on American retailing methods that prompted Marks and Spencer to review its own practices in light of these; but as the quality of goods improved both 'entered into direct competition with the department stores in a market which was becoming increasingly homogenous'.[28] Contemporary with the expansion of these multiple chains was the re-modelling, development and consolidation of London's central shopping streets and department stores: Regent Street, Oxford Street and the Strand between 1890 and 1930. A photograph from the British newspaper *The Daily Mirror* of Oxford St, London in 1909 captures very effectively this busy major shopping street. With both men and women walking along the street, some pausing to window-shop, others striding out purposefully, while some were taken to their destination by horse-drawn buses. Fashionable 'looks' are evident particularly among the young: blouses and skirts with straw boaters, while a few more elaborate hats, capes and gowns. Generational differences are also discernible particular with older women clad in dark clothes edged with lace (Figure 2.2). Similar street scenes were captured in New York at the same period.

Described as the centre of England's fin de siècle commercial culture, Regent Street was a vitally important shopping route.[29] Built in 1820 and rebuilt between 1880 and 1927, historically it had a number of different sections with distinct functions; in particular the south was predominantly masculine with banks, clubs and accommodation, while the central section particularly the Quadrant and those sections that bordered Oxford Street housed elite shops that catered to the needs of wealthy middle- and upper-class women. By the 1880s, as London's shopping routes shifted to the west and as Oxford Street dazzled with new stores and attractions, Regent Street's merchant tenants thought their shops were 'inconvenient and uncomfortable … mean and melancholy' and in dire need of rebuilding.[30]

Parallel factors contributed to the shifting landscape of both consumption and commercial development in the turn-of-the-century New York. The geography of New York City had changed radically by the end of the nineteenth century; at its core, like a crooked diagonal spine that ran from the Battery at its tip to

Figure 2.2 A Busy Oxford St, London, 1909. Mirrorpix.

upper Manhattan, was Broadway, the main thoroughfare that was consolidated in 1899 and re-named in its entirety. What had been a largely residential street became the city's centre for commerce and entertainment. Parks and urban squares were dotted along its route, including Columbus Circle, Union, Madison, Herald and Times squares, which became commercial hubs and the location of subway stations after 1904. The city's first theatres, which had opened on lower Broadway in the eighteenth century, migrated north throughout the nineteenth century, to be consolidated around Times Square in the early twentieth century. A study in 1918 by the city's deputy commissioner of traffic reported that Broadway was the busiest street in the world.[31] It figured significantly in the everyday lives of the many people who used it, but it was especially important in the late nineteenth century for shopping and leisure, performance and display, thanks in particular to the presence of theatres and department stores.

Contemporary accounts indicate the expansion of New York City retail business along Broadway by the 1850s,

> Broadway, which starts from Bowling Green, is one of the longest and grandest business thoroughfares in the world … Here is the retail shopping district, from 10th Street to above 23rd Street … [The] prominent retail establishments are the wonder and the admiration of all who see them, and in extent and variety of goods they are not surpassed elsewhere in the world.[32]

It was no surprise that lower Broadway was the location of New York's first grand department store that was opened by Alexander T. Stewart in 1846, as a testament to the popularity and liveliness of the area. A visitor to the city, English tourist Samuel Osgood, commented in 1866 on the vibrancy of Broadway, created by the unique juxtaposition of theatres, speciality shops, department stores, hotels, restaurants and cafes, and unlike in London with its distinct and separate theatre district. Marlis Schweitzer provides detailed insight into the close relationships between Broadway theatres and department stores. She references their close ties and joint mission to 'create an image of the city that encouraged middle-class consumers to by-pass its most troubling districts and to instead see New York as a "navigable, legible, and ultimately playful space"'. At the end of the nineteenth century, the vibrancy, excitement and confusion of Broadway in the presence of the matinee crowd was palpable:

> The walk down Broadway, then as now, was one of the remarkable features of the city. There gathered, before the matinee and afterwards, not only all the pretty women who love a showy parade, but the men who love to gaze upon and admire them. It was a very imposing procession of pretty faces and fine clothes. Women appeared in their very best hats, shoes, and gloves, and walked arm in arm on their way to the fine shops or theatres strung along from Fourteenth to Thirty-Fourth Streets. Equally the men paraded with the very latest they could afford. A tailor might have secured hints on suit measurements, a shoemaker on proper lasts and colors, a hatter on hats. It was literally true that if a lover of fine clothes secured a new suit, it was sure to have its first airing on Broadway.[33]

The area of Broadway referred to encompassed the fashionable Ladies Mile, an elaborate shopping district in the last decades of the nineteenth century, concentrating on women's clothing. Small shops and dressmakers were located on the cross streets, along with grander establishments, such as Redfern, the London couture house, which opened a branch near the popular Delmonico's restaurant in the mid-1880s.[34] Madame Demorest, the milliner who developed the paper dressmaking pattern, was located in 473 Broadway at 11th Street, in 1867.[35] The area catered initially for well-off local residents living around Madison Square Park. Their presence also attracted department stores to the neighbourhood, the first being R.H. Macy opening at Sixth Avenue and 14th Street in 1858. By the late 1880s, 'all the stores that made New York City the nation's shopping and fashion capital' had moved to this former residential area; the best known including Arnold Constable, B. Altman, the Adams Company, Best & Company, Bonwit Teller, Brooks Brothers, Ehrich Brothers, Greenhut, Herns, Lord & Taylor, James McCreery, McCutcheon, R.H. Macy & Co, Hugh O'Neill's, Simpson, Crawford & Simpson, Stern Brothers, Tiffany & Company and W & J Sloan.[36]

The supremacy of the Ladies Mile declined before the end of the nineteenth century as the centre of high-end fashion retail followed residential expansion further uptown.[37] Smaller shops had already begun to move north, motivated by the construction of the Sixth Avenue Elevated railway in 1878 and its extension north. The El marked a dramatic change to the City's geography of consumption, facilitating along its route, 'one of the world's longest and most diverse continuous shopping circuits'.[38] The 1902–1903 construction of the Flatiron Building at the junction of Broadway, Fifth Avenue and 23rd Streets spurred more commercial establishments, such as publishers and booksellers, which gradually replaced the residences on Fifth Avenue. Improvements in transportation meant that neither entertainment nor commerce relied so much on proximity to their clientele. By 1914, the Ladies Mile had been abandoned by department stores. Macy's was the first to strike out when it moved to Herald Square, at Sixth Avenue and 34th Street, in 1902 (initially, until the El expanded, arranging transportation up Sixth Avenue for shoppers). Gimbel Brothers joined it in 1909 with a large store between 32nd and 33rd Streets on Broadway. However, it was Fifth Avenue, between 34th and 57th Streets, that was to become the location of choice for most large Manhattan department stores and for specialty shops. The opening of B. Altman & Co on Fifth Avenue and 34th Street in 1906 signalled that midtown Manhattan, previously the city's 'most elegant residential neighbourhood', was becoming more commercial.[39] The change was reinforced when hotels such as the St Regis opened in 1904 on Fifth Avenue and 57th Street, and in 1907 the Plaza on Fifth and 59th Street. By 1916, the central geography of Manhattan was focussing further uptown; in the process the theatres and department stores were no longer part of the same commercial district.[40] The development of the subway system not only provided greater access to the whole city, but by 1910 shop windows were also placed below ground in the subway stations of many major US cities.[41]

Retailing strategies and practices – Department stores

The forthcoming commercial significance of the department store in New York was signalled in 1862 when A.T. Stewart, a shrewd businessman, moved his business into a 'white cast iron palace' that eventually occupied the whole block between East 9th and 10th Streets on Broadway. Probably the first building in the city with a cast iron front, its architecture enhanced the retail spectacle, with its five storeys of shopping floors, gas-lit interior and a large assortment of domestic and imported goods, including 'Belfast laces', silk gowns and expensive '$1,000 camel-hair shawls'. Carriages and fashionable women apparently thronged the surrounding streets to visit Stewart's, which for a short time was the largest, most innovative, and best-known dry goods store in the United States, and included among its customers Mary Todd Lincoln, the country's first lady.[42] Behind the scenes, on its fourth floor, women and children were working in the store's sewing workshop; such in-house clothes production being a common feature of department stores, including Macy's.[43] The theatrical analogy here is not happenstance; in common with his competitors, Stewart employed theatrical techniques to create an atmosphere of excitement in the store, for example using organ music to speed up the circulation of visitors.

While department stores appeared in the United States and in Europe at around the same time, different marketing strategies were developed in different places according to how customers were perceived. American store promotion has been referred to as 'a product of its own native environment' not a European import,[44] while English retail stores have been referred to as 'generally lagging behind' the continent.[45] Although such subjective comments could have been fired by xenophobia, there is no doubt that by the end of the nineteenth century many of the New York department stores were going to extraordinary lengths to promote themselves. Technology, lighting and the use of glass facilitated the design of stores as palaces of modernity. French plate-glass windows made the goods inside accessible to those who could not afford them, or did not have the courage to cross the thresholds, spurring the development of window-shopping as a popular leisure activity. Practicality and novelty overlapped one another; the steam elevator in Lord and Taylor's five-storey building, which opened on 20th Street and Broadway in 1872, carried 10,000 people in the first three days, drawing crowds in the hundreds of thousands who came just to look at it,[46] while an advertisement of 1878 asserted proudly that Macy's had 'the best lighted store in the city'.[47] Department stores took full advantage of the growing sophistication and latest innovations in advertising. Advertising cards, for example, were used in the 1880s and 1890s by department and dry goods stores, and also by circuses and theatres, reflecting the close ties in the period between commerce and popular culture.[48] Macy's in particular developed distinctive advertising strategies.

Specializing in 'fancy and imported dry goods for women' with an emphasis on good value, offering a money-back guarantee and a cash only policy into the 1950s, Macy's expanded from their original stock of flowers, feathers, ribbons, embroideries and lace goods, to offer gloves and hosiery for men, women and children, followed by home furnishings.[49] While the company could not surpass the advertising of larger and well-established department stores like Lord & Taylor and Arnold, Constable & Co, it strove to attract attention by producing classified advertisement that were untypically eye-catching and easy to read. Repeated words and phrases and layouts that included white spaces, as well as clever copywriting, were some of the devices it employed ahead of its competitors.[50]

Its first newspaper advertisement, dating 25 November 1858, a month after the store's opening, declared: 'CHEAP RIBBONS!! You want them, of course. Go to MACY'S'.[51] While Macy's advertised often, they strategically avoided dates when it was known that the newspapers would be crowded with advertisements for other dry goods establishments.[52]

Soon after it opened, Macy's announced that it was making men's shirts and women and children's underwear to order, and in 1859 added cloaks, skirts and dresses. Until the 1870s, it manufactured clothing off premises, probably using an independent contractor (Lord & Taylor had been doing much the same in 1866 if not earlier, as likely had other department stores).[53] By the early 1870s, it had developed in-house manufacturing, adding new personnel to an already complicated organization of male and female employees.[54] In 1873, a hat-trimming and millinery-manufacturing division was introduced at the store, which by 1877 employed 200 young women in the manufacture of ladies' underclothing and infants wear alone.[55] By 1879, another workshop was added to make men's shirts. In the middle of the following decade, Macy's in-store production included ladies and children's underwear, men's shirts, linen collars and cuffs for both men and women, women's dresses, bustles ('wire and others'), lace fichus, velvet wraps and linen handkerchiefs. The avowed purpose of in-house manufacture was to enable the firm to sell quality merchandise at low prices, although from 1887 accounts showed that this endeavour made a satisfactory profit.[56]

Macy's sold an increasing array of merchandise by other manufacturers but bearing its own brands, including La Forge kid gloves (1877) and Red Star silk (1878).[57] In 1888, at least part of their underwear manufacturing was transferred from Fourteenth Street to a factory in Wallingford, Connecticut, and the following spring another factory was opened in New Haven devoted to the same line. Moving out manufacturing created more sales space. Production continued to increase and led to new ventures; by 1890, it was also making corsets in one of its underwear factories.[58] Other developments in the 1890s included the acquisition of a, probably small, silk skirt and blouse factory in 1893 at 97 Bank Street not far from the store. By this date the store had also begun to make and remodel fur garments. In the late 1890s, Macy's made women's wear had expanded to include 'skirts, waists, petticoats and wrappers'.[59] Astutely, it responded 'to the growing fad for bicycles' by leasing a bicycle factory in Paterson, New Jersey in August 1895, which turned out thirty machines a week. Macy's entrepreneurship in manufacturing also reflected that of other stores.[60]

At the end of the nineteenth century, Macy's catered for a broad range of clientele. The store also placed increasing emphasis on custom dressmaking and ready-to-wear clothing for women. In a competitive attempt to offer his customers a wider and more distinctive range of goods, R.H. Macy himself or one of his subordinates made regular buying trips to Europe rather than relying on the selections offered by importers.[61] After 1880 formal openings became the regular means of introducing new models for fashion in the spring and fall. By 1882, if not before, cloaks and costumes from Paris were on sale. Nevertheless, Macy's policy was not exclusivity, but rather 'to offer a class of goods which will meet a popular demand rather than represent extreme style'.[62] Its more populist approach continued to be marked out through its promotional activities. The large window display of dolls in a series of tableaux in its Christmas season window for 1874, while not the first of its type, marked the start of the annual Macy's Christmas window event.[63] It paid attention to customer service as well as entertainment, offering free delivery in the city, which by 1875 was extended to Brooklyn, Williamsburg, Jersey City and Hoboken.[64] Before the founder's death in 1877, Macy's had instituted a low pricing policy that continued into the 1930s.

A sense of how the department store changed retailing on the Ladies Mile can be further enhanced by looking at Siegel Cooper, which opened a large store on Sixth Avenue between 18th and 19th Streets, next to the Elevated train, on September 12, 1896, announcing its presence with 'a heavy barrage of advertising',[65] and attracting enormous crowds (Figure 2.3). Siegel Cooper was not just large, but flamboyant in its promotional activities, as characterized by the architecture and design of the whole store. The report of its opening in

Figure 2.3 Opening of Siegel Cooper Co., 1896, Sixth Avenue, between 18th and 19th Streets looking south from 19th Street. 1896. Museum of the City of New York.

The New York Times called the 'Big Store' a 'shopping resort'.[66] Its spectacular architecture featured a tower at the top of building with a searchlight with a 36-inch diameter lens, 'the largest ever made' that could be seen from thirty miles away. The light was used to signal public notices and events like election results and for advertising at night (Figure 2.4). As well as selling the likes of 'feather boas,

Figure 2.4 Siegel Cooper building, 1910 (Spring/Summer Catalogue No. 49, 1910). Author's Collection.

birds and clothes', its offered substantial customer services including a bank, a telegraph office, dental parlours, a barbershop catering especially to children and a 350-seat restaurant.[67] The magnificence and modernity of such places captured the imaginations of newcomers to New York City. Immigrant Mina Friedman, whose clothes were either bought from pushcarts[68] or homemade, recalled being taken to Siegel Cooper by her father and being awed by the 'lovely fountain' and coloured lights as if she had entered 'fairyland'.[69]

Shoppers from the outer boroughs did not have to go to Manhattan to purchase fashionable clothes, but could make purchases in local department stores.[70] Along the IRT rail line to Brooklyn, store after store occupied 'stretches of brightly illuminated underground windows on display night and day'.[71] In downtown Brooklyn, on Fulton Street, Abraham and Strauss was the retail flagship, and apparently for many residents it was second in importance only to the Dodgers baseball team. For those without access to the city or its boroughs, Siegel Cooper and other department stores, and mail order companies shipped a huge range of merchandise, including food and furniture, across the United States. The New York City based Standard Mail Order Co. noted in its catalogue of 1913, 'We pay mail or expressage anywhere in the U.S. on anything in this book' (Figure 2.5).

In London, it was the opening of Selfridges on Oxford Street in 1909 that signalled the major transformation in the department store culture. Department stores had been in existence from the mid-nineteenth century in Britain, and indeed Bainbridge's of Newcastle-upon-Tyne, home to Joseph Swan, the inventor of the electric light bulb that was to make such a difference to department store windows and interiors, can make a strong claim to being one of the first in the world developing in the late 1830s into an expanded drapery business.[72] However, it was Selfridge's new store that marked the commercialization and Americanization of London's West End most profoundly. With large plate-glass windows lit up until midnight, it represented a new type of department store that challenged the ad hoc approach of London's existing stores. Located in the unfashionable western section of Oxford Street towards Marble Arch, Selfridges was unique as the first purpose-built department store in Britain. Contemporary to this and in part a response, a large number of London's existing stores were remodelled, expanded and re-located particularly on Oxford Street and due to competition, they adopted a range of new methods for selling their goods.[73] This latter group included Marshall and Snelgrove, John Lewis, Bourne and Hollingsworth, and Peter Robinson on Oxford Street, Barkers in Kensington, Army and Navy in Westminster, Whiteley's on Queensway and Harrods in Knightsbridge. A mixture of 'old-fashioned "bric-a-brac" Renaissance' and modern Art Nouveau, London's Harrods was remodelled, extended and modernized from 1901 to 1914.[74] Responding to increased competition, it offered modern conveniences such as lifts and escalators (introduced in 1898), comforts such as toilets,

WE PAY MAIL OR EXPRESSAGE ANYWHERE IN U. S. ON ANYTHING IN THIS BOOK.
55

Figure 2.5 Menswear, Standard Mail Order Co, New York City, 1913, p. 55. Author's Collection.

restrooms, cafes and tearooms and, from 1906, home delivery via motorized vehicles. Generally though London's West End department stores were neither architecturally impressive, purpose-built, or sited on grand Haussmann-style boulevards as could be seen with Bon Marché, Galeries Layfayette and Printemps in Paris. The few that were purpose-built were done so due to fire such as Whiteley's new store in Westbourne Grove, rather than merchandizing vision and entrepreneurial ambition. Whiteley's, opened in 1864, 'created Westbourne Grove as a major London shopping venue'.[75] Its customers came in huge numbers to enjoy not only the latest fashions produced at affordable prices by the 'Universal Provider', but hairdressing, tearooms and an estate agency. As Lancaster argued, Whiteley's offered spectacle and showmanship, rather than innovation, and it was New York and Chicago that provided the inspiration for this in London's newest stores. America's vast emporiums, particularly Macy's in New York and Marshall Field in Chicago,[76] offered the blueprint for the US businessman Gordon Selfridge who, with his new store on Oxford Street, signalled a revolution in store organization and display. Gordon Selfridge's success as retail manager at Marshall Field gave him the solid base from which to strike out on what was to become London's premier shopping street:

> Whether it was a plan for tearing out old counters and shelving, rearranging the display of goods, putting in a new system for marking sales slips, remodelling the main entrance to the store, developing a different kind of newspaper 'ad', putting in telephones and pneumatic tubes, or building an entire new building, Selfridge was in favour of it if it was new, sounded practical and stimulated sales.[77]

In 1906, two years after he had resigned from Marshall Field in Chicago, Gordon Selfridge arrived in London with the aim to build a million pound store 'which would be designed and operate on American principles'.[78] These principles involved imaginative advertising, creative window display, modern employee relations, a prolific degree of customer service that aimed to turn shopping into a pleasure all housed in a visually impressive new building that proclaimed the 'brand': 'the Oxford Street emporium towered over its neighbour with eight floors, six acres of floor space, nine passenger lifts, and one hundred departments. Eighty feet high, with huge stone columns and twenty-one of the largest plateglass windows in the world, Selfridge's struck even the most critical Londoner as an imposing visual spectacle'.[79] Designed by Frank Atkinson but advised by the Chicago architect Daniel Burnham, it was designed in 1907 and completed in 1909. Its façade comprised a ground floor of large windows and short pillars on which rested 'colossal Ionic columns richly decorated on shaft and capital and framing all-glass expanses except that the floors between the three storeys are concealed by metal panels'.[80] In marked contrast to the view that the West End – Bond Street, Burlington Arcade, Regent Street – was aristocratic, Gordon Selfridge set out to appeal to the mass market, to the middle classes and the better-off working class as the strategic siting of the store opened up Oxford Street westwards towards Marble Arch. He prioritized polished, sharp advertising that glamorized urban life and shopping in particular, and in the week prior to the opening he saturated the press with clever advertising by well-known illustrators. He employed the best window dressers who produced displays that made competitors' crowded windows look 'old-fashioned', he deployed media stunts such as the display of Bleriot's plane in the store the day after the famous flight, and he introduced novel features such as the American-style soda fountain. Spectacle was key and his new store drew people in. For women, in particular, responsible for the home, its decoration and comforts, the sheer opulence of the visual display and promise of luxury was highly seductive: 'the selling space had wide aisles, electric lighting, crystal chandeliers, and a striking colour scheme in which white walls contrasted with thick green carpets'.[81] This concentration on women from the middle and working classes helped to transform the West End of London particularly Oxford Street as a site for female pleasure and, inevitably, 'definitions of public and private, male and female, were necessarily renegotiated as women literally and metaphorically besieged the West End'.[82]

The activities of Gordon Selfridge and his competitors at the turn of the twentieth century helped to consolidate Oxford Street's position as London's premier shopping route and New York's importance for department store innovation. At the same time, they helped to democratize shopping for clothes, realigning it with mass-cultures rather than elite ones. Macy's and Siegel-Cooper in New York, and Selfridges and Harrods in London, reinforce a sense of the period from the 1880s to the 1910s as the 'golden age of department stores', when 'Plate glass, electric lights, and atrium construction made stores seem bigger and more spectacular. Elevators and escalators expanded shoppers' perceptions of moving rapidly through time and space'.[83] The profusion of goods from far and wide and literally piled up in displays made 'just looking' a popular pastime. Even for those without the wherewithal to enter the stores, their large plate-glass windows turned them into 'theatres of consumption', accessible to passers-by on the sidewalks. In the modernization process of the department stores, windows became primary selling tools.[84] Increasingly, merchants counted on the visual enhancement that plate glass provided. Windows distorted the goods, which often looked better behind glass and the use of theatrical principles gave these windows part of their enormous appeal. The new glass environment, outside and inside, began to change the way people related to goods. The windows mediated items from the streets, and glass cases separated shopper from potential purchases inside the stores.[85] While glass diminished the consumers' ability to touch and smell the items, it amplified the visual, 'transforming the already watching city person into a compulsive viewer'.[86] Well before the cinema became a widely popular pastime, the department store was educating people across the social spectrum to look and desire through glass, as window-shopping became a huge leisure pastime.

The department store served as a significant social space for men and women, rich and poor, but it was the relationship between women and the stores that effected a profound cultural transformation in both America and Britain, from making to consuming goods.[87] As Abelson has commented, not wearing the correct attire, for any occasion, 'became one with not knowing how to shop and not understanding how clothes had been transformed into a new symbol of middle class life'.[88] By the end of the nineteenth century, the main clientele of the large department stores were female and the majority of merchandise was targeted at female shoppers, as testified by the amount of women's fashion in store and mail order catalogues (Figure 2.6). Middle-class women have been described as shopping constantly, using the department stores as a form of cheap entertainment, to kill time and ease boredom, both to see what was available to wear and what was being worn. Department stores targeted women customers in particular, using luxury or pseudo luxury items and settings to transport beyond the drudgery of work 'and the humdrum everyday',[89] but they also 'eagerly accepted the dollars, whether proffered by the rough red hand of a charwoman or the kid-gloved hand of a millionaire's daughter'.[90] While on the other side of the counter, the shop girl – as well informed about clothing and appearance as the middle-class women she served – was distinctive in the modern department store, having replaced the male clerk (shop assistant) of the traditional dry goods or drapers store.[91] Typically young, single and primarily working class, by the 1890s the largest stores in New York and London employed young women in the thousands, while mature women held the more prestigious positions of buyers, floorwalkers and cashiers. It seems likely that clerks were eager and well-informed participants in the mass-culture of consumption. O. Henry (1910) writes in *The Trimmed Lamp* of Nancy, a twenty-year-old shop girl: 'She has the high-ratted pompadour, and the exaggerated straight-front. Her skirt is shoddy, but has the correct flare. No furs protect her against the bitter spring air, but she wears her short broadcloth jacket as jauntily as though it were Parisian lamb!'[92] Nancy earned $8.00 a week, a very modest sum compared to that of her nineteen-year-old friend Lou, who as a piece work ironer in a laundry earned $18.50 a week, which allowed her to dress in more ostentatious fashion, 'in a badly-fitting purple dress, and her hat plume is four inches too long; but her ermine muff and scarf cost $25'. Despite the considerably lower wages, Nancy preferred her job, with its potential to meet people, not least an eligible male:

> I like to be among nice things and swell people. And look what a chance I've got! Why, one of our glove girls married a Pittsburg-steel maker, or blacksmith or something – the other day worth a million dollars. I'll catch a swell myself some time. I ain't bragging on my looks or anything; but I'll take my chances where there's big prizes offered.[93]

Figure 2.6 'New York Styles' for Fall & Winter 1918–1919, The Bedell Company catalogue, p. 107. Author's Collection.

Shop girls working in the Ladies Mile were generally only allowed to use their small salaries to buy from their employing stores once a week, during an early hour set aside for them to shop. However, their work gave them access to female customers wearing the latest fashion, which could be replicated by those handy with a needle. While Lou learned about clothes as material things from working in the laundry her taste was for the showy. Nancy, by contrast, from her position on the shop floor, was able to discern how clothes were worn. She spoke of how one of her outfits, which Lou considered 'ugly' and 'plain', had been 'copied from one that Mrs. Van Alstyne Fisher was wearing. The girls say her bill in the store last year was $12,000. I made mine myself. It cost me $1.50. Ten feet away you couldn't tell it from hers'. Nancy is depicted in the novel as using her department store position to acquire the taste and refinement she would need to advance her social position and, as a result, 'She absorbed the educating influence of art wares, of costly and dainty fabrics, of adornments that are almost culture to women'.[94]

While sewing skills were of advantage to those who wanted to keep abreast of the latest styles, looking fashionable did not necessarily imply a total change of outfit. Fancy shoes and hats both enabled working-class women to participate in the consumption of fashion, 'Even newsgirls who could ill afford a presentable shirtwaist might splurge on an outrageous hat'.[95] Ironically, as with the case of Lou and Nancy, lower-class women often had more in common with the more showy fashion tastes of upper class women, showgirls, actresses or prostitutes, than with the more refined tastes of middle class women. For instance, the most stylish women seen wearing non-functional 'French heels', rather than boots, at the beginning of the twentieth century were typically from the upper and working classes. The latter could purchase the fashionable shoes for $1 or $2 a pair from pushcart vendors in their local neighbourhoods.[96] We can compare the prices of the leather boots, with French or Louis heels, shown in Figure 2.7 which range from $4.39 to $6.50, available by mail order from The Bedell Company, 1918–1919, which promoted 'New York Styles' and 'Money Saving Prices'.[97] According to Enstad, French heels were disdained by middle-class women, while for many young immigrant women they signalled Americanization and 'ladyhood', and such 'pretty shoes' were often one of their first purchases in the United States, which they wore both for work and leisure, not being able to afford more than one pair of shoes.[98] Peiss notes how the identification of working women with the rich was more 'playful and mediated than direct and calculated', echoing the style of prostitutes as well as socialites.[99] Nevertheless, in the modern cities of New York and London, 'anxiety was expressed by social observers and customers alike about the mingling of social classes within the confines of the stores and there were worries about the difficulties of "placing" some young women shoppers and shop-workers because of their respectable and fashionable appearances'.[100]

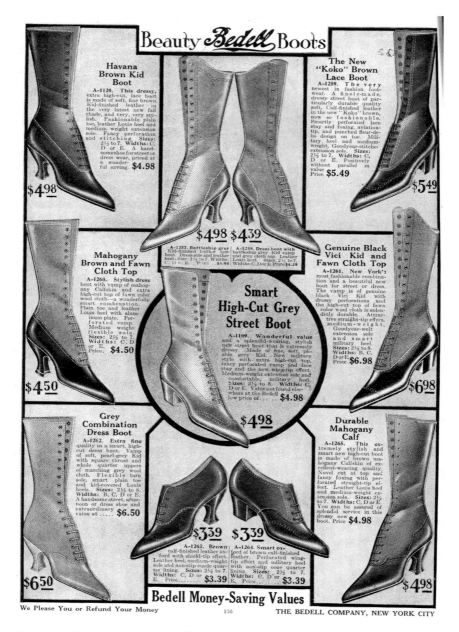

Figure 2.7 Boots and shoes with 'French' or 'Louis' heels, 'New York Styles, Fall & Winter 1918–19' The Bedell Company, New York City, catalogue. Author's Collection.

Enstad notes the similarities also between the ready-made evening gowns bought regularly by some working-class women, for instance to wear at balls on the Lower East Side, with the styles worn by the rich.[101] The lifestyles and taste of middle-class women did not allow for such garments. The disdain of middle-class women is reflected in a statement by Bertha Richardson that provides considerable insight into the hierarchy of fashion retail in New York at the turn of the twentieth century:

> Purposeless imitation!... The Fourth Avenue shop says to the Fourth Avenue buyer: 'Behold my clever imitation. For less than you could pay in a Fifth Avenue shop, I can give you a perfect imitation. You would not be behind the styles, I know. I can make you look like a real peacock'. The Third Avenue shop scans the windows of the Fourth Avenue shop and returns the same to its customers. The First Avenue shop has a still cheaper Imitation, and in Hester Street, on the pushcarts, ghosts of the real are 'Going, going, going' for thirty-nine cents.[102]

Fashion as street theatre

Describing shopping as 'middle-class women's entry into the nineteenth-century city', Nead identifies the chronology of this (the 1870s) and she points to the relative restrictions accompanying this.[103] This was in marked contrast to working-class women who occupied the city 'as a place of adventure, pleasure, excitement and risk... a place of economic and erotic possibilities'.[104] Women were increasingly visible on the streets of New York and London, with innovations such as the bicycle, the local railway and subway and underground bringing them greater mobility. Photographs taken in both cities show a similarity in fashion and reflect how respectable women would dress to literally walk the city streets. Two contrasting images from London dated 1890–1900 show fashionable young women out walking in the park and a throng of workers – men and women – arriving for work at the Army and Navy Stores in Westminster. In the first photograph (Figure 2.8) which was taken by a street photographer and is now in the City of Westminster archives, one of the two young women wears a light-coloured tailor-made costume with a high neck white blouse (shirtwaist) and stylish hat; the other wears a darker tailor-made, unbuttoned jacket but with a fox fur draped loosely around the shoulders. The demeanour of these two women is remarkably relaxed as they walk accompanied by a smart young man wearing a suit, waistcoat, cravat and collar and bowler hat. Notwithstanding the relatively elaborate hats, they evoke the image of the New Woman dressed fashionably, but also with some practicality so as to navigate the city with ease.[105] Photographs taken in New York at the same period reveal a

Figure 2.8 'Out walking', London, c. 1910. Westminster City Archives.

very similar demeanour. The second one (Figure 2.9) is a company photograph from the House of Fraser archives that captures the Army and Navy workforce arriving at the start of day. This mass of mainly young men and women range across the social spectrum: men wearing flat caps and kerchiefs around the neck and those with stiff collars, ties and bowler hats. The women – predominantly young – wear the uniform of the New Woman: shirt and shortened skirt, bow ties and belts, with straw boaters in abundance. These are 'the shock troops' of modernity.[106] The city could be both liberating and dangerous for women. Peiss comments on how young working-class women flocked to the streets for pleasure and amusement throughout the nineteenth century, 'using public spaces for flamboyant assertion'.[107] On the street, elegantly dressed women and men were both objects and subjects of the gaze; the street was not just a place to look but a place to stare. For the uninitiated and those not wearing fashionable clothes, such as Dreier's *Sister Carrie,* the experience could be a very uncomfortable one,

> Carrie found herself stared at and ogled. Men in flawless top-coats, high hats, and silver-headed walking sticks elbowed near and looked too often into conscious eyes. Ladies rustled by in dresses of stiff cloth, shedding affected

Figure 2.9 Army and Navy Store employees, Westminster, London, 1890s. Glasgow University Archive Services, House of Fraser Collection, GB 248 FRAS 538/12.

smiles and perfume. Carrie noticed among them the sprinkling of goodness and the heavy percentage of vice. The rouged and powdered cheeks and lips, the scented hair, the large, misty, and languorous eye, were common enough. With a start she awoke to find that she was in fashion's crowd, on parade in a show place – and such a show place![108]

Young women used the streets to search for men, to have a good time and to display their clothes in public. The attention they gave to how they looked could cause respectable women to be confused with the 'rowdy girls' who had long been targets of public commentary.[109] References to prostitutes recur in discussions of the city, with the individual woman walking alone, not as part of a family or kin group, continuing to be morally suspect.[110] Visitors to London from Britain's provinces could easily make the mistake of walking on the wrong side of the street at the wrong time; Regent Street was a case in point. A shopping street that adjoined Oxford Street, at mid-day it was the haunt prostitutes, whereas at mid-night they claimed the Haymarket in London's theatre district.[111] The proximity of brothels to theatres made it often impossible to distinguish society women and prostitutes as both groups strolled along important city streets including Broadway and Regent St.[112] Thomas Grattan, long-term British consul in Boston, observed in 1859 in New York that 'the flaunting airs of the ladies, their streaming feathers and flowers, silks and satins of all colors, and a rapid, dashing step as they walk along, give foreigners a wildly mistaken idea of them', akin in his eyes, to European prostitutes.[113] The Strand, London's main leisure area due to the plethora of theatres and music halls, was re-developed along with the Aldwych and Kingsway in the early twentieth century. On these and adjacent streets were numerous theatres that were remodelled and rebuilt to attract new clientele such as 'female parties, suburban couples and tourists' including the Aldwych in 1913, the Lyceum in 1904, the Playhouse in 1906–1907, the Strand in 1905 and the Gaiety in 1903.[114] In these less formal public spaces as people enjoyed themselves in the evening, the stars of both London and New York theatre such as Lily Elsie, Kitty Lord and Billie Burke, spearheaded the 'staging of fashion'.[115] These actresses also forged fashionable links between London and New York. Elsie de Wolfe, for example, while better known as a high-class interior designer and society figure in New York, London and Paris, began her professional life as an actress, appearing on the New York stage and throughout the United States. Belgian-American actress Camille Clifford, who performed on both sides of the Atlantic, was one of the most famous living models for the Gibson Girl, the popular image of American beauty at the turn of the twentieth century. The Gibson Girl provided one of a number of modern fashionable icons based on actresses as role models as their popularity was assured through a variety of promotional devices including the performances, postcards, photographs, advertisements and newspaper and magazine articles. In fact these 'public women' served, like the department stores, as an active and accurate point of reference for fashion, although they provided 'alternative models for stylish contemporary living' that was quite different to those determined by the aristocracy or by Paris.[116] Paris, the arbiter of women's fashion, was closely followed by London, with both cities influencing the fashions of New York. American actress Billie Burke patronized a London dressmaker, Mrs Hayward, who based her designs on what she had seen in Paris in the given season. Nevertheless, Burke could still be confident that when she wore the garments in New York, she would be at least a season ahead of the rest of America. Thus both cities' theatre districts and its actresses served as something of a 'school of fashion' for the whole country.[117] As Ewing put it, 'As far more people attended plays than could ever see the Society beauties and study their clothes, fashion was widely disseminated'.[118] However, by drawing instead on theatrical costume this 'presaged twentieth-century conceptions of fashion built around notions of celebrity, spectacle and the beguiling promises of commodity culture', rather than Paris.[119] Nevertheless, New York and London offered different theatre experiences.

Heritage, as well as newly developing metropolitan modernities, played an important part in London; indeed 'in the early twentieth century, Dickens still provided the paradigmatic image of the city'.[120] Observing Breward's list of occupations that were typical of the female theatre audience – showgirls, milliners, dressmakers, typists, stenographers, cashiers … telegraph and telephone girls – Nead explains that they are indicative of London's new modernity rather than a leisured elite.[121] These developed a style of modern dressing that crossed 'the boundary from stage to street and to play a formative role in the fashioning of modern femininity'.[122] This was underscored by American fashion merchandizing that promoted the democratization of desire by using 'theatrical strategy par excellence'.[123]

The assimilation of theatrical spectacle into dress in everyday life is no more evident than in the strategic product 'tie ins' between theatres and retailers, (long before such promotional devices began in the movies). Exemplified by the 'Merry Widow' hat, and an incident which occurred at the 275th performance of The Merry Widow in 1908 at the New Amsterdam Theatre at Broadway and 42nd Street, when female theatregoers were offered free hats 'from Paris' on the presentation of a coupon after the show. The hat, named after the show first staged in London, was designed by the prominent couturier Lucile (Lady Duff Gordon). While clothes by Lucile, who moved her business to New York in 1910, would be out of the financial reach of most women, her designs no doubt had a wide impact, not least via her theatrical work. The Merry Widow hat, for example, was parodied for its immense size, which reached as much as three feet in diameter.[124] At the 1908 performance something of a riot ensued as middle-class women demonstrated behaviour uncharacteristic to themselves and to a first-class theatre. The scene was more 'typical of the kind of counter crushes one might expect in a department store, where working and middle class women frequently battled over marked-down goods'.[125] Figure 2.10 from the U.S. Standard Mail Order catalogue of 1913 shows the variety of hats being worn at the time, which are also priced accordingly, from 59c to $3.29. They range from the cheap and simple (59c) hat at the top right, indicated for everyday wear, to the three very flamboyant hats in the centre, which much more resemble the fashionable Merry Widow styles.

The strategies created jointly and independently by the department store and the theatres, with their emphasis on display and the visual, informed women across the social classes. By c. 1910, for example, some stores had replaced their original open backed windows, which provided access to inside of the shop from the street, by enclosed versions. While the development of the use of display windows was uneven, the connections with the theatre were clear. Prominent American decorator, Arthur Fraser, head of display at Marshall Field's in Chicago and then in New York, and L Frank Baum (set designer for the Wizard of Oz) drew from their love of theatre to influence their store displays.[126] Schweitzer relates how he curtained the store windows on Sundays to reveal a new display on Mondays. By using effective backdrops also, he turned Field's windows into 'stages where commodities performed before an audience of delighted consumers'.[127]

SATISFACTION GUARANTEED OR YOUR MONEY BACK.   37

J358. For general knockabout, outing and everyday wear you'll find this one of the jauntiest, one of the most comfortable and most stylish hats made this season. Splendidly tailored of the fashionable **white Ratine** and is particularly becoming for misses and young women. The tailor-stitched brim may be turned in many graceful pretty ways and comes with blue, red or black stripes. The dainty coloured feather fancy provides a chic finish. Here's 79c. value, **reduced to** **55c**

33189. An ideal hat for general Mid-Summer wear. Effectively modelled of smart, light-weight "Madagascar" straw in a pretty natural tan. The becoming medium-broad brim is gracefully fashioned, and the crown is draped with a large tan silk scarf bordered with red rose and green foliage design. Serviceably lined and finished with a red velvet-piped brim. Very appropriate for the young and older woman, stylish and practical. Good value at even $2.50. **Reduced to $1.75**

N33169. A charming summer hat unusually becoming to both the younger and older woman. Made of a fancy, pretty tan straw with effectively turned brim that curves gracefully at the edge. A beautiful wreath of pink tea roses artistically trims the brim and wide rich lace drapes the crown. A large wired bow of pink taffeta ribbon is stylishly placed at side, adding a charming, dressy touch. You'll be immensely pleased with this excellent value. **Reduced to $1.49**

J33395. A lovely hat at a wonderfully **low price.** The shape is of splendid quality Chip, with medium-wide brim, artistically curved and dented. Trimmed with two large, stylish French 16½-inch "Featherette" plumes of strong, beautifully curled silky fibres, handsomer than real Ostrich, with the added advantage of being twice as durable. Attractively finished with pretty velvet bow. Black shape, with black or white "Featherette" plumes. A stunning $6.00 hat. **Reduced to $3.29**

33189 REDUCED TO $1.75

J358 REDUCED TO 55¢

J33395 REDUCED TO $3.29

N33169 REDUCED TO $1.49

N3298 REDUCED TO $2.48

X369 69¢

X369. Practical Summer Hat of pretty **white Ratine.** A soft, very comfortable shape, most becoming to the miss and young woman. The brim may be turned in several pretty ways and a full Bulgarian sash in neat dark shades is effectively employed. 89c. quality. **Special** **69c**

N3298. You'll greatly admire the charming style of this very handsome dress hat. It illustrates most cleverly the vogue for the smart flat shapes that are so effective to the younger and older woman. Fashioned of excellent **Neapolitan straw** with medium-wide, prettily turned brim. A beautiful Ostrich band trims the crown and a delightful color effect is provided in the large silk-and-velvet rose. The shape comes in all black, or black with tan flange. The Ostrich band comes in black, white, or black-and-white mixture. A splendid $4.50 hat. **Reduced to $2.48**

Figure 2.10 Hats, Standard Mail Order Co. catalogue 1913, p. 37. Author's Collection.

The 'window as stage' was further enhanced by a 'remarkable new store fixture': the live mannequin.[128] Leach refers to street crowding and even rioting in Spokane, Washington, when living models appeared in a local store window wearing fashionable Directoire gowns. While the public were entertained, moral heckles were raised, not least because store window display was a male occupation.[129] The live mannequin was a highly effective promotional device, which women could relate to directly. As Bertha June Richardson noted in 1904 in *The Woman Who Spends: A Study of Her Economic Motives,* 'women see themselves in store windows as they resolve others shall see them'.[130] The strategy assisted the ubiquity of fashion, as the latest styles could be seen from the street without an individual ever having to enter a store. For their regular female customers, stores offered in-house fashion shows. Gimbel's department store at 34 St and Seventh Avenue held its first 'Promenade des Toilettes' in 1910. Its success led to twenty variations in the next five years, when women apparently 'streamed into the store' to watch models parade daily on ramps 'in their fashionable Parisian costumes'.[131] In 1908, Macy's employed living models in their spring and fall 'style opening' to display imported gowns 'against an elaborately decorated background prepared especially for the occasion'.[132] The practice continued in subsequent years 'and helped to inform thousands of women about changes in styles, as well as to convey the idea that Macy's offered expensive, fashionable merchandise along with popularly priced staples'. In this sense, Macy's was 'trading up' by taking strategies from the higher end stores to inform its more diverse and mass-market clientele.

The physical transformations of New York and London that included transport infrastructure, new shopping streets and routes and changing patterns of consumption, alongside the expansion of opportunities for leisure as well as work, transformed these two major cities from the late nineteenth century. Traversed by people from diverse social, economic and ethnic backgrounds, this added to the sense of vitality coupled with attendant anxieties. London and New York were critically important cities in producing 'the maelstrom of modern life' that so perplexed writers, politicians and critics at the time and subsequently. Each brought something different to the mixture, but there were also as we have seen clear comparisons. London was a city founded upon and dependent on an Empire, whereas New York was a dynamic, modern city in the making with a population that was in constant flux. Both were heterogeneous and growing exponentially. Increasingly wealthy, but with huge economic disparities and social inequalities, they were to become ever more important in the twentieth century and, as we have argued in this chapter and Chapter 1, they were vitally important in developing fashion and fashionable identities, not only in selling clothes but in promoting and producing them too. In these cities, the mechanisms that enabled the wider availability and knowledge of fashionable clothes (department stores, new multiple stores, window displays and theatres) were consolidated and focused and, as we will see in Chapter 3, here existed the pre-conditions for mass culture and what we describe as the everyday modernity of fashion.

Notes

1   Erika Rappaport, 'Art, Commerce, or Empire? The Rebuilding of Regent Street, 1880–1927', *History Workshop Journal* 53, no. 1 (2002), 99.

2   Ibid.

3   Lynda Nead, 'Animating the Everyday: London on Camera circa 1900', *The Journal of British Studies* 43, no. 1 (2004), 65–90.

4   Barry Curtis, 'Response', in *Fashion and Modernity*, ed. Christopher Breward and Caroline Evans (Oxford: Berg, 2005), 194.

5   Ibid.

6   C. Breward, *Fashioning London: Clothing and the Modern Metropolis* (Oxford and New York: Berg, 2004), 66.

7   John Marriott, 'Sensation of the Abyss: The Urban Poor and Modernity', in *Modern Times: Reflections on a Century of English Modernity*, ed. Mica Nava and Alan O'Shea (London: Routledge, 1996), 77–100.

8   See for example: Erika D. Rappaport, 'A New Era of Shopping', in *Cinema and the Invention of Modern Life*, ed. Leo Charney and Vanessa R. Schwartz (Berkeley: University of California Press, 1995), 130–55; Judith R. Walkowitz, *City of Dreadful Delight: Narratives of Sexual Danger in Late-Victorian London* (London: Virago, 1992); Deborah Epstein Nord, *Walking the Victorian Streets: Women, Representation and the City* (New York: Cornell University Press, 1995); Deborah L. Parsons, *Streetwalking the Metropolis: Women, the City and Modernity* (Oxford: Oxford University Press, 2000); Lynda Nead, *Victorian Babylon: People, Streets and Images in Nineteenth-Century London* (New Haven and London: Yale University Press, 2000).

9   Lynda Nead, 'Response', in Fashion and Modernity, ed. Christopher Breward and Caroline Evans (Oxford: Berg, 2005), 123.

10   Jerry White, *London in the Twentieth Century: A City and its People* (London: Random House, 2008), 8.

11   Gavin Stamp, 'London 1900', *Architectural Design Profile* 46, no. 5–6 (1978), 322–323.

12   White, *London in the Twentieth Century,* 8.

13   Stamp, 'London 1900', 305.

14   Many of which still remain now as public institutions, including the Frick Museum just off Fifth Avenue at 70th Street, and the Carnegie Mansion at Fifth Avenue and 91st Street, the home of the Smithsonian Institute, Cooper Hewitt Smithsonian Design Museum.

15   Central Park opened in 1857 as a city-owned park, with its was extension and landscaping by Frederick Law Olmsted and Calvert Vaux being completed in 1873.

16   Marlis Schweitzer, *When Broadway Was the Runway: Theater, Fashion, and American Culture* (Philadelphia: University of Pennsylvania Press, 2009), 5.

17   Elizabeth Ewing, *History of 20th Century Fashion* (London: Batsford, 1989), 5.

18   Jane Beckett and Deborah Cherry (eds), *The Edwardian Era* (Oxford: Phaidon Press and the Barbican Art Gallery, 1987), 36.

19 F. Sheppard, *London: A History* (Oxford: Oxford University Press, 1998), 248.

20 Rappaport, 'Art, Commerce, or Empire?', 8–9.

21 Beckett and Cherry, *The Edwardian Era*, 37.

22 Breward, *Fashioning London*, 58–9.

23 Sheppard, *London: A History*, 292.

24 Beckett and Cherry, *The Edwardian Era*, 36.

25 Sheppard, *London: A History*, 272–7.

26 Sheppard, *London: A History*, 273.

27 Rachel Worth, *Fashion for the People: A History of Clothing at Marks and Spencer* (Oxford and New York: Berg, 2007), 24.

28 Goronwy Rees, *St Michael: A History of Marks and Spencer* (London: Pan Books Ltd, 1973).

29 Rappaport, 'Art, Commerce, or Empire?', 95.

30 Ibid., 99.

31 Kenneth T. Jackson (ed.) *The Encyclopedia of New York City*, 2nd edn. (New Haven and London: Yale University Press), 159.

32 A. Schoener, *New York: An Illustrated History of the People* (New York: W.W. Norton & Co, 1998), 192.

33 Theodore Dreiser, *Sister Carrie*, Clementine Classics (1900; repr., New York: Black Balloon Publishing, 2013), 230.

34 Caroline Rennolds Milbank, *New York Fashion The Evolution of American Style* (New York: Harry Abrams Inc., 1989), 32.

35 Ibid., 25.

36 Jackson, *The Encyclopedia of New York City* 201; 361.

37 Schweitzer, *When Broadway Was the Runway*, 58.

38 Ibid., 58.

39 Schoener, *New York*, 224.

40 William R. Leach, *Land of Desire: Merchants, Power, and the Rise of a New American Culture* (New York: Pantheon, 1993), 64.

41 Ibid.

42 Jackson, *The Encyclopedia of New York City*, 361.

43 Leach, *Land of Desire*, 21.

44 Ralph M. Hower, *History of Macy's of New York, 1858–1919* (Cambridge, MA: Harvard University Press, 1943), 142.

45 Ibid.,143.

46 Compare also Emile Zola, *Au Bonheur des dames (The Ladies' Delight)*, Penguin Classics (1883; repr., London: Penguin Group, 2001) description of a Parisian department store.

47 Hower, *History of Macy's of New York*, 165.

48 Leach, *Land of Desire*, 44.

49 Hower, *History of Macy's of New York*, 38.

50 Ibid., 59.

51 Ibid., 55.

52 Ibid., 59.

53 Ibid., 111.

54 Ibid., 115.

55 Ibid., 111, from *New York Tribune*, 20, 27 September and 16 December 1860.

56 Ibid., 161–2.

57 Ibid., 164.

58 Ibid., 246.

59 Ibid., 247.

60 Bon Marché, Paris, had also produced many of its own items as early as 1872, and Lord and Taylor made furniture in 1874 (Hower, *History of Macy's New York*, 249). In New York, A.T. Stewart operated a number of factories in connection with his mercantile business, although probably catering more to the wholesale trade.

61 Hower, *History of Macy's of New York*, 164. It has been noted how, by the middle of the nineteenth century, much of the structure of the American fashion market was in place, with fashion magazines, including *Peterson's, Harper's Bazaar, Godey's Lady's Book,* and *The Home Journal* informing urban women, through emissaries sent to Paris, seen as the world's fashion centre, for the latest trends. Specialized shops, fancy dry goods stores and department stores such as A.T. Stewart's also sent buyers to Paris to report back on the latest styles. The 'latest mode' from Paris being demanded for middle-class consumers at a third of the cost (Leach, *Land of Desire*, 95).

62 Hower, *History of Macy's of New York*, 163.

63 Ibid., 118.

64 Ibid., 119.

65 Ibid., 265.

66 'Notes on the Ladies Mile', *Museum of the City of New York, Department of Costumes and Textiles*.

67 Leach, *Land of Desire*, 45.

68 Peddlers with pushcarts continued as a main supplier of clothing, food, household and other items for working-class people into the twentieth century. In 1906, for instance, about 2,500 pushcarts were estimated to be on the Lower East Side, operated mainly by Jewish, Italian and Greek peddlers who provided the mainstays for life: 'Dried fruits, fresh fruit, pickles, preserves, vegetables, meat and fish alternate with household utensils, boots and shoes, jewellery and clothing, books and stationery' (quote from 'Thursday in Hester Street', *New York Tribune,* 15 September 1898, in Enstad, *Ladies of Labor*, 53). Some pushcart peddlers carried ready-made clothing, as well as fabric remnants, useful for making small items, and for trimming; others offered second-hand clothes, including the likes of items forgotten in the laundry (Enstad, *Ladies of Labor*, 65).

69 B.A. Schreier, *Becoming American Women: Clothing and the Jewish Immigrant Experience, 1880–1920* (Chicago: Chicago Historical Society, 1994), 73.

70 Brooklyn functioned quite independently through the nineteenth century, with major changes coming in 1883 when the opening of the Brooklyn Bridge linked it with Manhattan, followed by its annexation to New York City in 1898, which ended its independence as a city.

71 Ibid., 63.

72 Bill Lancaster, *The Department Store: A Social History* (Leicester: Leicester University Press, 1995), 7.

73 Mica Nava, 'Modernity's Disavowal: Women, the City and the Department Store', in *The Shopping Experience*, ed. Pasi Falk and Colin Campbell (London: Sage, 1997), 69.

74 Stamp, 'London 1900', 313.

75 Lancaster, *The Department Store*, 20.

76 Ibid., 21.

77 Ibid., 62.

78 Ibid., 68.

79 Rappaport, 'A New Era of Shopping', 133.

80 N. Pevsner, *The Buildings of England: London, Volume 1, The Cities of London and Westminster* (London: Penguin, 1957), 535.

81 Rappaport, 'A New Era of Shopping', 133.

82 Ibid., 148.

83 Sharon Zukin, *Point of Purchase; How Shopping Changed American Culture* (New York, Routledge, 2005), 20.

84 Elaine S. Abelson, *When Ladies Go A-Thieving: Middle-Class Shoplifters in the Victorian Department Store* (Oxford: Oxford University Press, 1990), 68.

85 Leach, *Land of Desire*, 46.

86 Ibid., 63.

87 Abelson, *When Ladies Go A-Thieving*, 40.

88 Ibid., 25.

89 Leach, *Land of Desire*, 91.

90 Susan Porter Benson, *Counter Cultures: Saleswomen, Managers, and Customers in American Department Stores, 1890–1940* (Illinois: University of Illinois Press, 1987), 89.

91 Jackson, *The Encyclopedia of New York City*, 201.

92 O. Henry, *The Trimmed Lamp* (1910), available online http://www.literaturecollection.com/a/o_henry/207/ (accessed January 14, 2016).

93 Ibid.

94 Ibid.

95 K.L. Peiss, *Cheap Amusements: Working Women and Leisure in Turn-of-the-Century New York* (Philadelphia: Temple University Press, 1986), 65.

96 This was a considerable percentage of a weekly salary, as Peiss (1986: 52) notes that a typical 'living wage' in New York in 1910 would be $9–10 a week, but many working women would be earning less, and for shop girls this would be around $6.50 a week (Peiss, 1986: 54).

97 The Bedell Company, *Fall & Winter 1918–19 catalogue* (New York: The Bedell Company, 1918).

98 N. Enstad, *Ladies of Labor, Girls of Adventure: Working Women, Popular Culture, and Labor Politics at the Turn of the Twentieth Century* (New York: Columbia University Press, 1999), 2.

99 Peiss, *Cheap Amusements*, 65.

100 Nava, 'Modernity's Disavowal', 69.

101 Enstad, *Ladies of Labor*, 29.

102 Bertha June Richardson, *The Woman Who Spends: A Study of Her Economic Functions* (Boston: Witcomb and Barrows, 1904), 75–76, quoted in Enstad, *Ladies of Labor*, 29.

103 Nead, 'Response', 69.

104 Ibid., 70.

105 See Ewing, *History of 20th Century Fashion*, chapter 1.

106 Sally Alexander originally used the term to describe women office cleaners, packers and shop assistants in the 1920s and 1930s as the 'shock troops' of industrial restructuring. See S. Alexander, *Becoming a Woman in London and Other Essays in 19th and 20th Century Feminist History* (London: Virago, 1994).

107 Peiss, *Cheap Amusements*, 58.

108 Dreier, *Sister Carrie*, 230–1.

109 Peiss, *Cheap Amusements*, 58.

110 Elizabeth Wilson, *The Sphinx in the City: Urban Life, the Control of Disorder, and Women* (Berkeley: University of California Press, 1992), 8.

111 Nead, 'Response', 65.

112 Katie Johnson, *Sisters in Sin: Brothel Drama in America, 1900–1920*, Vol. 24 (Cambridge: Cambridge University Press, 2006), 60.

113 Banner, *American Beauty A Social History Through Tow Centuries of the American Idea, Ideal, and Image of the Beautiful Woman* (New York: Knopf, 1983 [2006]), 109.

114 Breward, *Fashioning London,* 69–70.

115 Michele Majer (ed.), *Staging Fashion, 1880–1920: Jane Hading, Lily Elsie, Billie Burke* (New Haven and London: Yale University Press and Bard Graduate Center, 2012), 18.

116 Breward, *Fashioning London*, 72.

117 Marlis Schweitzer, 'Stylish Effervescence: Billie Burke and the Rise of the Fashionable Broadway Star', in *Staging Fashion, 1880–1920: Jane Hading, Lily Elsie, Billie Burke*, ed. Michele Majer (New Haven and London: Yale University Press and the Bard Graduate Center, 2012), 79.

118 Ewing, *History of 20th century Fashion*, 16.

119 Breward, *Fashion and Modernity*, 102.

120 Nead, 'Response', 122.

121 Ibid., 123.

122 Ibid., 122.

123 Leach, *Land of Desire*, 91.

124 Schweitzer, *When Broadway Was the Runway*, 1.

125 Ibid., 2 (note 9).

126 Ibid., 81.

127 Ibid., 82.

128 Leach, *Land of Desire*, 64.

129 Ibid., 69.

130 Abelson, *When Ladies Go A-Thieving*, 70.

131 Leach, *Land of Desire*, 102.

132 Hower, *History of Macy's of New York*, 334.

3
DREAMS TO REALITY

Introduction

Saturating everyday life, fashion as popular culture helped to subvert the high cultures of inter-war modernism and modernity. If 'mass culture [w]as woman: modernism's other', then fashion was the most 'female' aspect of that mass culture.[1] As a result of new technologies of cultural production, reproduction and dissemination, 1920s' and 1930s' fashion in New York and London effectively evoked the everyday as *mass experience*. For some writers and critics, for example, J.B. Priestley and Winifred Holtby in Britain, it was yet another example of what they considered to be the commercialization and trivialization of culture. As we argue in this chapter, hegemonic, but also democratized, fashion illuminated nuances of race and class, gender and generation particularly as it intersected with dance, cinema and print cultures. Articulating this alongside the notion of the 'Black Atlantic' that proposes race as 'a counter-culture of modernity', this chapter considers the ways in which aspects of African American culture in inter-war Harlem and its transatlantic mutations in 1920s' and 1930s' London helped to shape mass cultures.[2] Considering the 'two souls of black USA', Schwarz pinpointed the hybrid and diasporic qualities of this black counter culture: 'It is a culture characteristically based on the vernacular, where the complex cultural practices of the everyday contain within them an implicit critique of the abstractions of the ideologues of modernity'.[3] Looking in particular at dance and its relationship to fashion in the burgeoning dance halls of London and New York, we observe the importance – implicit and explicit – of non-white experiences at the level of everyday lives.[4]

In this chapter, we explore how popular visual cultures – found in print media (magazines and advertising), the cinema and dance (glimpsed in Hollywood and Harlem) – also subverted the perceived fashion dominance of Paris, exposed gender uncertainties and generational fault lines, and in London – at least – undermined the class distinction of the court and aristocracy. As we show, the everyday modernity of fashion offered its consumers a modest opportunity to transform dreams into reality. This chapter approaches fashion in everyday life through the prism of these three inter-connected forms of popular culture: magazines, cinema and dance. While window-shopping was an increasingly accessible means to see fashionable clothes, magazines, cinema and dancing provoked different relationships to fashion as consumers could scrutinize, rehearse and experience, enabling 'mimetic images of Harlow, Garbo and Crawford [to] parade ... the high street'.[5] Turning first to magazines, we look at their important role in disseminating and circulating particular types of visual images as well as stimulating social aspirations and economic mobility. The 1920s were a boom period for magazine publishing in Britain and the United States, and importantly New York and London were at the centre of this business.[6] Magazines such as *Home Chat, Good Housekeeping, Britannia & Eve, Harper's Bazaar, McCall's* and *Ladies Home Journal* were vital sources of knowledge about fashion and dress-making, especially as they provided up to the minute information through drawings and photographs, patterns and practical tips.[7] Dressmaking skills acquired from relatives, brought up to date by reference to magazines, and honed by continual practice allowed women some independence to choose style as well as colour and material. Image was pivotal, and for this the cinema led the way establishing new 'looks' and breaking established dress codes. As one woman put it, 'British fashion then was very old-fashioned and rules were rigid' but observing 'younger stars without gloves and hats – we soon copied them'.[8] This chapter re-thinks how Hollywood – marshalled as mass experience in these two increasingly important fashion cities – helped to position the everyday as a form of modernity via fashion and glamour, rather than to reassert entrenched codes that were grounded in tradition. [9]

The widespread popularity of the cinema was phenomenal. In London, in 1934, there was a cinema seat for every fourteen people with the majority of cinemagoers being under forty.[10] Initially the audience comprised those who were single and working class, but by the mid-1930s going to the movies attained a degree of respectability for married middle-class women and couples and it became 'part of the very fabric of new suburbia'.[11] The new 'dream palaces' – the Odeon, Paramount, Astoria, Granada, Roxy, Rialto and Alhambra – spoke of exotic places and conspicuous, almost indecent, luxury as they appeared in London's inner and outer suburbs at North Ilford, Tooting, Woolwich, Finsbury Park, Brixton, Rayner's Lane, Muswell Hill and Kingston on Thames (Figure 3.1). Atmospheric and modern with deep pile carpets and bewitching lighting, double sweeping staircases and ornate banisters 'one always felt like a Hollywood heroine descending into a ballroom'.[12] Undeniably modern, as we can see in this 1935 photograph of the Odeon on the High St at Kingston upon Thames, they provided a transitional space between the fantasy of Hollywood and everyday life, between dream and reality. These luxurious, spectacular designs allowed audiences to escape and imagine.[13] Discussing the impact of film on her life, one young housewife declared, 'I find myself comparing my home, my clothes, even my husband. I get extremely restless and have a longing to explore unchartered lands'.[14] In New York, and across the United States, in the 1930s, the movies provided brief escape from the everyday economic strains that resulted from

Figure 3.1 The Odeon Cinema in Kingston Upon Thames, March 1935. Mirrorpix.

the Depression. Many of the films were escapist in theme and content, and featured stylish or lavish costumes, as dictated by the plot. Film's visual images and dramatic stories were powerfully evocative for young lives yet to be lived as well as for those already enmeshed in marriage, children and jobs, and some 'drew a sharpened sense of self from the images on the screen and the stories they acted out'.[15]

Not surprisingly, this new sense of self provoked anxiety. Dancing and fashion, seen by some as symbolic of women's progress into a new modernity, also hinted at a recklessness that was debated in the newspapers of the period. In an article in 1920, the writer commented on these 'social butterflies [who were] frivolous, scantily-clad, jazzing flappers, irresponsible and undisciplined, to whom a new hat, a dance, or a man with a car are of more importance than the fate of the nation'.[16] As dancing became popular, integral to modern daily life, it too affected fashion. As the British newspaper the *Daily Mail* put it in 1919, 'Everyone dances in London now. We dance to the gramophone, the piano, the "Jazz" band ... We dance in our houses if they are of sufficient size ... we dance at "controlled dances" and uncontrolled dances in all sorts of little halls and studios'.[17] Indeed a form of everyday modernity was embodied in the escape from tradition represented by dances such as the foxtrot, and as the movements of new dances became 'symbolic and expressive of the breakdown of convention that was associated with the end of the war, and particularly with the increased independence enjoyed by women'.[18] The Shimmy, the Boston, the Charleston, the Hesitation, and the plethora of 'Rag' dances; 'like the majority of African American music and dance forms, ... represented a creolization of various African and European traditions ... while accompanying "rag" dances emerged out of working-class dance halls throughout the United States'.[19] In October 1919, the Hammersmith Palais de Danse opened in West London inaugurating a new era in popular dancing with numerous other venues opening on London's high streets including the Locarno in Streatham, the Lido in Croydon, the Paramount on Tottenham Court Road and the Astoria on Charing Cross Road. Capturing the popular imagination and made accessible with widening radio ownership (9 million licences in Britain by 1939), one could listen to 'syncopated music [and] enter this new world for sixpence'.[20] These dances were accentuated by hand-made or shop-bought dresses – shortened sparkling shifts and body-sculpted gowns – that shook and shimmered on the dance-floor. Provocative, suggestive and exhilarating to wear, a modern dress was essential for dances such as the Shimmy, named by the American performer Gilda Gray in 1918, as she shook her chemise as she danced. While magazines, cinema and dance were most sharply experienced within the city pointing to a modern, urban and metropolitan experience, tradition and continuity persisted particularly along generational, gender and class lines and these too remained integral to everyday lives: 'The new consumerism may be charted in reminiscence. Detonated by mass production, its growth was uneven and rooted in local traditions of distribution and desire'.[21] A *Daily Mirror* newspaper photograph from 1926 (Figure 3.2) showing the queue for public transport in London during the General Strike dramatically highlights the pervasiveness of 1920s' fashionable styles for women. While the wrap-around coats with shawl and fur collars reference high fashion via women's magazines and Hollywood,

Figure 3.2 Queuing for public transport on Mansion House Street on day two of the General Strike, London, 1926. Mirrorpix.

men's overcoats, suits and hats (note the working-man's flat cap as well as the bowlers) represented white-collar class identities that spoke of reliability and respectability.

Writing in 1942, Pearl Jephcott described 'Young Girls Growing Up' and, though she was critical of what she considered to be the false dreams offered by Hollywood and the mindlessness of dancing, she recounted the ordinariness of lives that were still locked down by precedent and dominated by tradition. Thus a London girl 'growing up' went to camp, sang and acted at the local youth club as well as attending dances (typically Scottish Country dancing).[22]

Magazines and fashion

American fashion magazines and home-dressmaking developed in tandem from the mid-nineteenth century: 'the history of United States fashion magazines is inextricably linked to the history of the United States pattern companies'.[23] One of the earliest pattern companies, Demorest, was established in 1854 and by 1860 it produced its own publication, *The Mirror of Fashion,* which was later incorporated into *Demorest's Monthly Magazine.* Butterick paper patterns established in 1863 by a tailor from Massachusetts moved into publishing in 1865 with the *Semi-annual Report of Gent's Fashions*, followed by the *Ladies Report of New York Fashions* in 1867 and *The Metropolitan* in 1868. Consolidated as

The Delineator, it ceased publication in 1937. McCall's Pattern Company was established in 1870 and by 1871, its owner James McCall advertised 'Bazaar Cut Patterns' in *Harper's Bazaar*.[24] Founded in 1867, *Harper's Bazaar* offered a pull-out pattern each week from the outset until it became a monthly periodical in 1901. In contrast, the patterns included in the *Ladies' Home Journal* and *Vogue* were a later addition. Begun as a society weekly in 1892, *Vogue* introduced patterns in 1899, whereas the *Ladies' Home Journal*, established in 1883, produced patterns from 1905. The plethora of new and established inter-war magazines that were produced predominantly in London and New York used new technologies of mass publishing as they imaginatively targeted a burgeoning, largely female, readership. Fashion was vital to this. Existing magazines in Britain included *Home Chat* (1895), *Woman's Weekly* (1911), *Peg's Paper* (1919), in addition to new titles *Good Housekeeping* (1922), *Modern Woman* (1925), *Woman and Home* (1926), *Woman's Own* (1932) and *Woman* (1937). Such 'women's' (as opposed to fashion) magazines can provide details about how the two cities were 'imagined' relative to one another through products, and it underscores the transatlantic interconnections during the 1920s and 1930s. An advertisement in *Woman and Home,* April 1936, for Yardley beauty products links London and New York with the latter represented by the skyscraper, an important image of modernity. Described as a 'city of enchanted towers, where the women seem to remain always lovely, young and fair', this revealing slogan set out to counter the idea of the city as a place of corruption and degradation (Figure 3.3).

   In the United States, the quintessential women's magazines of the nineteenth and twentieth centuries were known as the 'Seven Sisters', and included, in chronology of original publication date, *Ladies Home Journal* (1873), *McCall's* (1873), *Good Housekeeping* (1885), *Redbook* (1903), *Better Homes and Gardens* (1922), *Family Circle* (1932) and *Woman's Day* (1937). They 'devoted their monthly and general interest articles and columns toward improving the lives of the middle class suburban housewife (e.g. *Good Housekeeping* was aimed toward women of affluent backgrounds and *Better Homes and Gardens* inspired women with ideas on home economics and leisurely activities)'.[25] Writing of his Brooklyn childhood in the 1920s, Alfred Kazin recalls how his mother, a home dressmaker, consulted *McCall's* with her neighbourhood customers, who demanded she make them dresses like those illustrated in the magazine.[26] For high fashion, the most significant and influential magazine was, of course, *Vogue.* Begun in New York as a 'social gazette for a Eurocentric elite', it became a more 'professional and self-consciously patriotic' publication after its purchase by Condé Nast in 1909.[27] Less-expensive magazines, such as Edward Bok's popular *Ladies Home Journal* or *Munsey's*, were aimed at the largely rural middle-class population of the Midwest and western United States, while *Vogue* served as a bridge between the United States and Europe, with an upper-class New

Figure 3.3 Yardley advertisement, *Woman and Home*, UK, April 1936, p. 85. Author's Collection.

England readership.[28] While, as Matthews David has noted, *Vogue* positioned itself as an aloof and elite magazine, it gradually renounced Gilded Age snobbery to reflect a more encompassing understanding of American style and dress.[29]

In the 1920s, it started to cover New York fashion and designers. It reflected a US anti-European sentiment after the First World War, epitomized in its thirtieth birthday edition that appeared in the United States on 1 January 1923, in the United Kingdom on 1 February, and in France on 1 March of the same year.[30] Such was the power and impact of the magazine that its name and artwork were freely copied, as New York became a centre for the design and production of more expensive women's ready-to-wear fashion. The photograph (Figure 3.4) of the backs of two fashionably dressed women looking at an equally fashionable

Figure 3.4 Bonwit Teller, 1930. Museum of the City of New York.

evening dress in the window of Bonwit Teller is testament to New York as a centre of design. Bonwit was an established New York 'carriage trade' store, which had just moved to the location pictured on Fifth Avenue at 56th Street in the year that the photograph was taken. Designed the previous year, and then re-designed for Bonwit, the image shows how the building represents the confidence of New York modernity in architecture. Bonwit was also to mark itself among retailers when it appointed Hortense Odlum as its president in 1934, the first female to hold such a role anywhere in the United States. Odlum emphasized an atmosphere of style and elegance in the shop with the intention that every woman would feel welcome, irrespective of their income or social class.[31] Despite the Depression, under Odlum the store increased its market share and attracted customers by creating departments including Salon de Couture, Rendezvous, Debutante, College Girls Department, a beauty salon and the 721 Club, to cater to a varied clientele.[32] The department dedicated to women in college, opened in 1934, was particularly interesting in catering for a developing market created as more women were entering both co-educational and single-sex colleges across the country. Advertisements for the new shop showed the adoption of fabrics typically used for menswear, casual silhouettes and modest price points.[33]

The United States relied upon and fuelled interest and knowledge about fashion using various publishing devices. Featuring the latest styles from Paris, they also tantalized the reader with tales of Hollywood. Likewise, the British magazine *Peg's Paper* included a regular feature 'Peg Trots Around Hollywood' which covered the lives and attitudes of stars,[34] while movie magazines and pattern companies such as Butterick marketed 'Starred Patterns' that highlighted stars' designs from Hollywood films.[35] As Hackney has shown, information about what the stars were wearing 'established a discourse of modern femininity through consumption, employing a wider visual vocabulary of photography, new techniques of layout and design, and an increasing amount of display advertisements'.[36] Representing a 'modern femininity', these magazines were increasingly adept at using visual means to reach their intended audience and the new category of weekly magazines launched in Britain the 1930s had wide appeal due to their use of colour particularly *Woman* in 1937 which 'promoted a new form of modern femininity, one of style and appearance'.[37] Under the heading 'Gay London's Smartly Plain and Simple Styles', an article in the new monthly *Woman and Home* from December 1926 initially offered the reader free paper patterns: these 'Kut-Eezi' patterns 'have caught on!', declared the article's author. Advertised as being used by an actress, they offered ideas for the newest dance dresses (use the same material but in two different colours to highlight its design features). Based on Oxford Street, London, Kut-Eezi patterns could be obtained for 1/- or 1/6 by mail order, according to the feature writer: 'I have had scores of letters from readers who have made dresses for the first time from them. They say that until they used last month's free pattern they had no idea that dressmaking could be so easy'.[38] In the issue for April 1936, *Woman and Home* offered 'bargain priced' Bestway patterns for one shilling, or one shilling and nine pence overseas. Featuring 'A Gay Little Frock for Easter', the styles have a long, slim silhouette, with detail towards the neckline and shoulders, characteristic of the fashion of the period (Figure 3.5).[39] Three years later, in March 1939, a pattern

Figure 3.5 *Woman and Home*, UK, April 1936. Author's Collection.

for a 'Spring Foursome', comprising a frock, jumper suit, jacket and skirt, was available with a coupon, for just four pence halfpenny, or nine pence overseas (Figure 3.6).[40] The style is markedly different from three years previously, with shorter skirts and altogether simpler designs, foreshadowing the fashions of the next decade.

Figure 3.6 *Woman and Home*, UK, March 1939. Author's Collection.

As magazines such as *Britannia and Eve* illustrated the latest styles, they also advised customers where to buy fabric and which shops sold particular outfits. In 1933, an article entitled 'Sketches from the Winter Collections of the London Shops' in *Britannia and Eve* illustrated coats, gowns and day dresses, but a few pages further on, it offered 'Our Paper Pattern Service for the Home Dressmaker', including four day dresses.[41] Gowns were redolent of Hollywood glamour. An ankle-length pale-blue faille gown modelled in *Britannia and Eve* in 1930 was ideal for dances with asymmetric tiers swaying and swishing to the dance rhythm.[42] The soft light-ribbed fabric gown – most likely silk but possibly rayon – was tiered from the waist with a draped bodice clasped at the waist. Rayon, an increasingly ubiquitous 'modern' fabric, was also essential for the 'glamour' of these gowns and it was evident from the way it is advertised. The shingle-haired model was photographed 'Hollywood style' with dramatic lighting capturing both her profiled face and the cut of her gown, and while these patterns offered access to modernity, it was an everyday modernity – adaptable and attainable.[43]

Paper patterns were one of the most effective means by which fashion entered the everyday lives of women in this period as publishers included them for hard commercial reasons to woo their readership and to beat competitors. They were also an everyday investment. During the 1930s' Depression in the United States and in Britain, women were sewing more, but buying fewer patterns as they offered consumers great flexibility to adapt, re-model and revise elements of fashionable styles that were unsuitable or inappropriate. Equally, a dress could be 'freshened' with a change of collar or sleeve, especially when most pattern companies offered a variety of sleeve and collar choices with each pattern.[44] Indeed, many home dressmakers who often possessed large collections of paper patterns had a small number that were used repeatedly, particularly if these provided standard but essential templates for a particular style of dress, blouse or coat. As a result, fashionable features – seen in the movies, in magazines and on the dance-floor – could be creatively incorporated into standard items. In this way, 'the sewing-machine, mass-produced in the early twentieth century, often inherited from mother or mother-in-law, bought on hire-purchase, played its part' in democratizing glamour.[45] Armed with a paper pattern, young single women in particular could assert a self-image and independence that was at odds with the older generation for whom dress marked out particular ideals of class respectability and appropriate feminine appearance. In contrast to 'Court dressmakers [who] continued to turnout stiffened satins and brocades, and shop windows still displayed their clothes draped decorously on plaster busts', home dressmaking offered opportunities to be creative, economical and distinctive. [46] It wasn't just economy however, nor was it solely a working-class activity. Home-made clothing could also be the product of substantial skill in sewing, but also in knitting and crochet. An American pattern book from the mid-1930s for Bucilla brand knitting and crochet cottons depict garments that demand both skill and attention. A 'Sun Back Dress with Bolero' is also styled glamorously, with the model of the complete outfit wearing fashionable gauntlet gloves, and holding a rolled copy of *Harpers Bazaar* (Figure 3.7).[47] Another Bucilla leaflet for 'Advance Fashions in Hand Knits', featured a suit 'Design by Vera Heller Paris' which was being repeated by popular request from their collection of 'Couturier Fashions'.

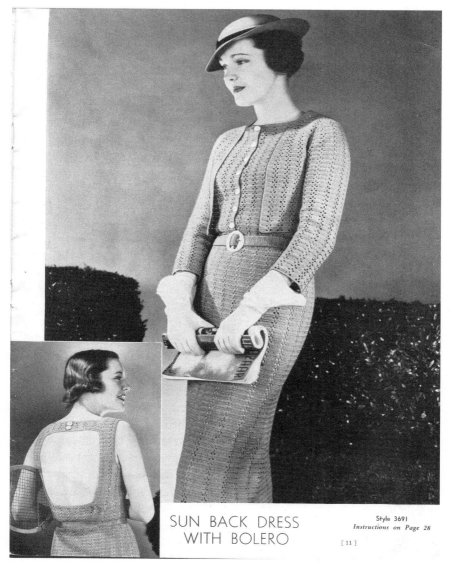

SUN BACK DRESS
WITH BOLERO

Style 3691
Instructions on Page 28
[11]

Figure 3.7 *Bucilla* 'Fashions Pet: Cotton Crochet', p. 11, n.d. Author's Collection.

Studying in London in the early 1930s, middle-class Rachel Rosta – from a Quaker family in the north of England – made her own clothes, as did her mother, Amy Wallis. While both bought clothes from local and London department and multiple stores wherever they lived (Binns in Darlington, Marks & Spencer in Cambridge, and Marshall & Snelgrove, John Lewis, Whiteley's and Barkers in London, as well as buying brands such as Horrockses), they both used paper patterns including McCalls, Vogue, Mabs Fashions and Butterick to make children's clothes, night wear, jackets, blouses, lounge pyjamas and dresses with such skill that it was difficult to differentiate home-made from bought clothes. Emphasizing the importance of oral evidence, the curator of the Wallis Archive which holds Rosta's collection observed that 'it would be hard to distinguish the bought dress, with its sleeveless bodice, net inset and intricately paneled skirt, from Rachel's home-made evening dresses on grounds of style, fabric, cut, construction or quality of finish'.[48] A salmon-pink rayon jersey evening dress bought from a London 'Guinea gown' shop in 1932 was described somewhat tellingly by Rachel as vulgar, whereas her home-made 1934 midnight-blue cotton velvet evening dress was glamorous.[49] A 1938 evening dress in red-brown moiré (artificial rather than silk) aimed for dramatic effect rather than high-quality finish and with a trained skirt, one can envisage Rachel taking to the dance-floor with some style and panache.[50] Rosta had a small number of patterns that she used repeatedly although she didn't copy them exactly; instead she modified or simplified them. The Vogue pattern (S3685) found in the Wallis collection for an ensemble of skirt, jacket, and blouse has a price of three shillings stamped on it, but the printed price on the pattern is for one dollar; another transatlantic exchange (Figure 3.8). Whereas her mother Amy Wallis sewed as a hobby, Rachel's sewing activities as a young woman in the 1930s were perhaps more linked to economy. Her personal geography took her away from the North East of England to London and Vienna to study music before switching to architecture, which she studied at the Bartlett School, the Architectural Association and Regent St Polytechnic School. During the Second World War, Rosta worked on the RIBA exhibition 'Rebuilding Britain', in addition to designing prefabricated houses with the company ARCON. Marriage to Lazslo Rosta, a Hungarian émigré, in 1944 led the family to move to Cambridge. Between 1946 and 1952, she had three daughters and, after being widowed in 1954, she began working for the British modernist architect Sir Leslie Martin; later in Cambridge, she designed her own modernist house in 16 Latham Road. As a working mother of three girls, few items were made at home between 1950 and 1970, but except for those twenty years, Rosta's dressmaking covered many years of her life. It changed as she grew up, became independent, married, widowed and worked, and her clothes held at the York Museums Trust capture her engagement with fashion over time as a child, a young woman, a working mother and as she became older.

Figure 3.8 *Vogue* pattern (S3685) for an ensemble of skirt, jacket, and blouse: 1930s (Rachel Rosta), York Museums Trust (York Castle Museum).

Going to the movies

Recounting a census of conversation among young women factory workers in Britain in 1934, Winifred Holtby found that cinema stars, men friends and private gossip came out top: 'When lives are restricted, the routine of work and leisure unvaried, limited and dull, it is not surprising that the vivid emotional romance of the Screen ... should capture the imagination'.[51] Shrewd and observant, Holtby noted the importance of fashion: 'Nowadays, thanks to the true democracy of the talkies, two penny fashion journals and inexpensive stores, it is possible for one fashion to affect a whole hemisphere with no distinction of class and little of pocket'.[52] This theme of homogeneity, characterized by fashion for Holtby, also resonated with other writers in 1930s' Britain including J. B. Priestley. America was a particular source of anxiety to Priestley; in fact he had complained in *An English Journey* of 1934 that parts of London looked more like California than England.

To those such as Priestley and Holtby, Hollywood films encapsulated the pernicious influence of American popular culture, but these transatlantic connections were already well established by the 1920s. Two-way business and cultural links were important as music, magazines, radio, film and fashion traversed the Atlantic. Described as 'the essential social habit of the age' by historian AJP Taylor,[53] it was suggested that 'only the Bible and the Koran have an indisputably larger circulation than that of the latest film from Los Angeles'.[54] Indeed, there was an escalating volume of Hollywood films into Britain particularly after the introduction of talkies in 1927. As with popular music, American film dominated British cinemas in the 1920s and 1930s, and cinema building gathered pace. By 1926, there were 3,000 in Britain and, by 1935, London had 258 cinemas that could accommodate a quarter of its population on any given day.[55] Some attended three times a week, and even those from poorer backgrounds went once a week. More importantly, unlike dancing, 'going to the pictures' was an activity that retained a degree of respectability thus allowing married women to carry on their cinema attendance after marriage and children. As Llewellyn Smith, author of *The New Survey of London Life and Labour*, put it in 1935, 'women mainly attend the afternoon performances. It is no uncommon sight to see women slipping into the cinema for an hour, after they have finished shopping and before the children come home from school'.[56] These mid-afternoon attendees were mainly women who didn't work outside the home, but nevertheless Londoners from all walks of life experienced the cinema regularly as a leisure activity. A report on cinema going in London's East End from 1936 found that audiences were very discerning. Generally they preferred 'good American pictures ... British pictures are disliked because the acting is wooden, because the actors and actresses talk "society fashion" and because they are too slow'.[57]

But the films were only half of the story. Audiences went for relaxation, for a good tale, as a respite from domesticity and to have some time with their partner, married or not. Dressing up and stepping out of everyday lives was one of the main motivations and the movie business recognized this. The stars' clothes tantalized the audience who became adept at recognizing designs by different Hollywood costumiers, which they then carefully noted, assessed and copied. Certain actresses gained a reputation, particularly in the 1930s, of being a 'clothes horse'. Joan Crawford was in this category, though Norma Shearer, Katherine Hepburn and Bette Davis were all leaders of fashion especially as, via Hollywood, America challenged the dominance of Paris. Pattern companies adapted the stars' gowns for mass-consumption and, as film historians have observed, the Letty Lynton dress worn by Crawford in the 1932 film of the same name appeared not just in Macy's shop window, but as a paper pattern version by Butterick from 1933 and even as an outfit for the ten-year-old Princess Elizabeth in 1936.[58] Crawford's personal story as a woman from an underprivileged background who had to work hard to 'make it' was vital to her star persona and, while she played heiresses and socialites, 'some of her more memorable lower-class parts were as stenographer' (*Grand Hotel*, 1932), factory worker (*Possessed*, 1931; *Mannequin*, 1938), maid (*Sadie McGee*, 1934), sales clerk (*Our Blushing Brides*, 1930; *The Women*, 1939) and cabaret singer (*The Bride Wore Red*, 1937).[59] It was these roles that allowed young working-class women to visualise their dreams particularly through the consumption of fashionable clothes.

As Joan Crawford had explained, her first chance came when a friend gave her money – $14 – to buy a handbag, gloves, shoes, hat, hose and dress.[60] At the same time, what mattered was that women should find and identify with a 'star' and his/her 'look'. As May Jones (one of Alexander's oral respondents) put it: 'You acted out what you saw the rest of the week … you probably saw the film round two or three times for sixpence, so you got the proper gist of it … and you used to walk along the road imbued with it, caught up in it'.[61] Likewise, Jackie Stacey's oral respondents in *Star Gazing* recounted, 'we copied whatever we could from the stars we saw in the films. We even sent off by post to Malta and Gibraltar for Hollywood Nylons'.[62] Another explained how 'it was fun trying to copy one's favourite stars with their clothes, hats and even make-up, especially eyebrows. Hats were much in vogue at that time and shops used to sell models similar to the styles that stars were wearing'.[63] Film magazines such as *Picturegoer* and women's magazines such as *Britannia and Eve* were commercial enterprises that fed off this desire for information about stars and their fashions. As one writer put it: 'the place to study glamour is the fan magazine … Everything is superlative, surprising, exciting … Nothing stands still, nothing ever rests, lest of all the sentences … Clothes of course are endlessly pictured and described usually with marble fountains, private swimming pools or limousines in the background'.[64] Indeed, by the 1920s and 1930s, these women, not the elite leisured classes, symbolized 'a new turn in London's modernity … and move[d] fashionability into the new mass market' that at the same time undermined both court manners and mores as well as generational protocols.[65] Movie and women's magazines emphasized rags-to-riches stories and dressing fashionably offered a chance to advance oneself. This cartoon 'The Craze for "Getting on the Films"' from the British *Daily Mirror* newspaper in 1922 captures the dual fascination with cinema – to watch but also to imagine oneself a star (Figure 3.9).

Figure 3.9 *Daily Mirror* cartoon by William Kerridge Haselden, January 20, 1922. Mirrorpix.

An article from 1929 in *Britannia and Eve,* entitled 'Hollywood: Through the Looking Glass', introduced the reader to a number of women who worked in Hollywood. These included the star Ruth Chatterton ('at work on her tenth talkie'), Kate Corbaley ('through her hands passes all the story material for endless films'), Ruth Harriet Louise ('the clever woman who turns out an annual average of five thousand photographs of a famous company's stars') and Charlotte Wood, who specialized in 'feminine fashion' publicity.[66] Wood's specialty was producing 'miles of print columns about the gowns and hats and shoes and "undies" which grace the ladies of her lot. Also she arranges the business details connected with those testimonials which stars give to face creams and eye-lash beautifiers – a profit-making arrangement for her studio'.[67] Through these determinedly commercial means, such 'looks' were democratized via Hollywood, disseminated by magazines, to be made or assembled at home or bought at a smart store.

Such strategies were equally important in the United States, where consumers still wanted to achieve the glamorous looks presented in the movies, despite the economic constraints of the Depression. Piece-goods stores offered a wide range of fabrics and other materials to enable women to update or create their own wardrobes. Large retailers, like Sears, encouraged this by featuring sewing, knitting and crochet supplies in their stores and their catalogues. Printed dress fabrics became more ubiquitous in the 1930s, having the practical advantage of being cheaper than embroidered designs and less likely to show stains than plain fabrics. Simple styles from synthetic fabrics such as rayon, cut to fit the average body, became very popular. Sears introduced its 'Sear-ettes' wraparound dresses, tied at the side, which became known as 'Hoverettes', after President Hoover, thus keeping in mind the state of the economy. The dresses were reversible to enable them to have a double wear before being washed and they sold at the very attractive price of two for 98c.[68] Needlework magazines provided transfers and instructions to enable women to purchase plain, cheap underwear to decorate by themselves, in order to save money. Despite the Depression, movie magazines such as *Hollywood, Modern Screen, Movie Mirror, Photoplay, Screenland* and *Silver Screen* served the same role as in Britain, of promoting the styles and looks of the stars. Hollywood was acknowledged, in April 1939 in the new monthly magazine, costing 15c, *Glamour of Hollywood,* as 'America's Glamour Center'.[69] Hollywood is described as offering the potential of glamour and of knowing, more than other places, 'the art of remaking men and women into a closer likeness of our wishful thinking'.[70] But the reader is advised that its temptations need to be used wisely and not imitated. Via the intervention of the magazine in question, Hollywood can give the reader 'your own personality and appearance a bit of the brilliance and radiance every woman needs in her own daily life'.[71] Another article in the same issue cautions that while there are 'prizes' there are also 'pitfalls' in borrowing styles from the movie stars, as the 'peculiar needs' of the camera require treatments that are not always applicable to what is worn in everyday life. Once again the reader is cautioned against 'careless copying' of clothes worn in the movies, offering particular 'dos and don'ts'.[72]

Fashion remained a strong presence in 1930s movies, with one Busby Berkeley spectacle, *Fashions of 1934,* addressing it directly as a subject. Even in financially hard times, so-called Cinema Fashions held sway in big cities and in particular in small American towns, where the movies had little competition as the dictators of what to wear.[73] On stylish Fifth Avenue in New York's Manhattan, a motion picture name could act to the advantage of fashion retailers. In 1939, Merle Oberon's wedding dress from *Wuthering Heights* was in the window of one store on upper Fifth Avenue, while hats from the film were shown in another and a reproduction of one of the rooms in a third.[74] The influence of Hollywood penetrated fashionable New York in different ways. One beauty salon is recorded as complaining how New York's smart debutantes were following Hollywood's stars in consistently ignoring the 'fashion edict for Up Hair', preferring to 'look young and pretty with their hair down than middle-aged with their hair up'.[75] Hollywood was also held responsible for greater informality of dress such as wearing suits for dinner or polo coats for parties as well as sports. Such practices discouraged new purchases, to the chagrin of the trade. Others were simply seen as a lowering of sartorial standards: Dorothy Lamour starting the 'cheap and convenient fashion' of wearing bandanas off-stage, instead of hats.[76] If standards were seen as slipping by retailers, they signalled not just a greater flexibility of everyday dress, but also the gradual move of fashion authority to the wearer. Hollywood also reflected the dance craze of the 1930s by featuring the Swing Era in dozens of movies, which also crossed the racial divide. Warner Brothers' *Hollywood Hotel* released in 1937, for instance, included the racially mixed Benny Goodman Quartet.[77]

Dancing

Describing a cleaner, lighter half-American London, Walter Burke observed in 1934 that

> the first quarter of this century…may be known to history as London's American Phase, since the major part of the many and rapid changes it has suffered may be traced to America. Our tube railways we owe to America. The bulk of our entertainment is American in quality and largely in personnel. All our latest hotels derive from American models. Our snack-bars and all-night supper-stands are pirated from America. Our electric night-signs are an American idea.[78]

With British war debt to America amounting to £900 million in 1920, its impact on British cultural life was both fraught and complex, but for many it was evoked most strongly by music and dance. Jazz arrived in London in 1919 with performances by the Original Dixieland Jazz Band at the Hippdrome, the London Palladium and the newly opened Hammersmith Palais de Danse (Figure 3.10).[79] Comprising white Italian-Americans from Chicago, this band was followed by an increasing number of bands that were uniformly African American including Will Cook's Southern Syncopated Orchestra with the talented clarinettist,

Figure 3.10 The annual Lyons 'Big Bang' held at the Hammersmith Palais de Danse, 18 January 1937. Mirrorpix.

Sidney Bechet. Black American musicians had arrived in Britain in considerable numbers after the war to replace the Germans who had previously staffed London's bands, and they brought with them a new syncopated sound that was lively and fast with unfamiliar rhythms.[80] To many this highly cosmopolitan sound that suggested Africa rather than urban America was fundamentally alien: 'Jazz's alien associations were further underlined by the link often made in the 1920s between jazz and Jewishness, due largely to the fact that popular music's finest composers, men such as George Gershwin, Irving Berlin and Cole Porter, were indeed Jewish'.[81] Racism and prejudice informed many of those who wrote about music and dance in inter-war London. Explaining that the 'Palais de Danse and the professional partner, now a regular feature of London life in all classes [had] set up temples to the negroid Priapus. And had canonised the dance-band', Burke commented that the older generation 'didn't like the Cake Walk; they didn't like the Turkey Trot or the Bunny Hug; they don't like the Fox Trot or the Charleston, and they can't do the Tango. They consider the Rumba vulgar, and could hardly bring themselves to mention the Black Bottom'.[82] Generally, American dances had to be toned down before they were adopted in Britain, as the American professional dancer Irene Castle explained: 'In the States we dance to jazz music, but there are no fixed steps for it. We get our new dances from the Barbary Coast. They reach New York in a very primitive condition and have to be toned down before they can used in the ballroom'.[83] Various adjectives used to describe these dances evoked racial anxieties – primitive, barbaric, wild, and simple.[84] Originating in the 'lowly dance-halls of African-Americans', these dances hinted at alternative worlds that seemed less constrained by society mores; but unsurprisingly given the national mood following the First World War, they rapidly gained popularity in Britain.[85] Prior to 1914, public dancing was not a widespread working-class activity; rather it was confined to the upper and middle classes who danced at prestigious hotels and private clubs.[86] It was the introduction of American music with its irregular syncopated sound, the commercialization of the dance hall business and the opening of purpose-built dance-halls such as the Palais de Danse 'that would, by the mid-1930s, make dancing a truly mass leisure pursuit'.[87] There was even a concern in the early 1920s that dance would outsell cinema, as cash-strapped post-war consumers spent their time dancing rather than going to the cinema. Dance and cinema were part of the 'cultural billiard table of the Atlantic' that saw ideas and people ricocheting between America and London.[88] Indeed as Abra argued:

> The public interest in American dances was connected to and ran parallel with a growing British fascination with American dance songs and Hollywood films, both of which streamed across the Atlantic at an escalating volume; at the same time, the commercial industries that developed around music, radio, and film were increasingly transatlantic enterprises. The result was that the popular dance culture being consumed by the British dancing public was often a hybrid of American and home-grown styles.[89]

Films that involved dancing were especially popular. Fred Astaire was already well known in Britain and the United States due to his performances with his sister on the London stage and Broadway, but from the early 1930s he made a succession of films with Ginger Rogers that were dancing spectacles including *Flying Down to Rio* (1933), *The Gay Divorcee* (1934), *Top Hat* (1935), *Swing Time* (1936) and, interestingly, *The Story of Vernon and Irene Castle* (1939), the biopic of the careers of the celebrated dance professionals. These 'dancing films exposed Britons to dance celebrities and new dance songs, and perhaps most significantly, to new dances'.[90] East-Ender May Jones went dancing to the People's Palace in the Mile End Road in Stepney; as she put it: 'we used to get ourselves three penn'orth of port to get ourselves in the mood, so we'd float away in the tango'.[91] Another recounted how 'I was enraptured by any star who appeared in a Hollywood musical. I was completely lost – it wasn't Ginger Rogers dancing with Fred Astaire, it was me'.[92] Ginger Rogers was a particular favourite for the dance fans: 'Ginger Rogers wore such wonderful clothes, and for a couple of hours or so, we could forget the terrible things that were happening'.[93] At the start of the dance craze, though, there was consternation from the dance teachers and professionals who abhorred the unruly movements and close physical contact of dances such as the Tango. Described by Cresswell as operating in a marginal space or liminal zone 'where the normal rules of acceptable conduct no longer hold sway', the Tango – characterized by irregular, novel rhythms – 'was brought about by the slave trade and the consequent introduction of negro folk rhythms into Latin America'.[94] This sense of otherness added to the risqué perception of the dance-halls and the attendant worries of some contemporary commentators that they were not only sterile and standardized forms of mass culture, but they weren't entirely respectable. Writing in 1942, Jephcott captured these anxieties:

> The commercial world offers two main anodynes, the cinema and the dance hall. Pictures provide a dreamland of romance, excitement, laughter, attractive clothes and sunlit gardens, as a relief for homes which are probably dull, and from jobs that are wearisome and binding. The girl can enter this new world for sixpence and once she is there nothing else is demanded of her...The dance hall offers the company of young people, an opportunity for rhythmical movement, a very considerable measure of emotional excitement, and, again, makes little demand on the dancer's mental capacity.[95]

While acknowledging that 'when a girl goes dancing it means that she can wear a smart frock and good stockings and try to look really glamorous', Jephcott underplays the bodily experience of dance and the tactile, sensory feel of dance-gowns that were cut to accentuate movement, to rustle, swish and sway.[96] Cut in layers, on the bias, with pointed segments, or clasped and draped, these dance dresses in tulle, moiré silk, rayon, faille and lace had fringes, beading, glitter, tassels and feathers. Often diaphanous, they could also be heavy with beads and decoration which hinted at traditional dressmaking skills, but which also drew on modern technologies of paper patterns, sewing machines, magazine photographs, and the glamour of Hollywood. Freedom was palpable as heavy layers and cumbersome petticoats disappeared, and the body was revealed as never before, either with short skirts that flashed dancing legs or by sculpting and wrapping the body to accentuate the waist, back, hips and breasts. These dresses symbolized a new form of modernity; one grounded firmly in the realm of the everyday, but one that resisted entrenched codes both of behaviour and appearance. Its origins lay in popular mass cultural forms particularly magazines, movies and dancing, and importantly it was transatlantic in orientation.

In New York City, Harlem was the major focus of the racial and cultural shift that occurred in the 1920s and was also influential on music, dancing and fashion on both sides of the Atlantic. From the end of the First World War until the Depression of 1929, Harlem changed radically from a white German Jewish enclave to become the centre of the city's African American population. Most of the new black residents were from the American South,[97] the Caribbean, or from other parts of the city, and included some major literary and artistic figures, such as Langston Hughes, Countee Cullen and Zora Neale Hurston, who contributed to the cultural outpouring in the 1920s that became known as the Harlem Renaissance. Not only restricted to high culture, however, Harlem became a centre of black identity, of political and economic life, of music, dancing and popular culture, and the foundation of the community that engaged in the Civil Rights struggles of the 1950s and 1960s. Even if they did not command high incomes, the ordinary residents of Harlem were very attentive to their personal appearance and style. On the streets they were seen 'parading their furs and feathers, their form-fitting dresses and bright shawls, checkered suits and gay parasols, their white spats and silk handkerchiefs protruding from a breast pocket – even a freshly washed gingham dress or a black suit looked elegant in the afternoon sun'.[98] Those sporting these elegant clothes might be earning less than $100 a month, as waitresses, redcaps or stevedores, and relying for their stylish clothes on instalment houses and the discount offered by Harlem's ubiquitous 'hot men'.[99] Across different income groups, in Harlem the performance of style was ubiquitous. Harlem Renaissance writer, Richard Bruce Nugent, commented how 'We all wore those monkey-backed suits, bell-bottomed trousers, pinch-backed suits'.[100] Nugent had one unforgettable suit made when he was in England, reminding us of the distinctive style and quality of British tailoring for men. Fortunately, many public displays of style have been recorded visually. In particular, the work of Harlem-based African American photographer James Van Der Zee (1886–1983) documented Harlem life with the opening of his first studio in 1917. One of his most fashionable images show what is believed to be dancers Paul and Thelma Meers, displaying their era's most fashionable status symbols, matching raccoon coats and a new Cadillac Coupe.[101] Dancers and dancing provided an essential link between music, fashion and the black and white bodies that wore the clothes. They assembled, across racial boundaries, in the many clubs that flourished in Harlem during the Prohibition era (1920–1933).

Ragtime music, so closely associated with Harlem, was already established in Brooklyn in the 1890s, and the Cakewalk had become the dance of choice in ballrooms nationwide.[102] By the fall of 1913, dancer Irene Castle observed that 'America had gone absolutely dance-mad', with the country divided between those for and those against, what to some appeared the Devil's work.[103] Edward Bok of the *Ladies Home Journal* remained unconvinced. So in 1914, when he finally ran a double-page spread on the fashionably dressed Irene Castle and her husband Vernon, it was evident that the power of dance, its impact on bodies, fashion, and above all the associated recognition of the rise of black culture, could no longer be ignored.[104] In midtown Manhattan, African American musicians played ragtime for Flo Ziegfeld's cabaret, but the sound could not compare to what was being played uptown in Harlem, at the likes of the Crescent, Lafayette and Lincoln theatres, where the sounds of jazz and blues were attracting white audiences just after the First World War.[105] In a basement next to the Lafayette Theatre on Seventh Avenue near West 131st Street was one of the most sophisticated Harlem nightspots, Connie's Inn. Opened in 1923 by a pair of local German-Jewish brothers, it was one of the first new Harlem jazz clubs for whites only, which attracted an international array of rich and famous clientele. The club later adopted a 'black and tan' policy, allowing light-skinned coloured customers in after hours, the quality and energy of the music in effect championing over the club's racism for local residents.[106] It was via such establishments that everyday black culture and style had an impact on the white population of New York and beyond. Perhaps the most famous establishment of all was the Cotton Club, which also opened in 1923, on the northeast corner of Lennox Avenue and West 142nd Street.

While the Cotton Club itself was hardly 'everyday', it was particularly distinctive. Its white-only clientele watched and listened to black performers (including those with light skin, like the singer Lena Horne). The décor, the work of modernist designer Joseph Urban, was created to resemble an old-time plantation, complete with a mural that depicted slave shacks and cotton fields, and a stage based on the veranda of a slave owner's mansion. While Connie's Inn was known for its floor shows, the Cotton Club was famous for its music, especially after Duke Ellington's orchestra began to perform there in 1927, putting Harlem on the music map for Swing, and making the club the most exclusive and best known in the city. Those who could not afford a ticket, or whose skin was too dark to gain them entry[107] could still take part by listening to its weekly celebrity night radio broadcasts, sponsored by Moe Levy's clothing shop on 149th Street.[108] In 1930, Cab Calloway replaced Ellington as bandleader and brought with him his characteristic improvised scat style of singing, and his distinctive style of dress.[109] But for those who wanted to dance, regardless of their race, the place to go was the Savoy Ballroom.

Opening on 12 March 1926, on Lennox Avenue between 140th and 141st Streets, the Savoy has been described as shaking America as profoundly as the 1913 Armory show did the world of mainstream art. Its spacious lobby, with its huge cut-glass chandelier and marble staircase, was echoed in scale by its orange and blue dance hall, which could accommodate 4000 people 'Stompin at the Savoy'.[110] Blacks and whites played and danced alongside one another at the club, named after London's Savoy Hotel, which made jazz a product for national consumption through their radio broadcasts.[111] The Track, as its dance floor was known, became the premier dance hall in the United States. While hostesses offered three dances for a quarter,[112] it was the regular clientele who performed the bodily extremes of the exuberant Lindy Hop, demonstrating why the dance had been named after Charles Lindbergh's first transatlantic flight, and featured moves named the Camelback, the Shimmy, the Stomp and the Jitterbug Jive.[113] In a photograph of three black women jitterbugging together in what appears to be a mixed race club in Harlem in 1939, we can notice the style and the practicality of their attire. They each wear dresses with belted waists and flared skirts with hems just below the knees, and wide sleeves, both to enable freedom of movement. Their shoes have small heels, appropriate for street walking, as well as for the fast moves on the dance floor (Figure 3.11).

Like the jazz dances that preceded it, including the Charleston and the Black Bottom, the Lindy Hop demanded its own functional dress code. In the 1930s, women wore sweaters, and skirts flared at the hem to enable the vigorous steps and movements of the dance, with bobby socks, and saddle shoes. To appear dressier the code was a one- or two-piece dress, blouse, hosiery and ankle-strap, medium-heeled shoes. Their male partners have been described as 'much more the peacocks', borrowed their dress styles from the musicians. They typically wore pleated, pegged trousers, wide at the knees and narrow at the cuffs (turn ups) with a key chain looped from the belt to the pocket, a double-breasted suit jacket, with wide padded shoulders and a long soft roll collar that closed at the waist with one button, described as 'the reat pleat with a drape shape' pre-empting, of course, the zoot suit (discussed in the next chapter).[114] Social class and economic wherewithal impacted the fashion choices of the dancers: 'College campus swingers and eastern Shag dancers favored the bobby-sox, saddle shoe,

Figure 3.11 Jitterbuggin' in Harlem, 1939. Museum of the City of New York.

clean-cut look, while the urban hepcat went for the sophisticated, sharp look'.[115] By running special nights, such as the 'kitchen mechanics'[116] nights, focused on a clientele who worked in kitchens downtown, the Savoy became the most integrated of dance establishments, culturally and racially. This significance would also have extended to disseminating what was being worn across social, racial and cultural boundaries. The 'culture of looking', referenced by Julie Malnig, was important in transmitting ways of dressing and moving from the African American population to its white counterparts. The Lindy Hop, or Jitterbug, was no social dance craze like the foxtrots, tangos and waltzes, featured in women's and dance magazines in the nineteen teens, which, for instance, Edward Bok in *The Ladies Home Journal* used to promote new merchandise from dance corsets to designer gowns.[117] The dances performed at the Savoy were highly energetic, sexually charged and open to all; on the dance floor everyone appeared equal, the class and economic and racial differences only being reinstated when the dancers returned to their seats.[118]

By the time the Savoy opened, many of the city's white population were already making the journey up to Harlem to drink, party and participate in a more lively and open atmosphere in the Prohibition period. The publication of the novel *Nigger Heaven* in 1926 by the wealthy, white writer Carl Van Vechten had contributed to opening Harlem to outsiders. While attempting to analyse the black community and its various social groups, Van Vechten projected a racist perspective of the black population, as expressive and sexual as reflected in the cabarets – a view that played a large part in the book's success.[119] As Erenberg put it:

Black entertainers were perceived as natural, uncivilized, uninhibited performers, naturally smiling, because they had what whites lacked: joy in life. Guidebooks advised visitors to go to Harlem late, after the unadventurous whites downtown had gone to bed. The lateness of the hour added to the sense that one was venturing to the heart of darkness, the city of night where all things forbidden during the day were available in those few hours stolen from conventional life. In hard-working New York, Harlem was the Montmartre of America, its dramatic counterpoint. The numerous descriptions of driving up to Harlem, through the park by cab, made it seem as if one journeyed out from civilization, to the heart of impulses.[120]

The clubs and dance halls of Harlem were indeed influential in defining a distinctly American (as opposed to imported European) popular culture and fashionable dress. These 'new experiences, newer personal styles often became the province of an expanding consumer economy, offering powerful visions of liberation and adjustment for personalities still trapped in the normal routines of everyday life'.[121]

Fashion and bodily comportment were indeed factors in this liberation. While recognizing the powerful impact of the Wall Street Crash and the Depression on everyday economics and lifestyle in 1930s America, what would have been dreams for some even a decade earlier had become reality. A photograph from 1935 demonstrates this; it shows world heavyweight boxing champion Joe Louis, the 'Brown Bomber', walking along a Harlem Street with his new wife Marva. The couple are stylishly dressed, he in a suit, overcoat and fedora, and she also in a fashionable suit and hat, with a large fox fur around her shoulders. What is noticeable is the large crowd of onlookers, women, men and children who had come to see this popular celebrity. Although originally from Detroit, Louis was 'adopted' by Harlem, where he opened a restaurant and bar in the 1940s, demonstrating how the credence of Harlem remained important for the heroes of black America.[122] A style icon to his black fans, Louis helped to popularize sports clothes for informal everyday occasions. This trend took polo coats, polo shirts, plus fours, tennis shoes and T-shirts and elevated them from the playing field to the street, in the 1940s and 1950s.

As this chapter has shown, new forms of mass culture contributed to change in fashion and fashionable looks in inter-war Britain and the United States. In particular, these were becoming more accessible to a younger generation and to those without considerable amounts of disposable income. The concept of a teenage market had been established in the United States in the 1930s, creating a demographic shift that was to be crucial for the growing significance of fashion in everyday life for the remainder of the twentieth century and for the twenty-first century.[123] A photograph of young women and men taken in July 1939 by Andrew Herman for the Federal Art Project, on the boardwalk at New York's working-class summer playground, Coney Island, reveals a distinctive everyday way of dressing (Figure 3.12). The two young women in the foreground are dressed casually, with shoulder-length hair, one with a headscarf tied under the chin. They have matching loose shirts, with drawn faces, which may be those of the wearers, with names and other words and images, including a truck on the shirt on the right. Each wears a skirt just below the knee, the one on the left carelessly creased. Both have ankle-length 'bobby sox' and flat shoes, those of the woman on the right appearing to be two toned saddle style. The young man to their left is also dressed casually, but much less individually. As this photograph shows, fashion was a reality in everyday life, but it was also distinct from the 'designer' system. The impact of mass culture, particularly women's magazines, cinema and dance, had challenged the hierarchies of couture and upper-class society norms. Access to popular representations of glamour and fashion coupled with greater opportunities to go to the dance or to see the latest movie contributed to the democratization of fashionable styles and looks. Striking too was the changing status of the body, which was not just manipulated, painted and fashioned, but it was also

Figure 3.12 Bobby Soxers, Coney Island, July 1939. Museum of the City of New York.

reconfigured. To the 'gazing' in department store windows were added the practical skills of adapting paper patterns and making fashionable clothes. With appropriate attire, 'becoming' a Hollywood lookalike or learning the plethora of new dances were within reach of a growing number of people. In her book *Rising Twenty: Notes on some ordinary girls*, Jephcott acknowledged that girls in Britain had been 'Americanised' by dancing and the cinema.[124] Written just after the Second World War, it was part of an attempt to understand the motivations of young people at that time. As she put it: 'One begins to realize, when talking with these girls, the amazing extent to which the minutiae of the clothes and hair arrangement of an American actress may affect the spending habits of a child in a mining village in Durham or a girl in a tenement in Central London'.[125] Signalling new and different forms of modernity, she described young working-class girls in Durham and London attending the cinema or jiving 'with skill, abandon and unselfconscious enjoyment'.[126] The consumption habits of this younger generation were under close scrutiny, not only by those such as Jephcott but, especially after 1945 in both the United States and Britain, as the consumption of new goods was vital in ensuring that the Depression years were not revisited by either, and also in reiterating the dominance of capitalism in the context of the Cold War. As Chapter 4 will show, the 'cultural billiard table of the Atlantic', quoted earlier by Ross, ensured that in these everyday activities of modern life, Britain and the United States remained closely connected.

Notes

1   Andreas Huyssen, *After the Great Divide: Modernism, Mass Culture, Postmodernism* (Bloomington and Indianapolis: Indiana University Press, 1987), quoted in *Modern Times: Reflections on a Century of English Modernity*, ed. Mica Nava and Alan O'Shea (London and New York: Routledge, 1996), 63.

2   Paul Gilroy, *The Black Atlantic: Modernity and Double Consciousness* (London: Verso, 1993).

3   Bill Schwarz, 'Black Metropolis, White England', in *Modern Times: Reflections on a century of English Modernity*, ed. Mica Nava and Alan O'Shea, 189.

4   Ben Highmore, *The Everyday Life Reader* (London and New York: Routledge, 2002), 18.

5   Sally, Alexander, *Becoming A Woman in London and Other Essays in 19th and 20th Century Feminist History* (London: Virago, 1994), 221.

6   Cynthia White, *Women's Magazines, 1693–1968* (London: Michael Joseph, 1970).

7   Fiona Hackney, 'Making Modern Women, Stitch by Stitch', in *The Culture of Sewing: Gender, Consumption and Home Dressmaking*, ed. Barbara Burman (Oxford and New York: Berg, 1999), 85.

8   Jackie Stacey, *Star Gazing: Hollywood Cinema and Female Spectatorship* (London and New York: Routledge, 1994), 204.

9   Highmore, *The Everyday Life Reader*, 10.

10 Jeffrey Richards, *The Age of the Dream Palace: Cinema and Society in Britain 1930–1939* (London: Routledge & Kegan Paul, 1984), 16.

11 Ibid.

12 Stacey, *Star Gazing*, 99.

13 Ibid.

14 Carol Dyhouse, *Glamour: Women, History and Feminism* (London and New York: Zed Books, 2011), 63.

15 Alexander, *Becoming A Woman in London*, 222.

16 Claire Langhammer, *Women's Leisure in England 1920–60* (Manchester: Manchester University Press, 2000), 53.

17 'How We Dance', *Daily Mail*, 15 January 1919, 4.

18 Allison Jean Abra, 'On With the Dance: Nation, Culture, and Popular Dancing in Britain, 1918-1945' (PhD diss., University of Michigan, Ann Arbor, 2009), 85.

19 Ibid., 34.

20 Pearl Jephcott, *Girls Growing Up* (London: Faber and Faber Ltd, 1942), 124.

21 Alexander, *Becoming A Woman in London*, 219.

22 Jephcott, *Girls Growing Up*, 143.

23 Joy Spanabel Emery, 'Dreams on Paper: A Story of the Commercial Pattern Industry', in *The Culture of Sewing*, ed. Burman, 238.

24 Ibid., 240.

25 Raymond Pun, 'The Story of the Seven Sisters: Women's Magazines at NYPL', *The Huffington Post*, March 31, 2013, available online: http://www.huffingtonpost. com/the-new-york-public-library/the-story-of-the-seven-si_b_2989101.html (accessed January 14, 2016). All continue in publication today with the exception of *McCall's*, which closed in 2002, having changed its name to Rosie in 2001, after the entertainer Rosie O'Donnell, appointed as its editorial director in 2000.

26 Alfred Kazin, *A Walker in the City* (New York: Harcourt Inc., 1951), 67.

27 Alison Matthews David, '*Vogue's* New World: American Fashionability and the Politics of Style', *Fashion Theory: The Journal of Dress, Body & Culture* 10, no. 1/2 (2006), 13.

28 Ibid., 17.

29 Ibid., 14.

30 Ibid., 31.

31 Michael Mamp and Sara B. Marcketti, 'Creating a *Woman's Place*: The Bonwit Teller Presidency of Hortense Odlum, 1934–1940', *Fashion, Style & Popular Culture* 2, no. 3 (2015), 304.

32 Ibid., 307.

33 Ibid., 311.

34 Deirdre Beddoe, *Back to Home & Duty: Women Between the Wars 1918–1939* (London: Pandora, 1989), 22.

35 Charlotte C. Herzog and Jane Gaines, '"Puffed Sleeves before tea-time": Joan Crawford, Adrian and Women Audiences', in *Stardom: Industry of Desire*, ed. Christine Gledhill (London and New York: Routledge, 1991), 82.

36 Hackney 'Making Modern Women', 75.

37 Ibid., 76

38 'Gay London's Smartly Plain and Beautifully Simple Styles. Kut-Eezi Patterns', *Woman and Home,* December 1926, 21.

39 'A Gay Little Frock for Easter', *Woman and Home*, April 1936.

40 'Spring Foursome', *Woman and Home*, March 1939.

41 *Britannia and Eve,* November 1933, 54–55, 70–71.

42 *Britannia and Eve,* June 1930, 64.

43 Advert, 'Courtaulds. The Greatest Name in Rayon', *Woman and Home,* U.K., April 1936, 1.

44 Joy Spanabel Emery, *A History of the Paper Pattern Industry: The Home Dressmaking Fashion Revolution* (London: Bloomsbury, 2014), 116.

45 Alexander, *Becoming A Woman in London*, 221–2.

46 Ibid., 221.

47 Leaflet for Bucilla, 'Fashions Pet: Cotton Crochet', 11.

48 Mary M. Brooks, 'Patterns of Choice: Women's and Children's Clothing in the Wallis Archive, York Castle Museum', in *The Culture of Sewing*, ed. Burman, 185.

49 bid.

50 Ibid., 186.

51 Winifred Holtby, *Women and a Changing Civilisation* (London: John Lane, 1934), 121.

52 Ibid., 118.

53 A.J.P. Taylor, *English History, 1914–1945* (London: Penguin, 1983), 392.

54 Richards, *The Age of the Dream Palace*, 11.

55 Langhammer, *Women's Leisure in England,* 58.

56 Ibid., 165

57 Richards, *The Age of the Dream Palace*, 26.

58 Herzog and Gaines, 'Puffed Sleeves before tea-time', 75.

59 Ibid., 86.

60 Ibid.

61 Alexander, *Becoming A Woman in London*, 222.

62 Stacey, *Star Gazing*, 200.

63 Ibid., 202.

64 Richards, *The Age of the Dream Palace*, 157.

65 Lynda Nead, 'Response', in *Fashion and Modernity*, ed. Christopher Breward and Caroline Evans (Oxford: Berg, 2005), 123–4.

66 Kathlyn Hayden, 'Hollywood Through the Looking Glass', *Britannia and Eve,* October 1929, 30–33.

67 Ibid., 33.

68 Stella Blum (ed.), *Everyday Fashions of the Thirties: As Pictured in Sears Catalogs* (New York: Dover Publications, 1981), 69, quoted in William H. Young and Nancy K. Young, *The 1930s* (Westport, CT: Greenwood Press, 2002), 83.

69 *Glamour of Hollywood,* April 1939, 35.

70 Ibid.

71 Ibid.

72 'Fashions From Hollywood: Prizes and Pitfalls in Borrowing Styles from the Stars', *Glamour of Hollywood*, April 1939, 48–51.

73 Margaret Farrand Thorp, *America At The Movies* (1939; repr. New York: Arno Press Inc., 1970), 110.

74 Ibid., 111.

75 Ibid.

76 Ibid. 118.

77 Ernie Smith, Preface to Norma Miller and Evette Jensen, *Swingin' at the Savoy: The Memoir of a Jazz Dancer* (Philadelphia: Temple University Press, 1996), xxvi.

78 Walter Burke, *London in My Time* (New York: Loring & Mussey, 1934), available online, https://ebooks.adelaide.edu.au/b/burke/thomas/london_in_my_time/ (accessed January 16, 2016).

79 Cathy Ross, *Twenties London: A City in the Jazz Age* (London: Museum of London, 2003), 28.

80 Ibid., 31.

81 Ibid.

82 Burke, *London in My Time.*

83 Tim Cresswell, '"You cannot shake that shimmie here": Producing Mobility on the Dance Floor', *Cultural Geographies* 13, no. 1 (2006), 69.

84 Ibid.

85 Ibid.

86 James J. Knott, *Music for the People: Popular Music and Dance in Interwar Britain* (Oxford: Oxford University Press, 2002), 149–50.

87 Ibid., 154.

88 Ross, *Twenties London,* 32.

89 Abra, 'On with the Dance', 161.

90 Ibid., 172.

91 Alexander, *Becoming a Woman in London*, 220.

92 Stacey, *Star Gazing*, 146.

93 Ibid., 111.

94 Cresswell, 'You cannot shake that shimmie here', 64.

95 Jephcott, *Girls Growing Up,* 125.

96 Ibid., 123.

97 Their numbers also increased the populations of cities such as Chicago, Philadelphia, and Cleveland, Ohio.

98 Steven Watson, *The Harlem Renaissance: Hub of African American Culture, 1920–1930* (New York: Pantheon Book, 1995), 7.

99 Ibid.

100 Ibid.

101 Carol Tulloch, *The Birth of Cool: Style Narratives of the African Diaspora* (London and New York: Bloomsbury, 2016), 59–62.

102 The Cakewalk apparently originated in slave plantations, and then became popular at the end of the nineteenth century among the lower- and middle-class urban white population who frequented bars and saloons where ragtime music was played. James Haskins, *Black Dance in America: A History Through Its People* (New York: Harper Collins, 1990), 22–3.

103 David Levering Lewis, *When Harlem Was in Vogue* (New York: Penguin, 1997), 30.

104 See image in Julie Malnig (ed.), *Ballroom, Boogie, Shimmy Sham, Shake: A Social and Popular Dance Reader* (Chicago: University of Illinois Press, 2009), 83,

Figure 4.1 caption 'Exhibition ballroom dance star Irene Castle models fashionable dance dress or the era. Circa 1913. Billy Rose Theatre Division, The New York Pubic Library for the Performing Arts, Astor, Lenox and Tilden Foundations.'

105 Ibid., 31.

106 Jonathan Gill, *Harlem: The Four Hundred Year History from Dutch Village to Capital of Black America* (New York: Grove Press, 2011), 267.

107 Most of the female performers being described as 'light or tan' skinned (Jeff Kisseloff, *You Must Remember This: An Oral History of Manhattan from the 1890s to World War II* [Baltimore, MD: Johns Hopkins University Press, 1989], 295)

108 Ibid., 268.

109 In 1935, soon after the Harlem riots, the Cotton Club moved to midtown, where it lasted only a year before closing for good (Kisseloff, *You Must Remember This*, 261).

110 The name of one of the key songs of the Swing era, by Andy Razaf and Edgar Sampson. Ibid., 269.

111 Ibid., 173.

112 Marshall Stearns and Jean Stearns, *Jazz Dance: The Story of American Vernacular Dance* (New York: Da Capo, 1994), 321.

113 Gill, *Harlem*, 270. Writer Langston Hughes, who lived in Harlem at the time, recalled how the lindy-hoppers at the Savoy practised their extreme routines for the entertainment of their white audiences, and would probably have never done so only for their own entertainment (Haskins, *Black Dance in America*, 40).

114 Ernie Smith, Preface to Miller and Jensen, *Swingin' at the Savoy*, xxiv.

115 Ibid., xxv.

116 Neil Shoemaker, *Harlem Heritage Guide*, 19 July 2013.

117 Julie Malnig, 'Athena Meets Venus: Visions of Women in Social Dancing in the Teens and Early 1920s', *Dance Research Journal* 31, no. 2 (1999), 37.

118 Rudolph Fisher, *The Walls of Jericho* (1928; repr., Ann Arbor: Ann Arbor paperbacks, University of Michigan Press), 74.

119 Lewis Erenberg, *Steppin' Out: New York Nightlife and the Transformation of American Culture, 1890–1930* (Westport, CT: Greenwood Press, 1981), 255.

120 Ibid., 255–6.

121 Ibid., 259.

122 A. Schoener, *New York: An Illustrated History of the People* (New York: W.W. Norton & Co, 1998), 286.

123 Emery, *A History of the Paper Pattern Industry*, 156.

124 Pearl Jephcott, *Rising Twenty: Notes on Some Ordinary Girls* (London: Faber & Faber, 1948), 155.

125 Ibid., 63.

126 Ibid., 150.

4
DRESSING UP

Introduction

Discussing costume and national identity in 1940s and 1950s British cinema, Pam Cook takes issue with film writers' lack of interest in what was worn on screen. Rehearsing a range of now familiar arguments, she proposes that the young woman who pieced together a look or identity drawn from film stars' images was not 'simply a stooge of consumerism', but 'a kind of performance artist, putting on and taking off different roles', sometimes on a daily basis.[1] These processes of 'dressing up' took on particular significance for both men and women in the 1940s and 1950s as fashion and clothes evoked patriotic intent, revealed local, national and transnational allegiances, negotiated race and class, as well as gender and generation, and highlighted a variety of consumption practices – both new and old. At the same time, these processes were responsive to broader social and cultural issues, including the concern for tradition in the face of accelerated modernity and the conflicting emotions of anxiety and optimism, in part due to political realignments both during and after the war, but also due to economic exigencies. Represented and articulated in film, news magazines, television (especially in the United States), amateur photography, advertising and retail promotional strategies, men and women's fashionable clothes and appearance spoke to the diversity of everyday lives. Ostensibly inhabiting a similar visual and material world, people in Britain and America were also remarkably diverse with fault-lines exposed around class, race, gender, ethnicity and geography. In large cities such as New York and London, these were exacerbated particularly so during wartime, but also in the peacetime rebuilding that followed. London was physically close to the war – close to the European mainland – but also its factories, houses and businesses were affected by German bombing. It offered a temporary home and stopping off point for refugees from Europe, for troops being moved to and from the battle zone; yet it remained home to a burgeoning population and diverse cultures. As Alistair O'Neill puts it, 'London, ravaged, if not razed by the Blitz, carved new pathways through the city' [and] 'offered libertines a new understanding of the broken city as a bountiful prospect'.[2] Depicted as physically damaged, but also as a playground instilled with tolerance and mischief, London allowed artists such as Francis Bacon, George Melly and Alberto Giacometti the spaces to develop a sense of style that was extraordinary rather than ordinary. Drawing upon the street performance of the 'spiv' and post-war Surrealism, it absorbed aspects of the visual style of recent West Indian immigrants that also nodded to America.[3] New York, in contrast, was a vital centre of business, media, transport and finance, as well as for the American fashion industry, which developed its confidence and independence during the war.

Focusing on London and New York, this chapter looks at dressing up during the middle of the twentieth century. Uniforms and uniformity for men and women were visually predominant for much of the war and during the immediate post-war years as rationing continued until 1952 in the United Kingdom and 1946 in the United States (where clothing rationing never impacted civilians as it did in Britain). With gender roles disrupted between 1939 and 1945, this proved to be a site of negotiation as sexual differences appeared – at first glance – to be played down. Demonstrating a high degree of subtlety, various strategies and devices were deployed to maintain the border that marked the difference between male and female. In fact, these boundaries between masculinity and femininity were repositioned and redrawn during this twenty-year period as central governments in both Britain and America via a plethora of agencies and departments set out to regulate gender excesses. Class remained a site of anxiety in Britain even though class distinctions in uniform were not so apparent as in earlier periods of conflict. Regulation during the war took place under the auspices of the Utility schemes in the United Kingdom and the War Production Board in the United States with both exhorting citizens to 'Make-do-and Mend' (UK) and 'Make and Mend' (US). While uniformity and uniforms were pervasive, and 'although all British citizens were technically bound by the same coupon restrictions, in no way was a uniformity of dress imposed across classes. Despite propaganda and subsequent nostalgic claims that social distinctions were suspended in the name of the war effort; dress remained very much a signifier of status, in both service and civilian contexts'.[4] As an advertisement for Austin Reed of London put it in 1943, 'Every woman knows – There's a world of difference between being in uniform, and wearing a uniform that fits you like your smartest tweeds'.[5] Needless to say, prior to the war not every woman had enjoyed the luxury of well-fitting, good-quality tweeds.

Following the war, the 'New Look' marked the promotion of an excessive hyper-femininity that had characterized dressing-up from the late 1930s and well into the 1950s, especially once popularized in TV and films such as *Gone with the Wind* (1939). In parallel, masculine identities were being re-drawn and there was a glamorized identification with everyday lives on the street particularly in terms of class and race. In London, this was particularly evoked by the wartime 'spiv' and the post-war Teddy Boy, while in New York's Harlem, it was the black, 'zoot' suit wearers who summed this up. Characterized by exaggerated and elaborate forms of dress and codes of appearance, these filtered into daily wear and challenged accepted formal models of masculine dress derived from business and social position in addition to the all-pervasive military uniform. On the street, through popular rituals, displays and ceremonies, a hyper-performativity pervaded aspects of the 'everyday' as lives were on the brink, especially during war-time, but also after the war as an accelerated desire for marriage and family took hold. These were underpinned by social policies that included better housing provision in both countries, and in the United States, the 1944 GI Bill that offered low-cost mortgages. VE Day and Coronation parties in May 1945 and June 1953 (in Britain) respectively, weekly dances and church outings, long-anticipated weddings and honeymoons, in addition to the annual Easter Parades (the latter particularly so in the United States), were an assertion of normality in uncertain times. This 'dressing up' was in part a response to the ubiquitousness of wartime uniforms and clothing restrictions, although these were frequently 'dressed-up' as beauty and femininity, especially fashionable hats, make-up and hair were deemed essential to female morale and the war effort.[6]

Everydayness, uniformity and design

In a post-war context where paradoxically both the political left and right feared mass culture and uniformity, influential figures in Britain worried about the impact of utility clothing. Writing in the British *Times* in 1947, the Archbishop of Canterbury, Dr Fisher, argued: 'if utility clothing went on for a century it would create a kind of utility in every mind' and, in his mind, these 'tend[ed] to produce a kind of uniformity of habit and attitude of life, and this created a need for those who were in a real sense able to resist the dominant forces of mass habits and opinions'.[7] Such comments are especially revealing in the complex political context following 1945, as both the collectivist, centralization of the Soviet Union and the uniformity and mass consciousness of fascist Germany had to be carefully negotiated in both America and Britain. For example, the right-leaning British *Daily Mail*, discussing the 'Welfarist' policies of the new Labour Government just after its election in 1945, declared that 'Socialism came to Britain in giant strides yesterday'.[8] As Britain's Labour Government introduced state planning on an unprecedented scale with new legislation for national insurance, the national health service and the nationalization of major industries, including coal, steel and transport, it was even more important to try to move towards less regulation in everyday dress. Rationing of clothes was introduced in June 1941 in Britain, but uniforms were already highly visible from the outset of war. To the writer Harry Hopkins, the epitome of the modern armed forces and consequent style was the Royal Air Force (RAF), which set the tone of the Second World War, especially as it was not homogeneous in its social constitution. Importantly, it didn't originate 'in the elementary schools or the playing fields of Eton, but in the grammar schools and technical colleges'.[9] This introduced a casual classlessness, as the young flyers took on responsibilities ahead of their years developing a persona for airborne daring and social irresponsibility. The RAF uniform summed up this modern armed force: 'the most beguiling emblem of the flyer's allure was their ashy-blue uniform with the Flying Badge worn above the right upper jacket pocket. The blue uniforms of the RAF were a dramatic contrast with the drab brown uniform of the army'.[10] After the Battle of Britain in the summer of 1941, the RAF flyer acquired an enviable reputation for bravery and glamour, especially as depicted in films such as *Dangerous Moonlight* (1941) and *The First of a Few* (1942). Uniforms were everywhere on the streets, and not just British ones, as an increasing number of US troops were to be found in Britain after 1942. The American GIs epitomized the allure of a culture that, to a British population, influenced by a weekly diet of Hollywood films, was both familiar and unfamiliar. It was also glamorous and abundant; the latter marked by the gifts of nylons, chocolate and chewing gum offered to a population whose morale and material resources had been eroded and depleted especially after 1941. By June 1944, a fifth of the British population was either in the armed forces or in industry supporting the war effort, and nearly half of women of working age were employed in women's services, civil defence or in war industry.[11] It is a truism that uniformity of appearance pervaded Britain during this period, and it was the case that being in uniform, wearing factory overalls and practical clothes was common particularly in the centres of population as people went to and from work or took shelter during bombing.[12] London, as Britain's capital, was a hub of troop movements as well as a target for sustained bombing that put pressure on finite resources. The introduction of rationing via the Utility schemes stemmed in part from this with the press as willing instruments in presenting the government's case for rationing. With a headline 'Double-breasted Coats Forbidden', the British *Times* newspaper announced a further reduction in the clothing ration by the President of the Board of Trade, Hugh Dalton:

> An Order would be made this week to prohibit the manufacture of double-breasted coats, turned-up trousers; limiting the number of buttons and doing away with a number of wasteful forms of garment construction. Those who had a reasonable amount of clothing would best serve the war effort if they did not buy anything more until we had won the war. For those who had to buy more clothes he recommended utility clothing.[13]

Eager to dispel the idea that utility represented 'standard' clothing, *The Times* writer claimed, 'It was not standard clothing: it comprised tasteful and attractive garments which he was sure would be popular'.[14] An earlier article in *The Times* in March 1942 made the case – a little unconvincingly – that utility clothing was not only about practicality but also adornment and comfort.[15] There was a particularly spirited discussion of the impracticalities of men's clothing and the improvements offered by utility clothing: 'many a sleeve has buttons but neither slit nor button-holes to justify them … Turned-up trousers are another affectation, or survival … The turn-up survived the muddy roads into the age of asphalt, and becoming a fiction, was not even an honest turn-up, but a mere tailored pretence. Let it go by all means'.[16] Indeed, reporting in *The Times* typically repeated the British Board of Trade's position, as it reiterated that control was merely common sense to reign in absurd and anachronistic aspects of fashion, but it still smacked of the imposition of someone else's taste. Without irony, Sir Thomas Barlow, Director-General of Civilian Clothing, pointed out that 'There were far too many shades of colour now in use'.[17]

Dressing up remained an important part of everyday lives not least for morale purposes, and it took on different meanings for different groups of people:

Becoming a Land Girl, for instance, gave many women from poor backgrounds a wardrobe – that is a *range* of different kinds of dress – for the first time. Standard 'issue' was generous: a hat, three shirts, one pullover, two pairs of breeches, two pairs of dungarees, two overall coats, six pairs of stockings, two pairs of slipper socks, one pair each of leather shoes and boots, leggings, gumboots, an oilskin or mackintosh and an overcoat.[18]

Advertisements in women's magazines and in the national press offer a rich source of evidence of how 'looking good' was still very much at the fore, in part to guard against women becoming overly masculine. An advertisement for the cosmetic company Yardley in *Good Housekeeping* insisted that 'War gives us a chance to show our mettle. We wanted equal rights with men; they took us at our word. We are proud to work for victory beside them … We must achieve masculine efficiency without hardness … Never must we consider careful grooming a quisling gesture'.[19] Looking at a photograph taken on the streets of London depicting people going about their lives, it is obvious that while uniforms were prominent, fashionable clothes were also to be seen (Figure 4.1). Titled 'Piccadilly Circus, Work and Play', the postcard dated 1944 shows a range of people traversing one of London's main public spaces: three or four men in uniform, two of them accompanied by fashionably dressed women (respectively they are wearing a dress with drop-waist pleats, and a suit with pleated skirt and jacket); a workman wearing a flat cap, jacket, but no tie; a number of women alone – three wearing what appear to be smart Utility suits that are narrowly cut with wide shoulders; another older woman wearing a coat that most likely dates from the 1930s; and an older man smoking a pipe and wearing a classic tweed jacket. Behind them is a poster with the slogan 'less shopping, more shipping'.

PICCADILLY CIRCUS, WORK AND PLAY

Figure 4.1 'Piccadilly Circus, Work and Play', 1944. Westminster City Archives.

Apparently un-posed, a depiction of everyday life, this offers a glimpse of war-time London and of fashions that might be seen and worn in the mid-1940s. Not of the 'moment' or the 'latest' looks, though evidently still connected to 'fashion' through the careful styling of the hair, the wearing of jewellery and hats (but few gloves), and the overall silhouette of the suits and dresses some of which nod to the 1930s, while others point to uniforms.

The situation in the United States was somewhat different, reflecting the country's dissimilar status in the war, which it did not enter until December 1941 after the Japanese bombing of the US Naval Base at Pearl Harbour. In the United States, the War Production Board (WPB) oversaw the rationing of clothing, giving the main responsibility to the industry, rather than to civilians. In April 1942, it issued regulation L-85, which restricted every item of women's clothing, and the overall fashion silhouette, but not specific details of style.[20] For the wearer the sanctions were much less intrusive than in Britain. While there were limits on the use of natural fibres, full skirts could have a 72-inch maximum hem circumference, and knife pleats and patch pockets were banned; this was minimal compared to Britain. On both sides of the Atlantic the wearer was encouraged to conserve, re-use and Make [do] and Mend. An article in the February 1945 issue of *Mademoiselle: The Magazine for Smart Young Women* pictures 'Joan [as she] makes over an old dress' to salvage winter clothes of good fabric to conserve wool (Figure 4.2). While encouraging conservation, the photograph also features for purchase garments made of mixed fibres, notably a 'wool jersey shirt tucked

JAMES ABBÉ, JR.

SCOOPS OF THE MONTH [*continued*]

Joan makes over an old dress. Now that conserving wool is so vital, she's salvaging all her winter clothes that are essentially good fabric. Her wool jersey shirt tucked into a wool-with-rayon skirt, kick-pleated fore and aft, by Joan Miller, in junior sizes, $14.95. Oppenheim Collins, New York; D. H. Holmes, New Orleans

Figure 4.2 *Mademoiselle: The Magazine for Smart Young Women*, February 1945, p. 172. Author's Collection.

into a wool-with-rayon skirt, kick-pleated fore and aft, by Joan Miller', priced at $14.95. Another article, featuring 'Mlle's Fashion Firsts' that had appeared on its pages since the magazine began in 1935, shows a 'wartime version of the blazer' from 1944. Cut shorter to conform to L85 regulations, it proved a best seller. In the same year, *Mademoiselle* also promoted a 'ballet-length dance skirt' that received the 'half-amused reception' afforded to the nightshirt featured in the same article.[21] The fact that the dimensions of the skirt appeared so contrary to wartime restrictions clearly demarcates the differences for wearers in the United States and Britain. It also brings to mind the full, circular felt 'poodle' skirts fashionable with teens in the United States in the 1950s, but originating in the 1940s, possibly utilizing felt intended for billiard tables, which was not subject to fabric control.[22] These fuller skirts also foreshadow the styles popular after restrictions ended, which as the magazine predicts, will soon be a 'fought-for-fashion'.[23] While Dior's New Look is typically credited with creating a fashion revolution after its introduction in 1947, the earlier ballet-length skirt indicates how American fashion styles were not simply 'trickling down' from Paris couture. Such garments also reinforce how sportswear had come to distinguish American fashion, and the New York-based, fashion industry.

From a business perspective, the war had a positive impact on American fashion design and on New York. It enabled designers finally to become independent from the influence of Europe (and Paris in particular) and to create appropriate and desirable garments for the working women who were involved in the civilian war effort.[24] Just before the United States entered the war in 1941, New York City Mayor Fiorella H. LaGuardia had acknowledged the substantial financial contribution made to the city's economy by the fashion industry. He also recognized the possible challenges posed by Hollywood and, especially, the influence of movie costumes on the ordinary consumer. The Mayor participated in fashion promotions and was even photographed attending fashion shows.[25] In August 1943, he announced a plan to establish a post-war building project called 'The World Fashion Center' (reported in *The New York Times* as the 'Style Center').[26] While LaGuardia's plan was never realized, it is evidence of the attention being given to fashion in wartime New York. Even *The New York Times* chose to expand its coverage of fashion during the war, despite the severe paper shortages that were beleaguering newspapers.[27] As Rebecca Arnold has noted, fashion was simultaneously and somewhat contradictorily used to encourage women to take an active party in the war effort, while emphasizing their 'natural' affinity to dress and appearance.[28] New York and American fashion as a whole became known for the design of sportswear. Originally created to allow the freedom of movement needed for active sports, it combined separate garments that also proved a practical combination for urban life. Sportswear had the practical advantage of enabling women to adapt and re-combine items for wear at home or at work. So fashion, as Arnold notes, could boost women's morale through identity construction, and through pleasure, just as it had done during the Depression.[29] Fashion also increasingly provided the same role for men.

Performing the street

Style and fashionability were not quashed during the war; in fact the contrary is true in the United States. A closer look at New York also reveals that it was not only the fashion industry that provided direction on what to wear. The development of the zoot suit in urban New York in the 1940s and the adaptation of this in relation to the drape suit in both the United States and Britain spoke to the strong desire to articulate new and varied masculine identities that resonated and reverberated in relation to class, race and generation. In different ways, both represent the embeddedness of fashion in everyday lives. The zoot suit provides an important case study of an everyday sartorial aesthetic as 'a device for living' and a 'practice of the self' within a racially segregated society.[30] Associated in particular with the eruptions of violence in Los Angeles in June 1943 in the midst of the Second World War, its origins and wear in New York City were much more associated with music and hipster cool. Influential bandleader Cab Calloway, referenced in the previous chapter, performed at Harlem's Cotton Club in the 1930s in attire that fits his own definition of the zoot suit. 'Zoot', according to Calloway's sixteen-page *The New Cab Calloway's Hepsters Dictionary: Language of Jive,* 1944, refers to an exaggerated action or style, such as 'the long killer-diller coat with a drape shape and wide shoulders; pants with reet-pleats,[31] billowing out at the knees, tightly tapered and pegged at the ankles; a porkpie or wide-brimmed hat; pointed or thick-soled shoes; and a long, dangling keychain'. As Peiss notes, the zoot suit 'was a striking urban look of the 1940s – a style created by African Americans that extended conventional menswear to the point of caricature'.[32] In *The Invisible Man,* set in the 1930s, Ralph Ellison describes three young African American men on a New York subway platform, as

> tall and slender, walking stiffly with swinging shoulders in their well-pressed, too-hot-cheap felt set upon the crowns of their heads with a severe formality about their hard conked hair? It was as though I'd never seen their like before: Walking hips in trousers that ballooned upward from cuffs fitting snug about their ankles; their coats long and hip-tight with shoulders far too broad to be those of natural western men.[33]

Like Ellison's characters, seventeen-year-old Malcolm X wore the full zoot attire when he arrived in Harlem in 1942.[34] His sharkskin grey 'Cab Calloway' zoot suit, long, narrow, knob-toed shoes, and pearl grey hat with a four-inch brim, worn on top of his fire-red hair, combined with his style of talking, had the effect of making people nervous and uncomfortable.[35] Having bought his clothes in a Boston department store, Malcolm X immediately took 'three of those twenty-five cent sepia-toned, while-you-wait pictures of myself, posed the way "hipsters" wearing their zoots would "cool it" – hat dangled, knees drawn together, feet wide apart, both index fingers jabbed toward the floor'. The suit was part of a total look, which included body, hair and stance, and one that he considered well worth capturing on film.[36]

African American historians have placed zoot suiters within 'a longstanding tradition of black style and performance, as well as in relation to the resurgent civil rights activism of the war years'.[37] The reading of the zoot suit in the context of sub-cultural style warfare is reinforced by the Mexican Americans in Los Angeles during the war, who were attacked, and their clothes damaged by white sailors and marines stationed in the city. The authors' own reading of the suit in New York corresponds to Peiss's more nuanced interpretation of 'an odd style of clothing created not by social elites and fashion designers but primarily by poor black youths and marginal tailors'.[38] Its adoption and meanings are complex and varied.[39] An example of extraordinary dress worn for everyday; the suit marked out the wearer for attention. It was indicative of how 'in everyday rituals[...] resistance can find natural and unconscious expression'.[40]

The adoption of the suit by African Americans, Mexican Americans, Filipinos, other people of colour and working-class whites was, 'as bound up in the choreography of sexual attraction, the negotiation of gender identity, conflict between generations, and the pursuit of pleasure within a specific music and dance culture as much if not more than it was motivated by a politics of opposition'.[41] Nevertheless, for some young non-white urban youths, wearing the suit to hang around on city streets not only demonstrated their indifference to clothing regulations, but to the country's patriotic expectation that they would fight for America and democracy.[42] On 14 February 1942, a cartoon in the *Amsterdam News*, an African American newspaper, shows a figure dressed strikingly similar to Eddie Rochester Andersons' character (mentioned below) hanging out on the street, having deferred his patriotic duty.[43] Likewise this photo was taken in Washington, D.C. in 1942 of a soldier inspecting a couple of 'zoot suits' at the Uline Arena during Woody Herman's Orchestra engagement there (Figure 4.3). The zoot suit's movement from Harlem and other urban centres to towns and cities across the nation was aided by a small section of the garment trade who specialized in the style, and by its media representation in movies, music and the press.[44] When, for example, Eddie Rochester Andersons' character wore a checked zoot suit to sing 'Sharp as a Tack' in the musical film *Star Spangled Rhythm,* a wartime morale booster released by Paramount Pictures in 1942, the number ends with his zoot being shed for an army uniform, more appropriate to the times and the pulse of the nation. The same year, in April, the wartime cloth conservation order made the zoot suit illegal.[45] On 24 September 1942, *Life* magazine reported how the War Production Board restrictions had infuriated young jive dancers, but predicted quite accurately that 'Despite the wails and whinnies of long-haired hepcats, the classy-cut but scandalously wasteful zoot suit is doomed'.[46] By 1943, the suit was considered distinctly unpatriotic, but its

Figure 4.3 Washington, D.C. soldier inspecting a couple of 'zoot suits', 1942.
Library of Congress.

style and meanings continued to change subtly, depending on context, wearer and place, as is true of all fashionable clothing.[47] While the zoot suit emerged as part of an African American tradition in the early 1940s in the United States, for a generation of young men it became a form of identification that cut across racial lines, to be worn by African Americans, Mexicans and 'second generation foreign-born whites'.[48] Referring in particular to the flamboyant dress of urban black men, or the Bowery Boys of mid-nineteenth-century New York, Peiss observes that 'For some men, then, fashion had long punctuated ordinary life with extraordinary looks'.[49] In the wider world, the zoot suit was firmly identified with American style by this period, and with popular music and performance. It inspired 'swing youth' in 1940s Europe, such as the *zazous* in France who wore elements of the style in defiance of the German Occupation,[50] as well as helping to give shape to the sharp sartorial styles adopted by several different social groups in late 1940s and 1950s Britain: white spivs, new black immigrants and white British Teddy Boys.[51]

By the late 1940s, the American men's fashion trade had adopted a modified version of the zoot suit described as the 'drape' suit that was distinguished as the 'bold look'.[52] This came from 'making everything bigger and brighter and bolder and louder than anyone has ever before attempted'.[53] Hollywood had made impeccable drape-style suits integral to the screen personas of matinee idols such as Cary Grant or Clark Gable in the 1930s. By 1949, the drape style, widely known as the 'American Cut', was closely associated with a national masculine ideal, which would continue through the 1950s in the United States and beyond, with the assistance of the media. The style emphasized male athleticism and virility, with the flow of the fabric on the body being described as easing men's stance and relaxing 'the way they inhabited their clothes, and swung with the body'.[54] By the early 1950s, the Ivy look, originating in the elite colleges on the East coast, had also made an impact on menswear nation-wide. Natural-shouldered suits became a new male uniform, with an article in *Life* commenting that 'The popularity of the natural-looking suit has widened quickly in the past two years as men became dissatisfied with pale bulky suits and flashy ties left over from their postwar splurge. To reaffirm their individualism, beleaguered Ivy Leaguers are considering adding a fourth button to their jackets or resorting to a radial new silhouette of "moderate Edwardian".'[55] Classic items, such as tweed jackets and polo coats, were appropriated from English male wardrobe and redesigned by pioneering American firms such as Brooks Brothers and J. Press, originally for male undergraduates at Ivy League colleges. After the war, however, until the late 1960s, the staples of the Ivy Style, Oxford cloth shirts, khaki pants and penny loafers were the everyday wear of a diverse group of men ranging from working-class GIs to jazz musicians. In this context, it is perhaps notable that Figure 4.4, a photograph of a man on a street in New York City, is dated c. 1940–1960, indicating how men's attire stayed fairly stable during the two decades. The man is smartly dressed in a tweed jacket, worn with high top trousers with a front crease and turn-ups, or cuffs. His pocket-handkerchief is patterned, as is his necktie, which is worn with a tiepin. His shoes are well shone and may be Oxfords (or brogues), which echo the shine of his hair. The precision of his hairstyle and the existence of a barber's sign behind him might also suggest that he has just visited that establishment. His attention to his appearance is not uncharacteristic of the everyday wear of men in the 1950s in New York and London.

With the zoot suit 'domesticated' in the United States, it was 'on the other side of the Atlantic [that] it retained its wild spirit and its capacity to shock'.[56] Whereas in the United States, the zoot suit's dominant meaning had been racial prior to its popularization as the 'drape suit', in Britain it was initially adopted by roguish working-class men, 'spivs', who sold black market goods in Britain's urban centres as rationing persisted. This meaning was subsequently overlaid with different ones with the arrival of the stylishly dressed new Caribbean immigrants from 1948 and the growing presence of white working-class teenagers particularly on the streets of London from the early 1950s. In discussing recent black history in Britain, Paul Gilroy proposed that 'Black expressive cultures affirm while they protest. The assimilation of blacks is not a process of acculturation but of cultural syncretism'.[57] The import of the zoot suit/drape suit into Britain is a

Figure 4.4 Man walking on a New York sidewalk, c. 1940–1960. Museum of the City of New York.

case in point. African American and Caribbean cultures that included fashionable clothes and style impacted on British streets during and after the Second World War particularly with American black GIs stationed in Britain and also black soldiers from Britain's colonies of which there were over 6,000 serving.[58] Adding to this, just after the war a growing number of people from the British colonies of Jamaica, Trinidad, Barbados, Guyana and Tobago came to Britain in response to the increased demands for labour to help in the rebuilding of Britain. This immigration from the West Indies was encouraged by the British Nationality Act of 1948, which gave all Commonwealth citizens free entry into Britain with 'the symbolic starting point of this mass migration to the "mother country" being the journey of the SS *Empire Windrush* from Kingston, Jamaica, to Tilbury, Essex, in June 1948. On board were almost 500 West Indians intent on starting new lives in Britain'. [59] Added to this was the wartime British experience of black American culture popularized in particular in Hollywood musicals such as *Stormy Weather* (1943) that starred Lena Horne, Bill Robinson and Cab Calloway and his Cotton Club Band. It is in such a context that the adaptation of the zoot suit into the 'drape' suit in Britain offers a revealing insight into the complexities of identities: class, race, generation and gender. To the 'wide-boy' spiv, on the criminal fringes 'wheeling and dealing from one fiddle to another', the exaggerated over-size drape suit with large jacket and wide trousers were an essential part of a persona that signalled an abundant colourful future rather than a rationed, grey past.[60]

It was East End Jewish tailor Cecil Gee at his Charing Cross Road shop who commercialized the look and brought the drape suit into the mainstream. Directly importing the accessories and making his own copies of the double-breasted drape, Gee sent his customers 'wild'.[61] As he put it: 'I was selling Manhattan shirts, Arrow shirts, Adam hats, Stetson hats, the glove shoe. Colourful satin shirts and wide satin painted ties'.[62] The suit spoke to a self-confidence and assertiveness that cut through class lines, although in Britain its racial, anti-authority and criminal connotations were never entirely effaced. During the 1950s, it became increasingly linked to sensationalized images of both petty and violent young criminals whose suits were redolent of a much harder American gang culture that was popularized in the cinema and which made them look much older and tougher than they were. Some elements of it were later taken up, modified and synthesized with upper-class styles by white working-class Teddy Boys, while other features were adapted and developed by incoming Caribbean immigrants.

As *The Tailor and Cutter* put it in 1948, the drape suit became synonymous with what the 'well-dressed Jamaican man-about-town is wearing these days'.[63] The double-breasted, wide-shouldered suit with boldly coloured tie lent an air of confidence to the wearer in this photograph (Figure 4.5). Arriving from Jamaica in 1954, Barrington Anthony Sherridan Young had this suit made by a 'Jamaican fella' on Denmark St, Moss-Side, Manchester, in 1955.[64] Visiting a friend in Tottenham, London, in 1955, he was 'snapped' by a street photographer as he walked around London while his friend was working. Describing how he felt wearing his suit, with its 'balloon peg' trousers worn with 'Jamaican style' perfumed handkerchief (one hanging out of his trouser pocket and one tucked into the top pocket of his jacket), he said that he 'looked sharp because in them days, the suit was Jamaican style and they didn't have that in England. So you stood out anywhere you went, you stood out because your clothing was different. Your

Figure 4.5 Barrington Young, London, 1955. Michaela Elli Young.

style was different'.[65] Interviewed by his daughter in December 2015, Barrington Young laughed as he explained his sense of style and, although he does not say it, it was obviously important to have with him something of 'Jamaica'.

The end of war in Europe marked by VE on 8 May 1945 brought party and performance onto the streets of both London and New York. In addition to street parties and spontaneous celebrations, there were a number of carefully choreographed events to mark the end of war. One such event was the dramatic lighting of London on 8 May 1945 to celebrate Victory in Europe. *The Illustrated London News* of 19 May 1945 contrasted the brilliance of the bold lighting with blackout Britain:

> As at the outbreak of war one of the most poignant phrases was 'The lights are going out all over Europe', so it was most fitting that the lights of London should blaze out to celebrate Victory in Europe: and Victory Night was celebrated with lights of every form, colour and source. That peculiarly modern art of peace floodlighting was used to illuminate and to illustrate all the main buildings of the metropolis. Some of the chief landmarks of London, glowing in the un-accustomed light [included]. Admiralty Arch, the Royal Exchange, Nelson's Column and the Houses of Parliament.[66]

Similar street events typified 'end of war' celebrations in the United States too. The New York City Victory Parade on 12 January 1946 was led by the 82nd Airborne Division and it included the African American 555th Parachute Infantry Battalion. Beginning in Washington Square and marching up Fifth Avenue, it was reportedly four miles long. These were spectacular and one-off events, which were captured on film creating what have become iconic images. One such photograph is of a sailor kissing a nurse in Times Square to celebrate the surrender of Japan on 14 August 1945. The formality of their uniforms is contrasted with the informality of the action – apparently a common form of celebration among strangers – at the time. With the resumption of regular street events, celebrations and parades, it was also a sign that normal life was being re-established. It is worthwhile to compare a more normalized view (Figure 4.6) of young women photographed probably on 14th Street near Union Square, possibly during their lunch break from work. They are dressed neatly, in either separates or dresses with slightly flared or pleated skirts, worn with low-heeled shoes, which include saddle style, and sandals, on what seems to be a warm summer day.

In its Spring Fashions issue of 15 April 1946, *Life* magazine reported that Americans would spend an estimated $2 billion that year on Sunday clothes, over double of what was spent in 1939, with most favoured items for women being new suits, coats and hats. Despite discarding many old customs before and during the war, American people still dressed up for their weekly visit to

Figure 4.6 Women near Union Square, Manhattan, photograph by Barbara Morgan, 1946. Library Special Collections, Young Research Library, UCLA.

church, with the high point of the year being Easter Sunday, 'when America puts on the world's greatest fashion show'.[67] A photograph of Al Smith, former Democratic governor of New York, and his wife leaving St Patrick's Cathedral on Easter Sunday, we assume in the early 1940s (Figure 4.7), demonstrates how people from all walks of life dressed up for the occasion. Mrs Smith wears a toning coat and dress, with a hat, long gloves, a patent leather handbag and matching shoes. The governor is formally dressed in a long jacket and a top hat, befitting

Figure 4.7 Al Smith with his wife leaving St. Patrick's Cathedral on Easter Sunday. Museum of the City of New York.

a man of more mature years (he died aged 70 in 1944, following the death of his wife earlier that year). While Sunday not being *every* day, the attention given to this weekly sartorial display, and at Easter in particular in New York in the 1940s, reinforces the importance of dressing up in the performance of the lives of ordinary people. For many, the high point of display was on Easter Sunday on Fifth Avenue. For the African American residents of Harlem, however, the Sunday stroll was already established as a regular weekly opportunity for showing off.

Novelist Rudolph Fisher observed, 'Indeed, even Fifth Avenue on Easter never quite attains this; practice makes perfect, and Harlem's Seventh Avenue boasts fifty-two Easters a year'.[68] Norma Mair, who emigrated from Jamaica to Harlem in 1922, commented how 'Everybody was dressed to the teeth. You would wear the finest you had, like chiffon dresses, white hats, new shoes, and everything matched, from your pocketbook on down'. Easter Sunday was the quintessential occasion for parading and display. On that day she saw a male friend from Africa 'wear cutaway, striped pants, top hat, white spats, and cane' as he strolled on Fifth Avenue.[69] Every northern American city had its equivalent of the Stroll, with Harlem being seen as the height of the realization of the imaginary. Born originally of poverty, the Stroll provided the opportunity to go out and socialize, with it being described, romantically, as 'not simply going out for a walk; it was more like going out for an adventure'.[70] Even those holding modest labouring jobs took the opportunity to dress up on Sunday, and in more fashionable and 'exaggerated styles and bright hues' than their white counterparts, according to articles in *The New York Times* in the late 1920s and early 1930s.[71] How African Americans should present themselves in public was nevertheless a problem, and especially for working-class people who, unlike their middle- and upper-class counterparts, did not readily adopt white manners and ways. While the majority of African Americans in the urban north were employed in menial and low-paid jobs as labourers, factory workers, domestic servants and the like, on Sundays and in their leisure hours they 'regained control of their bodies and of their souls' and dressed up like 'fashion plates'.[72] They gathered in 'convivial black spaces' in the first half of the twentieth century, as liberating rather than oppositional locations.[73] The Easter Parade in Harlem remained at the pinnacle of this sartorial display. Arriving there on Easter Sunday, probably in the early 1930s, black writer Elton Fax commented on 'people in the parade who were quite seriously elegant, in top hat, tails, cutaway coat, spats, cane – anything that mimicked white upper-class living, mimicry of that which was opulent, that which was approved, that which white folks aspired to be'.[74]

In the city as a whole, dressing up for Easter Sunday was an established practice by the late 1860s, and the secular Easter Parade on Fifth Avenue in Midtown Manhattan following Easter Sunday morning worship was being commented on at the end of the following decade.[75] In 1879, special 'Easter

Outfits' were being advertised by the department store Rogers, Peet & Co. The parade drew regular press attention in the early years of the twentieth century, and even elicited criticism in *The New York Times* in 1930 from a clergyman protesting that the religious occasion had become a fashion parade.[76] After the Second World War, the increased interest in the Easter Parade as a public secular celebration, an occasion for showing off new clothes often purchased specially for the day,[77] symbolized the city and the nation's new sense of optimism and prosperity. Fifth Avenue's parade was immortalized in the popular imagination in 1948, with the release of the movie musical, *Easter Parade,* starring Fred Astaire and Judy Garland, featuring the Irving Berlin title song. In its Spring Fashions issue that year, *Life* magazine featured 'New hats, frilly and frothy as ever … matched by frilly costumes'.[78] While the hat would disappear from the day-to-day wardrobes of most women, it continued its appearance at the Easter Parade. As an article in the *Saturday Evening Post* commented in 1955, New York's springtime pageant had become 'a reflection of the American Dream – that a person is as good as the clothes, car and home he is able to buy'.[79] The Easter Parade was also about women's visibility on the street. Parading in new and often extravagant millinery after the war was a symbolic act, no longer a response to a need to cover the head for modesty. 'The new world of Easter millinery was, in part, about the assertion of the self; about a world of mirrors and studies appearances … about self-transformation through bewitching lines, fabrics and colours; about fashioning of the self in a parade of protean styles'.[80]

Taken in 1944 by the U.S. Office of War Information, Figure 4.8 shows how fashion literally crossed the streets of New York when garment racks of fashionable clothing were wheeled between premises. As the fashion business grew in New York, an American 'look' developed, especially when Paris, the former arbiter of fashion, was no longer a viable point of reference during the Occupation.[81] Art schools such as Parsons School of Design, The Fashion Institute of Technology and Pratt Institute in New York as well as St Martin's School of Art, London College of Fashion and the Royal College of Art in London became important centres for training and innovation.[82] A studio at Parsons shows students well dressed in more mature styles, similar to that worn by the professional critic, wearing the hat, who may have been New York fashion designer Mildred Orrick (Figure 4.9). As graduating students from the art schools and colleges moved into the metropolitan fashion network in both cities, they bought for department stores, wrote and illustrated fashion for magazines, and designed for a range of companies. In particular, America's rapid economic recovery after the war, increased consumption and new and younger consumers stimulated New York's fashion production, retail, business and media.

While the lives of influential women in fashion have been researched,[83] there were many more anonymous women, and men, who contributed to the development of the fashion industry in London and New York at this time.[84]

Figure 4.8 New York Garment district, pushing racks through the streets, 1944.
Museum of the City of New York.

Professional fashion was very much part of its economy and image after the war, as off-the-peg American sportswear became the everyday wear of increasing numbers of young people in the United States and internationally. We can see this from an undated picture of two young women sitting on the steps of the fountain in Washington Square Park in lower Manhattan, dated c1956 (Figure 4.10). Their appearance is casual, as are their hairstyles, one with an Alice band and the other a ponytail, typically worn by teens at the time. Their coats and skirts are cut

Figure 4.9 Parsons School of Design, 410 E 54th Street, New York, Class Discussion of Student Designs, mid-1950s. Kellen Archive Parsons School of Design Alumni Association records.

straight and seem to have hemlines below the knee and are worn with flat-soled shoes. They might have been students, due to the location of the park close to New York University, or workers. While their appearance is not sophisticated, it is indicative of how different fashion groups, with their own 'looks' were coexisting in New York, and in London.

Young people were a target consumer group, and many young women aspired to work in the fashion business, to which they could also bring their own valuable insight into popular taste and lifestyle. *Mademoiselle* magazine, for instance, established in 1935 to target young college and career girls,[85] began producing an annual college issue in 1939, guest edited by summer interns.[86] Their life, work, attitudes and, moreover, their fashionable dress in the hot New York summer of 1953 provided the raw material for Sylvia Plath's *The Bell Jar.*

Figure 4.10 Two girls in coats sitting on fountain steps, Washington Square Park, c. 1956. Museum of the City of New York.

Based on her own intern experience, Plath provides careful details of clothes, demonstrating how professional young women (and young men) in New York were expected to dress formally at a time when leisure wear was becoming much more casual. Neva Nelson, who interned with Plath, describes walking to work on the 'hot steamy streets of New York' in June 1953, wearing 'a black sleeveless one-piece cotton sheath dress with a white collar with large black polka dots and a matching collarless short jacket, worn with a white eyelet hat with black velvet trim and short white gloves, sheer stockings and black patent leather shoes'.[87] But Nelson also chastised the magazine for being out of touch with the burgeoning California style of jeans, worn with penny loafers and no socks and the newest fad – tie-dyed T-shirts.[88] As the internship ends and Sylvia herself prepares to leave the city, she describes how, 'Piece by piece, I fed my wardrobe to the night wind, and flutteringly, like a loved one's ashes, the gray scraps were ferried off, to settle here, there, exactly where I would never know, in the dark heart of New York'.[89] Sylvia's clothes float off into the night, taking her New York identity with them, heavy with symbolism, and pre-empting the next and final chapter of her life. Most of the well-off young women who had interned with her would ultimately devote themselves to husbands and children, not career, despite their college educations, and they would likely go to live in the suburbs, where fashion would still play a part in their everyday lives, although the occasions and venues for dressing up were of a different nature than for city-dwellers.

Fashion and Suburbia

The return of enlisted men after the war and the opportunities provided with the passing of the GI Bill in 1944 had an enormous effect on their lives and those of the adult female population. The benefits provided by the government for war veterans (even those who had not seen active service) included low-cost mortgages, low-interest loans to start businesses, cash payments of tuition and living expenses to attend high education and unemployment compensation. The Bill was enormously effective and by the end of the decade the country's middle class flourished. Between 1947 and 1953, the number of middle-class families[90] increased from 12.5 million to 18 million, and salaried workers increased by 61 per cent, between 1947 and 1957 as business corporations expanded.[91] But the combination of the likes of GI loans and new planned infrastructure, including federally subsidized highway construction, led to middle-class 'white flight' from New York and other major cities to the newly developed and racially homogeneous suburbs. In the process, new market niches were created, facilitated by the lavish new suburban shopping malls. US clothing designers, who had previously focused on city dwellers, recognized that the 30 million Americans living in the suburbs by the early 1950s (43 per cent of them having arrived since 1947) with incomes 70 per cent higher than the US average presented a lucrative consumer market. City and suburban fashions began to overlap, with the latter having an impact on more casual dressing, leading to city cab riders in Manhattan being observed as dressing 'as casually as if they owned open sports cars'.[92]

In Long Island, the planned community of Levittown, built between 1947 and 1951, became the first mass-produced suburb, and the model for other suburban developments around the country. Created to provide for a specific need, at a time when there was a high demand for affordable housing after the war, the suburbs came to symbolize the American Dream, in allowing thousands of families to become home owners. Photographs from the period show the picture perfect nuclear family outside of their house, often with their automobile, always neatly dressed and racially white. Using new, widely available small cameras like the Kodak Brownie, some residents recorded their everyday lives. A snapshot from the family album of Charles Teluka jnr, born in 1951, was taken around 1959 of his aunt who worked as a photo girl at the famous, Latin-themed, Copacabana nightclub, which opened in midtown Manhattan in 1940, and featured major performers such as Frank Sinatra and Desi Arnaz. She was fashionably, but casually dressed in slacks and leans against a split windshield car. The photo caption refers to her as occupying 'the multiple universes of high celebrity and everyday suburban life'. Yet, as was also commented, perhaps for her at the time 'it was Levittown that seemed exotic, and the Copa was everyday'.[93] Following the war, at the height of the Cold War period, a white, suburban lifestyle epitomized the middle-class American family. Suburban life was about looking at and looking on, through the windshields of automobiles, the windows of stores in the mall, and on the screens of the televisions that were rapidly infiltrating homes. Television informed the American way of life, and also promoted the American Dream overseas.

The syndication of popular TV shows brought America to the living rooms of those British households that had the means to purchase televisions in the 1950s. The sitcom *I Love Lucy,* for example, starring Lucille Ball and her real-life husband Desi Arnaz, broadcast originally on CBS from 1951 to 1957, features a couple and their friends living on the east side of Midtown Manhattan. In the show, Arnaz played a Cuban-American bandleader, while Ball, true to the times, was a homemaker and as the show progressed became a mother. Also, predictably in the late 1950s, the show had the couple and their young family moving to the suburbs of Westport, Connecticut. Lucy always has an eye to her appearance, dressing typically in full-skirted, button down shirtwaist dresses, her hair neatly pinned up, with minimal jewellery, and full make up. Even when she is casual in trousers or in overalls for the sometimes messy clowning which her comedic role entailed, Ball's housewifely appearance was always put together. Like many women in America and in Britain, when she was seen wearing a sparkling clean apron, it was not so much for function, but as a sign of her status as housewife.[94] For actual housewives wanting to emulate Lucy's style and fashions, and those of other TV favourites, there continued be a substantial range of options for the home dressmaker and for those handy with knitting needles or a crochet hook. An issue of *Modern Needlecraft* from fall 1952 advocates separates as being both fashionable and economical choices for fall, and provides instructions for the knitted Chartreuse blouse and Dove

Grey skirt featured on the cover (Figure 4.11) The full skirt with the waist so tiny that it appears the image may have been altered is a reflection of the influence of the New Look, which was also evident in fashionable styles in Britain.

While the American ideal of suburban, domestic life was promoted in British women's magazines, fiction, film and, from the 1960s on television, the realities of everyday life were somewhat different. House building after 1945 had extended

Figure 4.11 Patterns for knitted separates, *Modern Needlecraft*, USA, Fall 1952. Author's Collection.

outwards from Britain's already established inter-war suburbs to new private housing estates that edged nearer to London's green belt, and to new high-rise estates such as Churchill Gardens in Pimlico (1946) and the Lansbury Estate, Tower Hamlet (1951). With the New Towns Act of 1945 this was extended north, south, east and west to a series of satellite towns outside London's green belt. These included Stevenage (designated 1946), Hemel Hempstead (1947), Crawley (1947), Harlow (1947), Basildon (1949) and Bracknell (1949). Much of this housing was to rent and it was funded by central government as part of the new Labour government's Welfare State that posited good housing as an essential element of a better peacetime Britain. However, with a population of roughly 50 million in 1951, Britain was barely back in business until the second half of the 1950s and, consequently, the paucity of new consumer goods was marked particularly in relation to the United States. Indeed indicative of the economy, and in contrast to the United States, were the number of TV sets in British homes; in 1947, they numbered 15,000 rising to 1.4 million by 1952 and 15.1 million by 1968. Equally, the launch of Dior's New Look in 1947 only exacerbated the difficulties of the British economy and, causing consternation in government circles as clothes rationing still persisted, the new style was well out of reach of most British women. It was only after 1956, and under the aegis of successive Conservative governments led first by Winston Churchill and then by Anthony Eden, that the economy began to expand as British manufacturing began to deliver the long-desired new goods, products and fashionable clothes. While the Incorporated Society of London Fashion Designers (founded in 1942) and, including at various times, Hardy Amies, Norman Hartnell, Digby Morton, Peter Russell, Victor Stiebel, Bianca Mosca, Worth, Edward Molyneux and Charles Creed interpreted the New Look for its wealthy clients, a plethora of companies began to produce versions of the style including, at the lower end, Marks and Spencer, and, in the middle, Ellis & Goldstein.

Ellis & Goldstein, whose labels included Dereta, Elgora and Eastex, was a particularly interesting company in terms of its market and age orientation and its interpretation of the New Look. Dependent on Jewish-family tailoring expertise that had been established in the early years of the twentieth century, Ellis and Goldstein was concentrated in the East End of London. It was a typically small-scale enterprise that was highly flexible, and well placed to respond to the dictates of fashion.[95] A Board of Trade survey of the women's-wear wholesale industry in 1939 found that 50 per cent of women's and girl's tailored outerwear was made in London.[96] As the women's-wear market grew rapidly in the first half of the twentieth century, it was the agile East End companies such as Mansfield and Ellis & Goldstein that responded to the challenges posed by 'fashion'. Most companies employed under fifty staff and rather than depending on new technologies as did the large companies based in the north of England, these London-based firms depended on a highly skilled, flexible workforce which could react quickly to the nuances of fashion change. These encouraged companies to pursue 'individual market niches' and as 'a consequence there was more market co-ordination'.[97] Mansfield and Ellis & Goldstein were typical of this group of manufacturers and in the 1950s, their ranges responded to changing fashion and to new markets. The founder of Mansfield, Frank Russell had learned tailoring skills from his father, the son of a Jewish immigrant from Eastern Europe who then worked as a tailor in the East End. With a background in tailoring that began at the age of fourteen years and that was augmented by pattern cutting lessons, Russell worked as a pattern cutter for a number of companies in the 1920s and 1930s, eventually becoming head of design and patterns for a company named Davis and Frost following military service in the Second World War. In 1950, he seized the opportunity to establish his own company, Mansfield, initially making women's outerwear (coats and suits) under the labels 'Mansfield Couture' and 'Mansfield Originals'. For design ideas,

> instead of going to Paris I could go to New York a few weeks later where they had line for line copies at $105 which was much cheaper than going to Paris to get two rotten paper patterns one month earlier. In one particular week in New York all the major stores showed their line for line copies and they were televised as well ... So I'd go to Macy's one day, then Altmans and Saks the next day and so on and I'd spend a whole week in New York buying the best of the line for line copies which were really much more commercial that the paper patterns.[98]

Russell's experience of looking to New York rather than Paris is indicative of the loosening of Paris' domination of fashion after the war, New York's gaining confidence and the democratization of fashion knowledge via magazines, film and television. At the same time, new ranges developed for new markets, and companies were acquired, re-shaped and consolidated after 1945 in response to economic and social changes. Mansfield's 'Junior Miss' range is indicative of new lines for newly emerging markets while Ellis & Goldstein's acquisition of Laura Lee Frocks Ltd, Dereta (London) and Rembrandt Dresses Ltd., between 1947 and 1957, is representative of the restructuring of sectors of the industry that saw new premises built on London's outer periphery in rapidly expanding towns such as Luton. Ellis & Goldstein had built a new factory in Commercial St in London's East End in 1928, but in 1939, factory space in Luton was bought for the production of uniforms. This factory became one of the most modern in Britain as it adapted to the production of double-knit jersey and a range of new materials including Crimplene and Terylene in the 1950s.

Following de-restriction in 1949, Ellis & Goldstein resumed production introducing new collections of women's coats, suits, dresses and separates with the labels: Elgora, Dereta and Lisscraft Sportswear. Promotional brochures for Elgora's Spring/Summer and Autumn/Winter ranges of 1951 included New Look – inspired coats with long, wide skirts and nipped in waists illustrated in the loose graphic style popular in fashion magazines at the time (Figure 4.12). The nipped waist of the New Look became very popular and it was adapted for all occasions, from wedding dresses to simple cotton dresses to patterned dirndl

Figure 4.12 Elgora range, Spring 1951 promotional brochure, manufactured by Ellis & Goldstein, London. Jacques Vert Group.

skirts, in the mid- to late 1950s through to the 1960s. A photograph from the London Metropolitan archives show this very effectively. In this, a group of young women who were part of the London Secondary Girls School Choir depart for a tour of Sweden in 1955 (Figure 4.13). The five young women setting out on their trip are dressed in a range of styles that illustrate the impact of fashion in everyday lives. Their clothes are remarkably varied, and show how dressing in 1955 drew on fashionable outlines that came from the 1940s as well as the 1950s. More contemporary in appearance was the young woman on the right, who wears a printed dirndl skirt with the popular nipped in waist. The persistence of this particular outline is interesting, and worthy of further discussion. The New Look had attracted a great deal of approbation when it first appeared in 1947; it was attacked in the British press and in the British Houses of Parliament for its wastefulness and frivolity. At the same time to some, particularly women who had been involved in politics and the various campaigns for political equality before the war, the decorativeness seemed to represent a reassertion of traditional feminine values at the wrong time. The style had widespread popular appeal, however, and there were numerous paper pattern versions, which could be adapted and worn as appropriate by women across the social spectrum, as well as knitted versions, already mentioned above. It was this adaptability and wearability that most likely appealed; and women's capacity to dispense with the

Figure 4.13 Young women members of the London Secondary Girls School Choir departing from London for a tour of Sweden, 1955. Alpha Press.

elements of the style that weren't thought suitable shouldn't be under estimated. Thus the peculiar corset that was worn by New Look models was not essential for everyday wear, while the extra material in the gathered waisted skirt could be adapted and reduced as necessary.

This waistline was also apparent in the ranges produced by Ellis & Goldstein, such as Lisscraft Sportswear range. This range from the autumn of 1951 had button-through dresses that owed as much to New York fashions as to Paris. Made in the finest Utility worsted in a range of colours, these were suitable for 'the office or goes equally well to golf'.[99] The Eastex brand, with a distinct marketing approach, was launched in 1952. Apparently based on information from the 1952 census which revealed that the average height of women in Britain was 5'2", it was 'designed exclusively for women of 5 feet 2 inches or less' and as an alternative to having to 'make do' (Figure 4.14).[100] A promotional brochure for Spring and Summer 1954 depicted two smart women wearing sharply tailored fashionable suits that speak to New York glamour mediated by actresses such as Doris Day. In fact, returning to our image of the young women's choir, the dissemination of these fashionable lines is recognizable in the stylish clothes of the young woman on the second left with her cropped jacket and pencil skirt. Ellis & Goldstein catered for this demand for greater choice with their various labels: model dresses by Lisscraft, inexpensive dresses by Laura Lee and coats and suits by Ellis & Goldstein.

It is a truism to point to wartime as disruptive: prompting, if not accelerating, change. Reflecting on fashion in everyday lives in mid-century Britain and America, it was perhaps the feeling of being in transition that was most apparent. The gap between young and older adults seemed to grow, markers of gender appeared to sharpen, but at the same time men and women had been changed by war in ways that were not immediately obvious, informality in fashion and everyday life was more discernible, and the persuasiveness of mass culture especially television but also popular music gathered pace. In both the United States and Britain, major cities such as New York and London were the focus for the spectacular and the ordinary. New York offered a space in which the fashion business and fashionable style were on a bolder footing, less constrained by Europe and attuned to the complexities of modern urban lives. London was a different place, bombed and wrecked, but also providing diverse social and cultural spaces that accommodated, albeit uneasily, new Afro-Caribbean immigrants, young families in new housing estates, and the idea of the 'New Jerusalem' that posited a better world for all rather than just the few. Apparent in this discussion of fashion in the 1940s and 1950s is that, while a level of fashionability was evident as people went about their everyday lives in the 1950s, it was also the case that particular outlines and shapes persisted over time, though these were adapted and re-shaped especially by the young – the New Look outline being a case in point. Alongside this, a growing informality and casualness was discernible that was well served

Figure 4.14 Eastex Range 52, Spring-Summer 1954 promotional brochure, manufactured by Ellis & Goldstein, London. Jacques Vert Group.

by the burgeoning ready-to-wear business that especially in New York excelled in the production of leisure and sport clothes as well as well-tailored classic men's suits. While ready-to-wear companies such as Ellis and Goldstein imaginatively developed its markets (sportswear and the 5'2" woman) and its business from its metropolitan base, London became a site for new styles that came as much from the streets as from the salons providing a foundation for the innovations of the 1960s. As Caroline Evans interpreted 1960s London as quintessentially youthful with retailers, designers and photographers from the same age group as their audience, she also proposed that 'many of the decade's novelties originated in the late fifties, that bridge between forties austerity and sixties affluence'.[101] It is easy to forget that Mary Quant's first shop opened in 1955 as we think of her as a 1960s designer and her iconic clothes as typically 1960s. Similarly, socialite Joan 'Tiger' Morse had opened her pop boutique 'Teeny-Weeny' on New York's Upper East Side at Madison Avenue and 73rd Street in 1958.[102] Indeed, to an extent, the 1950s has been understood in relation to the 1960s, and the latter is presented in terms of one-off boutique items that ignore the plethora of ready-to-wear companies that manufactured fashionable clothes for all aspects of the sector and for a range of markets and ages. Indeed as we will see in Chapter 5, trying to neatly separate the 1950s and 1960s is not especially useful, nor is it helpful to read the 1950s as an episode 'towards the 1960s'. What is apparent is that when we are dealing with the 1960s particular types of myth-making took place about the avant-garde nature of 1960s' fashion that has its origins in the 'media-isation' of that decade; a tactic compounded by a Janus tendency to see the future in the present and to forget continuities with the past.

Notes

1   Pam Cook, *Fashioning the Nation: Costume and Identity in British Cinema* (London: British Film Institute, 1996), 47.

2   Alistair O'Neill, *London: After a Fashion* (London: ReaKtion, 2007), 102.

3   Ibid.; Breward, *Fashioning London.*

4   Peter McNeil, '"Put Your Best Face Forward": The Impact of the Second World War on British Dress', *Journal of Design History* 6, no. 4 (1993), 286.

5   Ibid., 287.

6   Pat Kirkham, 'Fashion, Femininity and Consumption', in *Utility Reassessed: The role of Ethics in the Practice of Design*, ed. Judy Attfield (Manchester: Manchester University Press, 1999), 143–156; McNeil, 'Put Your Best Face Forward', 283–299.

7   'Danger of Uniformity', *The Times*, July 12, 1947, 3.

8   Harry Hopkins, *The New Look: A Social History of the Forties and Fifties* (London: Secker & Warburg, 1964), 53.

9   Ibid., 19.

10 Martin Francis, *The Flyer. British Culture and the Royal Air Force, 1939–1945* (Oxford: Oxford University Press, 2008), p. 23.

11 Asa Briggs, *Go To It: Working for Victory on the Home Front, 1939–1945* (London: Imperial War Museum/Mitchell Beazley, 2000), 18–19.

12 Julie Summers, *Fashion on the Ration: Style in the Second World War* (London: Profile Books in partnership with the Imperial War Museum, 2015); Geraldine Howell, *Wartime Fashion: From Haute Couture to Home-made, 1939–1941* (London and New York: Berg, 2012).

13 'Less Material for Clothes. Big Saving by Cut in Ration. Double-Breasted Coats Forbidden', *The Times,* September 4, 1942, 5.

14 Ibid.

15 'Utility Clothing', *The Times,* March 4, 1942, 5.

16 Ibid., 5.

17 'Simpler Clothes', *The Times*, March 4, 1942, 2.

18 Colin McDowell, *Forties Fashion and the New Look* (London: Bloomsbury, 1997), 54.

19 Ibid.

20 Rebecca Arnold, *The American Look: Fashion, Sportswear and the Image of Women in 1930s and 1940s New York* (London: I.B. Tauris, 2009), 142.

21 *Mademoiselle,* February 1945, 113.

22 Reference form Phyllis Magidson, Curator of Costumes and Textiles, The Museum of the City of New York, in conversation with Hazel Clark, January 7, 2016.

23 Kay Silver, 'Mlle's Fashion Firsts', *Mademoiselle: The Magazine for Smart Young Women*, February 1945, 113.

24 Sandra Stansberry Buckland, 'Promoting American Designers, 1940–44: Building Our Own House', in *Twentieth-Century American Fashion*, ed. Lynda Welters and Patricia A. Cunningham (Oxford and New York: Berg, 2005), 116.

25 Ibid., 110.

26 Ibid., 116.

27 Ibid., 116–17.

28 Arnold, *The American Look*, 140.

29 Ibid.

30 Ian Hunter, 'Aesthetics and Cultural Studies', in *Cultural Studies*, ed. Lawrence Grossberg, Cary Nelson and Paula A. Treichler (New York: Routledge, 1991), 348–349, quoted in Kathy L. Peiss, *Zoot Suit: The Enigmatic Career of an Extreme Style* (Philadelphia: University of Pennsylvania Press, 2011), 21.

31 Peiss, *Zoot Suit*, 10.

32 Ibid., 9.

33 Ralph Ellison, *The Invisible Man* (1952; repr., New York: Vintage Books, 1995), 440–441.

34 Alford notes how the suit 'was usually worn by boys ages sixteen to twenty'. Holly Alford, 'The Zoot Suit Its History and Influence', *Fashion Theory: The Journal of Dress, Body & Culture* 8, no. 2 (2004): 226.

35 Alex Haley and Malcolm X, *The Autobiography of Malcolm X* (New York: Ballantine Books, 1964), 82.

36 Shane White and Graham White, *Stylin': African American Expressive Culture from Its Beginnings to the Zoot Suit* (Ithaca and London: Cornell University Press, 1998), 253–254.

37 Ibid., 10–11.

38 Ibid., 11

39 It is not sufficient to apply to it only the Marxist reading of the cultural practices of the post-war working class in Britain adopted by Dick Hebdidge and other British scholars associated with the Centre for Cultural Studies at the University of Birmingham. While the zoot suit has been interpreted as a sub-cultural style of resistance, Thornton has cautioned that 'subcultures' is a term applied from the outside, not by participants, Sarah Thornton, *Club Cultures: Music, Media and Subcultural Capital* (Middletown, CT: Wesleyan University Press, 1996), 20.

40 Stuart Cosgrove, 'The Zoot Suit and Style Warfare', in *Zoot Suits and Second-Hand Dresses: An Anthology of Fashion and Music*, ed. Angela McRobbie (London: Macmillan, 1989), 20.

41 Peiss, *Zoot Suit*, 20.

42 White and White, *Stylin'*, 249.

43 Ibid., 250 (figure 55).

44 Famously as worn by Cab Calloway in *Stormy Weather,* the 1943 20th Century Fox movie featuring a high-calibre African American cast.

45 White and White, *Stylin'*, 254.

46 'Zoot Suits: WPB Order Ending Jive-Garb Production Outrages Nation's Teen-Age Jitterbugs', *Life*, September 24, 1942, 44–5.

47 White and White, *Stylin'*, 256.

48 Ibid., 261.

49 Peiss, *Zoot Suit,* 25.

50 Ibid., 10

51 Somewhat ironically perhaps, as one of the style originators of the zoot suit is typically cited as the British Duke of Windsor, later King Edward VIII; see White and White, *Stylin'*, 251.

52 Steve Chibnall, 'Whistle and Zoot: The Changing Meaning of a Suit of Clothes', *History Workshop Journal* 20, no. 1 (1985); 61.

53 Ibid.

54 Peiss, *Zoot Suit*, 26.

55 *Life*, 22 November 1954, 68–72.

56 Chibnall, 'Whistle and Zoot', 62.

57 Paul Gilroy, *There Ain't No Black in the Union Jack. The Cultural Politics of Race and Nation* (London: Unwin Hyman, 1987), 155.

58 '1944–1950: Black GIs, English Women, and "brown babies"', *Mix-d: Museum*, Timeline 1900–2016, available online http://www.mix-d.org/museum/timeline/black-gis-english-women-and-brown-babies (accessed December 3, 2015).

59 'Citizenship: Brave New World: Postwar Immigration', *The National Archives*, available online http://www.nationalarchives.gov.uk/pathways/citizenship/brave_new_world/immigration.htm (accessed December 3, 2015).

60 Chibnall, 'Whistle and Zoot', 66.

61 Ibid., 68.

62 Ibid.

63 Ibid., 73.

64   Michaela Elli Young with Barrington Young, Interview, 14 December 2015.

65   Ibid.

66   'The lights of London: Famous Buildings Floodlit on Victory Night', *Illustrated London News*, 19 May 1945, 523.

67   *Life,* 15 April 1946, cover and 77–82.

68   R. Fisher, *The Walls of Jericho* (Ann Arbor: Ann Arbor paperbacks, University of Michigan Press, 1928, repr.), 189.

69   Nora Mair, quoted in Kisseloff, *You Must Remember This*, 282.

70   James Weldon Johnson, *Black Manhattan* (1930; repr., New York: Arno Press, 1991), 162–3.

71   White and White, *Stylin'*, 234–5.

72   Ibid., 245.

73   Ibid., 245–246.

74   Quoted by Jeff Kisseloff, *You Must Remember This,* 282.

75   Originally instituted as a promenade between churches to see their Easter floral displays. Leigh Eric Schmidt, 'The Easter Parade: Piety, Fashion, and Display', *Religion and American Culture: A Journal of Interpretation* 4, no. 2 (1994): 148.

76   James H. Barnett, 'The Easter Festival—A Study in Cultural Change', *American Sociological Review* 14, no. 1 (1949): 65.

77   A practice with deep roots in European religious traditions and folk customs at Easter. Schmidt, 'The Easter Parade', 148.

78   *Life*, April 1948, 90–2.

79   Schmidt, 'The Easter Parade', 154.

80   Ibid., 155.

81   Elizabeth Wilson and Lou Taylor, *Through the Looking Glass: A History of Dress from 1860 to the Present Day* (London: BBC Books, 1989), 122.

82   Ibid., 31; Christopher Breward, 'In the Eye of the Storm. Oxford Circus and the Fashioning of Modernity', *Fashion Theory: The Journal for Dress, Body & Culture* 4, no. 1 (2000): 3–26.

83   McRobbie, *British Fashion Design*, 31.

84   Tiffany Webber-Hanchett, 'Dorothy Shaver: Promoter of "The American Look"', *Dress* 30 (2003): 80–90.

85   Arnold, 2009: 87

86   Elizabeth Winder, *Pain, Parties, Work: Sylvia Plath in New York, Summer 1953* (New York: Harper Collins, 2013), 36, points out that this was the innovation of the magazine's far-sighted Editor in Chief Betsy Talbot Blackwell, who would later be the first women's magazine editor to publish Gloria Steinem and Betty Friedan.

87   Winder, *Pain, Parties, Work: Sylvia Plath in New York, Summer 1953,* 98.

88   Ibid., 100.

89   Sylvia Plath, *The Bell Jar* (1971; repr., New York: Harper Perennial, 2005), 111.

90   With annual incomes from $4 to $7,500, see Bill Osgerby, *Playboys in Paradise: Masculinity, Youth and Leisure-Style in Modern America* (New York: Berg, 2001), 80.

91 Ibid., 80.

92 'Suburban stylishness goes to Town: Informality from Out of Town Converts the City', *Life,* October 11, 1954, 114–20.

93 Available online http://tigger.uic.edu/%7Epbhales/Levittown/levitek.html (accessed July 25, 2013).

94 New York designer Claire McCardell's well-known popover housedress of 1942 was designed with a detachable oven mitt, as were other garments of the period aimed at the 'housewife'.

95 Godley, 'Immigrant Entrepreneurs'.

96 Ibid., 42.

97 Ibid., 43.

98 A.J. Kershen, *Off the Peg: The Story of the Women's Wholesale Clothing Industry 1880 to the 1960s* (London: The Jewish Museum, 1988), 9.

99 Ellis and Goldstein, 'Lisscraft brochure Autumn 1951-2', Jewish Museum, London.

100 Ellis and Goldstein, 'Eastex brochure Spring and Summer 1954', Jewish Museum, London.

101 C. Breward, E. Erhman and C. Evans (eds), *The London Look: Fashion From Street to Catwalk* (New Haven and London: Yale University Press with Museum of London, 2004), 117.

102 Thanks to Phyllis Magidson, Curator of Textiles and Costumes, The Museum of the City of New York, for this reference and date; conversation with Hazel Clark, January 7, 2016. See also Anne Morra, 'Tiger Morse: Fashion Guru and Andy Warhol Star', *MoMA*, July 23, 2014, available online http://www.moma.org/explore/inside_out/2014/07/23/tiger-morse-fashion-guru-and-andy-warhol-star (accessed January 7, 2016).

5
DRESSING DOWN

Introduction

This chapter looks at how fashion was negotiated and embedded in everyday life in Britain and the United States from the late 1950s to the early 1970s. Expectations about who you were and who you might become had been changing from the start of the twentieth century, but this gathered momentum after 1945. Fashion played a vital role in this, and its potency seemed ever more powerful to various groups of people: working-class and middle-class men and women, young and middle-aged alike, and those who were gaining new civil rights or emigrating from former colonies. Negotiating this was hardly straightforward, but the expansion in popular media – magazines and TV in particular – provided instruction, advice, role models and, above all, a vast array of visual images. Describing how she and her mother pored over the fashion pages in *Woman* and *Woman's Own* in her early teens, British, Hilary Fawcett wrote: 'my love of fashion was part of the tension between the achieving me and the traditionally feminine me, the me that would be the first woman in my family to enter higher education and the me that identified with my housewife mother and her engagement with the rules of style and good taste'.[1] Young people were a particular source of anxiety especially in the popular press as they seemed intent on breaking rule after rule: 'Older generations might deplore the new assertiveness of the young: the lack of deference to established authority, trouser suits and miniskirts (making girls look unladylike), the long hair on boys (making them look like girls) and so forth, but the carnival of youth and the new permissiveness seemed unstoppable'.[2] Towards the end of the 1960s, as the young contested mainstream politics and economics, their anti-establishment stance also impacted upon the lives of those who were less radical, including those from different classes, colour and sexual orientation: fashion was an obvious indicator of this. Within the metropolitan centres and suburbs of London and New York, from the late 1950s, and certainly by the early 1960s, various social groups and communities were less constrained by established social mores, and some enjoyed increased social and geographical mobility, but at the same time their positions could be somewhat precarious and in transition due to the economy, new types of migration and shifting demographics as well as changing family structures. Crucially as 1960s' fashion in New York and London ran counter to the apparent conformity of 1950s' fashion, so the late 1960s saw growing reactions to the earlier part of the 1960s and the preoccupation with progress and modernity that characterized, for example, the conspicuous consumption of the post-war baby boomers and the ambitious urban renewal projects of post-war planners. By wearing second-hand, 'retro' and non-Western forms of dress, some groups within society managed to create alternative identities. The focus of this chapter is the assimilation of fashionable looks and ideas into everyday lives. London and New York are viewed as two major cities in which the fashions that were initially associated with the young became routinized and assimilated. The increasingly pervasive and diverse media – music, magazines, TV, film – was critical to this, particularly by popularizing, celebrating and commercializing fashion, especially in London, which was seen to lead the world by the mid-1960s. As we will see from the late 1950s to the early 1970s, as politics was a catalyst for change, and music a backdrop, so fashion represented and embodied the complexities in everyday life.

The election of the young John F. Kennedy as President of the United States in January 1961 signalled for many an optimism that was reflected in the domestic agenda he had promised during his presidential campaign, but was marred by his assassination in 1963. The passing of the Civil Rights Act in 1964, outlawing discrimination based on race, colour, sex, religion or national origin, characterized the decade and marked the start of a new chapter in American history. More radical politics developed as Black Power became a central focus of the Civil Rights Movement. Gender politics also gained traction in the United States in the wake of Betty Friedan's groundbreaking book *The Feminine Mystique,* published in 1963, which was to be instrumental in the beginnings of second-wave feminism (although also later criticized for its privileged white, middle- and upper-class perspective).[3] Likewise, the raiding by police in June 1969 of the Stonewall Inn, a gay bar in New York City's Greenwich Village, was seen as the beginning of the gay rights movement. Also, student activists became more radical in the United States, as they did in Europe. In the United States, a major target of concern was the country's involvement in the Vietnam War (1954–1973), which intensified from 1964 to 1968, and had a direct impact on young men in particular who were subject to conscription. While a counter-culture had identified itself in the United States, and was evident in New York City as well as on the West coast, the spirit of optimism that it engendered had begun to dissipate by the end of the 1960s. Markers included the assassination of Civil Rights leader Dr Martin Luther King in April 1968. A year later the Woodstock pop festival, held in upstate New York in summer 1969, attracted more than 400,000 young people, and became in retrospect something of a last breath of hopefulness, which was never fully to be reinstated.

At the same time, social, political and cultural lives in Britain were in transition as class boundaries blurred, greater numbers of women worked – albeit in low paid jobs – and the racial mix of the country was transformed by several phases of immigration from former colonies, beginning in the mid-1950s. The attitude to such change was ambivalent and varied, but legislation – both permissive and restrictive – played a critical role. Permissive legislation included the Wolfenden Report of 1957 that recommended the decriminalization of all forms of consensual homosexual behaviour between adult men in private, the introduction of the Abortion Act in 1967 and the Divorce Act of 1969. Restrictive legislation included the Commonwealth Immigration Acts of 1962 and 1968, which sought to limit immigration into Britain. Nevertheless, there was growing permissiveness particularly around sex and personal relationships, and while 'the laws that changed society did not come in a single package [they] were fudges, compromises', they undoubtedly contributed to changing perceptions of Britain and what it meant to be 'British'.[4] However, the British economy, with London at the forefront, had been hit by the combination of loss of imperial power and the diminution of its manufacturing base and markets. Indeed, it 'ceased to be the imperial city without becoming anything else in particular; and her economy began to wilt'.[5] Trade from the port of London to the Commonwealth between 1959 and 1975 fell by 50 per cent, leading to the closure of various docks (East India, St Katharine's, and the London) and the decline of manufacturing in Greater London by a third that also included the garment industry. [6]

While London in the 1960s was a byword for fashion, the banner of 'The Swinging City', was symbolic of Britain in transition, shedding in the process 'much of its smugness, much of the arrogance that often went with the stamp of privilege, much of its false pride'.[7] Indeed, as Piri Halasz wrote in an oft-cited issue of *Time* in 1966, it still had 'a large measure of … civility … tolerance … simple humanity … gentleness … ease, a cosiness and a mixture of different social circles that totally eludes New York'.[8] Emerging in the 1960s as culturally adventurous, it seemed surprising given Britain's political and economic position just after the Second World War. This was dramatically symbolized by the 'British Invasion' of the United States. Initiated by The Beatles first visit to New York in 1964, this delivered across the Atlantic not only pop music but also fashion that was distinctly young and seemingly egalitarian across the Atlantic. The role of fashion and popular culture in the resurgence of London was striking, but retrospectively it could be seen to have been built upon pre-existing foundations. These included a long connection with the popular music industry and a garment industry that was 'strongly-rooted [and] flexible' and therefore 'well-placed to respond to quick-change fashion and style from the late 1940s'.[9] At the same time, changing city geographies after 1945 saw marginal and previously dubious districts and spaces of the city come to the fore offering opportunities for designers, artists, musicians and entrepreneurs (the myriad of streets in Soho – behind Regent St and south of Oxford St – were a case in point).

Focusing on London's liminal spaces, some writers have challenged 'histories of fashionable London by presenting them from a perspective that makes them appear strange and unfamiliar'.[10] Grey and austere, as well as vibrant and youthful, O'Neill's cityscape is a place in which fashion – as a vehicle of change – 'propels the multifarious attitudes and beliefs that shape the evolving fabric of London'.[11] Notable for him is the heightened sense of masculinity captured best by the menswear designer John Stephen. As he puts it, 'John Stephen is credited with the title of "King of Carnaby Street" for his swift commercial assault on dressing the modern male youth of London in the 1960s. He was largely responsible for transforming a low-rent street of tobacconists into the central site of the consumption of "Swinging London"'.[12] While there has been debate about the extent to which London was 'swinging', various writers have noted that London in the 1960s 'built on home-grown talent emerging from the capital's art and fashion colleges'.[13] Presented as part of a 'social revolution', it drew upon creative young talent from London's working-class areas of East Ham, Tottenham, Stepney, Dartford and Neasdon, and it included photographers, actors and filmmakers, musicians, fashion designers and models. Green suggests however that 'Swinging London lasted perhaps two years. Elitist, style-obsessed, hedonistic and apolitical, it was not destined to survive'.[14]

New York was changing too. In the Bronx and Harlem, the Black Power movement gathered political momentum and economic influence, pioneering the concept of 'Black is Beautiful' in the early 1960s. In 1969, the riots at the Stonewall Inn was the much needed catalyst for the gay liberation movement and begged an all important question of what to wear – not just for those 'coming out', but for everyone. *Life* summed up 'The 1960s: A Decade of Tumult and Change' in the cover headline for its last issue of 1969.[15] While the physical mapping of New York took different forms to that of London, it too was a city under transformation. Race riots in Harlem in the 1960s preceded a long period of social and economic decline in the neighbourhood. Yet it was also a time when the fashion and appearance of black Americans was to gain more attention and respect. Likewise, downtown in Greenwich Village, the gay community finally took a stand against police harassment, a move that summoned the beginning of gay pride. Uptown and downtown, and across the Atlantic, fashion mattered in the context of everyday experience and enabled the representation of new modes of youth, masculinity and femininity, at once more complex and more interesting than what had gone before. Singular items of dress or particular hairstyles could be indicative of these new aspirations, and also resistant to existing mores. As the thirteen-year-old British Sheila Rowbotham gazed at 'my friend Pam's cousin Malcolm who had a Tony Curtis and a bootlace tie', she also craved 'a sling-back coat and high heels'.[16] At boarding school in the 1950s, Rowbotham's experience encapsulated both the social, economic and political opportunities and insecurities of this period and, as this chapter will show, both modernity and the 'counter-cultural' as a harbinger of post-modernity permeated everyday life via fashion. At first glance, fashion was antithetical to this counter-cultural questioning: it was intimately linked to mass-culture and consumerism; it was symbolic of conformity and compliance; and it was redolent of power structures related to class, race, sexuality and gender that had led to the critical questioning that characterized the 1968 generation. It was, however, also pervasive, in some ways democratic, easily disseminated and a viable means of change.

Selling the look(s): The media-isation of fashion in everyday life

If 'Swinging London' didn't last for very long, or swing in its entirety, then it was still, as Brenda Polan put it, an 'instant media myth'.[17] This instant media myth described by Polan was extremely powerful; and glamour, celebrity and commerce were vital in popularizing and embedding this in everyday lives; be it through grand statements or modest tokens. Ordinary men and women going about their everyday lives negotiated – consciously and unconsciously – the plethora of what could legitimately be described as a 'fashion system'. Better standards of living allowed for greater and more diverse methods of consumption; home dressmaking remained, but the fashion business (manufacturers, shops, magazines, paper patterns) jostled to be ahead of the game. By the 1950s and 1960s, however, there were marked differences in the media, particularly in its ubiquity and pervasiveness that was accelerated by technological change – in advertising and publishing, and in television and photography with the use of the telephoto lens. While Britain had undoubtedly lagged behind the United States both before and after the war in terms of media technologies, by the 1960s it was these media – both new and revamped – that enabled London to be presented as 'swinging': 'The 1960s was perhaps the first decade created in the media. It was "invented", chronicled and examined whilst it was unfolding, rather than labelled and analysed with the benefit of hindsight'.[18]

Newspapers jumped on the bandwagon producing women's sections and fashion features particularly in the emerging colour supplements. *The New York Times* had led the way introducing an illustrated Sunday magazine in 1896 followed by its *Fashions of the Times* magazine in 1946. In Britain, *The Sunday Times* launched its colour supplement in 1962 as cheap colour printing allowed for the wider media representation of fashion. At the same time, popular tabloid newspapers such as the British *Daily Mirror* had women fashion editors – Marjorie Proops had that role before becoming the eponymous agony aunt, and the *Daily Mail* and *Daily Mirror* touched on stories that related fashion if only for sensational purposes. These fed 'the fears of their "Middle England" readership that constantly bemoaned the seeming collapse of civilisation' as Beatlemania took hold, the mini skirt continued to rise (albeit modestly compared to its height at the end of the 60s) and Mods and Rockers battled it out on the English coast.[19] In multiple ways and with various audiences, this media-isation of fashion, of music (discussed later) and of the young transformed popular perceptions of London as a grey, rationed, bomb-damaged city to one that was vibrant and economically resurgent. 'Sixties London' rippled out to the periphery and British cities such as Manchester, Birmingham, Newcastle and Leeds developed their own boutiques on alternative but soon to be fashionable streets. It was London, however, that caught the popular imagination as it became symbolic of the youthful enterprise of post-war Britain, bustling with cultural energy and economic potential.

New magazines emerged for new markets and old ones were revamped to appeal to a wider readership: *Vogue* and *Queen* were in the latter category, whereas the new youth-oriented magazine *Honey* appeared in 1960, with its spin-off *Petticoat* published in 1966 (aimed at teens) and *19* in 1968. Stalwarts of the women's magazine market in Britain were *Woman* and *Woman's Own* and, like their predecessors in the previous two centuries, they were interested in all that was feminine. In this respect, women's magazines were vital arenas in which fashion was represented and, significantly in the 1960s, readership of these magazines reached a high that was not repeated.[20] Winship attributes the circulation climb that gathered pace in the 1950s to an expansion in the wider commodity market, but she argues that it was in the 1960s that 'the beauty and fashion trades mushroomed with products aimed at young and largely unmarried women across the class spectrum'.[21] She goes on to identify products that were intended for working-class consumers on local high streets, as well as those found in boutiques and multiple chain stores (C&A, Marks and Spencer, British Home Stores). Featuring images of fashionable young women on their packaging and advertising, leading make up brands included Rimmel, Outdoor Girl and Miners. The plethora of magazines excelled in visually articulating new fashionable styles and, with coverage across age and class groups, they were immensely powerful. Notwithstanding promotions and advertising for particular retailers, they also offered advice about home dressmaking as well as tips as to where cheaper versions might be found, such as in mail order catalogues.

The US magazine publishing industry based predominantly in New York had seen its own markets threatened in the wake of post-war social and economic change. It too had had to adapt to develop existing markets and explore new ones. In the 1950s, *Look* (1937–1971), a bi-weekly general interest magazine, with a greater emphasis on photographs than articles, that was in the shadow of *Life*, made a concerted effort to appeal to women, particularly in their roles as consumers. In the 'For Women Only' section it highlighted consumer goods and services including fashion for new as well as existing markets. *Look* is an excellent visual source for the lives of New Yorkers, of how they looked and what they wore, presenting a picture of a city both tough and human, and essentially visual. Particular neighbourhoods provided the material for visual essays for many documentary photographers. In 1968, Magnum photographer Eve Arnold went to Harlem to shoot a collection that featured the actress Cicely Tyson wearing her hair in a natural Afro style and serving as a role model for 'go Afro'.[22] In the previous decade, Arnold had photographed fashion shows in Harlem, accompanied by music and dancing, held in church-halls, Elks' meeting halls and gymnasiums. Published in the British photo-journal *Picture Post* in 1950, the associated article had a distinctly racist tone, but noted nevertheless how the African American dressmakers who produced the garments for the shows were at a disadvantage when whites owned over 90 per cent of the shops and businesses in Harlem.[23] The photographs from the 1968 shoot celebrated 'Black is Beautiful', marking the profound changes in American racial politics, fashion and the body that had occurred in the wake of the Civil Rights Movement.[24] When *Look* magazine published a photograph of a black model wearing an evening gown in 1958, the image was unprecedented in the white media.[25] It was a sign that black people were also becoming recognized for their economic potential, no more so than by Chicago publisher John Johnson, who had been instrumental in developing the black media and consumer market in the United States.[26]

From these early days, Johnson Publishing strove to create an authentic and positive image of African Americans for its readership, highlighting the lives and achievements of black celebrities and heroes. *Ebony* magazine, first published in November 1945, became a popular equivalent to pictorial magazines such as *Life* and *Look* that were popular among the white community. Followed by *Jet* (1951), *Tan Confessions* (1950) – renamed *Tan* (1952) – and *Hue* (1953), these periodicals reflected black life as a shared experience, rather than as a societal problem fuelled by racism. Black celebrities, such as Lena Horne, who appeared on *Ebony's* first colour cover in 1946, demonstrated the possibilities for African Americans in post-war consumer culture.[27] Fashion played a role in this positive self-representation. By the mid-1950s, *Ebony* included a regular fashion feature, entitled Fashion Fair, which showed the latest styles on elegant black models, as well as instituting an annual feature on the nation's best-dressed women. An even greater contribution by Johnson Publishing Company to fashion was the launch of the Ebony Fashion Fair in 1958.

The brainchild of Eunice Walker Johnson, wife of John Johnson, the Ebony Fashion Fair (1958–2008) brought the latest designer fashion to largely black audiences across the United States, Canada and the Caribbean. Travelling to major and also minor cities and towns, staged in theatres and church halls, the show raised money for African American charities and promoted Johnson Publishing, but more significantly, created a positive image of black Americans by and for themselves, through fashion. When the Fashion Fair began, racial discrimination affected every aspect of black life in America. An African American consumer market had not yet been articulated, and racism meant that in many places black shoppers could not even try on clothes and accessories in department stores before making a purchase.[28] During the '60s numerous *Ebony* cover spreads were devoted to the Fair, bringing them to a wider audience via a magazine that became ubiquitous in most African American households. As the decade progressed more colourful clothes were introduced, moving away from the expectation in the late 1950s that dark skinned women should not draw attention to themselves by wearing bright clothes'.[29] Contemporary photographs of the Fashion Fair's audiences show black women and some men, all very well dressed, demonstrating the importance of their clothing in reflecting self-esteem, gaining respect, and also as a source of pleasure.[30] At its height in 1987, the fair visited 200 cities, always starting out at more modest locations, such as Rochester or Buffalo, New York, rather than in Manhattan. Eunice Johnson was instrumental in bringing fashion to African Americans, and in employing black fashion models, such as Donyale Luna, the daughter of a Ford car plant manager from Detroit, who appeared on the cover of British *Vogue* in 1966.[31] In 1974, Beverly Johnson became the first black model to appear on the cover of American *Vogue*. Ebony Fashion Fair had helped to break professional racial barriers; as one commentator noted: 'Ebony Fashion Fair represented and propelled so much more than fashion alone; it harnessed the power of fashion as a super-fuelled allegory for social change'.[32]

Photographs taken in public places in New York and London demonstrate the pace and nature of change, which is especially evident in the clothing of fashionable young women. The photograph of a busy Fenchurch St Railway station in London from the mid-1960s (Figure 5.1) captures the new London. Unlike images of established shopping streets, the railway station was a transitional space as people went to and from work, or set out for a day in the city. Walking down the stairs towards the trains, it is striking how many of the women wear mini-skirts and dresses. The young woman on the right-hand staircase has a 'Twiggy' style haircut, while to our left on the other staircase, a young woman wears a bold psychedelic-printed mini-shift dress. These were not dissimilar to those wore by Jean Shrimpton or made by Mary Quant and sold at her shop Bazaar on the fashionable Kings Road. This image conforms to the popular perception that these fashionable styles were more free and easier to wear than styles from the preceding decades. Unstructured shift dresses and mini-skirts, casual three-quarter coats, loose cardigans and sweaters reinforce the truism that attributes the success of the 'sixties' styles for women to the freedom that these type of dresses and skirts offered. Looking more closely, the

Figure 5.1 A busy Fenchurch St railway station, London, mid-1960s. John Gay. Getty Images.

young woman on the right has put together a number of fashionable items to create a distinctive, though relaxed stance. The silhouette in this photograph is linear, not curving and nipped in, but most importantly, this youthful mini-skirted look was ubiquitous; reiterated again and again in media representations on TV, in magazines, and in the cinema, it was part of everyday life.

Another photograph from the London Metropolitan archives (Figure 5.2) shows various groups of people enjoying a day out at a fair on Hampstead Heath in 1963. The image, fascinating in what it tells us about fashion in everyday lives, comprises a black older woman accompanied most likely by her daughter, a group of young men, an older white woman and a man standing separately, families – some with small children – and a group of young women. The fashions worn by all are remarkably varied and date from the 1940s to the present day of 1963; in them we see a snapshot of generational differences with the two women

Figure 5.2 A day out at Hampstead Heath Fair, London, August 1963. London Metropolitan Archives.

in the foreground representing two generations through age and through their clothes. The younger woman with dark flicked hair, a style reminiscent of US soul singer Gladys Knight, sunglasses and a pale shift dress shows the influence and popularization of Mary Quant's late 1950s shift dresses. Probably her mother, alongside, wears what appears to be a 1940s' button-through dress with a darker edging that is structured but now worn loosely most likely the result of changing stature due to age. The groups of young men and women dress fashionably in styles from the late 1950s to the early 1960s: the younger women are wearing full-skirts and flat-laced pumps, but in a casual and informal way, and the men wearing narrow-lapelled suits with tapered trousers and pointed shoes, hair combed back in the manner of the British pop star Billy Fury. Most revealing is the co-existence of looks that in numerous ways represent some form of engagement with fashion. Fashion is built into the clothes worn by all the people in this photograph, but few are completely of the 'moment'. More typical is the combination of old and new.

Nevertheless, it is a youthful London that, for obvious reasons, has preoccupied fashion writers, but as historians have begun to revise their accounts of this decade, so it is also useful to question how and why these new images and styles shaped everyday lives. Notable is the spread of the 'sixties' look beyond the youth generation and its relative longevity. This was aided by mail order catalogues in which pop singers such as Lulu modelled styles for working-class consumption. Also contributing to this democratization of fashionable looks was the widespread availability of Style and Simplicity paper patterns for new fabrics that enabled 'cut and sew' shift dresses to be quickly made at home. Knitting patterns were also popular and available and were sold through the numerous wool shops with companies, such as Sirdar and Robin, leading the way. In the United States, a knitting pattern leaflet produced by New York–based Columbia Minerva indicated how 'hot pants' were briefly fashionable in the early 1970s. Four different styles showed shorts worn either alone for the bold, baring the thighs, or with a covering skirt for more modest wearers. This was definitely a fashion for the young, as is emphasized in the bodies, faces and hairstyles of the models, and the accessories of knee-length boots and socks, and socks pulled over the knee, or panty hose. A picture of a pair of knitted hot pants and vest top worn in Britain in 1971 (Figure 5.3) shows how such fashionable styles were evident on both sides of the Atlantic, with their origins often closely determined by different forms of media.

Figure 5.3 Kay Reid models a pair of knitted hot pants with matching vest top, UK 1971, M. McKeown /Daily Express. Getty Images.

Another example in the early 1970s was the development of 'blaxploitation', the term for a genre of films originally targeted at a black urban audience, which soon crossed racial lines, and were popular viewing across the Atlantic. One of the most successful was *Shaft* (1971), directed by photographer Gordon Parks and set in Harlem, where black private detective John Shaft worked with the local mob against the downtown Mafia. It presented an image of black masculinity as tough, cool, sexy, well dressed and all together fashionable. In his turtleneck sweater, jacket and full-length leather trench coat, the combination of John Shaft's clothing, body language and race contributed to the presence and power of the character. Such depictions were not restricted to a cinematic genre, but can been seen in the style being worn everyday on the streets of Harlem. Three men (Figure 5.4) pictured in the early to mid-1970s, in an image titled 'Sharply Dressed', show the same qualities. Their clothes vary from the casual to the more formal, worn on bodies that appear relaxed and confident. What is evident is that their appearance matters to who they are and how they are seen. In its increasingly varied forms, the media provides valuable records of the appearance of fashion in everyday life, both as social documentation and through the promotion of new styles.

Going about their everyday lives, even older people's dressing responded in modest ways to styles that had been initially associated with the young. In Britain, middle-aged, married women wore popular retailer C&A adaptations of the mini-skirt, produced in new materials such as Crimplene, and styled their hair like Jackie Kennedy. Those who were a little better-off wore clothes by companies such as Eastex that produced versions of these styles for the middle-class married woman who wanted to signal knowledge and understanding of fashion, but also

Figure 5.4 'Sharply Dressed', New York City, 1970s. Museum of the City of New York.

expected the high-quality finish of manufacturers such as Ellis and Goldstein (Figure 5.5). This brochure from the Ellis and Goldstein archive at the Jewish Museum in London shows the diffusion of elements of the '60s look' to a slightly older, more affluent market. The three-quarter-sleeve dress with large repeat print in coordinating beige, rust and cream is slightly fitted around the body to give some definition to the figure. With dark eyes, long blonde hair and a youthful pose, the model is a more mature version of Jean Shrimpton or Twiggy. Eastex was a reputable company that sold through department stores and smaller shops around Britain, but this promotional brochure is indicative of the ways in which it too responded to this step-change in fashion. Importantly, it wasn't just women who were keen to connect in some ways with fashion; it was older men as well as young men. Colour, pattern, style and 'pose' impacted on menswear in different markets in subtle ways – Terylene shirts in various hues, worn with slim, coloured ties, tapered trousers and jackets that were cut in towards the waist, and hairstyles that, while not long, pointed to an informality that was casual, less formal and avowedly not 'military'. While youth styles were taken up by a plethora of fashionable retailers and boutiques – Bus Stop, Biba, Etam, Dorothy Perkins, and Miss Selfridges – that increasingly dominated the streets of London and of provincial towns and cities, they also had an impact on the established shops and manufacturers to affect the lives of older women through styles that came from Eastex, Windsmoor, Marks and Spencer, C&A, British Home Stores and Littlewood, as well as mail order catalogues such as Grattan and Freeman.

Media images of Jack and Jackie Kennedy, John Paul Sartre and Simone de Beauvoir, James Dean and Marlon Brando, Brigitte Bardot and Juliette Greco, Joan Baez and Bob Dylan found eager audiences via the popular media: magazines, daily newspapers, film, music and TV. Even in the later 1960s, various iterations of the counter-culture began to be incorporated, assimilated and commodified; importantly, improving manufacturing techniques and materials brought high fashion 'looks' quickly into the realm of everyday life. The impact of radical and alternative politics both before and after 1968 added layers of complexity, diversity and contradiction that also connected in a variety of ways to fashion within everyday lives. Some manifestations of this were accentuated and extreme: the bohemianism of the Beat Generation, the anti-capitalist stance of hippies and the affirmation of Black Power. Alongside this, the controversy and associated demonstrations of second-wave feminism and the Gay Liberation movement brought knowledge and awareness of these issues into the public domain. Ethnic and floral prints based on Art Nouveau patterns, mauve and pink shirts for men and bias cut skirts that looked back to the 1930s seeped into everyday lives losing their radical meanings on the way. Art students attending the wedding of friends in the north east of England in summer 1974 show the variety of fashionable styles then acceptable (Figure 5.6). While the bride is traditionally dressed in a long white gown, the groom wears

Figure 5.5 Eastex Dresses, Spring 1967, promotional brochure, manufactured by Ellis & Goldstein, London. Jacques Vert Group.

Figure 5.6 Art student friends, North East England wedding photo 1974. Linda and Martin Collier.

a dark blue velvet suit with flared trousers and a broad neck tie, the latter also worn by the other male guest. Two of the female guests choose knee-length outfits, from the fashionable high street label Bus Stop, or similar. The woman on the far left pairs her grey dress with a short fox fur and crepe jacket from the 1930s, bought second hand a few years before. The woman second from the left wears a lightweight two-piece suit probably from Biba in London, her favourite brand at the time. The guest on the groom's left wears a full-length loose dress from Laura Ashley. Everyone seems to be wearing shoes or boots with platform soles, of various heights, which were fashionably popular at the time. Thus fashion brands, second-hand and traditional garments are all in evidence, as sources of fashion and fashion knowledge became more diverse. Despite her traditional appearance, the bride pictured typically shopped second hand at 'jumble sales', had a penchant for wearing a different colour hose on each leg, and took her stylistic references from the music and flamboyance of the likes of performers David Bowie, and Roxy Music.

Popular music and fashion

Pop stars and popular music had a dynamic effect on fashion in the United States and Britain; the latter being focused mainly on London, although due to the Beatles, Liverpool was a centre too. Similarly in segregated America, a completely new and innovative style of music issued from the centre of auto production, Detroit. This new music both helped to draw attention to racial diversity and to promote youthful fashion to a wide audience, especially when television entered American homes, in 1947, immediately after the Second World War. The male and female artists who Berry Gordy signed up on his Motown record label in Detroit (the 'Motor City') from January 1959 took advantage of the fact that they would be seen as much as heard. Some became fashion as well as music icons, in particular The Supremes (originally, Diana Ross, Mary Wilson and Florence Ballard), who were the subject of a fashion exhibition at the Victoria and Albert Museum, London in 2008. Their outfits reflected the 'Motown Look' that Gordy styled carefully to appeal to the widest possible audience, rather than to consciously promote race and colour. He instituted a special 'Artist Development' programme, which resembled the Hollywood charm schools of the 1930s and 1940s. Maxine Powell taught the musicians, many from working-class backgrounds, how to dress, eat, sit, walk and how to appear on television.[33] By 1965, The Supremes had made history by achieving five consecutive number one hits, and Motown had become the most successful black-owned enterprise in America. Music generated by black culture cut across race and class to become 'The Sound of Young America'.[34] According to Supreme Mary Wilson, they all liked fashion; in fact, Diana Ross had been studying fashion before the group was formed. At first they made their own stage clothes, then bought them from Saks Fifth Avenue and later commissioned them from major costume designers like Bob Mackie.[35] Ms Powell schooled them as representatives of the black race who had to act appropriately, but the musicians also wanted to look different, 'They wanted to glitter'.[36] And they did. The full-length, high-necked, long-sleeved, beaded dresses that The Supremes wore to meet Queen Elizabeth, the Queen Mother, at the Royal Variety Performance at the London Palladium in November 1968, while modest in design, were jewel-encrusted and each weighed 35 lbs.[37] The fact that this annual show was family viewing indicated the popularity of Motown music in Britain and the close relationship between pop music and fashion. It also reinforced the role of television in giving fashion and style a presence in everyday life in the United States and in Britain, especially when broadcasting in colour became more widely available in the 1970s.

For Americans, Sunday night prime time viewing came in the form of the popular *Ed Sullivan Show* (1948–1971) broadcast by CBS from its New York studio, first in black and white and then in colour from the second half of the 1960s. The show promoted popular musicians in the 1950s and 1960s, priding itself on having 'bucked the system' to include African American performers and to give their 'first television breaks' to Motown artists including The Supremes, Stevie Wonder, The Four Tops, Gladys Knight and the Pips, and The Jackson Five.[38] But one of the most memorable shows, on 9 February 1964, was when The Beatles played live, marking their first visit to the United States with a performance that was watched by an estimate of over 73 million Americans[39] and signalling the start of the 'British Invasion'. Dressed in matching slim-fitting Italian-style suits, worn with skinny neckties and 'mop top haircuts',[40] their appearance and that of their thousands of female fans echoed what was also being worn on another popular American television show, *American Bandstand*. First broadcast in 1952, and from 1956 until its close in 1989, hosted and produced by Dick Clark, *American Bandstand* provided a non-threatening image of teenagers for their parents. It introduced the American public to rock 'n' roll, and provided the first national exposure for Jerry Lee Lewis, Buddy Holly and, for Motown artists, guaranteeing stardom. While breaking racial ground, Clark virtually ignored the British Invasion and The Beatles never appeared on his show. He tended towards the tamer pop acts, always trying to appeal to the mainstream and therefore ensure his success.[41] While both black and white teenagers appeared as dancers on the show, their demeanour and body language was reserved, certainly in comparison with the screaming girls who welcomed The Beatles to New York. On a show in March 1963, for example, female dancers were wearing knee-length skirts, long-sleeved tops and cardigans, many with their hair flipped (or flicked) at the bottom. The young men sported long jackets, slim trousers and skinny ties,[42] reflecting the Italian look worn in Britain, the style of The Beatles and of the Mods. Although, as Cunningham notes, the collarless, single-breasted corduroy jackets were made popular by the Beatles, they owed their origins to the mean's ready-to-wear styles introduced by Pierre Cardin in 1960.[43]

Appearing on US television panel game *To Tell the Truth* in March 1964, Cathy McGowan, host of the British pop music show *Ready Steady Go* (broadcast August 1963 to December 1966), declared herself the 'Queen of Mod' in front of the distinctly older and more conservatively dressed panelists, Tom Poston, Peggy Cass, Orson Bean and Kitty Carlisle, the latter wearing a low-cut cocktail dress and a diamond necklace. By contrast, McGowan wore a full-length skirt, a slim sweater, and a chin-length bob. She described the female Mod teenager as generally wearing no lipstick, lots of eye make-up, having straight hair, liking light-sleeved crepe shirts, ankle-length skirts, white stockings and granny shoes. Mod music followers listened to The Beatles and The Dave Clark Five, and young men followed their fashion style.[44] Although *Ready Steady Go* was short-lived and was never shown in the United States, being broadcast in black and white at a time when the US networks were converting to full colour, it provided an important expression of fashion and music. Its BBC rival, *Top of the Pops*, which began on 1 January 1964 and continued until 2006, did not have the strong and more cultish identity of *Ready Steady Go*. With its radio programming under threat from pirate radio (*Radio Caroline* in 1963), the BBC also offered the new Radio One in 1967. All of this cemented the relationship of pop music and fashion, not least in the self-presentation and empowerment of working-class kids in Britain, and also Stateside, with the so-called British Invasion.

Many British pop groups soon followed the 'Fab Four' across the Atlantic, including The Dave Clark Five, Herman and the Hermits, Freddie and the Dreamers, the Rolling Stones and Billy J. Kramer. Like The Beatles, a number came from Liverpool on Merseyside, a gritty working-class port, which like Detroit was not known previously for popular music or culture. While British fashion was more associated with London, there fashionable geographies were also shifting. Having opened her boutique Bazaar on the King's Road, Chelsea in 1955, designer Mary Quant was later to note how

> Chelsea suddenly became Britain's San Francisco, Greenwich Village and the Left Bank. The Press publicized its cellars, its beat joints, its girls and their clothes. Chelsea ceased to be a small part of London; it became international; its name interpreted a way of living and a way of dressing far more than a geographical area.[45]

The fashion of the original Chelsea girl, with her leather boots and black stockings, was copied in London, watched by the rest of Britain, and soon moved to New York.

In October 1963, *Life* magazine reported from London on the work of young fashion designers, including Quant, Jean Muir, Sally Tuffin and Marion Foale, who were responsible for the 'Chelsea Look', which was already available at moderate prices in 'scores of U.S. cities'.[46] Photographed by Norman Parkinson, the featured dresses included a sleeveless Shetland wool sheath with a high turtle (polo) neck by Sambo, available from Saks Fifth Avenue for $35, and for the same price a sleeveless tweed dress with a fashionable scoop neckline and small collar, by Polly Peck, from Bloomingdale's. Like all of the daywear featured, both of the dresses were knee length. When *Life* returned to the same designers in September 1965, it was to report how in 1963 'They were so promptly and widely copied that a swift demise was predicted. The giants of the U.S. ready-to-wear industry now think otherwise. They have imported the young British designers themselves to do this fall's clothes'.[47] In 1962, Mary Quant was given an initial order for 6,235 junior-size garments, aimed at teenagers, by J.C. Penney, then America's biggest chain store. The order was large for Quant at the time and had been secured via an introduction from Paul Young, then a Penney's employee who went on to stock Quant's designs in his Paraphernalia boutique, which opened in Manhattan on Madison Avenue in 1965.[48] While influenced by the development of boutiques in London, including Biba, Young also sought out young American talent, to create clothes that would not retail for more than $99 (teasingly priced to be less than a round trip flight to Puerto Rico) and were expected to be relatively short-lived. Betsey Johnson (later to have her own label) joined from the art department of *Mademoiselle,* as did Joel Schumacher (later the Hollywood movie director), a Parsons School of Design graduate employed in creating window displays for another leading fashion retailer, Henri Bendel.[49] Mary Quant also credited the help she and other young British designers received in the United States in negotiating international fashion business and mass-production.[50] She was impressed by the professionalism of American businesswomen, and by the accuracy of garment sizing:

> They seem to know how to mass produce for every possible female shape. I found that if a woman knew her size she could just walk into any shop and buy off the peg without trying on. The most she might have to do would be to turn up the hem or shorten the sleeves. Buying a new dress was as simple as walking into an electrical department to buy a new plug for a standard lamp.[51]

In 1963, Quant's diffusion label Ginger Group became available at in-store boutiques in 160 department stores around Britain.[52] In the same year, Barbara Hulanicki started Biba's Postal Boutique, which began what was to become a hugely successful business with its famous Biba boutique and then a full-scale department store in London's Kensington. Her original media exposure was in the popular British tabloid the *Daily Mirror,* whose fashion editor Felicity Green ordered a simple pink gingham shift and matching kerchief from Hulanicki, which was retailed at 25 shillings mail order to readers.[53] Hulanicki's later designs were typically angular and intentionally 'skinny-looking', an effect achieved by cutting armholes very high and sleeves so narrow that they were often too small to accommodate average-sized bodies.[54] The most fashionable clothes of the time were created for youthful, even infantile, bodies characterized by British model Twiggy, who wore her mini skirts shorter and shorter as the decade progressed. When economist E.P. Schumacher published *Small is Beautiful: A Study of* Economics *as if People Mattered* in 1973, the title seemed to sum up the late 1960s. Small clothes (the mini skirt), products (the mini car), fashion models (the ultra thin, sixteen-year-old Twiggy), pop musicians (the British Small Faces, and singer Millie Small) were fashionable in Britain, and America took readily to these products of the British Invasion. For fashion in particular, role models were in demand. On 22 November 1963, when John F Kennedy was assassinated, the nation lost not only its own youthful President but also an influential fashion icon in his wife Jackie. The night after the Kennedy assassination, American folk singer Bob Dylan opened a concert with a song he had recorded less than a month before, 'The Times They Are a-Changin'. The lyrics and the sentiments were prescient on both sides of the Atlantic.[55]

Fashion and empowerment

Moving to Greenwich Village in 1961, from Minnesota, Robert Zimmerman (later Bob Dylan) encountered a thriving folk music scene at the heart of the city's bohemian culture, centred on the Beat Generation. Frequenting coffee shops, clubs and bars such as the famous Cedar Tavern on University Place, they were stereotyped as the 'fellow in beard and sandals, or a "chick" with scraggly hair, long black stockings, heavy eye make-up and a expression which could indicate either hauteur or uneasy digestion'.[56] *Life* compared them unfavourably to 'England's Angry Young Men who know what they want from society and bay for it with vehemence'.[57] The Beats had more in common, intellectually and sartorially, with CND protesters in Britain, many of whom were students, who did not eschew fashion, but sought an 'arty alternative'[58] to the mainstream. In the late 1950s, 'arty' young British women were described as wearing thick black, dark green or maroon stockings, and full dirndl skirts. Their male counterparts sported check shirts, oiled wool fishermen's jerseys from Norway (or from Marks and Spencer), duffle coats from Millets or other army surplus stores, with tight 'drainpipe' trousers made of velvet or Black Watch tartan, or, for some, blue jeans.[59]

In post-war America, while the specific political issues were different from Britain – the Cold War, Civil Rights, the Vietnam War (1959–1975) – the fashion of the counter culture was similar and can also be compared with what was being worn by young left-wingers on the Left Bank in Paris. At the level of personal and state identity politics, Britain and America were also addressing homosexuality by the end of the 1960s, with its recognition having a liberating effect on men's fashion in particular.[60] The passing of the Sexual Offences Act in England and Wales in 1967 decriminalized sex in private between males aged over 21. Legislature in the United States came a few years later and was instituted on a state-by-state basis. Yet it was in New York that one of the most formative events occurred, in Greenwich Village in 1969, which kick-started the Gay Liberation Movement and a concerted campaign for gay rights.

Gay bars, which had functioned covertly in the Village since after World War I, were frequently subject to police raids. But the raid on the Stonewall Inn in June 1969 was to prove historic, because the mostly male customers fought back and a riot ensued that led to demonstrations by gay men and women throughout the city in the following days. The riots inspired LGBT people across the country to organize in support of gay civil rights, and within two years gay rights groups had been started in most every major US city.[61] This was an enormous change. As Shaun Cole has noted in his insightful research on gay men's dress in the twentieth century, from the 1930s to the 1950s gay males in Britain and America suffered the very real fear of exposure, blackmail and imprisonment. As a result, the everyday dress of most gay men followed the conventions of prevailing fashion. One of Cole's respondents, John Hardy, commented: 'when you were out and about in the streets and going about your ordinary day-to-day business you wouldn't think of wearing anything really outrageous. You tended to dress down and look like everyone else'.[62] The Mattachine Society, one of the earliest homosexual societies in the United States founded in 1950, required that male participants in gay demonstrations wore suits and ties, and women wore dresses, to look 'ordinary' and get bystanders to listen to them, rather than being prematurely turned off by how they looked.[63] While there were insider sartorial signifiers, such as suede shoes in 1950s Britain, a declaration of homosexuality was often through stance and gesture, as many gay men did not want to announce their sexuality via their appearance.[64]

By contrast, the fashionable styles worn by young men in the 1960s were increasingly self-conscious and flamboyant, bringing the sartorial preferences associated with gay men into the fashion mainstream. Male Mods in particular were fastidious dressers, earning them the description of 'working class dandies'.[65] By the early 1960s, the Mods 'were wearing the more effeminate and colourful clothes of Carnaby Street'.[66] Cole notes how the flourishing of Carnaby Street men's shops brought 'an essentially "queer" look to a heterosexual market' and how similar shops and gay men's style had an impact in America.[67] John Stephen provides an interesting case study as his casual separates permeated menswear styles in the 1960s bringing pattern and colour to everyday male dress. As O'Neill puts it, 'Stephen earned a special place for offering an accelerated choice to young men eager for difference…but [he] applied a greater degree of business acumen so that … largely homoerotic style was filtered for mass consumption'.[68] Establishing a single shop on Carnaby Street in 1957, he went on to open thirty shops in Europe and the United States by 1975 when his company closed. The sartorial impact of designers such as Stephen was wide and several other boutiques for men built on his success, including Michael Rainey's Hung On You. At the same time, aspects of the look affected menswear more widely. Sirdar Yarns, for example, sold wool and patterns for home knitting during the 1960s. Pattern 2151 showing a sharp 'mod' man wearing a yellow cable V-neck sweater pictured in front of a black and white photograph of a sixties 'dolly bird' with dark eyes and open pouting mouth highlights the clear impact of this new group of designers (Figure 5.7).

In 1963, *Harper's* magazine was commenting how in the Village and on Manhattan's Upper East Side, a number of smart men's shops were featuring 'slim cut and youthfully styled clothing designed to appeal to homosexuals'.[69]

Figure 5.7 Sirdar Yarns knitting pattern 2151, mid-1960s. Sirdar.

The following year, in an article on 'Homosexuality in America', *Life* magazine showed photographs of 'brawny young men in their leather caps, jackets and pants [who] are practising homosexuals', as well as 'two fluffy-sweatered young men' strolling in what appears to be Washington Square Park in the Village, to the stares of a 'straight' couple. The same article described, 'swarms of young, college-age homosexuals wearing tight pants, baggy sweaters and sneakers [who] cluster in a ragged phalanx along Greenwich Avenue in the Village'.[70] The different looks and styles worn by various groups of gay males in the 1960s were beginning to help establish more stylistic diversity in men's fashion as a whole and were placing greater emphasis on the physical form of the body.[71] Pre-Stonewall, lesbians also had equally to conform to gender norms in dressing in their everyday lives.

In November 1968, *Life* published a feature on the lesbian movie *The Killing of Sister George,* an adaptation of a play that had opened in London's West End in 1964, which it cited as one of a spate of recent films about male and female sexuality.[72] Each of the three main lesbian characters wore female gendered outfits, with two being fashionable. Beryl Reid, the oldest of the three who played Sister George, wore tweed suits with simple sweaters and a trench coat, she smoked cigars and had a partiality to gin. Her outfit, body and age contrasted markedly with that of her partner, the infantile Alice McNaught, nicknamed 'Childe' (played by Susannah York), who wore short baby doll night dresses, mini-skirts, with a gamine hairstyle and pale makeup, *à la* Twiggy. Mercy Croft (actress Coral Browne) was dressed in slightly more mature, but distinctly fashionable, knee-length shifts and coats worn with contrasting hats. It was not until George and Childe (dressed as comedians Laurel and Hardy) went to Gateways, a genuine private women-only London nightclub, that the audience gained insight into contemporary butch and femme style. While providing only a modest insight into reality (even though the film was X rated and restricted to an adult audience in the United Kingdom and not widely shown in the United States), it was arguably acceptable in the context of the changing social mores and fashions of the late 1960s, not least the greater acceptance of women wearing trousers and less overtly feminized styles.

Likewise, during the 1969 Stonewall riots, gay men were observed to be wearing more informal and less conventionally male-identifying fashions: 'the hippie, long-haired, bell-bottomed, laid-back, and likely to have "weird," radical views'.[73] This description could equally be of the more androgynous mainstream male fashions of the early 1970s, in particular the longer hairstyles. Continuing the more casual and anti-establishment styles of the Beats, the hippie style contrasted with the male gay clone look.[74] The masculinization of gay culture in the 1970s drew on macho archetypes from American culture such as the cowboy, the lumberjack and the biker. The clones, especially in US cities such as New York and San Francisco, broke away from the effeminate homosexual sartorial clichés associated with the 1950s.[75] In the mainstream, the popular American disco group Village People (named after Greenwich Village), formed in 1977, came to represent the clone look, not least when their 1978 song 'YMCA' became a huge hit in Britain and America. Yet the gay butch appearance was transgressive, it subverted the dress norms of straight males, comprising flannel shirts, jeans, boots or construction workers shoes, wearing them according to particular insider semiotic codes. Equally, the uniform of lesbians in 1970s America comprised flannel shirts, t-shirts and blue jeans, Birkenstocks, tennis shoes or Frye boots, worn with short hair.[76] For many gay women, the casual freedom of the lesbian uniform helped to structure community solidarity post-Stonewall. But others soon found the clone look oppressive and ostracizing, especially those who wanted to wear feminine gendered clothing.[77] At the same time as the prevailing fashions for gay men became hyper-masculinized, heterosexual men were adopting more feminine-identified signifiers (colourful and floral fabrics, for example). Established gender norms in fashion were beginning to change.

While the media in Britain and America were at pains to point out that an interest in fashion was not necessarily homosexual and that homosexuals did not set fashion trends, gay liberation demonstrated how social changes did actually impact fashion, and in unpredictable ways.[78] The effect of gay culture on majority fashion, for instance, signalled the greater individualization of fashion in everyday life. Not only were given fashion trends less consistent and less ubiquitous than in the past; they were being challenged and broken down, especially as gender, sexual, racial and other social givens changed in Britain and America. Access to travel was also having an impact on British society. Cheap package tours started to introduce summer fashions and the potential of a suntan, neither previously available to many ordinary working-class Britons, especially in the North. Some of the young and adventurous made the trek overland to India, returning with 'Afghan' coats, kaftans, beads and other exotica. (At the same time, many of their American male counterparts were having a decidedly less exotic experience serving in Vietnam). Alma Rangel (born 1930), named on *Ebony* magazine's best-dressed list in the late 1960s, recalled also how, in the 1970s, 'black style was all about influences from Africa and the Middle East. Everything was supposed to be exotic'.[79] For those without the means or the desire to travel, markets and second-hand shops were ready sources for the 'alternative' wardrobes sought by young people with more hippie-inclined affiliations.[80] Hand-made clothes, for instance, were no longer seen as inferior to ready-made, but rather offered the potential for the desired 'uniqueness', which was to continue to infuse fashion going forward. Ethnic inspired looks also filtered into the mainstream. A special issue of US magazine *Woman's Day* published in 1973, featuring '101 Sweaters You Can Knit & Crochet', reflects these trends. Included is a pattern for a one size crocheted 'Lacy Poncho' (Figure 5.8) and a 'Mexican Jacket' knitted in bulky yarn (Figure 5.9). Music events provided ready venues for dressing down, particularly pop festivals, famously Woodstock (1969) in upstate New York, and the Isle of Wright Festivals (1968–1970) in Britain. On the British high street and on American main street or in the mall, exotic and nostalgic influences were also evident. The eponymous Laura Ashley, for example, was a British favourite for her romantic, Edwardian-inspired long printed cotton dresses. As second-wave feminism took hold and more women in Britain and America – across income and class lines – expanded their horizons beyond the home, taking on full-time paid jobs, and as

Figure 5.8 *Woman's Day* 101, 1973. Pattern 44. Author's Collection.

Figure 5.9 *Woman's Day* 101, 1973. Pattern 58. Author's Collection.

they began to exercise control over their fertility with the wider availability of the contraceptive pill, fashion both seemed to reflect and also contradict what was happening in the everyday lives of many British and American citizens.

By the late 1960s, second-wave feminists in the United States and Britain had begun to systematically examine the home, the family and the body as sites of women's oppression. At the core of this was the belief that 'the personal is political'. In this context, an interest in beauty, appearance and fashion as constituent factors in the formation of feminine identities was a strong theme in the work of writers and feminists Betty Friedan and Kate Millet, writing in the United States, Juliet Mitchell and Germaine Greer, writing in Britain, and Simone de Beauvoir in France in her pioneering 1949 work, *The Second Sex.*[81] In this she set the tone:

> Woman…is…required by society to make herself an erotic object. The purpose of the fashions to which she is enslaved is not to reveal her as an independent individual, but rather to offer her as prey to male desires; thus society is not seeking to further her projects but to thwart them. The skirt is less convenient than trousers, high-heeled shoes impede walking; the least practical of gowns and dress shoes, the most fragile of hats and stockings; are the most elegant; the costume may disguise the body, deform it, or follow its curves; in any case it puts it on display.[82]

Taking this up in 1971 in her book *Woman's Estate,* Juliet Mitchell also discussed the role of fashion, arguing that, although youth cultures and hippies had been influential on fashion and appearance, and the 'ex-Empire (or its remains) has been re-raided to reproduce itself in miniature concentration in Oxford Street…*beauty is all'*. As she put it, 'having been offered all possibilities for self-glorification, having produced the sexually radiant you, the commercial dimension of capitalism can re-use you…to sell the drabber products: cars, washing machines, life insurance'.[83] In this type of analysis, fashion was at the frontline of women's oppression, a powerful weapon deployed to shape women's lives and consciousness within patriarchy and capitalism. It was in response to this that a group of women in Britain organized a demonstration at the Miss World contest at the Royal Albert Hall in London in 1970, throwing smoke bombs, flour and leaflets and stopping the compere, Bob Hope in his tracks.[84] But paradoxically to other feminists – including some who had supported the Miss World protests – fashion was an important, though contentious part of being a woman. For British socialist-feminist historian Sheila Rowbotham, it marked her engagement with alternative cultures that did not originate in Leeds nor belong to her parents' world. As a teenager in the northern British city of Leeds, she described her experimentation with various feminine identities; as she put it: 'how was I to turn into Juliette Greco and Brigitte Bardot and Simone de Beauvoir all rolled into one? Leeds C&A cheaper separates just did not stretch far enough'.[85]

Summarizing the problematic of feminist responses to fashion in her book *Adorned in Dreams* in 1985, Elizabeth Wilson wrote:

> the thesis is that fashion is oppressive, the antithesis that we find it pleasurable; again no synthesis is possible…Either the products of popular culture are the supports of a monolithic male ideology, or they are there to be enjoyed and justified…To care about dress and our appearance is oppressive, this argument goes, and our love of clothes is a form of false consciousness.[86]

Wilson's work in this area from the early 1980s marked a clear attempt to move beyond the anti-fashion stance articulated by some feminists in the early 1970s. Arguing persuasively about the complexity and importance of fashion in forging new identities, she proposed, 'One dimension of fashion is the history of individuals who created this world in which reality and fantasy mingle and become confused, a world in which we go adorned into our dreams'.[87] Looking carefully at the ways in which second-wave feminists dressed, Wilson observed: 'in so far as feminists have dressed differently from other women (and most have not), their style of dress has still borne a close relationship to circulating styles'.[88] Tellingly these styles were circulated in a context of political activism, not just around gender but also in terms of the counter-cultural critique of consumerism, anti-Vietnam war demonstrations, nuclear disarmament, civil rights, student unrest and the left. As Sara Evans argued, 'in Western Europe, Japan, and parts of Latin America, histories of contemporary feminism invariably place its origins in 1968, even if the movements themselves usually emerged a year or two later'.[89] This is a view reiterated by Rowbotham: 'The extraordinary sequence of events during 1968 led my generation to believe we were moving in the same direction as history ... We were convinced that we could make everything anew'.[90] Within this context, and reflecting on her own approach to fashion as part of her everyday existence as a feminist, British-based Lynne Segal was nevertheless aware of unspoken rules and rituals of engagement that had to be traversed to be accepted; this was 'evident in the dress code of the day – loose, practical, relatively unadorned and economical'.[91] But while her friend Liz Heron 'bought some denim dungarees, a red-necked cowboy-style shirt and some brown "desert boots"', Segal commented: 'some of us preferred the round plunging necklines of the Biba T-shirt, or floppy, floral tops, even the broad flowing skirt and occasional mini dress'.[92] Segal was never 'without some subtle form of high heels, lipstick and eyeliner'.[93]

In Rowbotham's account of her life, fashion plays a huge part in the making of her identity as she moved from Leeds to Paris to Oxford to Hackney. Acutely aware of fashion's semantic power (to reference Barthes), she experimented with the revivals and sub-cultural re-appropriations of particular looks at the end of the 1960s and early 1970s. Arriving at St Hilda's College, Oxford, in the early 1960s, she

> unpacked my antique washed Levi's, my shift dress with muddy gold and wine stripes bought in the Bon Marché in Paris, and my black tight dress with its halter-neck collar, which, despite its origins in Leeds Lewis's, had an existential look, and hung them in the wardrobe ... They dangled there in culture shock, waiting for someone with the requisite discrimination to open the door and appreciate the nuances of my carefully assembled beat identity.[94]

That there was a multiplicity of responses to fashion within second-wave feminism and knowingness about its language is obvious when scrutinizing photographs from key events: the demonstration at the Miss World contest at the Albert Hall in 1970, the first Women's Liberation conference in Oxford in 1970, a Women's Liberation March in Hyde Park, London, in 1972 (Figure 5.10)

Figure 5.10 Women's Liberation March, Hyde Park, London, 1972. Getty Images.

or, indeed, the front cover of the British feminist *Spare Rib* magazine in 1973 [https://journalarchives.jisc.ac.uk/britishlibrary/sparerib]. The photograph of the women's liberation march exposes the complexity of feminist interactions with fashion. The clothes worn by this group of five women varied from a patterned woven cape, a long shaggy-fur sleeveless coat with Oxford bags, a plain coloured cape with shortened dress and calf-length boots, a suede midi coat, and black shortened jacket and trousers. These women have not rejected fashion, nor have they adopted a feminist uniform; rather they creatively use the plethora of possible styles. Similarly the cover of *Spare Rib* captures a romanticized, natural look that marks the turn from modernity in the late 1960s towards a softer retro look comprising a hand-knitted cropped jumper that looks back to the 1940s and an unstructured floral skirt and long flowing hair redolent of the Aesthetic Movement at the end of the nineteenth century. Both images point to the Janus-faced nature of fashion as it simultaneously looked backwards (via certain colours, patterns and shapes of garments) and forwards (in terms of the silhouette, pose and overall look), but also beyond Britain and the West. They demonstrate that an engagement with fashion was pervasive even when intertwined with questions of empowerment. Indeed a knitting pattern, available in the United States in the same year, 1973, for a 'Striped Over-Sweater', (Figure 5.11) shows the similarity of fashionable 'looks' in Britain and the States. It also emphasizes how stylistic differences could enable individuals and groups to engage with fashion more selectively than in the past.

In the fifteen or so years from the end of the 1950s to the early 1970s, distinct sartorial changes had taken place, in both London and New York and the countries at large. Whether one wore the very latest designs from current designers, or you were just 'checking in' with fashion for special occasions or for new purchases, or you were wilfully challenging fashion's orthodoxies, it was apparent that 'fashion's rules' had been resolutely broken. Informality and casualness, coupled with changing perceptions of the body, both complex and contradictory, ensured that fashion was increasingly part of everyday lives, and not just of those 'dedicated followers of fashion' – young women. Characteristically multi-coded, and with the capacity for critically questioning, fashion was increasingly available wherever you were. At certain points during this short period, London gained a mythical position as a centre of fashion but, as we have seen, New York was also the springboard for the emergence of alternative fashionable identities particularly towards the end of the 1960s. While a variety of media (newspapers, magazines, film, music, photography and TV) were pivotal in the commodification of fashionable styles and looks, the ways that people engaged with fashion was polyvalent. It was paradoxically compliant and oppositional, reinforcing certain norms and also undermining them. Most importantly it had become yet more routinized and integral to everyday life even in the most modest of ways. In the introduction to *Swinging Sixties,* Breward proposed that 'the old always informed the new', but

Figure 5.11 *Woman's Day* 101, 1973. Pattern 87. Author's Collection.

perhaps what this chapter hints at is their co-existence.[95] We have seen this in archival photographs, in knitting and sewing patterns and in magazine covers. At the same time, important global events that were reported in newspapers and on TV generated different types of understandings and, importantly, visual images of the wider world. Complicated post-colonial geographies confronted both Britain and America, with further anxieties threatening both, as Fordism was revealed as fallible. This wider context presented social challenges that affected the young – but also older – men and women, people from diverse racial and ethnic backgrounds, as well as those questioning dominant gender and sexual values, and not only those in the West. Fashion played a significant part as it also seeped and soaked into people's daily lives. This chapter has highlighted the numerous ways in which the emergence of identity politics (in various manifestations), the ubiquity of the media and the proliferation of the processes and mechanisms of fashion production and dissemination broke the dominance of one particular idea of fashion. In Chapter 6 we will see further implications of this process, including the impact of the shift from an industrial to a post-industrial economy particularly as it affected London and New York as they developed to become known as 'fashion cities'.

Notes

1 Cheryl Buckley and Hilary Fawcett, *Fashioning the Feminine: Representation and Women's Fashion from the Fin de Siècle to the Present* (London: I.B.Tauris, 2002), 122.

2 Carol Dyhouse, *Glamour: Women, History and Feminism* (London and New York: Zed Books, 2011), 143.

3 bell hooks, *Feminist Theory: From Margin to Center* (1984; repr., London: Pluto Press, 2000).

4 Jonathon Green, *All Dressed Up: The Sixties and the Counterculture* (London: Pimlico, 1999), 312.

5 Francis Sheppard, *London: A History* (Oxford: Oxford University Press, 1998), 343.

6 Ibid.

7 White, *London in the Twentieth Century: A City and Its People* (London: Random House, 2008), 342.

8 Ibid., 341–342.

9 Ibid., 343.

10 O'Neill, *London: After a Fashion* (London: Reaktion, 2007), 22.

11 Ibid., 9.

12 Ibid.,130.

13 White, *London,* 342–3.

14 Green, *All Dressed Up,* 86.

15 *Life,* 26 December 1969.

16 Liz Heron (ed.), *Truth, Dare or Promise: Girls Growing up in the 50s* (London: Virago, 1985), 198.

17 Green, *All Dressed Up,* 84.

18 Christopher Breward, David Gilbert and Jenny Lister (eds), *Swinging Sixties: Fashion in London and beyond 1955–1970* (London: V&A Publications, 2006), 80.

19 Ibid., 84.

20 Marjorie Ferguson, *Forever Feminine: Women's Magazines and the Cult of Femininity* (London: Heinemann, 1983), 207.

21 Janice Winship, *Inside Women's Magazines* (London: Pandora Press, 1987), 42–4.

22 'Exhibition – Magnum in Harlem. Magnum Photographers', *Magnum Photos*, available online, http://www.magnumphotos.com/C.aspx?VP3=SearchResult&ALID =2TYRYD938QCL (accessed June 6, 2014).

23 Nontando Jabavu, 'Fashion Show In Harlem', *Picture Post*, 25 March 1950, Issue 12, 42–5.

24 Eve Arnold, 'USA. NYC. Black Is Beautiful. 1968', *Magnum Photos*, available online, https://www.magnumphotos.com/Catalogue/Eve-Arnold/1968/USA-NYC-Black-is-Beautiful-1968-NN112537.html (accessed January 18, 2016). The origin of the term 'Black is Beautiful' is attributed to the Apollo Theatre.

25 *Black Style Now,* Museum of the City of New York, 2006, exhibition text, 21.

26 *Inspiring Beauty: 50 Years of Ebony Fashion Fair,* Video, Chicago History Museum, March 16, 2013–11 May 2014.

27 Joy L. Bivins, 'Style and Substance: Ebony's *Fashion Fair*', in *Inspiring Beauty: 50 Years of Ebony Fashion Fair*, ed. Joy L. Bivins and Rosemary K. Adams (Chicago: Chicago History Museum, 2013), 13–15.

28 Ibid., 18; 23 (note 15).

29 Thank you to Joy Bivins for both of these insights; interviewed by Hazel Clark, Chicago, 28 March 2014.

30 Maxine Leeds Craig, 'Respect and Pleasure: The Meaning of Style in African American Life', in *Inspiring beauty: 50 Years of Ebony Fashion Fair*, ed. Joy L. Bivins and Rosemary K. Adams (Chicago: Chicago History Museum, 2013), 25.

31 *Black Style Now,* 23, which also quotes Richard Avedon, the photographer for the 1965 shoot, as commenting 'For reasons of racial prejudice and the economics of the fashion business … I was never able to photograph her for publication again.'

32 Virginia Heaven, 'The Power of Fashion: Ebony Fashion Fair', in *Inspiring beauty: 50 Years of Ebony Fashion Fair*, ed. Joy L. Bivins and Rosemary K. Adams (Chicago: Chicago History Museum, 2013), 48.

33 'The Story of The Supremes', *Victoria and Albert Museum*, available online, http://www.vam.ac.uk/content/articles/t/the-story-of-the-supremes-from-the-mary-wilson-collection/ (accessed June 10, 2014).

34 Ibid.

35 Mary Wilson, in conversation with Stuart Cosgrove, Director of Nations and Regions for Channel 4, video, Victoria and Albert Museum, May 13, 2008, available online, http://www.vam.ac.uk/content/articles/t/the-story-of-the-supremes-from-the-mary-wilson-collection/ (accessed June 10, 2014).

36 Maxine Powell discussing image with Mary Wilson, video, Victoria and Albert Museum, available online, http://www.vam.ac.uk/content/articles/t/the-story-of-the-supremes-from-the-mary-wilson-collection/ (accessed June 10, 2014).

37 'The Supremes Meet Queen Elizabeth, The Queen Mother: Black History Photo of the Day', *Hufftington Post*, July 2, 2007, available online, http://www.huffingtonpost.com/2013/02/07/the-supremes-meet-queen-elizabeth-queen-mother_n_2638297.html (accessed June 10, 2014).

38   'Ed Sullivan (1902–1974): "Master of Variety"', *The Official Ed Sullivan Site*, available online, http://www.edsullivan.com/about-ed-sullivan/ (accessed June 10, 2014).

39   'The Beatles', *The Official Ed Sullivan Site*, available online, http://www.edsullivan.com/artists/the-beatles (accessed June 10, 2014).

40   Ibid.

41   Ann Oldenburg and Gary Levin, 'Curtain Falls on Dick Clark, but Not on His Legacy', Obituary, *USA Today*, April 18, 2014, available online, http://usatoday30.usatoday.com/life/people/obit/story/2012-04-18/dick-clark-dies-at-82/54390716/1 (accessed June 10, 2014).

42   http://www.youtube.com/watch?v=oxrnr-P8plc (accessed June 10, 2014).

43   Patricia A. Cunningham, 'Dressing for Success', in *Twentieth Century American Fashion*, ed. L. Welters and P.A. Cunningham (New York: Berg, 2005), 194.

44   'Cathy McGowan on "To Tell the Truth" (23 March 1964)', video, available online, http://www.youtube.com/watch?v=PIqZUbk3G9E (accessed June 10, 2014).

45   Mary Quant, *Quant By Quant* (London: Pan Books, 1966), 78.

46   'Brash New Breed of British Designers', *Life,* October 18, 1963, 79, available online, http://books.google.com/books?id=XlIEAAAAMBAJ&printsec=frontcover&source=gbs_ge_summary_r&cad=0#v=onepage&q&f=false (accessed June 11, 2014).

47   'British – and Dizzier Than Ever', *Life,* September 17, 1965, 65, available online, http://books.google.com/books?id=7FIEAAAAMBAJ&printsec=frontcover&source=gbs_ge_summary_r&cad=0#v=onepage&q&f=false (accessed June 11, 2014).

48   David Gilbert, 'Out of London', in *Swinging Sixties: Fashion in London and Beyond 1955–1970*, ed. Christopher Breward, David Gilbert and Jenny Lister (London: V&A Publications, 2006), 109.

49   Amy Larocca, 'The House of Mod', *New York Magazine*, available online, http://nymag.com/nymetro/shopping/fashion/spring03/n_8337/index1.html (accessed January 7, 2015). See also 'Women in New York Fashion: A Research Agenda', *Geraldine Stutz Fellowship*, available online, http://adht.parsons.edu/GeraldineStutz/ (accessed January 7, 2016).

50   Quant, *Quant By Quant,* 119–20.

51   Ibid., 113.

52   Jenny Lister, 'Kaleidesope: Fashion in Sixties London', in *Swinging Sixties: Fashion in London and Beyond 1955–1970*, ed. Christopher Breward, David Gilbert and Jenny Lister (London: V&A Publications, 2006), 40.

53   Barbara Hulanicki, *From A to Biba* (London: Hutchinson & Co, 1983), 71–2.

54   Ibid., 74.

55   Anthony Scaduto, *Bob Dylan* (1972; repr., New York: Helter Skelter Publishing, 2001), 160.

56   Paul O'Neill, 'The Only Rebellion Around: But the Shabby Beats Bungle the Job in Arguing, Sulking and Bad Poetry', *Life*, 30 November 1959, 117, available online, http://books.google.com/books?id=T1UEAAAAMBAJ&pg=PA114&dq=Beat+generation&hl=en&sa=X&ei=jUWbU8_kCoikyATTgYLgBg&ved=0CB4Q6AEwAA#v=onepage&q=Beat%20generation&f=false (accessed June 13, 2014).

57   Ibid., 115.

58 Elizabeth Wilson and Lou Taylor, *Through the Looking Glass: A History of Dress from 1860 to the Present Day* (London: BBC Books, 1989), 161.

59 Ibid., 161.

60 '… [I]n the beginning of the new men's wear fashion evolution the homosexual played a very important part … the homosexual in the creative community, that is. They were the first to snap up new ideas and give them exposure', in Robert J. Lukey, 'Homosexuality in Menswear', *Menswear*, February 1970, 73 quoted in Shaun Cole, *Now We Don Our Gay Apparel: Gay Men's Dress in the Twentieth Century* (Oxford and New York: Berg, 2000), 74 (note 22).

61 'Stonewall Riots: The Beginning of the LGBT Movement', *The Leadership Conference*, June 22, 2009, available online, http://www.civilrights.org/archives/2009/06/449-stonewall.html (accessed June 16, 2014).

62 Shaun Cole, *Now We Don Our Gay Apparel: Gay Men's Dress in the Twentieth Century* (Oxford and New York: Berg, 2000), 60.

63 Martin Duberman, *Stonewall* (New York: Dutton, 1993), 111.

64 Cole, *Now We Don Our Gay Apparel,* 65.

65 Dick Hebdidge, 'The Meaning of Mod', in *Resistance through Rituals: Youth Subcultures in Post-War Britain*, ed. Stuart Hall and Tony Jefferson (New York: Routledge, 2005), 87, quoting a remark made by musician George Melly in 1972.

66 Richard Barnes, *Mods!* (London: Plexus, 1979), 10.

67 Cole, *Now We Don Our Gay Apparel,* 74 (note 22).

68 O'Neill, *London,* 131.

69 William J. Helmer, 'New York's "Middle Class" Homosexuals', *Harpers*, March 1963, 85–92, quoted in Cole, *Now We Don Our Gay Apparel*, 76 (note 43).

70 Paul Welch, 'Homosexuality in America', *Life*, June 1964, 66–74.

71 R. Lukey, quoted in Cole, *Now We Don Our Gay Apparel*, 77 (note 41).

72 Richard Schikel, 'Shock of Seeing a Hidden World', *Life*, November 1, 1968, 34–38.

73 Duberman, *Stonewall*, 189–90.

74 Cole, *Now We Don Our Gay Apparel*, 84.

75 Ibid., 94.

76 Karen Everett, *Framing Lesbian Fashion*, documentary, 1992.

77 Author Laura Frederico in conversation with author and therapist JoAnn Loulan. Ibid.

78 Cole, *Now We Don Our Gay Apparel*, 89 (note 37), referring to an article in the American trade magazine *Menswear* in 1970, and an editorial *Style* in Britain in 1974.

79 *Black Style Now*, 20.

80 See Angela McRobbie, 'Second-Hand Dresses and the Role of the Ragmarket', in *Zoot Suits and Second-Hand Dresses* (London: MacMillan, 1989), 23–49. For wider discussion of second hand fashion, see Alexandra Palmer and Hazel Clark (eds), *Old Clothes, New Looks: Second Hand Fashion* (Oxford and New York: Berg, 2005).

81 Betty Friedan, *The Feminine Mystique* (New York: Norton, 1963); Kaye Millet, *Sexual Politics* (London: Abacus, 1972); Juliet Mitchell, *Woman's Estate* (London: Penguin, 1971); Germaine Greer, *The Female Eunuch* (London: Paladin, 1971); Simone de Beauvoir, *The Second Sex* (1949; repr., London: Penguin, 1981).

82 de Beauvoir, *The Second Sex*, 543.

83 Mitchell, *Woman's Estate,* 141.

84 Sheila Rowbotham, Lynne Segal and Hilary Wainwright, *Beyond the Fragments: Feminism and the Making of Socialism* (London: Merlin Press, 1979), 158.

85 Heron, *Truth,* 208.

86 Elizabeth Wilson, *Adorned in Dreams: Fashion and Modernity* (London: Virago, 1985), 232.

87 Ibid., 228.

88 Ibid., 240.

89 Sara M. Evans, 'Sons, Daughters, and Patriarchy: Gender and the 1968 Generation', *The American Historical Review* 114, no. 2 (2009): 331.

90 Sheila Rowbotham, *Promise of a Dream: Remembering the Sixties* (London: Penguin, 2000), 191.

91 Lynne Segal, *Making Trouble* (London: Serpent's Tail, Profile Books, 2007), 80.

92 Ibid.

93 Ibid.

94 Rowbotham, *Promise of a Dream*, 43.

95 Breward, Gilbert and Lister, *Swinging Sixties,* 15.

6
GOING OUT

Introduction

Marked political similarities between Britain and America characterized the late 1970s and 1980s. Britain's Conservative and first female Prime Minister Margaret Thatcher and US President and former movie star Ronald Reagan were each distinctive personalities who governed two nations with deepening social and economic divisions. The election of Reagan to his first term in 1980 (a year after Margaret Thatcher who had two further election wins in 1983 and 1987) marked the beginning of a predominantly conservative period and a 'right turn' in US and British culture, although counter-cultural stances continued to permeate fashion and popular culture, especially music. The global oil and Iran hostage crises of 1979, the US invasion of Iran and the subsequent war in 1980, Britain's invasion of the Falkland Isles in 1982 and Prime Minister Thatcher's confrontations with the trade union movement (in particular the National Union of Mineworkers), followed by Reagan's election to a second term in 1984, reinforced a world view of both nations in an imperialist, authoritarian mode. Increasingly important as fashion cities, the development of a post-industrial economy in both London and New York brought an influx of people into the city highlighting extreme contrasts. Both cities experienced social and urban decline that brought a number of inner city disturbances and riots. At the same time, the last quarter of the twentieth century saw both experience urban renewal that gathered pace with the potential to bring huge financial and cultural benefits if not social ones.

London experienced renewed cultural and artistic vitality that seemed to offer a continuation of 'the boom business of fashion, design, and music, together with photography, modelling, magazine publishing and advertising' of the 1960s.[1] Yet alongside this, historians observed that its manufacturing base was disintegrating as it shifted from 'an industrial to a post-industrial economy based on financial, business and creative services'.[2] Whereas in the mid-1960s, London was a major centre of light industrial production with a third of its workforce engaged in this, by 1981 one in ten of its workforce was involved in financial services and by the end of the century, it was one in five.[3] Alongside the demise of London as a manufacturing centre, it became subject to a 'sequence of middle-class colonisation' that moved 'north across Camden, Islington and western Haringey; east into Hackney, Stoke Newington and Docklands; west into Hammersmith and Fulham, North Kensington and Ealing; north-west in Kilburn; south into Vauxhall, Bermondsey, Clapham and the whole river strip, and back into inner areas of the East End adjacent to the City of London'.[4] As the social class composition of inner London became more mixed than it was thirty years ago, it was also the case that by the end of the twentieth century, economic segregation had risen 'between wealthy home-owners in one street and low-income council tenants a few streets away'.[5]

In parallel, by 1975 New York City was bankrupt and dangerous; apparently neglected by the federal administration that was echoed in the now notorious *New York Daily News* headline of 30 October 1975, quoting President Gerald Ford: 'Ford to City: Drop Dead'. As in London, gentrification came to New York with the economic boom of the 1980s, but it was from the mid-1990s and with 'renewed intensity' that it swept across Manhattan, Morningside Heights, Lower East Side, Chelsea, Williamsburg, Fort Greene, Park Slope and Central Harlem.[6] Central Harlem, for example, received an influx of middle-class residents throughout the 1970s and 1980s, but 'the changes during the late 1990s and 2000s are different', as incomers sought manageable commutes: Midtown in 15 minutes, Wall St in 30 minutes and La Guardia only 20 minutes away in a cab.[7] The fashion geographies of both cities developed in relation to these processes of social change and gentrification – with newly regenerated areas and districts such as Covent Garden and Hoxton in London, and in New York, SoHo and the East Village in Manhattan and later Williamsburg in Brooklyn. In London, these became part of the everyday shopping terrain as they extended established shopping routes and streets such as Oxford St/Regent St/Bond St, Kings Road/Kensington High St/Knightsbridge. In New York, artists occupied lofts and semi-derelict buildings, prior to gentrification and fashion consumption taking hold.

In this changing context, fashion was increasingly a means of 'producing' an individual identity, not only for those in the public eye – designers, musicians and other performers – but also for ordinary people. The media provided the role models, consumption the means, and going out, be it to clubs or simply appearing on the streets, provided the onus for fashion to make an imprint on everyday life. In the last decades of the twentieth century, as Church Gibson noted, the fashion-centred consumption of goods was not only conspicuous (in Veblen's terms) but also continuous as celebrity culture 'seeped into every conceivable nook and cranny within the public sphere'.[8] At the same time, there was a growing awareness of 'the designer, the brand, the characteristic style and the relevant logo' that led to a consumer – men and women, young and old, wealthy and impoverished – that was more knowing and literate about design.[9] In the US 'images from popular music figures sometimes cut across the conservative grain', fuelling forms and venues for music and creativity, which encompassed extremes of personal appearance.[10] With some irony – given the advent of punk rock in the 1970s – London was also home to the epitome of the mundane in the form of the Sloane Ranger. While simultaneously parodying and celebrating class distinctions, Sloane Rangers reached their zenith with the cult of Princess Diana; a royal who was at once extraordinary and ordinary both in her mode of being and in her interest in fashion.[11]

From the late 1970s, fashion had become a greater part of everyday life for previously disparate ages, classes, races and neighbourhoods in New York City. Dressing for going out had its own fashion codes, often depending on what sort of music and dancing was involved. The blend of fact and fiction, ordinary and extraordinary dressing and performance, was exemplified in the 1977 dance movie *Saturday Night Fever*. Set in Bay Ridge, Brooklyn, and starring John Travolta as its hero Tony Manero, an immature young man who was transported from his mundane everyday existence by his weekend visits to a local discothèque, where dressed in a tight fitting white suit and performing fast moves, he became the disco king. Inevitably the movie heightened the reality. In fact, the 'Brooklyn nightclubs were a neighbourhood thing, a place among friends. You came with your tribe but you were only in competition with yourself: how well you could dress, how smooth you could dance, how sweet you could talk. Everybody knew each other. Anything outside the neighbourhood wasn't Brooklyn anyhow, not to the Italians'.[12] *Saturday Night Fever* was a huge commercial success. It helped to popularize disco music around the world in addition to its associated fashion and sexually liberated lifestyle, before the early 1980s AIDS epidemic.[13] It provided a New York parallel to glam rock (or glitter rock) that developed in the United Kingdom in the early 1970s. Characterized by androgynous and sometimes camp styles, male performers wore extravagant and colourful costumes, platform soled shoes, make-up and glitter, enabled by new perspectives on gender roles and appearance. British musicians and bands included David Bowie, T.Rex, Sweet, Roxy Music, Gary Glitter and Queen. Formed in London in 1970, Queen became one of the most successful stadium rock bands in the world, with an enormous following in the United Kingdom and the United States. David Bowie was a pioneer of the edgier glam style; by taking on alter egos such as Ziggy Stardust and Aladdin Sane, he pushed the boundaries of gender roles and dressing on stage, serving as a model for his followers to do the same when they dressed to go out.

Music continued to play a huge role in bringing the diversity of fashion into everyday lives, especially for those under thirty-five. In Britain, from the mid-1970s through the 1980s, punk (The Clash, Sex Pistols, The Jam), Ska (UB40, The Specials and Madness), the New Romantics (Adam and the Ants, Duran, Duran, Boy George and Culture Club), New Wave (The Police, Eurythmics, Elvis Costello) and individuals such as Bowie all articulated a plethora of identities that could be subversive either in their ordinariness or in their extraordinariness.

Stateside, the eponymous New York Dolls, Lou Reed and the Velvet Underground, developed more edgy and street-style looks, which resonated with their less populist sounds, and paved the way for glam metal, the New Romantic style, and especially Punk. New York's Punk music scene began in the mid-1970s (although never achieving the sartorial impact it had in London), followed by post-punk New Wave. Its geographical centre was downtown, in clubs such as CBGBs on the Bowery or Max's Kansas City on Park Avenue South. While this was one of the worst social, economic and crime-ridden times in the city's history, it was also one of its most creative in music, fashion and personal style.[14]

Clubbing

Both uptown and downtown, New York clubs were *the* places to go out and show off, with different neighbourhoods attracting different crowds. From when it opened in 1978 to its closure in 1983, the Mudd Club in TriBeCa was a major venue for the downtown underground music scene, and for some extraordinary attire (Figure 6.1). It provided a cultural and geographic counterpoint to Steve Rubell and Ian Schrager's glitzy Studio 54 on West 54th Street, whose famous clientele included Andy Warhol and the fashion designer Diane von Furstenberg. At the Mudd Club's upstairs gallery, Keith Haring curated catwalk shows of the work of young fashion designers such as New York–based Anna Sui or London-based Jasper Conran. Figure 6.2 shows an outfit designed by Anna Sui worn at the club, which bears a striking resemblance to Vivienne Westwood and Malcolm McClaren's first 'Pirates' collection for Autumn/Winter 1982/3.[15] Students were important to the existence of the Mudd Club. Founder Steve Mass not only showed their work but made a point of circulating invitations to the club's events to students studying at Parsons and at the FIT (Fashion Institute of Technology). The club even issued a 'Mudd Club College of Deviant Checks' ID.[16] The fashion, performance of style and featured cult musicians, including Lou Reed, Debbie Harry, David Byrne, Nico, and Lydia Lunch, caused *People* magazine to liken the club to the decadence of Berlin cabaret in the 1920s.[17] Different styles of music and appearance were morphing and blending. After the Punk sessions had ended, Hip Hop DJ Afrika Bambatta started his set, and the Punk kids stayed around to listen (Figure 6.3).[18] As Carlo McCormick wrote in *Paper* magazine: 'All modes of cultural production were in the same room sharing the same space'.[19] There was an apparently seamless connection between cultural producers and their audiences, with everyone being a participant. Key downtown geographies were also changing, with young artists and cultural producers occupying territories where rents were cheap and crime was rife, first in SoHo in the late 1970s and then the Bowery and East Village in the 1980s.

During the late 1970s, New York had experienced an unprecedented migration of young people, who followed the avant-garde that started to populate downtown (south of Fourteenth Street) after the Second World War.[20] Music and dancing were points of reference and communication, with different genres developing and connecting members of different style groups. Clubs were the spaces where encounters took place and served as invisible boundaries of a hip downtown universe, described by participant and reporter Chi Chi Valenti as spanning 'from the Mudd Club to the south, Danceteria to the north, the Pyramid Club to the east, and the desolate stretches of the after hours Wild West'.[21] There, dressing up was elevated to an art form extraordinaire, which the proponents employed to make and remake themselves, rather than to reflect statement fashion. These looks were not happenstance: some required weeks of planning for a single event and could involve the bricolage of everyday items that provided the palette for an eclectic performative style. Materials might come from the bargain stores on Fourteenth Street, from the industrial suppliers on Canal Street, or from a dumpster, brought together with assistance from a sewing machine or a hot-glue-gun. 'Inspiration was everywhere, from aluminum-foil baked-potato wrappers to Lord Byron's waistcoat'.[22] Chi Chi Valenti comments how new arrivals to the city were inspired by this Do-It-Yourself (DIY) ethos to form 'their own tribes of like-minded dressers, who in turn started magazines, club nights, and bands. Low-budgets and happy accidents fashioned The New – such as the now iconic Punk portrait of Debbie Harry, draped in a zebra-print pillowcase straight out of a Bowery garbage can'.[23] Arguably, this was a time when self-made statements had meanings to those in the clique, before stylists reduced them to commodities, and 'personal invention had become a mere marketing device' in the 1990s.[24]

In London, a similar DIY aesthetic prevailed and was at its creative zenith in the club scene. Specialist club nights offered opportunities for dressing up in the company of a like-minded set. Louise's, a lesbian club on Poland Street, run by the eponymous Frenchwoman who played host to her friend the artist Francis Bacon, was probably the first to draw attention. There, Punks could be found inventing themselves in the seminal summer of '76, in styles which were far from homogeneous.[25] Yet within a few months the media had reduced this sartorial anarchy to a stereotype. What Polhemus describes as 'Media Punk' was transmitted by newspapers, magazines and television, throughout Britain and, by 1978, had reached the United States.[26] But it was not only Punks that gathered at Louise's; her clientele included the self-proclaimed Posers, such as Steve Strange and George O'Dowd, who would soon become known as the Blitz Kids (after the Blitz Club in Covent Garden that they frequented after Louise's closed in 1978) or the New Romantics. Other venues, such as Billy's, and the Club for Heroes, were small, had selective groups of patrons and were known for their own niche styles, which filtered into the mainstream through the media and

Figure 6.1 'New Wave Hits Party Goers at Mudd Club, 1980'. Stephen Mass.

Figure 6.2 Outfit designed by Anna Sui for a fashion show at the Mudd Club, c. 1982. Stephen Mass.

Figure 6.3 New York Punk. Cynthia MacAdams, 1987. New York Public Library.

music. (One popular figure was George O'Dowd, the androgynous Boy George of the band Culture Club.) Stevie Stewart, of the fashion designer duo Body Map, noted how 'each group of people, whether they were fashion designers, musicians or dancers, filmmakers, living together and going out together had a passion for creating something new that was almost infectious'.[27] Later, new and larger venues opened, such as the Camden Palace, and one-off warehouse parties began. They perpetuated the creative link between music, clubs and fashion, bringing it to a larger audience (and foreshadowing rave culture).

Profiles of young clubbers reveal their investment in fashion as personal style and also as a source of income. Jane, who lived in an attic flat in North Islington, made patchwork quilts and cushions, which she sold at Camden Market. She used to go out to the Camden Palace, but had started to find the music boring, preferring the Hippodrome in Leicester Square after going to a wine bar with friends on Tuesdays, but not on weekends when it was crowded with tourists. Jane was very conscious of her own style and how to achieve it:

Personally, I like to wear my own clothes. I pinch ideas from magazines, make up my own patterns, it's quite simple really. Joseph is my favourite if I'm buying. I could spend hours trying things on in Pour la Maison. I find muted subtle colours suit me best, I dislike shocking pinks, fluorescent and shiny things. Cotton is very nice to work with, comfortable to wear. I steer clear of satin, lace, rubber, that sort of thing. I go for plain shoes too, flat soled Ravels, Russell and Bromley, they're my favourites, and jewellery – usually inexpensive junk, old silver, large earrings.[28]

Describing Leigh Bowery, infamous clubber and fashion designer, O'Neill observed that the slippery extraordinariness of the night-time club scene depended on the 'feasibility of the day … For Bowery, his East End days were the unremarkable and unseen flipside to the fantastic notoriety of his West End Nights'.[29] Leigh, 'a seasoned club going professional' who spent his days designing clothes and his nights 'out on the town', reinforced the importance of developing an individual and often spectacular look. He is described as always wearing his own, distinctly extravagant, designs: 'currently a collection of exaggerated shouldered suits, cut above the knee in checked worsted with spots and stripes, polka dotted silk scarves and matching stencilled face and neck, shorts and knee length socks, topped off with blue rinse granny wigs'.[30] The music and fashion scenes were intertwined with the growing prominence of London's art schools that became the springboard for a new wave of highly creative artists and fashion designers. Many of the club goers were students, including those studying fashion at St Martin's School of Art on the Charing Cross Road and at the Royal College of Art in South Kensington, both of which taught essential skills while encouraging creativity and individuality. The proximity of some of the most fashionable clubs to St Martin's School of Art made them a social extension of the college and an outlet for the greater extremes of creativity. John Galliano is quoted as recalling how 'Thursday and Friday at St Martin's, the college was almost deserted. Everybody was at home working on their costumes for the weekend'.[31] As fashion designer Georgina Godley remembered, 'Young London was all about taking risks and creating something out of nothing through passion and ambition'.[32] Key to this was a burgeoning style press, particularly *i-D*, *Blitz* and *The Face* that eagerly reported music, fashion collections and clubs. The 'Scarlett Dress', a hobble style with 3/4-length sleeves and a low back, originally designed and made by Juliana Sissons as a birthday present for Scarlett Cannon, club host of the Cha Cha's night at Heaven night club, Charing Cross Road, was widely photographed and featured in numerous magazines throughout the 1980s. It was worn to celebrate Scarlett's twenty-first birthday at two parties: first at the Slum it in Style club night at the Camden Palace hosted by Steve Strange and Rusty Egan, and then at a private party held for her at Bolts night club in North London. In 1982, Juliana Sissons had her own fashion outlet, Call me Madam, situated in Heaven nightclub, which opened every Thursday evening and was frequented by 'club kids', who included socialites, artists, dancers, fire-eaters and drag queens.

The shop was a meeting place and a private party room for friends to hang out. It was described as looking 'like a glorious dressing up box, with vintage glass cabinets displaying tiaras, false eyelashes and evening gloves. The rails were filled with one off items from elaborate "glamour" dresses and corsets to accessories such as black feather boas and pink plastic rain caps'.[33] Extreme and provocative, these ensembles of clothes had a wider impact on everyday fashionable 'looks'. Indeed in February 1985, under the headline 'Fine and Dandy', the British mass-market newspaper *The Daily Mirror* reported on 'the chintzy look that's sparked off a romantic revival'.[34] Described as 'Lording it up in silk', 'Stand and Deliver' and 'Belle in Brocade' (Figure 6. 4), three ensembles perfectly captured the widespread popularization of this complex eclecticism, in this instance with a 'New Romantic' feature. Comprising cream lace, red and pink brocade and chintz trousers sourced from lower-end market stores such as Hobbs and Warehouse, as well as Liberty & Co, these marked the assimilation of retro and heritage themes into everyday life. Discussing the use of chintz in Scott Crolla's summer collection from 1985, O'Neill proposed that 'this kind of visual quotation is very much emblematic of how the past was integrated into the present in the 1980s', but he also argued, the chintz was redolent of a different London.[35] Not only a garden village, but also at the centre of a post-colonial, post-Empire network of exchange.

Tales of two cities

London

Students and young people in search of new and individual fashion looks, but with limited budgets, patronized second-hand shops, army-surplus stores, jumble sales and rag markets. Christopher Breward writes of the range and diversity of used clothing he witnessed when he moved to London as a student in the mid-1980s, available from the 'down-at-heels stalls in Bell Street, Brick Lane, Greenwich and Portobello, or sourced among the organized chaos of such canny importers of Americana as Flip and American retro in Covent Garden'.[36] These retail venues were in stark contrast to the smart fashion stores opening in the West End, on South Molton Street and St Christopher's Place and 'the corporate blandness of the emerging "label" culture'.[37] Some of the merchandise was ex-military, such as functional Army greatcoats. The range of menswear alone was vast and included: 'rubbed Levi's 501 jeans worn with bulky turn ups', collarless 'granddad' shirts, Jazz-style silk ties, 'ox-blood Doc Marten shoes, thick woollen hiking socks, battered leather satchels, peaked flannel caps and lapel-pins from the communist Eastern bloc'.[38] Street markets, including the popular weekend Camden Lock market, were the source of unique used items,

Figure 6.4 Fine and Dandy, 'Old Style … New fashion', February 1985. Mirrorpix.

and venues for creative people to sell their work. As McRobbie noted, 'Most of the youth subcultures of the post-war period have relied on second-hand clothes found in jumble sales and ragmarkets as the raw material for the creation of style'.[39] While clubs were the quintessential place for extremes of dressing among young people, what was worn on the city streets and in certain retail places and spaces must not be under estimated. While the street was a place for hanging out, 'the place you go when you aren't old enough or rich enough to get in somewhere'[40] according to Ted Polhemus, retail venues were not just for shopping but also places to be seen and could be selected according to personal style, be it actual or aspirational.

Eclecticism and retrospection provided a strong visual theme that impacted upon high street fashions. This continued to be influenced by Hollywood movies – the American actress Diane Keaton in the 1977 Woody Allen film *Annie Hall* springs to mind, sporting a casual, layered masculine look that entered the mass market. Fashion 'looks' were becoming more diverse, and varied, as more choices were available. From late 1973 to 1975 when it closed, Barbara Hulanicki's 'Big Biba' in the former Derry and Toms department store building on Kensington High Street was *the* place to go. London residents and out-of-towners went there to shop, browse or merely to pose in the Roof Garden. Biba continued to exert an influence on UK fashion chains during the late 1970s and 1980s, with companies such as Chelsea Girl, Warehouse, Miss Selfridge and Wallis responding to its tendency towards 'strong dark clothes in plain fabrics and bold shapes, which encourage girls to look different and interesting'.[41] Chelsea Girl, which began in 1965 and developed from Lewis Separates, was the place where cheaper fashionable clothes could be found in the 1970s and 1980s. Influenced by Biba, but more stylistically varied and less ostensibly 'retro', it offered accessible glamour across British cities with its highly distinctive shop fronts combining the red heart symbol and post-modern/high-tech fascia, darkened interiors and stylish mix of velvet midi skirts, floral printed shirts, crocheted tops and faux suede culottes (Figure 6.5).[42] While mothers headed for the big chains, such as C&A and Marks & Spencer, this growing group of boutique chains drew in their daughters. In these, the retro decadence of 'Biba' was redefined and updated; its suggestive edges smoothed off, and thus more able to infiltrate the everyday lives of those in their teens and twenties.

Second-hand clothes remained a vital source of this simultaneous process of looking back and looking forward. As McRobbie noted of Camden Lock market, 'Young people go there to see and be seen if for any other reason than that fashion and style invariably look better worn than they do on the rails or in the shop windows'.[43] Yet she also observed how 'The unemployed and semi-employed have been cast adrift, and for many young men and women their attention has turned inwards towards the body. Wild peacock punk dressing of the type seen on the streets in the early 1980s signified this body politics, this making strange through an excessive marvellous, a "quotidien marvellous".'[44] Quoting Angela Carter writing in *New Society* in 1983, McRobbie highlights the irony of rich girls who 'swan about in rancid long johns with ribbons in their hair, when the greatest influence on working class girls would appear to be Princess Di'.[45] After her marriage in 1981 to Prince Charles, the British heir to the throne,

Figure 6.5 Chelsea Girl shop front, London, late 1970s. River Island.

Princess Diana served as a popular fashion icon in Britain throughout the 1980s. Her dress code and items of clothing were copied endlessly. She was capitalized on as a fashion role model for ordinary women, via manuals such as *The Princess of Wales Fashion Handbook* (1984).[46] According to one source, '1981 was declared, thanks to Di, the Year of the Hat'.[47] Her hat styles were reproduced in British high street chain stores such as BHS (known as British Home Stores until 1986, and after 2005), and no doubt featured in many wedding photos of the period. A version of the blouse she wore for her engagement photographs sold in the popular chain store Marks and Spencer for £9.99. The Senior Selector for the company's Ladies Blouse Department recalled how 'As soon as Diana did that engagement picture, our fastest-selling style was a side-tying Lady Di blouse'.[48] Subsequently Marks and Spencer, which had built its success on selling good-quality and well-designed clothes to low income customers across a broad demographic, began to upgrade its somewhat dowdy image in response to competition.

From the 1970s, its design department was led by art school-educated Brian Godbold whose brief was to update and reform it. Twenty years earlier the company had followed and interpreted fashion for a mass market that included the whole family.[49] Then it had a strong reputation for regular standard items that were of good value and quality, and, combined with synthetic fabrics such as Acrilan, Orlon and polyester, these helped Marks and Spencer to maintain its appeal as these were hardwearing and practical. By the early 1970s with a resurgence of interest in natural materials, Marks and Spencer's challenge was to upgrade its fashion content without being too extreme, develop its natural but washable fabrics, and to hold on to its established market for quality staples. As Figure 6.6 shows, the design department did respond to the latest fashions but it combined this with classic looks; in this case, Yves St Laurent's masculinized styles from the late 1960s and early 1970s, and Burberry. The outcome, as this photograph shows and as Rachel Worth explained, 'was that the company marketed watered-down versions that were less attractive precisely because they

Figure. 6.6 Marks and Spencer latest coats, London, 1970. Mirrorpix.

lacked the flair of the original'.[50] However, by the end of the decade, Marks and Spencer had reappraised its image and its design perspective, and through the 1990s it employed consultants such as designers Paul Smith, Betty Jackson and Bruce Oldfield, the latter having designed clothes for Princess Diana.[51] Reflecting on Marks and Spencer's attempt to negotiate fashionable styles from high end to everyday, we see an effective illustration of the ongoing embeddedness of fashion in ordinary lives. This did not just apply to women. In both countries, men were much more subject to fashion's variation and change and were dressing less formally in everyday life. A group of men leaving the Irish bar, McSorley's Old Ale House on E 7th Street, in New York's East Village in 1978, are dressed in the casual styles then fashionable (Figure 6.7). What is most noticeable are

Figure 6.7 Men leaving McSorley's Old Ale House, East Village, 1978. Museum of the City of New York.

their waist-length jackets, worn not with a shirt and tie, but with a crew necked or turtle (polo) necked sweater. In fact, the appearance of the man in front brings to mind relaxed but distinctly masculine style of *Shaft,* mentioned in the previous chapter. The hems of the trousers worn by the men in the photograph have width and a slight flare and no cuffs (turn ups). Their hairstyles are neat but more natural looking and longer than had been typical until the previous decade. Such developments in style and attention to fashion were reflected in changes in retail both in the United States and in Britain.

The identification of new groups of fashion-conscious consumers fuelled the emergence of new companies on the British high street and as mail order businesses with a brief to produce fashionable clothes specifically for women over twenty-five, who had been to some extent neglected by retailers in favour of the youth market.[52] Under the leadership of chief executive George Davies, Next developed a new retail store concept featuring in-house designed and branded items. It totally revitalized Hepworth's the nationwide men's wear chain that had acquired the women's wear retailers Kendalls in 1981. In February 1982, seven Next shops had opened in former Kendalls locations and by the end of the year more than seventy stores had been converted, with a turnover of over 82 million GBP, two and a half times of what was anticipated. Next for Men stores followed, numbering 130 by the end of 1985, then department stores, offering women's, men's and home ware under the Next Interiors label. By overseeing its own production, Next PLC offered the consumer quality designs at affordable prices, in stylish retail environments, as well as the hugely successful Next Directory mail order catalogue launched in 1988.[53] Other high street names soon followed suit. Burton's men's tailors launched their Principles women's range nationwide and Habitat Mothercare revamped the Richard Shops chain.[54] Demographics was an important factor in these new retail strategies; in 1985, it was estimated that the 25–45-year-olds would increase to constitute 28 per cent of the British population by the end of the century, while 16–24-year-olds would drop from 15–13 per cent.[55] For retailers, strategy was all, evidenced by the fact that when British designer Jeff Banks opened the first American branch of his Warehouse fashion retail brand in 1984, he eschewed a floor at Macy's in Manhattan, in favour of a more 'ordinary' shopping mall in Paramus, New Jersey.[56]

This demographic shift was also marked by the emergence of new women's magazines in both the United States and Britain. Launched in Britain and targeting the 25–35 age group were *Elle* (1985) and *Marie Claire* (1988). Both were aimed at women in ABC 1 social classes: educated and independent as interested in politics as relationships, but crucially with disposable income. With a content target of 40 per cent fashion and 'focusing on how people live their lives', these two magazines depicted women as informed and knowledgeable consumers of fashion who dressed with style and intelligence and bought from a range of retailers.[57] The success of these two titles prompted a broader re-thinking that influenced established titles such as *Cosmopolitan, Honey* and *Woman*, led to new launches such as *Options*, and contributed to changes to the wider magazine market that saw new categories of magazine emerge. Focusing on style, fashion, music and contemporary consumer cultures, as well as male and female readers, these titles, including *The Face* (1980), *Arena* (1986) and *i-D* (1986), articulated new ideas of masculinity that were at odds with the older generation. Typically young, these men were potential consumers not only of music and sport but also of cosmetics, stylish goods for the home and fashion. Notably, this plethora of magazines brought fashion knowledge into a variety of everyday lives as they championed lifestyle and choice, rather than prescribed roles and rules.

Importantly for individuals, what distinguished their own fashion identity or that of their reference group was not necessarily the specific items they were wearing, but how they put them together to form a 'look'. Be it from a high street retailer like Next, or a more expensive designer brand, a fashion look could be an attempt to reflect an individual's social role and status or an intentional masquerade. Responding in some ways to earlier sub-cultural groups and signalling the symbiotic relationship that existed between sport, music (particularly Northern Soul) and fashion in everyday lives were the Casuals. These were 'hard-core members of the "unofficial" football supporters' clubs',[58] formed in the late 1970s, who favoured mainstream and, often expensive, branded fashion items that offered a smart though under-stated masculinity. In London, Casuals sported a 'more luxurious' image than in the Northern cities of Liverpool and Manchester, preferring 'an incongruous mixture of Nike trainers, frayed Lois jeans, Lacoste shirts worn with cashmere scarves and sweaters, often with the Pringle label, and long Burberry raincoats'.[59] In Britain, the Casuals boosted the popularity of brand-name sportswear, and by 1985 had moved on to patronize top menswear shops in London's West End such as Browns, Giorgio Armani, Ebony and Woodhouse.[60] While their smart clothes could belie violent and anti-social behaviour, often including their wearing stolen items, the Casuals had a substantial influence on British menswear (which Polhemus goes as far as to call a long overdue 'revolution'). Their sharp style and attention to detail, which also characterized the early Mods, paved the way for the huge success in the 1990s of brands such as Chipie, Chevignon, Diesel, and Soviet.[61] They have also been situated as part of the 'good taste revolution' happening on the British high street via lifestyle brands such as Next or Habitat. Importantly neither the Casuals nor this expanding market were comprised solely of the young; as with Next and Habitat, the consumers of these distinctive and relatively expensive branded goods were in their later twenties and early thirties. In this way, these designer fashion brands were a response to the *embourgeoisement* of 1980s Britain, when 'many people want to be on a ladder upward at a time when the economic structure of society is directing them downwards'.[62]

The media continued to provide points of fashion reference and potential sartorial role modes, often far from the reality of the everyday life of most people in Britain, or in the United States. In the US soap opera *Dallas,* oil-magnate real estate – for both the office and the home – was equally matched by the glamorous, power-playing female leads including Linda Gray as Sue Ellen Ewing. Showing in British homes from its start in 1978 until 1991, wide-shouldered, sharply tailored suits and glittering evening wear with nipped in waists and sculpted bodices were quickly adapted in cheaper polyester fabrics by High Street stores such as Richards and Principles. As Carol Dyhouse put it, 'glamour was cranked up and camped up ... the word glamour so widely used that it came to dominate the discourse of magazines aimed at women, whatever their class, age or colour'.[63] Recycled in magazines such as *Marie Claire* as well as lower-market, *Heat*, these epitomized the 'overiding pre-occupation with glamour and sex' that was dependent upon a spectacularized female body, distinct from that of the 1960s.[64]

Catering for a distinctive middle-aged and older market was the British fashion company Ellis & Goldstein that traded through this period. Its output under the auspices of the Eastex label was distinctly middle-of-the road with a nod to fashionable silhouettes. According to Samuel Goldstein, who was Chair of the company until the late 1960s, its peak profit year had been in 1965. However, in an unpublished memoir written at the time of his retirement in 1968, he wrote: 'between 1965 and today there was a dramatic change which arose in the ladies fashion trade due to the advent of special teenage fashions'.[65] This put pressure on the company to carefully define its market, company structure and retailing policy. Company brochures from the 1960s show that it continued to design for a smart, metropolitan woman who was most likely middle-aged, middle-class and married. Fashions referenced 1960s' styles – just above the knee Crimpelene suits, tailored wool dresses and full, tubular coats with large buttons – but it maintained the slogan, 'If you're about 5'2" then Eastex is designed for you'. Throughout the 1970s, Ellis Goldstein 'tracked' the market. A brochure for the Eastex's Autumn-Winter collection of 1970 showed the impact of high fashion particularly Yves Saint Laurent's classic cut and tailoring, for example an A-line black and white, herring-bone-fitted wool coats, and strong-coloured wool trouser suits with single and double-breasted jackets and large rounded collars worn with slightly flared trousers. Following rather than leading, its cautious approach and its concentration on an older woman chimed with the changing demographics in the 1980s as a company promotional brochure aimed at fashion buyers and published in 1988 made clear. With the slogan 'She'll make you rich', the brochure described the Eastex woman: 'She's a 45+, middle class, shorter woman. She wants to look and feel her best, without standing out in a crowd. She wants quality tailored clothes, that reflect the current fashion trends ... She has more money than ever before. She's ready to pay to get the clothes she wants'.[66] The designs promoted in this brochure encapsulate Ellis-Goldstein's caution in terms of fashion, but also the eclectic array of styles in the 1980s (Figure 6.8). Included were ultra-feminine 'Lady Di' suits and blouses; pleated skirts and cropped jackets with pussy-cat bows redolent of Margaret Thatcher's outfits, well-fitted outlines extenuated by padded shoulders in soft fabrics, and solid but subtle colours that were clearly based on TV series such as

Figure 6.8 Eastex range promotional brochure, produced by Ellis & Goldstein, London, 1988. Jacques Vert Group.

Dallas and Dynasty, and inside the brochure, unstructured shirt-waisted dresses in large check print and coordinated jacket and dress in a William Morris style floral print. Offering a bigger range of sizes (8–24), Eastex provided fashion for a distinctive but growing market that wanted clothes that could be assimilated into wardrobes rather than standing out.

New York

Contrasts of style according to geography, economic and cultural capital are reinforced in contemporary factual and fictional accounts of London and New York. Tom Wolfe's novel *The Bonfire of the Vanities* (1987) characterizes New York in the 1980s as a city in decay, but also one with huge wealth in the pockets of a powerful minority. Moving – as Wolfe does in his narrative – between the burnt out tenements of the South Bronx and the luxury mansions of the wealthy on the Upper East Side of Manhattan serves as something of a metaphor for New York City and for the times. Previously distinct sartorial codes, inscribed according to gender, class and income, were changing here as they were in London. Summing up the times, fashion historian Caroline Rennolds Milbank felt that:

> Most high-school students, at least in New York, have dressed down in the 1980s, wearing jeans, thrift-shop overcoats, men's undershirts and dark glasses for a look of deliberately uncool cool (exceptions include their experimental punk-style haircuts and wearing of multiple earrings). Although a sense of how to put clothes together still tends to emanate from the street, and, even more from the new phenomenon of MTV, the most intense trends of the decade, such as Hermès scarves and Kelly bags, Chanel suits, quilted pocketbooks, and gold chains strung with baroque pearls, have trickled down into inexpensive fashion from Fifty-seventh Street.[67]

In New York, the advice for those wanting to be 'Truly Cool' was to wear 'one-of-a-kind garments from downtown design collectives or thrift stores'.[68] Karen Moline, fashion writer for *The Village Voice,* identifies three categories of street dress to be found in NYC: All-American, East Village and SoHo. The All-American 'collegiate/preppie brigade' wore jeans, athletic shoes, tee shirt or a button-down oxford shirt, and a leather jacket if it was cold, with the only 'permitted' accessory being a Sony Walkman. S/he was advised to buy items which were 'cheap, cool and disposable after a season' at Unique and Canal Jeans, where an eclectic range could be found, including 'Katharine Hamnett ripoffs, baggy Jap looks, dayglo socks, studded biker jewelry, pseudo African prints, mesh tanks, overdyed tees, rayon Hawaiian shirts, army fatigues, pith safari hats'.[69] For a more British-influenced style, closer to London's King's Road, the advice was to hang out in the East Village. Consumers were referred to the shop that Patricia Field[70] had run on 8th Street for ten years, stocking 'everything from oversize white sportswear, huge droopy hand-knits, Williwear, sophisticated linen suits, rubber wetsuits, plaid boxer shorts, one-piece wrestling suits, and crayon-coloured wigs to chunky space-age jewelry'.[71] Other choice retail outlets were Trash and Vaudeville on St Marks Place (Figure 6.9), as well as the original New York punk store Manic Panic, which purchased much of its newer stock from 'people who come in from off the streets'.[72] Better-off shoppers were referred to SoHo (South of Houston Street) as the most European of NYC's downtown neighbourhoods, then the centre of the downtown gallery scene with exclusive boutiques featuring European and American fashion designers. 'On weekends, SoHo becomes a veritable feast for the senses. The teeming masses from suburbia descend to buy an outfit and accessories in which they can return the following weekend in an attempt to be trendy'.[73] The most interesting clothes on the SoHo streets were said to include 'Japanese silhouettes, turbans and fantastic jewelry from Artwear', which was 'sported by gallery groupies on their way to openings'.[74]

For many less sartorially adventurous women, a staple garment for going out to work or to socialize was the wrap dress. Created in 1973 by New York designer Diane von Furstenberg, it has been lauded as a modern and versatile

Figure 6.9 Trash & Vaudeville, St Mark's Place, East Village, Manhattan, NYC.
John Huntington, March 1981.

garment that changed American women's apparel (Figure 6.10). By 1976, over a million of the dresses had been sold,[75] and von Furstenberg had been featured on the cover of *Newsweek*.[76] Made in drip-dry cotton jersey, the style of the dress proved easy to wear and comfortable on different body types and sizes, and became something of an everyday uniform for a variety of women.[77] The versatility of the style made it a popular alternative to the shirtwaist in and beyond the United States, in its original and in copies. By the end of the 1970s, the dress

Figure 6.10 Diane von Furstenberg wearing the wrap dress, 1973. Diane von Furstenberg.

had become a media icon of women's liberation and female empowerment, with the designer describing it in retrospect as 'more than just a dress; it's a spirit', to British daily newspaper *The Independent* in 2008.[78] This distinctly feminine garment complied with the gendered 'power dressing' of the time, which 'called on career women to think about and act upon their bodies in particular ways as part of an overall "project of the self" in order to maximize one's chances of career success'.[79] It is perhaps no surprise therefore that John Molloy could find a ready market for *The Women's Dress for Success Book* (1977), two years after publishing the original *Dress for Success* (1975) for men. Appearance had become a competitive issue for corporate advancement, and also simply for getting a job at a time when the American economy was failing and unemployment rates were high. Not only was this to the advantage of established men's retailers and manufacturers such as Brooks Brothers, but it generated many new companies, such as Liz Claiborne and Jones of New York, which specialized in business wear for the increasing numbers of women entering professions.[80] By 1978, women comprised 41 per cent of the US workforce and 1 out of 6 were in a profession.[81] This was increasingly evident in the financial centre of Manhattan, which belied the more impoverished economic status of much of the city.

Art historian Debora Silverman saw Ronald Reagan's arrival at the White House in 1981 as solidifying an 'aristocratic strain' apparent in the high culture and consumerism of New York City, reflective of the 'visible wealth' and an unchecked 'new luxury'.[82] Collaborations in the first half of the 1980s, between Upper East Side department store Bloomingdales and the Costume Institute of the Metropolitan Museum of Art, facilitated by Diana Vreeland, its special museum consultant and the former editor of American *Vogue*, reflected the elision of high and consumer culture. One target of Silverman's fierce critique was Mrs Vreeland's 1983/4 exhibition of the work of Yves St Laurent, which is described as celebrating 'elite opulence and visualizing a world of permanent leisure and privilege without responsibility'.[83] Silverman takes aim at the show's celebration of St Laurent as 'an haute couture artist' while 'obscuring the dialectic between exclusive design and mass merchandising at the heart of his success',[84] and missing entirely the designer's 'genuine innovations in fashion, and his flirtation with the "street" and with the 1960s counterculture'.[85] Silverman points out how high culture and commerce, the museum and the department store had the power to present their own fictions of fashion, in common with advertising and the media. She compares Nancy Reagan's White House with the television soap opera *Dynasty* and its star Krystle Carrington (televised in the United States from 1981 to 1986), a top-rated show in the United States and equally popular in Britain (as was its effective companion piece, *Dallas*). The series spawned The Dynasty Collection of women's wear, premiered at Bloomingdales in 1984.[86] The style epitomized the power dressing of the 1970s and 1980s, which in New York City was the social style of the Upper East Side, and the business style of

Midtown or Wall Street. Elsewhere in the city, fashion and its role in everyday life continued to be markedly different.

It was not the borough of Manhattan that spawned one of the most substantial fashion influences to come out of the city in the late twentieth century, but rather the geographic and social margins of the South Bronx. The neighbourhood was created by the construction of the ambitious Cross Bronx Expressway (1948–1972), cutting through upper Manhattan to link New Jersey and Queens, under the grand scheme of planner Robert Moses. Produced by the demolition of lower middle-class apartments and the exodus of 60,000 largely white Jewish and Irish residents, the vast modernist-inspired vertical public housing complexes of the South Bronx attracted poor African-American, Jewish and Puerto Rican families, but no jobs. By the end of the 1960s, half of its former white residents had moved out to suburban Westchester County, to New Jersey, Queens and Long Island. Racial tension flared in the city when African-American, Afro-Caribbean and Latino families moved into formerly Jewish, Irish and Italian neighbourhoods, and gangs of youths came into conflict.[87] As one commentator described it: 'Here was the unreconstructed *South* – the south Bronx, a spectacular set of ruins, a mythical wasteland, and infectious disease, and, as Robert Jensen observed, "a condition of poverty and social collapse, more than a geographical place".'[88]

While disco was still dominating the downtown club scene, South Bronx gang culture provided a rich and enervating source of style in New York in the 1970s through the emergence of hip-hop. Its development as a sub-culture among black and Latino youth has been well documented,[89] as has its continued appropriation by mainstream culture and corporate mass production.[90] At its point of emergence, it was signified by music (rap and D-Jing), dancing (breaking) and by its associations with graffiti writing. Like rap music, a new mode of street-influenced dress relied on 'sampling' that is improvising with ordinary clothes, as a way of displaying individuality.[91] Among black youth it has been described as more potent in galvanizing black social identity than the civil rights movement of the 1960s.[92] Proponents wore casual, functional sportswear items; particularly those designed for basketball, a game omnipresent in urban New York as it demanded no special or expensive equipment, other than a ball and a hoop. Established sportswear and fashion brands, such as Le Coq Sportif, Kangol, Adidas and Pro-Keds, rapidly associated themselves with the emerging hip-hop scene, astutely recognizing its commercial potential. As a result, sneakers became essential wear on New York City streets, worn in pristine condition as sartorial signs of the hip-hop look, not least by breakdancers and B-boys (Figure 6.11).

The origin of the sneaker craze in the city is dated to 1973, when New York Knicks basketball player Walt 'Clyde' Frazier requested a custom version of the PUMA suede shoe, which became known as the PUMA 'Clyde'. It took

Figure 6.11 Breakdancers, B-Boys, on the street, New York, USA 1981. Getty Images.

little time before break-dancers and DJs adopted the Clyde and customized it with fat laces in various colour combinations. Another style turning point came in 1984, when young and emerging basketball star Michael Jordan flouted the NBA's (National Basketball Association) rule prohibiting players from wearing black sneakers during games, to wear red and black Nike-sponsored high-tops. Despite the steep fine of up to $5000 each time, Jordan's infringement increased enormously the desirability of the shoes and the willingness of so-called 'sneakerheads' to pay $100 (over $200 at current prices) a pair.[93] Athletic footwear companies quickly capitalized on the trend, introducing new designs often in limited editions that sold out immediately to those who could afford them. For those without the means, stealing sneakers, sometimes off the feet of their wearers, became a strategy for their acquisition.[94] One of the most popular styles was the Nike Air Force One, named after the plane that carries the President of the United States. Produced first in 1982, discontinued the following year, then re-released again in 1986 with the addition of the Nike Swoosh logo, it is now considered a classic example of a sneaker fashion launched strategically by Nike through controlled supply in response to excessive demand. Originally considered the favoured shoes of inner city youths, especially in Harlem, they gained the popular moniker 'Uptowns'. Rappers wrote songs about their shoes. Run-D.M.C. released 'My Adidas' in 1986, while rapper Nelly and his group St. Lunatics celebrated Air Force Ones on a 2002 single.

Sneakers were not only worn in New York City for their style status. They became a practical necessity in April 1980 when a mass transportation strike crippled the city for ten days as contracted transit workers petitioned for higher wages. New York Mayor Ed Koch was photographed with thousands of fellow commuters walking to work across the Brooklyn Bridge.[95] The popular image of a woman wearing a business suit and sneakers was reinforced during this event, when footwear purchased for aerobics and other fitness classes graduated to the city streets. Going out or getting on takes on a whole new meaning here as men and women from various social and ethnic groups and from all ages took on this practical, but highly fashionable footwear. By the time Tom Wolfe published *The Bonfire of the Vanities* in 1987, sneakers had become ubiquitous, but were equally markers of economic and social status:

> The old man was wearing a pair of purple-and-white-striped running sneakers. They looked weird on such an old man, but there was nothing really odd about them, not on the D train…Half the people in the car were wearing sneakers with splashy designs on them and molded soles that looked like gravy boats. Young people were wearing them, old men were wearing them, mothers with children on their laps were wearing them, and for that matter, the children were wearing them. This was not for reasons of Young Fit & Firm Chic, the way it was downtown, where you saw a lot of well-dressed young white people going off to work in the morning wearing these sneakers. No, on the D train the reason was, they were cheap. On the D train these sneakers were like a sign around the neck reading SLUM or EL BARRIO.[96]

While sneakers were the most notable sportswear item to transfer from functional to fashionable wear, they were not the only ones. Blue jeans also crossed gender, age and income distinctions and continued to signify different forms of 'Americanness'.[97]

Performing fashion

Lee jeans were the classic '"old school" hip hop uniform',[98] but by the mid- to late 1980s, hip-hop style was beginning to impact the fashion establishment of Seventh Avenue, with designer brands such as Tommy Hilfiger and Ralph Lauren being among the first to identify this new market segment. Jeans in particular continued to be worn everyday for function, but also increasingly as fashion items. Signifiers of resistance on the one hand and of status on the other, their cultural and economic values became more complicated as the fashion industry appropriated one of the most commonplace garments of all time. The licensing of her name by New York socialite and designer Gloria Vanderbilt to

Murjani jeans in 1976 marked a distinct functional, semiotic and economic shift. The coming into existence of 'designer jeans' transformed an everyday garment into a fashionable one, as demonstrated in the advertisement from the British department store chain Debenhams (Figure 6.12). Jeans became associated with upscale urban lifestyles (as well as with downtown and alternative ones), became socially distinctive, feminized and were worn, not just as work wear, but to go out. In this process, the sartorial tactics of the socially and economically

Figure 6.12 Gloria Vanderbilt jeans at Debenhams, UK, 1980s. Advertising Archives, UK.

disempowered (such as wearing worn or torn jeans) were appropriated by the powerful, in this case the fashion industry. As a result, Macy's could advertise, 'Expressions – Faded attraction…the worn out jean from Calvin Klein Sport', 'Worn out in all the right places'.[99]

Social differentiation still remained between the wearers of 'really' old, torn jeans, and those purchased by Macy's customers; jeans served to reflect the complex and shifting relationships between fashion and everyday life. By the 1980s, as Fiske points out, 'the ads for designer jeans consistently stress how they will fit YOU; the physicality of the body is more than a sign of nature, vigour, and sexuality, it becomes a sign of individuality'.[100] Jeans were being designed for different (female) body types. An advert for Wrangler promoted sizes 'Misses Full', 'Misses Regular' and 'Juniors' to ensure 'a fit for every (female) body', no matter who or what it was doing.[101] In Britain, the quintessential comparative example was the 1985 Levi's 501s advertising campaign, by Bartle Bogle Hegarty and featuring musician and model Nick Kamen. Styled as the 1950s, one advertisement featured Kamen sitting in a bathtub full of water to shrink his new 501s. The other had him going to the public launderette to wash his jeans, which he removed in public view and then sat down with the other customers to watch them in the machine. With supporting music from the 1960s, Marvyn Gaye's *Heard it Through the Grapevine* (1968) and Sam Cooke's *Wonderful World* (1963), the intention of the advertisement was to restore consumer interest in denim, not historical accuracy.[102] The backdrop for this advertising industry appropriation of US black soul music to revitalize Levi's blue jeans was the unprecedented riots in British inner cities in the 1980s that resulted from racist policing combined with inner city decline. Declaring that '[s]omething is happening to "menswear"; something is happening to young men', Frank Mort identified the plethora of influences: 'from Tottenham High Road to *The Face.* Fashion spreads of Doc Martens and cycle shorts. Citywide boys and black rappers. Soul boys, wallies and razor partings, dancing late night. Soho clubs as metropolitan style'.[103] Not only were young men experiencing the sharp end of commercialism as retro imagery was used to advertise all manner of products: 'the choice of the 50s and 60s has been no accident (whether 70s revivalism is a passing fad or something more significant remains to be seen). Ironically it is there as a crucial signifier of youth and modernity'.[104]

Through the 1970s and 1980s, to speak of 'Black' identity was complex and troubled, not least because of the increasingly racist policies of Margaret Thatcher's Conservative government that affected those from former (and socially and culturally diverse) British colonies in the Caribbean, the Indian sub-continent and Africa. Discussing 'Black Style' in her book of the same name, Tulloch quoted Stuart Hall and Mark Sealy who defined 'Black' as the shared understanding that stemmed from 'the historical experience of living in a racialized world'.[105] Although people of colour in London and New York shared some similar experiences of a racialized world, there were some key differences. In Britain, especially on the streets of south London, the East End and Notting Hill, reggae and ska provided the context 'around which another culture, another set of values and self-definitions could cluster. These changes were subtly registered in the style of black youth; in the gait, the manner, the voice which seemed overnight to become less anglicized'.[106] Imported Chicago and Southern blues, Detroit soul, were joined by Bob Marley, Burning Spear and Prince Buster, but also home-grown reggae bands such as the Birmingham band Steel Pulse, formed in 1975, that resonated with this second generation whose parents had been in that first exodus from the Caribbean to Britain in the 1950s. Young men wore oversized Tams, khaki camouflage, dreadlocks and a red, gold and green colours, while young women's hair was left unstraightened or 'short or plaited into intricately parted arabesques, capillary tributes to an imagined Africa'.[107] As Punk in Britain took up the cause 'Rock Against Racism', they also identified with black West Indian rude and Rasta styles adapting these in their Mohican hairstyles.

Performative practices on the sub-cultural threshold reached and influenced the mainstream through the media and in doing so emphasized the growing significance of the recognition of the body and of the fashion system in everyday lives. In 1990, director Jennie Livingstone's documentary film *Paris Is Burning*, for example, chronicles the end of ball culture in the African American, Latino, gay and transgender communities from 1986 to 1989. A poignant exploration of race, class, and gender, the film is set in Harlem, portrayed as 'the New York ghetto and slum, the district of poverty, fear and homosexuality'.[108] Fantasies are evoked of Paris 'the distant city of cities, city of luxury, of fashion and beautiful women' through performances that mimic the glamour of high fashion promoted by the likes of *Vogue* magazine, which are also redolent of the gay drag balls held in Harlem since the late nineteenth century.[109] But the spectacularization of the sub-cultural communities or 'Houses' (as in fashion houses), criticized in particular by bell hooks, is also redolent of the assimilation of British Punks into the mainstream by the mid-1980s.[110] No longer purveyors of sartorial and corporeal signs of resistance, they had become just another London tourist attraction. Yet, instantiations of sub-cultural style and high fashion were reaching everyday life more rapidly and comprehensively than ever before through the media, and as international travel became economically within the reach of more people and electronic communications created connections and a greater sense of immediacy.

The proliferation and widening reach of the media was critical to the dissemination of the 'fitness craze', which hit the United States by the beginning of the 1980s according to *Time* magazine.[111] Celebrities, movies, television shows and advertising promoted fitness in various forms, making sweat pants, spandex, leg warmers and high top sneakers everyday street wear for women in

New York, London and beyond. A fit and 'toned' body came to be an aspiration promoted by the media. In New York City, as in London, and in other towns and cities in each country, fitness studios and gyms became lucrative businesses. While actress Jane Fonda would probably be credited with originating the aerobics classes, which became hugely popular for women, their place of origin was New Jersey, where Jacki Sorensen began an Aerobic Dancing class there at a local YMCA in 1971. Her method was based on a fitness television programme she had developed for the wives of Air Force servicemen in Puerto Rico, where she was stationed with her husband in 1969.[112] Images of fit female bodies abounded, such as a contemporary advertisement for P.S. Gitano jeans that shows three women wearing skin-tight jeans and t-shirts posed at a barre, arguably moving 'the masculine ruggedness of the West into the feminine fitness center of the city'.[113]

Noting that the 'early 1980s saw the mass popularity of dance exercise style', Angela McRobbie charts the success of *Fame,* the 1980 musical movie based in New York City, which became a highly popular television show on both sides of the Atlantic.[114] *Fame* follows a group of students through their studies at the fictional New York City High School for the Performing Arts.[115] Not only a showcase for pop music and dance performances, 'it also worked visually as a high fashion text' for the dance exercise style.[116] Broadcast in the United Kingdom in 1982 and 1983, the show was an immediate success, particularly with young girls, and it 'added momentum to the exercise craze of the early 1980s'.[117] Equally popular was the 1982 movie *Flashdance,* marketed to a slightly older and less exclusively female teen viewer, it became an international box office success. Set in the steel mills of Pittsburgh, Pennsylvania, it was 'a narrative of desired social mobility' by female welder Alex Owens (played by Jennifer Beale) to a professional contemporary style dancer.[118] It demonstrates the power of dance, as practice and spectacle, to relate to its audiences, as McRobbie has noted, in referencing Peter Wollen's comparison between the balletic body of 1912–1913 and 'the ambiguously extravagant body which was part of punk style in the early 1980s'.[119] As with this reference, the films and TV series that served to promote dance and exercise, located 'ballet outside of the sterile terms of high culture, and instead posits it as something which has connections with the aesthetics of everyday life'.[120] In tandem, sport and outdoor leisure clothing infiltrated everyday lives, so that not only the 'performance' of the clothes but also how they were 'fashioned' became important. In addition to outdoor brands such as Patagonia, The North Face, Berghaus and Timberland (which began in the 1960s and 1970s as specialist, high-performance clothing), and the widening global appeal of soccer, football and baseball and the concurrent retailing of kits, clothing associated with running and snow-boarding has been accommodated in everyday wardrobes. Directly and indirectly this has drawn further attention to the body, and to the necessity for it to be healthy and fit. Under control, toned and muscular, as several commentators have argued, the body is now a site of regulation principally by diet and exercise rather than corsets and cut. Certainly in New York and London, the increasing commodification of dance, exercise and sport served to reiterate and connect fashion to popular culture and the everyday.

Shifting geographies of place have enabled both London and New York to retain and develop distinctive identities as fashion cities through the late 1970s to the early 1990s. Counter-cultures in various guises (music and dance in particular, but also in both cities in the 1990s a vibrant, emergent art scene) helped to stimulate the revival of peripheral and run-down streets and districts. These formerly liminal spaces retained a distinctive sense of place until they became assimilated and joined established shopping routes – such as Oxford St and Fifth Avenue – as part of the fashion geography of both cities. Yet paradoxically as the millennium approached, fashion moved well beyond the physical constraints of national borders as its global scope intensified with the growing impact of the Internet. As Chapter 7 will show, web-based retailing, social media and blogs ostensibly challenged the idea of distinctive fashion cities, while at the same time the desire for individualism and personal identity that stemmed from being connected to a particular place remained. Thus London and New York's inner suburbs gained in importance as vital elements of what helped to constitute these as fashion cities particularly as gentrification speeded up (for example, Brixton, Balham, and Shoreditch in London, or Williamsburg in Brooklyn, New York). As star fashion designers came to the fore and then slipped out of focus, some enjoying extraordinary fame as they were celebrated in the media and in influential cultural institutions, the ubiquity of fashion in everyday lives remained. Indeed, as we will see in Chapter 7, it gathered pace and momentum.

Notes

1   David Gilbert, '"The Youngest Legend in History": Culture of Consumption and the Mythologies of Swinging London', *The London Journal* 31, no. 1 (2006), 9.

2   Chris Hamnett, 'Gentrification and the Middle-class Remaking of Inner London, 1961–2001', *Urban Studies* 40, no. 12 (2003), 2404.

3   Ibid.

4   Ibid., 2416.

5   Ibid., 2417.

6   Kathe Newman and Elvin K. Wyly, 'The Right to Stay Put, Revisited: Gentrification and Resistance to Displacement in New York City', *Urban Studies* 43, no. 1 (2006), 23–57.

7   Ibid., 45.

8   Pamela Church Gibson, *Fashion and Celebrity Culture* (London and New York: Berg, 2012), 2–3.

9 Ibid., 13–17.

10 Douglas Kellner, 'Madonna, Fashion, and Identity', in *On Fashion*, ed. Shari Benstock and Suzanne Ferriss (New Brunswick, NJ: Rutgers University Press, 1994), 162.

11 Peter York, *The Sloane Ranger Handbook: The First Guide to What Really Matters in Life* (London: Ebury Press, 1982).

12 Charlie LeDuff, 'Saturday Night Fever: Live', *The New York Times,* June 9, 1996, available online: http://www.nytimes.com/1996/06/09/nyregion/saturday-night-fever-the-life.html (accessed November 20, 2013).

13 An interesting transatlantic footnote is that the movie story was based on a 1976 *New York Magazine* article 'Tribal Rites of the New Saturday Night' by British writer Nik Cohn, later acknowledged to be fabricated. A newcomer to the United States, Cohn was unable to make any sense of the disco subculture and rather based the main character that became Tony Manero on a British Mod acquaintance. Mark Rozzo, 'Nik Cohn's Fever Dream', *New York Magazine*, 2 December 2011, available online: http://www.nytimes.com/2011/12/04/magazine/nik-cohn-fever-dream.html (accessed November 20, 2013).

14 Elizabeth Currid, *The Warhol Economy How Fashion and Music Drive New York City* (Princeton, NJ: Princeton University Press, 2007), 30.

15 Later, in conversation with the Mudd Club's owner Stephen Mass, Vivienne Westwood accused Sui of 'ripping off' her Pirates collection. (Hazel Clark in conversation with Stephen Mass, January 21, 2016).

16 Stephen Mass, interview with Hazel Clark, New York, November 6, 2015.

17 'Why Are Lines Shorter for Gas Than the Mudd Club in New York? Because Every Night Is Odd There', *People,* July 16 1979, available online: http://www.people.com/people/archive/article/0,,20074119,00.html (accessed November 20, 2015).

18 Elizabeth Currid, *The Warhol Economy: How Fashion and Music Drive New York City* (Princeton, NJ: Princeton University Press, 2007), 31.

19 Ibid., 31.

20 Performance artist Eric Bogosian, in Marvin J. Taylor, *The Downtown Book: The New York Art Scene 1974–1984* (Princeton and Oxford: Princeton University Press, 2009), 149.

21 Chi Chi Valenti, in Taylor, *The Downtown Book*, 64.

22 Ibid.

23 Ibid.

24 Ibid.

25 Ted Polhemus, *Street Style* (London: Thames and Hudson, 1994), 91–2.

26 Ibid., 93.

27 'Club to Catwalk: London Fashion in the 1980s', *Victoria and Albert Museum*, available online: http://www.vam.ac.uk/content/exhibitions/exhibition-from-club-to-catwalk-london-fashion-in-the-80s/about-the-exhibition/ (accessed January 10 2014).Similar observations were made by New York fashion designer Stephen Burrows, recalling the elaborate shared dressing up ritual of he and his friends to go out at night in the city in the 1980s. 'Stephen Burrows in conversation with Kim Jenkins', 24 April 2013, Museum of the City of New York, in collaboration with the exhibition, *Stephen Burrows: When Fashion Danced,* March 22–July 28, 2013.

28 Vaughan Toulouse, 'Clubbed to Death: Why be in When You could be Out', in *The Fashion Year, Volume III*, ed. Lorraine Johnston (London: Zomba Books, 1985), 66.

29 A. O'Neill, *London: After a Fashion* (London: Reaktion, 2007), 200–203.

30 Ibid., 62.

31 'Club to Catwalk'.

32 Ibid.

33 Ibid.

34 Lesley Ebbetts, 'Fine and Dandy', *The Daily Mirror,* February 28, 1985, 17.

35 O'Neill, *London*, 178.

36 Christopher Breward, *Fashioning London: Clothing and the Modern Metropolis* (Oxford and New York: Berg, 2004), 178.

37 Ibid., 179.

38 Ibid., 178–179.

39 Angela McRobbie, 'Second-Hand Dresses and the Role of the Ragmarket', in *Zoot Suits and Second-Hand Dresses: An Anthology of Fashion and Music*, ed. Angela McRobbie (London: Macmillan, 1989), 24.

40 Polhemus, *Street Style,* 7.

41 Catherine Ross, 'Biba, Black Dwarf, Black Magic Women', in *Biba: The Label, The Lifestyle, The Look* (Newcastle upon Tyne: Tyne and Wear Museums, 1993), 14.

42 Harriet Walter, 'Let's Twist Again', *The Independent Newspaper,* October 22, 2011,1

43 McRobbie, 'Second-Hand Dresses and the Role of the Ragmarket', 32.

44 André Breton, *What is Surrealism?* (London: Pluto Press, 1981), quoted in McRobbie, 'Second-Hand Dresses and the Role of the Ragmarket', 47.

45 McRobbie, *Zoot Suits,* 46.

46 Sue Orbis, *The Princess of Wales Fashion Handbook* (London: Orbis, 1984), quoted in Lee Barron, 'The Habitus of Elizabeth Hurley: Celebrity, Fashion, and Identity Branding', *Fashion Theory: The Journal of Dress, Body and Culture* 11, no. 4 (2007), 482.

47 Jackie Modlinger, 'Diana: Princess Superstar', in *The Fashion Year*, ed. Brenda Polan (London: Zomba Books, 1983), 99.

48 Ibid.

49 Rachel Worth, *Fashion for the People: A History of Clothing at Marks and Spencer* (Oxford and New York: Berg, 2007), 79–80.

50 Ibid., 81.

51 Ibid., 82–3.

52 Cheryl Buckley, *Designing Modern Britain* (London: Reaktion Books, 2007), 223.

53 Robert O'Bryne, *Style City: How London Became a Fashion Capital* (London: Francis Lincoln Limited, 2009), 119–20.

54 Jon Savage, 'Golden Oldies of '85', *The Observer,* February 10, 1985, 23.

55 Ibid.

56 Brenda Polan, 'Putting a Kick in the Mall', *The Guardian,* August 16, 1984

57 Anna Gough-Yates, *Understanding Women's Magazines: Publishing, Markets and Readership* (London: Routledge, 2003),105.

58 Deborah Lloyd, 'Assemblage and Subculture: The Casuals and their Clothing', in *Components of Dress*, ed. Juliet Ash and Lee Wright (London and New York: Comedia [Routledge], 1988), 101.

59 Ibid., 102.

60 Ibid., 103.

61 Polhemus, *Street Style,* 101.

62 Lloyd, 'Assemblage and Subculture', 106.

63 Dyhouse, *Glamour,* 6.

64 Hilary Fawcett, 'Fashioning the Second Wave: Issue across Generations', *Studies in the Literary Imagination* 39, no. 2 (2006), 104.

65 'Resume of the life, business and social activities of Mr Samuel Goldstein', unpublished memoir, 26 November 1968, Ellis & Goldstein archive, Jewish Museum, London, 9.

66 'Eastex sales brochure', undated but c. 1988, Ellis and Goldstein Archive, Jewish Museum, London (2010.68.3.14), 3.

67 Rennolds Milbank, *New York Fashion*, 265–6.

68 Karen Moline, 'Street Fashion NYC', in *The Fashion Year: Volume Two*, ed. Emily White (London: Zomba Books, 1984), 69.

69 Ibid., 70

70 Later better known as the costume designer for the television series and movies, *Sex and the City*.

71 Moline, 'Street Fashion NYC', 72.

72 Ibid., 72.

73 Ibid., 74.

74 Ibid.

75 'I Just Felt Flawless', *Financial Times, Style,* January 11/12, 2014, 4.

76 *Newsweek*, March 22, 1976.

77 The forty-year history of the dress was celebrated in the exhibition, *Journey of a Dress,* LA County Museum of Art, January 11–1 April 2014.

78 Justin Howard, 'Diane von Furstenberg – The Wrap Dress', *About Style*, available online: http://fashiondesigners.about.com/od/Fashion-History/a/Diane-Von-Furstenberg-The-Wrap-Dress.htm (accessed January 21, 2016).

79 Anthony Giddens, *Modernity and Self-Identity: Self and Society in the Late Modern Age* (Cambridge: Polity, 1991), quoted in Joanne Entwistle, 'Fashion and the Fleshy Body: Dress as Embodied Practice', *Fashion Theory: The Journal of Dress, Body and Culture* 4, no. 3 (2000), 330.

80 Cunningham, 'Dressing for Success', 192.

81 Ibid., 203.

82 Debora Silverman, *Selling Culture: Bloomingdale's, Diana Vreeland, and the New Aristocracy of Taste in Reagan's America* (New York, Pantheon Books, 1986), 5.

83 Ibid., 83.

84 Ibid., 90.

85 Ibid., 93.

86 Ibid., 152.

87 Jeff Chang, *Can't Stop Won't Stop: A History of the Hip-Hop Generation* (New York: St. Martin's Press, 2006), 9.

88 Ibid., 17.

89 In particular, George Nelson, *Hip Hop America* (New York: Viking, 1998).

90 Susan Kaiser, Leslie Rabine, Carol Hall and Karyl Ketchum, 'Beyond Binaries: Respecting the Improvisation in African-American Style', in *Black Style*, ed. Carol Tulloch (London: V&A Publications, 2005), 65.

91 *Black Style Now*, Museum of the City of New York, 2006. Exhibition text, 28.

92 Van Dyk Lewis, 'Hip-Hop Fashion', in *Encyclopedia of Clothing and Fashion*, Volume II, ed. Valerie Steele (New York: Thomson Gale, 2005), 214.

93 *Just for Kicks,* 2005 movie.

94 *Black Style Now*, 32.

95 'Commuters on the Queensboro Bridge', image, *The New York Times*, available online, http://graphics8.nytimes.com/images/2005/12/14/nyregion/15strike.5.jpg (accessed January 22, 2016).

96 Tom Wolfe, *The Bonfire of the Vanities* (New York: Farrar, Straus and Giroux, 1987), 36.

97 John Fiske, *Understanding Popular Culture* (London and New York: Routledge, 1989), 4.

98 *Black Style Now*, 29.

99 Fiske, *Understanding Popular Culture*, 18.

100 Ibid.

101 Ibid., 13.

102 Helen Rees, *British Youth Culture* (London: The Conran Foundation, 1986), 14–24.

103 Frank C. Mort, 'Boy's Own? Masculinity, Style and Popular Culture', in *Male Order. Unwrapping Masculinity*, ed. Rowena Chapman and Jonathan Rutherford (London: Lawrence and Wishart, 1988), 193.

104 Ibid., 199.

105 Carol Tulloch (ed.), *Black Style* (London: V&A Publications, 2005), 11.

106 Dick Hebdige, *Subculture: The Meaning of Style* (London & New York: Methuen, 1979), 40.

107 Ibid., 43.

108 Barbara Vinken, *Fashion Zeitgeist: Trends and Cycles in the Fashion System* (Oxford and New York: Berg, 2005), 50.

109 Adam Geczy and Vicki Karaminas, *Queer Style* (London, New Delhi, New York, Sydney: Bloomsbury, 2013), 116–17.

110 bell hooks, 'Is Paris Burning?', *Black Looks: Race and Representation* (Boston, MA: South End Press, 1992), 145–56.

111 *Time c*over story, November 2, 1981.

112 'Team Sorensen Bios: Jacki Sorensen, President', *Jacki Sorensen's Fitness Classes*, available online, http://www.jackis.com/about/team-sorenson-bios (accessed January 23, 2016).

113 Fiske, *Understanding Popular Culture*, 12.

114 Angela McRobbie, '*Fame, Flashdance,* and Fantasies of Acheivement', in *Fabrications: Costume and the Female Body*, ed. Jane Gaines and Charlotte Herzog (New York and London: Routledge, 1990), 48.

115 Based on the *Fiorello H. LaGuardia High School of Music & Art and Performing Arts*, in New York City.

116 McRobbie, '*Fame*', 48.

117 Ibid., 51.

118 Ibid., 57.

119 Ibid., 41.

120 Ibid.

7
SHOWING OFF

Introduction

In its reportage of London Fashion Week in February 2014, the popular British tabloid newspaper *The Sun* included advice for women on what to 'Wear in the World',[1] specifically in London, Paris, New York, and Milan, the world's 'fashion capitals' and hosts to the biannual fashion weeks.[2] To pass fashion muster in London, *The Sun* recommended a surprisingly casual look comprising a baseball cap, blue Nike trainers, a purple jumper and grey trousers both from Topshop. For Paris, the newspaper suggested a striped matelot-style sweater from Mango, a Marc by Marc Jacobs phone case bearing an image of the Eiffel Tower, which incidentally cost over twice as much as the sweater, a Fedora from Zara and walking brogues. By contrast, the footwear suggested for New York and Milan was to wear 5-inch heels, which seemed to have stepped, or rather teetered, off the set of *Sex and the City.* For New York, the stilettos accompanied a long blazer, while in Milan the other recommended accessories were 'drop gem earrings' and a 'metallic clutch'. Yet it was not just the unpredictable predictability of the pairing of the outfits with each city that was notable, but the very fact that *The Sun,* best known for 'Showbiz, babes, celebrities, sport and racing, national and international news', was covering Fashion Week at all, and moreover, as 'the most anticipated event in every fashionista's diary'.[3] The feature underscored how fashion had become so ubiquitous and the fashion city had entered the popular imagination. By the millennium fashion was more newsworthy than ever, in part because the vehicles for its dissemination were greater in type and impact. Fashion was both on show, that is a more visible and consistent part of lives, as well as a means by which more people could 'show off' in public than ever before in our period. Not only in newspapers, which were fast disappearing in their printed form, but via the Internet, television, movies, social media and exhibitions, fashion was gaining more of a place in everyday life – a phenomenon *The New York Times,* and former *Financial Times,* fashion journalist Vanessa Friedman, called 'fashionisation'.[4]

Fashion was a means for (modern and post-modern) individuals to distinguish themselves, while at the same time an increasingly powerful *lingua franca* uniting groups in different places as the subjects and objects of fashion production, consumption and media. The appearance of the same big brands, high fashion and 'fast fashion' labels on the shopping streets of London and New York created an impression that what was being worn in urban centres was becoming more similar. In London the 'everydayness' of business attire and casual wear was interpreted as 'Everybody looks like everybody else',[5] and also as a sign of people dressing 'badly' having lost the capacity for individualism.[6] Yet fashion's potential for showing off provided the means for injecting the extraordinary into the everyday. Changes in fashion's social, cultural, economic and geographical significance by the millennium were made manifest in London and New York, not just by courtesy of the fashion industry, but through the creativity of wearers. More people were able to gain access to fashion, not only through what they wore and where they lived but also as a vicarious pleasure through its mass media presence and spectacle. Fashion became more transitory, both as 'Cheap, ubiquitous clothes which lack artistic merit of any kind',[7] which were destined for landfills, and as fleeting images – signifiers of status, economic and cultural capital. 'Surculture',[8] the neologism for the annexation of high and popular culture, which playfully celebrated and critiqued dominant culture, was reflected in mainstream fashion. It also characterized what was being worn, and photographed on the streets of London and New York, which by the twenty-first century had increasing similarities, but also continuing differences.

Back *On the Street*

The documentary film *Bill Cunningham New York* (2010), directed by Richard Press, became something of a cult sensation in New York City. It followed the working life and history of photographer Bill Cunningham (1929–2016), whose photo column *On the Street* had appeared in *The New York Times* every Sunday for over thirty years.[9] The column began after Cunningham, then a New York-based fashion journalist for *The Chicago Tribune* and *Women's Wear Daily,* took a chance street photograph of Greta Garbo, which was published as part of a group of impromptu pictures in *The New York Times* in December 1978.[10] His editor Arthur Gelb described the photographs as 'a turning point for the *Times,* because it was the first time the paper had run pictures of well-known people without getting their permission'.[11] Subsequently, Cunningham continued to photograph people on the streets of New York (mostly in Midtown Manhattan, around 57th Street and Fifth Avenue) and at society events, as well as covering the runway shows. Cunningham had an educated eye for fashion, selecting for his column 'two groups of New Yorkers' described as 'the fashionable people, whose style changes more rapidly than that of the masses, and the truly creative ones, whose style, while outré, in its theatricality never really changes at all'.[12] From the vantage point of the bicycle that he rode around the city, taking often-unexpected shots of unsuspecting subjects (Figure 7.1), Cunningham was a

Figure 7.1 Bill Cunningham photographing women's shoes, New York City. Courtesy of Zeitgeist Films.

self-designated 'record keeper' of 'historical knowledge'[13] of fashion, which he described, pointedly, as 'the armor to survive the reality of everyday life'.[14]

Around the same time as Cunningham's column began, photographer Amy Arbus was taking street shots for the monthly fashion section of *The Village Voice*. Her *On the Street: 1980–1990*, a collection of 70 of more than 500 black-and-white portraits, provided a downtown East Village parallel to Bill Cunningham's midtown perspectives. Included were Madonna, captured in 1983 on St Mark's Place (Figure 7.2), carrying a bowling bag, and wearing a stained overcoat, over what appears to be legwear akin to the 'rancid long johns', which Angela McRobbie is quoted in the previous chapter as referencing being worn at the same time in London. Yet, Madonna's look is also distinctive and prescient of the fashion influence she would become on young women. Amy Arbus also photographed, among others, the designer Anna Sui wearing a tent dress, as part of the developing 'straight-up' genre of photography. Defined as a 'style of dress worn by ordinary people as opposed to professional models, combined in apparent disregard of dominant fashion codes and celebrated in the streets rather than in the rarefied spaces in which fashion was usually found', 'straight-up' photography originated with the 1980s British cult-style magazine *i-D*.[15] Since then it has become a staple of fashion journalism, offering the masque of authenticity of ordinary people going about their lives on city streets. The technique began in the first issue of *i-D*, which celebrated 'the people's everyday creativity, their "know-how"'.[16] Rocamora and O'Neill have commented how journalists have used street-fashion images in an attempt to make sense of the anonymity, chaos and disorder of the city. Borrowing from de Certeau, they

Figure 7.2 Madonna, St Mark's Place, New York, 1983. Amy Arbus.

present these images as a vantage point or prospect from which to capture and comprehend city streets.[17] Such images were visually arresting, but as these authors note, they were hardly 'authentic' or everyday, rather they were chosen consciously with a fashion insider's eye, à la Bill Cunningham.

The same covert intentionality applied to *The Sartorialist,* the pioneering street-style fashion blog begun in 2005 by New Yorker Scott Schuman, 'with the idea of creating a two-way dialogue about the world of fashion and its relationship to daily life' (Figure 7.3).[18] Schuman moved on to capture what people were wearing on the streets of major cities around the world, including London. Since then the form has been emulated by others to record people on the streets of major international cities, not least those places hosting the seasonal runway shows. The growing numbers of street style bloggers in the 2000s led potential subjects to situate themselves *outside* of the biannual fashion show locations, in anticipation of being photographed. As Anna Wintour, editor of American *Vogue,* quipped in *Bill Cunningham New York,* 'we all dress for Bill'.[19] While she is referring to fashion professionals and fashionistas, by the end of the decade capturing 'real people' on the streets of New York had become an occupation for some. The popular blog *Humans of New York*[20] featured short profiles of subjects, as well as their photographs, providing insights into their characters and lives, rather than highlighting only how they dressed and looked. Other more niche fashion and style blogs developed such as *Hijabi Street Style*, disseminated through the visual-based Tumblr and Pinterest, and as print publications.[21] Similar blogs, which combined advice on style and dressing with where to buy items, and whose street shots and images were redolent of fashion photographs, provided evidence of the fashion consumer as 'self-stylist',[22] and of the overlapping of the everyday and the aspirational through fashion. More will be said below of the role of personal style and fashion blogs in that process, but first some words on the developing role of popular media in promoting the greater relationship between fashion and everyday life.

The real and the unreal

Even a cursory glance at American and British television comedies, dramas and movies in the 1990s and 2000s reveals an increasing number of fashion-centric programmes and much more sophisticated fashion and media 'tie ins' than those referred to in Chapter 3.[23] Even non-fashion focused programmes could set unexpected fashion trends. Famously, *The Cosby Show* (1984–1992), based on the lives of an upper-middle-class African American family living in Brooklyn Heights, New York, featured a collection of 'Cosby sweaters' worn by the main character Cliff (played by Bill Cosby). These vibrantly coloured boldly patterned sweaters, created by New York–based fashion designer Koos van den Akker

Figure 7.3 The Sartorialist, Broadway, New York, 2015. Scott Schuman.

and friend of Bill Cosby's, proved a commercial hit. The show also presented Cliff's wife Clair as a smartly and fashionably dressed style icon for the black female body.

In the year *The Cosby Show* ended, an entirely different and markedly dysfunctional family was at the centre of the British cult comedy *Absolutely Fabulous* (1992–1995). The show also presented a hilarious and irreverent insider view of the fashion business, care of its two main characters. At once knowing and foolish, with personas and names based on real-life fashion mavens, Edina Monsoon (Jennifer Saunders) ran a high-powered fashion PR company and her friend Patsy Stone (Joanna Lumley) had some vague sinecure on a fashion magazine. With London as the backdrop ('performing' as fashion city *par excellence*), they were the epitome of fashionable 'showing off'. (Figure 7.4). They drank champagne all day, shopped at only the most fashionable and/or expensive stores, sported bright and outrageous clothes and mixed with the whacky and the famous; all of which served as metaphors for their metropolitan lifestyles. Through them fashion was the subject of spectacle and the object of mild derision and ridicule, but the show was a huge success, ranking among the 'Top Cult Shows Ever' by *TV Guide*,[24] and paving a way for several fashion-centric TV shows. Avowedly tongue-in-cheek, *Absolutely Fabulous* also played on London's ascendancy as the creative nerve-centre of Britain, if not Europe,

Figure 7.4 Patsy and Edina (Joanna Lumley and Jennifer Saunders), Absolutely Fabulous, BBC Television. BBC television.

in the wake of the success of the YBAs (Young British Artists) group. Many were graduates of London's art colleges, and included Damien Hirst, Tracey Emin, Sam Taylor-Wood and Sarah Lucas. Together they revitalized the art world with their challenging and provocative approach that included found-objects, throw-away materials and conceptual art. Beginning in 1988 with exhibitions at the Saatchi Gallery, and the Frieze Art Fair, the culmination was the major Royal Academy exhibition, Sensation in 1997. (The show caused a similar 'sensation' when it was shown, under the same name, at the Brooklyn Museum of Art, from October 1999 to January 2000.)

With the spectacular general election win of New Labour's Tony Blair in 1997, London appeared to evoke youth and change not just in politics but also in pop music which enjoyed a renaissance under the guise of BritPop. Comprising the groups Oasis, Pulp, Blur, The Verve and the Spice Girls, it augured a changing conception of Britishness: Cool Britannia rather than Rule Britannia, more introspective, less socially divisive and bombastic. The Spice Girls (Scary, Posh, Sporty, Ginger and Baby) had their debut single Wannabe in 1996 and under the banner of 'Girl Power' they were part of a changing consciousness among young girls and women. Criticized by some for its shallow consumerism and overly sexualized feminine images, retrospectively it is part of a continuum that includes Madonna and Lady Gaga and is a contributory factor in the emergence of third-wave feminism. Wearing a cross section of contemporary fashion – sportswear (Melanie 'Sporty' Chisholm), stilettos and high style (Victoria 'Posh' Adams – later Victoria Beckham), leopard-skin pant-suits and afro (Melanie 'Scary' Brown), pig-tails and girly dresses (Emma 'Baby' Bunton), and glitzy stage outfits including the 'Union Jack' mini-dress (Geri 'Ginger' Halliwell) – the Spice Girls had a huge impact on the everyday dressing of young women as well as high street stores such as New Look and Miss Selfridge.

For New York, the cult TV show equivalent of Absolutely Fabulous, although not focused directly on the fashion industry, was Sex and the City (1998–2004). Following the lives of four single female friends who lived in Manhattan, the series was based on the book of the same name by Candace Bushnell. Transformed as a professional writer, the lead character Carrie Bradshaw (Sarah Jessica Parker) served as the narrator. Her individualistic style was for expensive designer labels, with her commodity fetishism being focused on shoes in particular. As a consequence, established high-end brands such as Prada and Gucci, and shoemaker Manolo Blahnik, came to the attention of 'women who lived in small towns in the American heartland'.[25] After Carrie Bradshaw screamed, 'I lost my Choo!' while running for the Staten Island Ferry, in the episode first screened on 5 July 1998, the visibility of the Jimmy Choo shoe brand skyrocketed, without it paying anything for the product placement on the show.[26] Church Gibson points out how women in the United Kingdom also responded to Carrie Bradshaw's style that was 'overtly promoted on the British high street'. Midrange department store Debenhams hosted evenings for their store cardholders to promote the first *Sex and the City* movie (2008). Marks and Spencer produced a thirty-five piece collection titled 'Destination Style: New York', in collaboration with the show's costume designer Patricia Field.[27]

Following the success of *Sex and the City*, Patricia Field, a native New Yorker with her own eponymous fashion brand, went on to design the costumes for the movie *The Devil Wears Prada* (2006) and the television show *Ugly Betty* (2006–2010). Both were staged in the offices of fictional fashion magazines, *Runway* and *Mode* respectively, and projected stereotypical images of fashion as glamorous and bitchy, as a business populated by women and gay men. Miranda Priestly, the fictional editor-in-chief of *Runway,* played by Meryl Streep, was assumed to have been based on Anna Wintour, who had briefly employed at *Vogue* Lauren Weisberger, author of the 2003 book on which the film was based. While Miranda was portrayed as hard and tyrannical, the character helped to make Anna Wintour something of a household name[28]: 'Besides the gilded venues of New York, London, Paris, and Milan, Anna was now known and talked about over Big Macs and fries under the Golden Arches by young fashionistas in Wal-Mart denim in Davenport and Dubuque'.[29] Three years later, the documentary film *The September Issue* (2009) starring Anna Wintour and Grace Coddington, the creative director of *Vogue*, traced the making of the magazine's September 2007 issue (traditionally the largest annually and most packed with advertising). The credibility or apparent authenticity of that movie was validated by the inclusion of many well-known fashion designers, models and photographers. Taken together, *The Devil Wears Prada, The September Issue* and *Ugly Betty* provided some insights into the production of a fashion magazine, while also blurring fashion fact and fiction for public entertainment; a deceit enhanced by fashion professionals and celebrities appearing as themselves on fictional fashion shows.[30] Nowhere did this blurring take place more effectively than in the spate of highly successful fashion reality television shows which were broadcast from around 2000.

One of the most successful fashion reality TV shows of the first decade of the twenty-first century was *Project Runway* (2004–). Following, typically twelve, contestants through a series of fashion design challenges, the show culminated with the final three being invited to present a collection at New York Fashion Week, and to be eligible to win a prize of $100,000 or more to start their own fashion brand. Recorded originally in workrooms of the School of Fashion at Parsons School of Design in New York, its hosts were former fashion model Heidi Klum and Tim Gunn, Chair of Fashion Design at Parsons when the series began (Figure 7.5). The show proved enormously successful and was syndicated worldwide with local contestants and judges, as well as producing spin-offs in the United States such as *Project Accessory* (2011). Viewers responded to the purported 'insider view' of fashion and the creativity of contestants who were

Figure 7.5 Project Runway. Season 6, Episode 14, Aired 19 November 2009. Barbara Nitke ©2011 A+E Networks.

given unusual design briefs such as to design a garment using items purchased in a grocery store (*Project Runway* Seasons 1 and 5). Yet the reality was subtly belied. Parsons was only the set for the show, with the presence of cameras, props and stars interrupting the everyday workings of the actual design school. While the winners of the US competition had varying degrees of professional success, it was the show's host Tim Gunn who became a media star and fashion gatekeeper. Books followed, such as *Tim Gunn: A Guide to Quality, Taste & Style* (2007),[31] and television shows included *Tim Gunn's Guide to Style* (2007–2008) and *Under the Gunn* (2014). As well as bringing notoriety to their hosts, this genre of show also generated more interest in and knowledge about the fashion industry among a widely distributed viewing public.[32]

By 2010, fashion formed a substantial part of everyday entertainment, a vicarious visual pleasure for anyone with access to a screen, be they sitting at home wearing pajamas, or standing on a crowded subway train looking at their phone screen. What was interesting was how the media had developed fashion, and fashion in the city in particular, as a new 'spectator sport'. Being 'fashionable' could be predicated on having and demonstrating fashion knowledge, not just dressing fashionably. Importantly whether in London or New York, the entertainment industry's perspective had affected the definition and identification of the 'fashion city'. It created new tourist venues. As the New York garment industry struggled to survive, the Parsons 'Project Runway building' south of Times Square became a feature of city bus tours. *Sex and the City* also spawned its own dedicated tour, still being offered in 2014, which included forty sites from the series.[33] Fashion was becoming a vehicle for 'making over' New York and London in its own image, with fictional sites of fashion becoming more powerful and more glamorous in the public imagination than the reality of the sharp decline in local garment manufacturing. Ironically as clothing production moved out of the East End of London to the Far East, its run-down streets such as Redchurch St, Calvert Ave and Shoreditch High St became the focus for the edgier fashion stores.[34] With regeneration and gentrification, the East End districts of Dalston, Hoxton and Shoreditch have become revitalized centres with numerous upper-end boutiques and vintage shops, and as *Time Out* put it, 'What east London lacks in big brand chain stores, it more than makes up for with its wide choice of independent boutiques and some of the capital's coolest clothing shops'.[35]

The fact and fiction of fashion and everyday life also engaged one another powerfully through the vehicle of makeover shows, which aimed to change and ostensibly improve individuals' appearance through instilling a sense of fashion and style. One of the earliest and most successful in the millennium was the BBC UK show *What Not to Wear* (2001–2007). The show offered fashion judgement and makeovers to ordinary people as well as to celebrities, and made fashion authorities of its presenters, Trinny Woodall and Susannah Constantine. BBC Entertainment broadcast the show around the world, and the successful format influenced many other similar programs. In North America, *What Not to Wear* (2003–2013), aired by TLC in the United States and Canada, featured the secret filming of contributors who had been nominated by family or friends. Once 'ambushed' by the show's stylists (Stacy and Clinton), they were flown to New York City, with their offending wardrobes, for a weeklong overhaul. After a swingeing critique of what they wore, they were provided with two days of supervised shopping, and a new hair do and makeup. While purporting to help ordinary women to be better dressed and maybe more fashionable, such shows played on class, privilege and power in setting standards of taste. As Angela McRobbie has observed, 'What emerges is a new régime of more sharply polarized class positions, shabby failure or well-groomed success'.[36] Although originally popular in the United Kingdom, *What Not to Wear* was dropped due to increasing complaints about its presenters.[37]

The general commercial success of the makeover programme resulted in the entertainment industry creating new and unexpected fashion gatekeepers for popular audiences. Joan Rivers, the viciously sharp-tongued American comedian, was joined as co-host on the US *Fashion Police* (2002–) by British media star Kelly Osbourne.[38] Rivers was well into her sixties when the show first aired, while Osbourne displayed her tattoos and her distinctly average (as opposed to rail thin) body shape. The show denounced the sartorial choices of celebrities, with the support of their peers. Guest hosts included rap music star Nicki Minaj, Kimora Lee Simmons, former model and founder of the hip-hop brand *Bay Phat* (both of whom are mixed race), reality TV personalities, Kim Kardashian (*Keeping Up With the Kardashians)*, Nicole 'Snooki' Polizzi (*Jersey Shore)* and Ali Fedotowsky (*The Bachelor* and *The Bachelorette*), all of which proved evidence of 'the elevation of the celebrity status and the desire of consumers to become stars themselves'.[39]

In the first decade of the twenty-first century, the connections between media, celebrity and the fashion industry were becoming forged more tightly, sometimes overtly on screen, as well as behind the scenes. The discount fashion retail chain T.K. Maxx,[40] for instance, sponsored the second season of the British *Frock Me* (2010), which linked fashion and music, and was hosted by fashion media icon Alexa Chung and designer Henry Holland. Their approach has been described as 'more democratic' and in 'sharp contrast' to Trinny and Susannah's.[41] At the same time, a number of celebrities, often with their roots in music or TV, were forming their own fashion brands. They included the eponymous Victoria Beckham, the Olson twins (The Row), and Sarah Jessica Parker (Bitten). Parker, a former spokeswoman for Gap Inc, featured intentionally low-priced items, with the tagline, 'Fashion is not a luxury, it's a right'.[42] Yet in the 2000s, the same consumers (even those with relatively modest incomes) who were purchasing from mass brands were also being encouraged to acquire, or aspire to acquire, the products of luxury labels. This blending of 'high' and 'low' in the consumer market owed its origins in part to sub-cultural trends, and in particular the continuing influence of hip-hop.

Hip – Again

Hip-hop

By the late 1990s, the dominant influence on American youth culture was undoubtedly hip-hop, which had formed its own niche in the urban-wear market. Yet there was no one fixed hip-hop fashion, rather the term describes 'a popularization of styles',[43] which was to come to be seen as expressing 'the status of African-Americans at the beginning of the twenty-first century'.[44] As Van Dyk Lewis noted, 'The everyday fashion expressions of the English-speaking African Diaspora offer examples both of dislocation from the mainstream culture and of attempts to regain lost identities through the manufacture of fashion'.[45] The hip-hop influenced aesthetic, originating with the music and dance of the 'B-boys' and 'B-girls' in the 1980s and early 1990s,[46] clearly challenged and transformed the accepted rules of mainstream fashion. Clothes were worn oversize, to hang from the body; men's pants famously 'sagged' below the natural waistline, revealing underwear, sometimes in its entirety. Diamonds (either real or fake) became acceptable for everyday wear, men sported heavy gold chains and women huge earrings, all in the desire to 'bling', whether to show off wealth and status, or just to catch the eye. The hip-hop sub-cultural aesthetic also changed, to appropriate familiar status objects including 'designer clothing, imported champagne, Cuban cigars, luxury automobiles, and fine jewelry – all the things that prove how successful you are by American Dream standards'.[47] The media and fashion industries rapidly commercialized a hip-hop look, characterized by certain fashion brands in the 1990s. Shrewd businesses tapped into urban youth trends with remarkable success, giving away their products to key 'influencers' in local neighbourhoods, and promoting their lines without the use of traditional advertising. Some established fashion brands, including Polo by Ralph Lauren, Tommy Hilfiger, Nautica by David Chu, as well as DKNY, were appropriated as part of hip-hop style, and in its turn 'hip hop would start to change the sartorial landscape of Seventh Avenue, Paris, and Milan'.[48] Tommy Hilfiger became the sportswear designer of choice. Ironically, its all-American, exclusive Ivy-style look, symbolic of the East coast WASP, was the brand favoured predominantly by African American men. Hilfiger actively embraced hip-hop, using black models in advertising campaigns, and having celebrities such as Sean (Puff Daddy or P. Diddy) Coombs, rapper Coolio, and members of the band Jodeci as runway models for his Americana collection.[49] Timberland, another popular brand with an outdoor, casual aesthetic, did not embrace hip-hop in the same way, 'perceived as being afraid of the hardcore urban attitude'.[50] Hilfiger was astute in recognizing the potential of celebrity product placement and new market sectors. It provided the lead for many urban sportswear brands such as FUBU (For Us By Us), Ecko Unlimited, Mecca USA, Lugz, Walker Wear, Boss Jeans by IG Design and Enyce, to produce sweatshirts, denim and clothing items bearing huge logos across the chest, back and legs. New York-based FUBU became highly successful in the 1990s, securing a distribution agreement with Samsung, and product placement in over 100 Macy's outlets and more than 300 J.C. Penney stores, bringing New York inner city street style to the suburbs and the fashion mainstream,[51] characterized by the style of its creators, with their casual urban style, with a touch of bling (Figure 7.6). The Fall 1998 collections, for example, typically featured hoodies, cargo pants, bomber jackets, shearling coats, and sneakers, all garments associated with hip-hop.[52]

By the 2000s, a number of hip-hop and black music industry stars were running very successful fashion companies. Among the most prominent brands were Sean John (Sean 'Diddy' Combs), House of Deréon (Beyoncé), Baby Phat (Kimora Lee Simmons), Rocawear (Jay-Z, Damon Dash, and Kareem 'Biggs' Burke) and Todd Smith (LL Cool J). Each of them featured the glamorous lifestyles of their founders as a marketing tool and encompassed formal wear as well as casual wear to create their own distinctive blend of street fashion and high fashion.[53] Kimora Lee Simmons' Baby Phat label moved hip-hop style

Figure 7.6 The creators of the urban clothing line FUBU, Essence Awards, Radio City Music Hall, New York, 2000. Scott Gries. Getty Images.

very effectively to women's wear. With higher waisted jeans, tighter T-shirts and larger jackets, it provided a feminine version of the simple white T-shirt, jeans and baseball cap that constitute the, now globally recognizable, signifiers of hip-hop. The brand has been described as 'an ever-changing amalgam of the street and the avenue, self-expression imported directly from New York courtesy of up-to-the-minute media and the internet – untamed, unfiltered, and unstoppable'.[54] Hip-hop's fashion direction also changed, especially in the early 2000s, when its consumers began to move away from casual wear in favour of more tailored styles.[55] Its ethnic and demographic profile had also expanded beyond the African American and teen populations, to include the earlier adopters who had matured in age and had entered establishment occupations.[56] Hip-hop brands also entered the retail mainstream, with Russell Simmons Argyleculture and Sean Combs Sean John labels being prominently placed on the menswear floors at Macy's, and with Kanye West producing a women's wear line, Dw.[57] Hip-hop fashion became a ubiquitous delineator of 'cool'. Even the British royal princes, William and Harry, were seen wearing baseball caps and adopting 'homeboy gestures', presumably gleaned from music videos.[58] The media was central to the promotion of all things Hip in the millennium, not least the re-emergence of the term *hipster*. With its semantic origins in the first half of the twentieth century, the fact that the twenty-first-century hipster seemed both ubiquitous and hard to define was itself a revealing sign of the times.

Hipsters

Contemporary hipsters have been identified generationally as Millennials, and in New York City they are associated in particular with the East Village, the Lower East Side and Williamsburg, Brooklyn. In the late 1990s, Brooklyn's former industrial neighbourhood was attracting artists and musicians into large warehouse spaces with low rents. Ten years later, the hipster sub-culture (if there ever truly was one) had been so parodied and commercialized that it was designated as being completely 'over'.[59] But hipster style had its origins not in hip-hop and the South Bronx, but in the bohemian culture of 1950s Greenwich Village. In 1998, the population of the North side of Williamsburg was already being described as 'a mix of young artists and professionals, of Italian immigrants and Polish immigrants with relatives in nearby Greenpoint'.[60] They sported brightly coloured hair and wore retro-style clothes bought at local second-hand shops. Yet, in contradictory fashion, the White Hipster image that emerged in 1999 was also represented by

> trucker hats; undershirts called 'wifebeaters', worn alone; the aesthetic of basement rec-room pornography, flash-lit Polaroids, and fake-wood paneling; Pabst Blue Ribbon[61]; 'porno' or 'pedophile' mustaches; aviator glasses; Americana T-shirts from church socials, et cetera; tube socks; the late albums of Johnny Cash, produced by Rick Rubin; and tattoos.[62]

Just as the 'White Negro'[63] had once fetishized blackness, 'the White Hipster fetishized the violence, instinctiveness, and rebelliousness of lower-middle-class "white trash"'. Its media channel was the fashion magazine *Vice,* which moved to New York from Montreal in 1999 and 'drew on casual racism and porn to refresh traditional women's-magazine features'.[64] Millennial hipsters, unlike the musicians and writers who bore the name in the 1950s, were not artists, but 'hip consumers' who employed their creativity carefully to select the products of mass-consumption as 'a form of art'.[65] Their mainstream fashion icon was American Apparel, the low-priced casual brand founded in Los Angeles in 1997, which originally promoted its local anti-sweatshop manufacturing, but gradually moved its advertising images to more 'amateur soft-core porn'.[66] The cognoscenti also looked to Urban Outfitters, and its sub- brands[67] that targeted college students in its urban retail locations, favouring a nostalgic re-cycled look. It appealed to a consumer demographic, in the United States, but also through its outlets in Canada and Europe, as well as through its online retail.

By 2003, hipsterdom had been commercialized, globalized and had had a substantial consumer impact, thanks in no small part to the Internet, which 'deregulated' subculture and disseminated its codes and symbols (Figure 7.7).[68] Hipster ironic nostalgia had become mainstream, with LP records and record

Figure 7.7 Hipster couple on Carnaby Street, Soho, London, 2013. Getty Images.

players being sought-after commodities, and fixed gear bicycles without brakes or other interference, becoming popular. In sartorial terms, skinny jeans became so ubiquitous as to virtually obliterate other styles from the mass-market. At the corporeal level, no self-respecting white or light-skinned woman or man aged 18–30 would be seen without a tattoo. So much so that in *The Hipster Handbook* (2002), Robert Lanham advised (ironically, of course) that 'Hipsters today must be more discriminating when selecting a tattoo for themselves' as tattoos had 'gone suburban'.[69] While declaring that hipsters were 'everywhere', from New York to New Zealand,[70] Lanham (wisely) did not advise on their dress code. In London, hipsters had their geographical origins in Shoreditch and the East End, on Old Street, and in the retail outlets on and around Brick Lane. Interestingly, the tongue-in-cheek online quiz 'Are You a British Hipster?' offered respondents shopping choices that included thrift stores, Ebay, and international brands including American Apparel, New Look, River Island and GAP, as well as Uniqlo, Urban Outfitters and Reiss.[71]

Hipsterdom burgeoned as a fashion and lifestyle influence in the 'oughts', so much so that 'Everything becomes just another signifier of personal identity. Thus hipsterdom forces on us a sense of the burden of identity, of constantly having to curate it if only to avoid seeming like a hipster'.[72] The dissemination of hipster style owed a considerable debt to mainstream and social media, and to commerce, which even resulted in the reproduction of formerly defunct products, such as the typewriter, record player and Polaroid camera.[73] While hipsterdom targeted 18–30–year-olds and was evident in London and New York, certain less mainstream locations became particularly iconic to the style. The US satirical television sketch comedy *Portlandia* that debuted on the Independent Film Channel (IFC) on 21 January 2011, based in and around Portland, Oregon, was a successful and hugely entertaining parody of hipster lifestyle. But it was not the only cultural development that had a wider impact on fashion and consumption. In London Chavs, and in New York Normcore, each had distinct style and product manifestations, while drawing their references from everyday life.

Chavs and Normcore

In February 2004, British tabloid *The Daily Mirror* headlined 'How to Spot a Chav. You may know them as Kevs, Slappers, Neds, Townies, or Scallies – but a new Internet website has branded them Chavs, from an old gypsy word for child'.[74] It was this same year that apparently the word 'chav' entered the *Oxford English Dictionary* and was defined as 'In the United Kingdom (originally the south of England): a young person of a type characterized by brash and loutish behaviour and the wearing of designer-style clothes (esp. sportswear); usually with connotations of a low social status'.[75] Key elements of chavs and their sartorial appearance were fashion and language. Poked fun at in a British TV in series such as *Little Britain* chavs were typically white working-class, and their language, Chavspeak 'is "hybrid cockney" taking in "Jamaican Yardie"'. Inevitably the 'young chav will ditch his middle-England accent and suddenly take on the voice and characteristics of his LA [Gangsta Rap] heroes'.[76] Also drawing from US urban black cultures was an excessive use of jewellery and branded sportswear (trainers/sneakers, baseball caps) combined with luxury brands such as Burberry that had previously been associated with 'the smart set' (paralleling the consumer preferences of the British Casuals mentioned in Chapter 6). In consuming such products within this distinctive sub-culture, chavs changed the meanings of powerful brands in ways that were not anticipated.[77] Indeed due to this growing association between what were seen by politicians and social observers as short-hand for a group of dysfunctional, inadequate, poor young people, Burberry withdrew its renowned fabric design 'Nova' from the market as it had become the brand of choice for Chavs.[78] Burberry's products with this infamous check experienced enormous reputational damage due to this association; however, by 2014, with Romeo Beckham modelling in the company's new advertisement, the Burberry brand made a comeback re-establishing itself as the ubiquitous high fashion brand.[79] As the Daily Mail Online put it in November 2014, 'In the current advert, Romeo Beckham wears the £315 "icon" cashmere scarf in Burberry's distinctive camel, black, white and red check. Hard to believe that it was only a decade ago that the brand seemed in crisis and that check was less icon, more albatross. Far too widespread for its own good, it had become known as "chav check".'[80]

Although Chavs represented a specific and distinctive group, the wearing of expensive brands in everyday life had become commonplace in the early twenty-first century and not just among a younger generation. Following from consumer practices established in previous decades, in Britain and the United States, sports and outdoor brands such as Nike or The North Face continued to provide clothes that could be either fashionable or ordinary. New brands also appeared on the market, such as the Japanese fast fashion brand Uniqlo, which had a vast international expansion in the second decade of the twenty-first century. Opening its first store in London (and China) in 2002 and then New York in 2005, it produced a casual 'street style' that was priced for most pockets and styled and sized to suit most generations, following retailers such as Marks and Spencer in the United Kingdom and GAP in the United States.[81] Whether strictly a fashion brand or a producer of Unique Clothing (originally named the Unique Clothing Warehouse), Uniqlo's products became a part of functional and fashionable urban street wear in London, New York and way beyond. Completely anonymous in terms of brand identity, Uniqlo captured the fashion moment, as did 'Normcore', in its referencing of the most ordinary of everyday dress.

Coming ten years after the identification of hipsters and chavs, Normcore was coined by the Brooklyn-based forecasting group K-Hole, who originated the neologism in a report called Youth Mode: A Report of Freedom, which they produced in October 2013 for an exhibition at London's Serpentine Gallery.[82] Or, arguably, the term was coined in London in 2011 in Alice Goddard's magazine *Hot and Cool*.[83] A synthesis of 'normal' and 'hardcore', it had *The Guardian* journalist Richard Bensen asking in February 2014, 'Normcore: the next big fashion movement?' while describing it as '2014's most forced of forced memes'.[84] Its featuring of 'normal clothes', could be disconcerting, as New York journalist Fiona Duncan described an experience in summer 2013: 'Sometime last summer I realized that, from behind, I could no longer tell if my fellow Soho pedestrians were art kids or middle-aged, middle-American tourists. Clad in stonewash jeans, fleece, and comfortable sneakers, both types looked like they might've just stepped off an R-train after shopping in Times Square'.[85] Confusions could occur when the motivation was to look as ordinary as possible, rather than seeking to look 'different' or 'authentic'. As twenty-six-year-old New York fashion designer Kristine Guico, pictured in the same article wearing a long-sleeved blue denim shirt, and a white Nike baseball cap pulled over her eyes, was quoted as saying, 'Everyone's so unique that it's not unique anymore. Especially in New York'. And we could add also, in London. Normcore clothes of choice were bland, the sartorial role models being Jerry Seinfeld and the characters of the New York-based sit-com *Seinfeld* (1989–1998). To achieve their look, followers should sport, 'mock turtlenecks with Tevas and Patagonia windbreakers; Uniqlo khakis with New Balance sneakers or Crocs and souvenir-stand baseball caps'.[86] The fashion 'look' was not distinction, but sameness, with the idea not to stand out, but rather to completely blend in, as here where the appearance of British singer Alexandra Burke blends with that of her fan (Figure 7.8). As Lipovetsky noted of the late twentieth century, 'Everything goes, and yet the streets look drab, devoid of originality for the most part: designers follies are countered by the monotony of everyday appearance'.[87] 'Sameness' and 'monotony' might also be seen to be reactions to what was taking place in the commercial fashion arena, where change appeared to be more rapid than ever before.

Brand new

Once the preserve of a small wealthy consumer niche, the luxury market had been transformed early in the millennium, as consumers demonstrated their purchasing power in what might be termed, new fashion geographies, including for example nations in the Middle East. Strategic product development, plus digital information and communications, had broadened the marketing platform for luxury brands bringing them global exposure. Mass fashion labels adopted business strategies that resembled those of luxury brands by offering similar goods at lower prices.[88] A huge mass-market change occurred with the

Figure 7.8 The British singer Alexandra Burke with a fan while promoting her new album 'Heartbreak on Hold' at an HMV store, Market Street, 6 June 2012, Manchester, England. Getty Images.

development of 'fast fashion' in the twenty-first century, which brought new merchandise into stores every few weeks instead of every fashion season. Zara was the fast fashion market leader in the early years of the millennium, reputed to have the most effective and responsive operations techniques, enabling production of new designs approximately every three weeks.[89] Spanish in origin, the brand transcended any national identification, expanding into Europe, the United States and beyond. Swedish-based, global fashion brand H&M went further by collaborating with prestigious fashion designers beginning with Karl Lagerfeld, then Stella McCartney, Viktor and Rolf, and Rei Kawakubo of Comme des Garçons, as well as with celebrities including Madonna. The same approach was utilized by Target, the United States' second-largest discount retailer after Walmart. Target had already hired product designer Michael Graves to create their homewares collection, but it was with its commissioning of New York designer Isaac Mizrahi in 2003 that it began to produce celebrity fashion collections.[90] Fashion designers were being employed by mass-market brands as a strategic tool to increase profits. Fast fashion's marketing strategies spread; Dorothy Perkins, a mainstay of the British high street, ran special in store customer product discount events with free cocktails. Even Primark, regarded as one of Britain's lowest status fashion brands, showed at London Fashion Week,[91] providing it kudos in the fashion system and thus with its customers.

Some brands also made the, commercially risky, retail leap across the 'pond'. Topshop, from Britain, opened its first US store in New York on Broadway in 2009, the year after the American brand Banana Republic had opened a flagship store on London's Regent Street. Both brands were well established in their home countries for affordable fashion. As one journalist commented, 'Just like Topshop for Americans visiting Britain, Banana Republic was a first port of call for Brits visiting the US'.[92] Top Shop (later changed to Topshop) began in the early 1960s, in the basement of the Peter Robinson department store (part of the larger Burton Group) at London's Oxford Circus, targeting the developing young fashion market.[93] By the early 1970s, Top Shop was so successful that stores were opening around Britain, to gradually replace the parent brand.[94] Although its trade declined in the late 1970s and 1980s, the brand was revived in the 1990s under the direction of Jane Shepherdson, who was attributed in the British press as 'democratising style and changing the way we buy and wear fashion'.[95] Shepherdson made the brand a high street fashion leader again. 'Its huge Oxford Circus store became famous as the first place fashion editors visited when they arrived in London for the biannual fashion-week shows. Everyone-everyone-shopped at Topshop'.[96] The store received a very positive consumer response when it opened in New York in April 2009. Despite the continuing recession, Topshop benefitted from existing awareness of the UK brand, as well as from consumers 'trending down' and away from more expensive New York fashion retailers such as Saks or Barneys.[97] Described as bringing 'over-the-top rock "n" roll merchandising' the shop location had historical significance, relative to the 1980s downtown scene, and to the development of fashion retail on Broadway over a century before. By making available 'two-for-$18 jerseys and a $500 dress within 15 feet of each other', Sir Philip Green, the owner of the parent company Arcadia, rightly described its success as having 'something for everyone'.[98] Each brand was distinguished by a particular fashion identity: Topshop's edgy 'rock "n" roll' style was paralleled by Banana Republic's 'preppy', casual look.

Banana Republic is a long-standing fashion brand in the United States, founded in 1978, and acquired by Gap Inc. in 1983. It was credited in the British press as doing 'what US fashion does best: efficient, well-cut, on-trend workwear and accessories for men and women'.[99] As Banana Republic was getting ready for its debut in London, the brand was also preparing another initiative, which was playing on mythic 'New Yorkness' as well as utilizing the established fashion retail practice of the tie in. The venture with AMC, the US cable TV network, was for limited edition men's and women's wear collections in collaboration with series Mad Men.[100] Centred on a Madison Avenue advertising agency and set in the late 1950s and early 1960s, the series ran for seven seasons (2007–2015). The collaboration resulted in two collections, in 2011 (Figure 7.9) and in 2012, devised by the show's costume designer and Banana Republic's brand's creative team. The venture also reflected the growing popularity of 'heritage' in fashion, whereby companies were re-issuing versions of items from their history. This could result in clothing, which had been ubiquitous but also utilitarian, being re-launched as *fashion* items. One of many examples was the American Sperry Top Sider footwear, first made in 1935. History and national favourites were revitalized for international markets, in what appeared as a search, by brands and consumers, for greater credibility and authenticity in the early twenty-first century.

Lamrad and Hanlon noted how the search for authenticity, evident in some fashion trends, 'resolves the tension between the need for freedom expressed through individuality and the need for security and a sense of belonging to an imagined community'.[101] The fashion business referenced imagined community in a range of different ways, as noted from the beginning of this chapter – not only by way of the (mythic) fashion city, or national identity, but via the Internet, which gave consumers access to a greater range and diversity of fashion knowledge and items, to fuel a desire for products and for social, cultural, economic and ethical capital. The latter could be provided by the 'fashion for development' model, of which Lamrad and Hanlon write, where with a purchase consumers 'give back' or 'pay the membership fee to be inducted into the imagined community'.[102] After the millennium, there were many and varied ways to do this, such as the 'One for One' model where an equivalent item was donated to those deemed in need for one purchased by those who were not (TOMS shoes, for example). Others, such as Etsy, the e-commerce website founded in 2005, featured peer-to-peer trading of handmade and used items, as well as mass-produced equivalents that were somehow deemed unusual or unique. Such initiatives were also evidence of attention being paid to fashion as material *clothing*, not just as image, as part of a developing ethical awareness, at the level of production and consumption.

The tragic collapse of the Rana Plaza clothing factory, killing more than 1,100 workers and injuring 2,500 in Bangladesh on 23 April 2013 drew a chilling

Figure 7.9 Banana Republic 'Mad Men' 2011 collection. Getty Images.

parallel to the Triangle Shirtwaist fire in New York City just over a century before. Extensive media coverage of Rana Plaza revealed the reach and intricacy of global production and supply chains, with thirty-two companies being found to have links with the factory complex. Two years after the disaster around a third of those companies, associated with fast fashion, had failed to contribute to the trust fund set up to compensate victims and their families.[103] The tragedy drew attention to global labour conditions and exploitation, as well as to the diverse and widespread points of origin of fashionable clothes, cheap ones in particular. While this did not necessarily dent the commercial fashion market, it did reinforce the amount of waste – human and material that fashion, especially fast fashion, engendered and depended upon. In parallel, however, a small but significant shift was becoming evident, at the level of consumers and producers, of the greater visibility of the darker side of the fashion system. Alternative and 'slower' approaches to fashion were gaining attention, and highlighted more transparent production systems, local resources, and the need for closer relationships between wearers and their clothes.[104] Biographies of clothes were also becoming of interest academically[105] and to a wider readership.[106] The latter resonated with a greater interest by consumers in second-hand clothes, for ethical as well as fashionable reasons, but it also led to some new retail initiatives, such as providing mending. New York-based retailer Eileen Fisher established a service where its customers could return brand items to its shops for repair. The company also established its Green Eileen recycling initiative that bought back and re-sold gently used Eileen Fisher items.

Eileen Fisher was an eponymous brand started in the late 1980s, known for comfortable clothes favoured by older women, it was neither considered 'fashion forward' nor associated with a younger wearer. The brand underwent something of a facelift in 2009 with the stock market crash, but also apparently due to a damning line by a character in an off-Broadway play by Nora and Delia Ephron, *Love, Loss, and What I Wore,* who commented, 'When you start wearing Eileen Fisher, you might as well say, "I give up".'[107] In-house research revealed that it was not just the middle aged and well off who liked the brand's comfortable clothes. Some younger wearers wanted comfortable, well-made clothes, but could not always find items in the stores. Stores were gradually re-designed, advertising campaigns started to feature younger models (Figure 7.10) and by 2010 profits had increased.[108] The brand also opened its first shops outside of North America, in London's Covent Garden and on Marylebone High Street in 2011, and began to sell wholesale to Fenwick's of Bond Street. The London fashion trade news outlet, *Drapers,* considered London a logical step, commenting that, 'The cultural connection between the US and UK made that first step a little easier; there's a similar way of doing business'.[109] The same article also referred to how the Fifth Avenue store in New York had newly reopened after refurbishing with what the company called the 'London Approach'. This approach, which was to be used

Figure 7.10 Eileen Fisher Advertising Campaign, Fall 2015. Eileen Fisher, Inc.

in all Eileen Fisher US stores, involved 'a more heavily curated' layout, with fewer sizes out on the rails and more emphasis on contemporary store design, as typical of the UK premium market.[110] That the stores were described as being 'curated' spoke to the fact that the term 'curation'[111] had saturated fashion, art, business and everyday life. While dismissed as an over-used buzzword,[112] it nevertheless signalled new connections that united different practices across time and space; not least the affiliations that luxury fashion brands were making with art and museums, each it seems in search of greater publicity and economic return.

Fashion – Curation

A retrospective of the work of Takashi Murakami, the Japanese pop culture artist, at the Brooklyn Museum of Art (April 5–13 July 2008), which originated at the Museum of Contemporary Art, Los Angeles, in 2007, helped to attract new audiences to the museum. © *MURAKAMI* sponsored by Louis Vuitton, featured a shop in the middle of the show, selling Murakami's designs for the brand, an affiliation that began in 2003 and which included handbags ranging in price from $1,310 to $2,210.[113] Just as the Los Angeles show had attracted young people who had never been to the museum, 'because they heard about the show through various kinds of cross-branding ... Names like Louis Vuitton, Kanye West and eBay',[114] the Brooklyn exhibition did the same. One visitor, 'Roderick A', a self-described 'art novice' considered it 'one of the best exhibits I have ever been to', even though 'the only reason I heard of Murakami was because he designed Louis Vuitton bags, which became heavily bootlegged, and he did the cover of Kanye West's "Graduation".'[115]

In the autumn of 2008 an altogether more ambitious collaboration between a luxury fashion brand and artists took place in New York's Central Park. *Mobile Art* was staged in a purpose-built temporary pavilion designed by architect Zaha Hadid in collaboration with Karl Lagerfeld, chief designer of Chanel who sponsored the event. Artists, including the French Sophie Calle and the Swiss Sylvie Fleury, were commissioned to create pieces inspired by Chanel's classic 2.55 quilted handbag with a chain strap. An overt advertisement for the brand, additional artists' installations were staged in the Chanel shops in midtown and in SoHo. Although originally scheduled to continue to London, Moscow and finally Paris, New York proved the last stop of the show (which had previously visited Hong Kong and Tokyo) as the change in the global economic climate made this extravagance no longer financially viable, even for Chanel. Nevertheless, it was evidence of a closer and increasingly more ambiguous association between fashion brands, and art, as well as of the rising tide of celebrity culture. When the Costume Institute at the Metropolitan Museum of Art staged *Alexander McQueen: Savage Beauty* in the summer of 2011, it had to extend its daily visiting hours as well as the length of the show to cope with the unprecedented number of visitors. The combination of the tragic suicide of the designer in 2010, the choice of Sarah Burton, McQueen's successor as chief designer, to create the dress for Katherine Middleton's April 2011 wedding to Prince William, plus the spectacular beauty of the show, completely captured the public imagination.

In London also, exhibitions devoted to fashion and fashion icons were becoming more frequent. The Victoria and Albert Museum opened its refurbished 'Fashion Galleries' in 2012 where, according to one review, 'the grandeur and exuberance of the fashions on display will ultimately win over any critics'.[116] The museum staged fashion-focused shows on a regular basis, including: *Black Style* (2004), *Swinging Sixties'* (2006–2007), *The Concise Dictionary of Dress* (2010), *Hollywood Costume* (2012–2013), *Club to Catwalk: London Fashion in the 1980s* (2013–2014) and *Alexander McQueen: Savage Beauty* (2015). During the same period, the revamped neoclassical Somerset House on The Strand became a regular venue for fashion exhibitions, including *SHOWstudio: Fashion Revolution* (2009), *Martin Margiela '20' The Exhibition* (2010), *Valentino: Master of Couture* (2012) and *Isabella Blow: Fashion Galore!* (2013–2014), and from 2009, it hosted London Fashion Week. Showing the extensive fashion wardrobe of the late Isabella Blow, a former fashion journalist and muse of Alexander McQueen drew attention to the contemporary significance of fashion's gatekeepers and influencers. Heiress Daphne Guinness, who had acquired her friend Isabella's private fashion collection after her death, owned many of the pieces on display.

She had already had an exhibition of her own wardrobe at the Museum of the Fashion Institute of Technology (FIT) in New York (2011–2012). In the millennium, who and what was impacting fashion was becoming much more disparate, as well as encompassing a wider range and diversity of participants, aided especially by the Internet, social media and blogging.

On 18 June 2012, journalist Judith Thurman hosted a conversation entitled 'Good Taste/Bad Taste: The Evolution of Contemporary Chic' between New York personality and fashion maven Iris Apfel, aged 90, and fashion style blogger Tavi Gevinson, aged 16. Despite the contrast in their ages, each of the women was a fashion authority with her own individual style, sanctioned by the Costume Institute of The Metropolitan Museum of Art where the event was held, and by the fashion industry. To attend the talk, Mrs Apfel wore items from her extensive wardrobe of fashion and ethnic items, which had been the subject of the exhibition *Rara Avis: Selections from the Iris Apfel Collection,* at the Costume Institute (2005-2006) and then at the Peabody Essex Museum in Salem, Massachusetts (2009-2010) (Figure 7.11). Miss Gevinson's outfit included a pleated 'lips' skirt from Miucia Prada's 2000 collection, given to her by the designer. After the formal conversation ended, Miss Gevinson's young female fans in the audience rushed forward to get more time with the *Style Rookie,* who began writing her blog in 2008, at the age of 11, from her home in the suburbs of Chicago. Gevinson was the youngest independent style blogger to gain fame through a genre 'chiefly

Figure 7.11 Iris Apfel, *Rare Bird of Fashion: The Irreverent Iris Apfel,* 17 October 2009 - 7 February 2010, The Peabody Essex Museum, Salem, Massachusetts. Getty Images.

devoted to their authors' everyday life, to the ordinary practices and moments it is made of',[117] which had become part of fashion discourse and of the everyday lives of many young women by the second decade of the twenty-first century.

Of the two main genres of fashion blogs which developed, the independent and the corporate, it is the first category, and particularly the individual personal fashion of style blog[118] that shed most light on what ordinary individuals (as opposed to fashion professionals such as Scott Schuman of *The Sartorialist*) were buying, wearing and thinking about fashion. Of course, for some such as Tavi or Susanna Lau, known as Susie Bubble, of the blog *Style Bubble,* the popularity of their blogs transformed them into fashion and media stardom. For others, personal blogs served as sartorial and consumer diaries and autobiographies, offering the opportunity to display and share the triumphs and anxieties of their identity construction and display from the safety of their bedroom, living room or back garden. Writing before the emergence of the first fashion blog in 2003,[119] Sherry Turkle noted in 1995 how already 'The Internet has become a significant social laboratory for experimenting with the constructions and reconstructions of self that characterize postmodern life. In its virtual reality, we self-fashion and self create'.[120] By the 2000s, social media offered previously unforeseen opportunities to share fashion 'looks' by means of the substantially visual form of some of the microblogs such as *Tumblr* (2007), *Instagram* (2010) and *Pinterest* (2010). The availability and sophistication of the technology influenced the diversity of the productions, and increased the currency of still and moving images. A simple webcam was all that was needed to document the 'shopping haul' phenomenon that was particularly popular with teenage girls, who shared what they had bought via homemade YouTube videos. Sixteen-year-old Blair Fowler showed a haul from Forever 21, which included tops, skirts and skinny jeans bought for $6.99, chosen according to her criteria that they were 'cute'. The 500 *YouTube* videos posted by Blair and her sister Elle received over 750 million views from fans. Such popularity alerted large fashion retailers to the huge advertising potential of social media.[121] As a result they offered free items to popular 'haulers' and bloggers in a contemporary version of the commodity tie-ins previously used in movies and on television shows. The difference here was that peers were speaking directly to peers, literally using their own language, and in doing so were reinforcing the simultaneously individual and collective appeal of fashion, referenced by Simmel over a century before.

Blogs also extended the scope of who and what might be considered fashionable and stylish. Ari Seth Cohen's *Advanced Style* added a new demographic to street photography. Inspired by his grandmothers, his blog featured 'the over-60 set in the world's most stylish locales',[122] although here the subjects were the spectacle, rather than the originators of their own images and texts. Blogs and social media offered the potential for empowerment through fashion, especially for women who were typically disenfranchised, due to age or body type or size. As Julia Twigg has noted, the women featured on Advanced Style display 'a self-conscious, edgy, performative look that makes sense in an urban centre like New York'.[123] They are not fashion followers, but could be described rather as unabashed individualists who bring extraordinarily creative approaches to their everyday outfits, and who love showing them off. Twigg raises the question of what is being performed, is it age, or an alternative vision of age, or youth? The answer is not clear or fixed, depending in part on the intention of the subjects and the nature of their audiences. What is important is how a New York–specific phenomenon has been shared, through a range of media including the website, books and a movie (2014). This serves as an example of how fashion can provide agency to individuals and media-isation can be a form of sharing and community building. It also indicates how despite the spatial and locational ambiguity of virtual communication and of globalization, place continued to retain an important role for fashion in everyday life in the millennium. While stereotypes of the 'fashion city' might, on the one hand, have been reinforced in the popular media, as demonstrated in *The Sun* article that introduced this chapter, other more interesting dimensions should not be overlooked. Social media in particular offered the potential for more particular or niche fashion communities to be established and for new locations to be identified and communicated. This was demonstrated at an event at the Brooklyn Museum of Art in December 2013, where a panel made up of local bloggers, stylists, photographers and fashion retailers showed the diversity of 'Brooklyn Style'.[124] The presenters reinforced a perspective that was distinct from the familiar fashion stereotypes of New York, which through its very existence could provide a model of how more ordinary modes of dress could be both distinct and extraordinary. Through social media, other styles and fashions that were created within communities rather than by the fashion system could be disseminated within and well beyond their places of origin. This served not only as evidence of a greater democratization of fashion but also of the changing nature of what constituted 'fashion' and how it was defined, and of its greater evidence in everyday life (Figure 7.12). Fashion impacted upon the young and middle-aged of different classes and ethnicities, black and white, men and women, affirming McRobbie's proposition that 'the cleavages of class, race and sex can also be read in and through the parades of fashion and style of the post-war years'.[125]

In London and New York, the ubiquity and pervasiveness of fashion (making, advising, informing, accessing, fashioning) that we highlight in this chapter and throughout the book begs the question about the nature of the everyday as it intersects with fashion. Related to this, is the question of how the ordinary maps onto fashion? Seigworth and Gardiner, who posed a set of questions that have informed our thinking in this book: about how everyday life is transformed under the conditions of modernity (we would add post-modernity to this); how everyday life is manifested in particular geographies; and how 'emancipatory possibilities'

Figure 7.12 'Harlem Style', 2015. Photographer Marcqui Akins for The Common Thread Project © Mikaila Brown.

have been inscribed and taken up in everyday practices, mentions the ordinary only once as the counterpoint to 'remarkable?'[126] In contrast, Sandywell appears to draw a distinction as he wrote, '*ordinary* implicates a cluster of significations indexing the habitual, customary, regular, usual, or normal'.[127] Indeed, although he doesn't reference fashion, he should. It is and it has been throughout our period an exemplar of his proposition that 'where ordinary is exemplified by commonplace phenomena that are taken for granted and unnoticed, the extraordinary marks the disturbing eruption of the rare and the highly valued. Like other forms of extravagant experience, the extraordinary exceeds the limits and boundaries of ordinariness'.[128] This is the dialectic of fashion, or perhaps we should say, it has been commonly perceived to be so. In fact, we contend that in the long twentieth century, fashion operated along a continuum, moving back and forth, up and down from extraordinary to ordinary. In fact the principal driver for this has been the proliferation of knowledge and widening access to fashion that has been one of the major characteristics of the twentieth century. While attempting to claim a privileged place as art, it has in fact yielded its uniqueness in the face of its permeability in the diversity of everyday, on-going lives. By focusing on two major fashion cities that were subject to significant change, it is clear that fashion has become embedded in the 'grammar of everyday life' in these cities, and it has taken particular forms as a result of this; but perhaps fundamental and at its core has been the precarious and transitory nature of its relationship to tradition and modernity.[129] Fashion has been both endlessly repetitive and shockingly aberrant. Paradoxically as we progress beyond the millennium, we discern fashion's increasing preoccupation with the 'real': 'real people' as bloggers, photographers and filmmakers; yet, we have argued, fashion has been 'writing the real' by helping to articulate and shape everyday lives over the preceding hundred years.

Notes

1   'Wear in the World', *The Sun,* February 17, 2013, 39.

2   See, for example, Christopher Breward and David Gilbert (eds) *Fashion's World Cities* (Oxford and New York: Berg, 2006).

3   *The Sun*, available online, http://www.thesun.co.uk/sol/homepage/ (accessed March 18, 2014).

4   Vanessa Freidman speaking at the Fashion Benefit, Parsons School of Design, May 19, 2015.

5   Gilles Lipovetsky, *The Empire of Fashion: Dressing Modern Democracy* (Princeton: Princeton University Press, 1994), 123, quoted in Andrew Hill, 'People Dress So Badly Nowadays: Fashion and Late Modernity', in *Fashion and Modernity*, ed. Christopher Breward and Caroline Evans (Oxford and New York: Berg, 2005), 68.

6   Hill, 'People Dress So Badly Nowadays', 67–77.

7   Pamela Church Gibson, *Fashion and Celebrity Culture* (London and New York: Berg, 2012), 18.

8   Cesar Harada, 'Surculture', available online, http://cesarharada.com/pearls/surculture/ (accessed March 18, 2014).

9   As did his column 'Evening Hours' which features photographs from selected recent society charity events.

10 '57th and Fifth: A Holiday Magnet for the World', *The New York Times*, December 30, 1978, 21.

11 *Bill Cunningham New York, a Film by Richard Press*, available online, http://www.zeitgeistfilms.com/billcunninghamnewyork/aboutbill.html (accessed January 21, 2014).

12 Lauren Collins, 'Man on the Street Bill Cunningham Takes Manhattan', *The New Yorker*, March 16, 2009, available online, http://www.newyorker.com/reporting/2009/03/16/090316fa_fact_collins?currentPage=all (accessed January 21, 2014).

13 'Bill on Bill', *The New York Times*, 27 October 2002, available online, http://www.nytimes.com/2002/10/27/style/bill-on-bill.html?pagewanted=4&src=pm (accessed January 21, 2014).

14 Bill Cunningham in *Bill Cunningham New York,* a film by Richard Press, 2010.

15 Agnès Rocamora and Alistair O'Neill, 'Fashioning the Street: Images of the Street in the Fashion Media', in *Fashion as Photograph: Viewing and Reviewing Images of Fashion*, ed. Eugenie Shinkle (London: I.B. Tauris, 2008), 186.

16 Ibid., 190.

17 M de Certeau, 'Walking in the City', in *The Practice of Everyday Life* (London: University of California Press, 1988), 92, quoted in Rocamora and O'Neill, 'Fashioning the Street', 192.

18 'Biography', *The Sartorialist*, available online, http://www.thesartorialist.com/biography/ (accessed February 13, 2014).

19 Anna Wintour in *Bill Cunningham New York,* a film by Richard Press, 2010.

20 *Humans of New York*, available online, www.humansofnewyork.com (accessed February 13, 2014).

21 *Hijabi Street Style*, available online, http://hijabistreetstyle.tumblr.com/ (accessed February 13, 2014). Dian Pelangi, *Hijab Street Style* (Jakarta: Penerbit, 2014).

22 Uché Okonkwo, *Luxury Fashion Branding: Trends, Tactics, Techniques* (New York: Palgrave Macmillan, 2007), 225.

23 See also, Jane Gaines and Charlotte Herzog (eds) *Fabrications: Costume and the Female Body* (New York and London: Routledge, 1990).

24 Ranked 29th on *TV Guide*'s 'Top Cult Shows Ever' list in 2007. 'Top Cult Shows Ever', *TV Guide*, available online, http://www.tvguide.com/news/top-cult-shows-40239.aspx (accessed February 6, 2014). 'Ab Fab' was revived in 2001–2004, and in 2011–2012, latterly to coincide with the London Olympics, featuring the same cast, who while older, remained just as fashion-fixated. 2016 saw the release of *Absolutely Fabulous: The Movie*.

25 Tamara Mellon, *In My Shoes* (New York: Portfolio/Penguin, 2013), 64.

26 Its appearance was initiated by Candace Bushnell having visited the Jimmy Choo shop in London's Motcomb Street and fallen in love with the product. The brand went on to be mentioned on the show thirty four times in total. Mellon, *In My Shoes*, 64.

27 Church Gibson, *Fashion and Celebrity Culture*, 107.

28 On January 14, 2014, The Metropolitan Museum of Art announced that it would designate the Costume Institute's refurbished space, to be opened in the Spring, the Anna Wintour Costume Center, in recognition of her advocacy and fund-raising towards the space. Much of the $125 million raised had come from the annual Costume Institute Benefit, which she co-organized. 'Metropolitan Museum to Designate Renovated Costume Institute the Anna Wintour Costume Center', *The Metropolitan Museum of Art*, available online, http://www.metmuseum.org/aboutthe-museum/press-room/news/2014/anna-wintour-costume-center (accessed January 24, 2014).

29 Jerry Oppenheimer, *Front Row: Anna Wintour, the Cool Life and Hot Times of Vogue's Editor-in-Chief* (New York: St Martin's Press, 2005), 363.

30 For example, New York-based Martha Stewart, fashion designer Isaac Mizrahi, and fashion celebrity Tim Gunn played themselves on *Ugly Betty.*

31 Tim Gunn and Kate Moloney, *Tim Gunn: A Guide to Quality, Taste & Style* (New York: Harry N. Abrams, Inc., 2007).

32 Fashion journalist Vanessa Friedman noted likewise how Tyra Banks, host of the TV show *America's Next Top Model* (2003–2015) gained much more notoriety than the winners of the show's competitions, and how the show itself shaped viewers perception of the fashion industry.Vanessa Friedman, '"America's Next Top Model," Deconstructed', *The New York Times*, December 16, 2015, 14.

33 'Sex and the City Tour', *CitySights*, available online, http://www.citysightsny.com/tourpage.php?ref=cj&item=SCT&gclid=COSm0OL2wbwCFXNp7Aod71EAkQ (accessed February 10, 2014).

34 See Adam Hart, 'A neighbourhood Renewal in Dalston, Hackney: Towards a form of Partnership for Inner City Regeneration', *Journal of Retail and Leisure Property* 3, no. 1 (2003): 237–245; Michael Moran, 'Regional Trends. The Central London Retail Property Market: A Fresh Perspective', *Journal of Retail and Leisure Property* 5, no. 1 (2005): 78–89.

35 'East London Shopping', *TimeOut London*, available online, http://www.timeout.com/london/shopping/east-london-shopping (accessed January 17, 2016).

36 Angela McRobbie, 'Notes on What Not to Wear and Post-feminist Symbolic Violence', in *Feminism After Bourdieu*, ed. Lisa Adkins and Beverly Skeggs (Oxford: Blackwell, 2004), 1.

37 Church Gibson, *Fashion and Celebrity Culture*, 148. (By the end of the show's run Trinny and Susannah had been replaced by co-hosts Lisa Butcher and Mica Paris.)

38 Daughter of celebrities Ozzy and Sharon Osbourne, and stars of their own family soap opera, *The Osbournes*.

39 Okonkwo, *Luxury Fashion Branding*, 36.

40 The name for the British branch of the U.S. T.J.Maxx.

41 Church Gibson, *Fashion and Celebrity Culture*, 148.

42 'Sarah Jessica Parker to Launch Low-End Clothing Line', *Sarah J Parker*, available online, http://sarahjparker.hollywood.com/press/sarah-jessica-parker-to-launch-low-end-clothing-line/ (accessed February 10, 2014).

43 Tasha Lewis and Natalie Gray, 'The Maturation of Hip-Hop's Menswear Brands: Outfitting the Urban Consumer', *Fashion Practice: The Journal of Design, Creative Process and the Fashion Industry* 5, no. 2 (2013): 231.

44 *Black Style Now*, Museum of the City of New York, 2006. Exhibition text, 231.

45 Van Dyk Lewis, 'Dilemmas in African Diaspora Fashion', *Fashion Theory: The Journal of Dress, Body and Culture* 7, no. 2 (2003), 164.

46 Listed in detail by ibid., 167–169.

47 Emil Wilbekin, 'Great Aspirations: Hip Hop and Fashion Dress for Excess', in *The Vibe History of Hip Hop*, ed. Alan Light (New York: Three Rivers Press, 1999), 278.

48 Ibid., 279.

49 Ibid., 282.

50 Ibid.

51 'Fubu History', *Funding Universe*, available online, http://www.fundinguniverse.com/company-histories/fubu-history/ (accessed January 22, 2014).

52 Wilbekin, 'Great Aspirations', 283.

53 *Black Style Now*, 58–59.

54 Ibid., 62.

55 Lewis and Gray, 'The Maturation of Hip-Hop's Menswear Brands', 233.

56 Ibid., 234.

57 Ibid., 238–239.

58 Van Dyk Lewis, 'Hip-Hop Fashion', in *Encyclopedia of Clothing and Fashion*, Vol. II, ed. Valerie Steele (New York: Thomson Gale, 2005), 217.

59 See, for example, Mark Greif, Kathleen Ross and Dayna Tortorici (eds), *What was the Hipster: A Sociological Investigation* (New York: n+1 Foundation, 2010).

60 John B. Manbeck (ed.), *The Neighborhoods of Brooklyn* (New Haven and London: Yale University Press, 1998), 211.

61 A 'classic' American beer since the mid-nineteenth century that had been undergoing a sales slump before being adopted by Hipsters, raising its profile and its sales.

62 Mark Greif, 'Positions', in *What was the Hipster?*, ed. Grief et al., 9.

63 Norman Mailer, 'The White Negro', *Dissent (Fall 1957)*, available online, http://www.dissentmagazine.org/online_articles/the-white-negro-fall-1957 (accessed February 13, 2014).

64 Mark Greif, 'What was the Hipster?' *The New York Times*, 24 October 2010, available online, http://nymag.com/news/features/69129/ (accessed February 6, 2014).

65 Greif, 'Positions', 12.

66 Ibid.

67 Namely, Anthropologie, Free People, Terrain and BHLDN.

68 Grief et al. *What was the Hipster?*, 43.

69 Robert Lanham, *The Hipster Handbook* (New York: Anchor Books, 2002), 68.

70 Ibid., 6.

71 'Are You a British Hipster?' *Go To Quiz*, available online, http://www.gotoquiz.com/are_you_a_british_hipster/ (accessed December 1, 2015).

72 Grief et al., *What was the Hipster?*, 81.

73 Karen von Hahn, 'Mama, Don't Take My Polaroid Away', *Globe and Mail*, 5 September 2009, L3.

74 'How to Spot a Chav', *Mirror*, available online, http://www.mirror.co.uk/news/world-news/how-to-spot-a-chav-1597537 (accessed January 17, 2016).

75 'Chav', *Oxford Dictionaries*, available online, http://www.oxforddictionaries.com/definition/english/chav (accessed January 17, 2016).

76 Mia Wallace and Clint Spanner, *Chav! A User's Guide to Britain's New Ruling Class* (London: Bantam, 2004), 29; 91.

77 Roger B. Mason and Gemma Wigley, 'The "Chav" Subculture: Branded Clothing as an Extension of the Self', *Journal of Economics and Behavioral Studies* 5, no. 3 (2013), 175–176.

78 Catherine Ostler, 'As Romeo Beckham Stars in their New Ad, How Burberry Went from Chic to Chav to Chic again', *Daily Mail*, November 5, 2014, available online, http://www.dailymail.co.uk/femail/article-2822546/As-Romeo-Beckham-stars-new-ad-Burberry-went-chic-chav-chic-again.html (accessed January 18, 2016).

79 Ibid.

80 Ten year old Romeo Beckham modelled Burberry's 2013 spring/summer range. Romeo is the son of England footballer, David Beckham and designer Victoria Beckham, (formerly 'Posh Spice' of the Spice Girls).

81 Jeff Chu, 'Cheap, Chic, and Made for All: How Uniqlo Plans to take Over Casual Fashion', *Fast Company*, available online, http://www.fastcompany.com/1839302/cheap-chic-and-made-all-how-uniqlo-plans-take-over-casual-fashion (accessed December 1, 2015).

82 Richard Benson, 'Normcore: How a Spoof Marketing Term Grew Into a Fashion Phenomenon', *The Guardian,* December 17, 2014, available online, http://www.theguardian.com/fashion/2014/dec/17/normcore-spoof-marketing-term-fashion-phenomenon (accessed December 1, 2015).

83 Fiona Duncan, 'Normcore: Fashion for Those Who Realize They're One in 7 Billion', *The Cut,* February 26, 2014, available online, http://nymag.com/thecut/2014/02/normcore-fashion-trend.html (accessed December 1, 2015).

84 Benson, 'Normcore'.

85 Duncan, 'Normcore'.

86 Ibid.

87 Lipovetsky, *The Empire of Fashion*, 127.

88 Okonkwo, *Luxury Fashion Branding*, 225–56.

89 Ibid., 227.

90 'Isaac Mizrahi', *Vogue*, available online, http://www.vogue.com/voguepedia/Isaac_Mizrahi (accessed January 28, 2016).

91 Ibid.

92 'Banana Republic Opens First British Store', *The Telegraph*, March 20, 2008, available online, http://www.telegraph.co.uk/news/uknews/1582259/Banana-Republic-opens-first-British-store.html (accessed December 3, 2015).

93 'Raymond Burton Obituary', *The Guardian*, March 15, 2011, available online, http://www.theguardian.com/lifeandstyle/2011/mar/15/raymond-burton-obituary (accessed December 3, 2015).

94 Sonia Ashmore, '"I think they're all mad": Shopping in Swinging London', in *Swinging Sixties*, ed. Breward et al., 73.

95 Cat Callender, 'Jane Shepherdson: From Oxford to Oxfam', *The Telegraph*, May 11, 2008, available online, http://fashion.telegraph.co.uk/article/TMG3364886/Jane-Shepherdson-from-Topshop-to-Oxfam.html (accessed December 3, 2015).

96 Polly Vernon, 'Jane Shepherdson', *The Guardian*, March 8, 2008, available online, http://www.theguardian.com/lifeandstyle/2008/mar/09/fashion.women2 (accessed December 3, 2015).

97 Sir Philip Green, 'Topshop Bites Into the Big Apple', *The Guardian*, April 2, 2009, available online, http://www.theguardian.com/business/2009/apr/02/top-shop-opens-in-new-york (accessed December 3, 2015).

98 David Moin, 'Topshop Lands in New York', *WWD*, March 31, 2009, available online, http://wwd.com/globe-news/retail-features/topshop-lands-in-new-york-2087669/ (accessed December 3, 2015).

99 'Banana Republic Opens First British Store'.

100 'Banana Republic Launches First-Ever 'Mad Men' Series-Inspired Collection in Collaboration with AMC and 'Mad Men' Costume Designer Janie Bryant', *Gap Inc.*, Press Release, June 22, 2011, available online, http://www.gapinc.com/content/

gapinc/html/media/pressrelease/2011/med_pr_Banana_Republic_Mad_Men_Collection.html (accessed December 3, 2015).

101 Nadira Lamrad and Mary Hanlon, 'Untangling Fashion for Development', *Fashion Theory: The Journal of Dress, Body and Culture* 18, no. 5 (2014), 610.

102 Ibid., 618.

103 Jonathan Owen, 'Bangladeshi Factory Collapse: Clothing companies fail to pay into Rana Plaza fund that provides compensation for victims of 2013 disaster', *Independent*, April 18, 2015, available online, http://www.independent.co.uk/news/world/asia/bangladeshi-factory-collapse-clothing-companies-fail-to-pay-into-rana-plaza-fund-that-provides-10187129.html (accessed December 4, 2015).

104 Hazel Clark, 'Slow + Fashion – an Oxymoron – or a Promise for the Future …?' *Fashion Theory: The Journal of Dress, Body and Culture* 12, no. 4 (2008), 427–46

105 Sophie Woodward, *Why Women Wear What They Wear* (Oxford & New York: Berg, 2007).

106 Emily Spivak, *Worn Stories* (New York: Princeton Architectural Press, 2014); Sheila Heti, Heidi Julavits and Leanne Shapton, *Women in Clothes* (New York: Blue Rider Press/Penguin, 2014).

107 Ellie Pithers, 'Lessons from the stylish: Eileen Fisher, 63, designer', *Telegraph*, January 4, 2014, available online, http://fashion.telegraph.co.uk/columns/ellie-pithers/TMG10548575/Lessons-from-the-stylish-Eileen-Fisher-63-designer.html (accessed December 4, 2015).

108 Ibid.

109 Emily Norval, 'The Drapers Interview: Eileen Fisher', *Drapers Online*, October 5, 2013, available online, http://www.drapersonline.com/the-drapers-interview-eileen-fisher/5053587.fullarticle (accessed December 3, 2015).

110 Ibid.

111 See, for example, David Balzer, *Curationism: How Curation Took Over the Art World and Everything Else* (London: Pluto Press, 2015).

112 David Balzer, 'Reading Lists, Outfits, Even Salads are Curated – It's Absurd', *The Guardian*, April 18, 2015, available online, http://www.theguardian.com/books/2015/apr/18/david-balzer-curation-social-media-kanye-west (accessed December 4, 2015).

113 Carol Vogel, 'Watch Out, Warhol, Here's Japanese Shock Pop', *The New York Times,* April 2, 2008, available online, http://www.nytimes.com/2008/04/02/arts/design/02mura.html?pagewanted=all (accessed March 20, 2014).

114 Ibid.

115 A. Roderick, 'Takashi Murakami Exhibit, Brooklyn Museum', posting on *Yelp*, April 6, 2008 http://www.yelp.com/biz/takashi-murakami-exhibit-brooklyn-museum-brooklyn?hrid=5o_aS7rXUsQRksdIAenztQ&rh_ident=louis%20vuitton (accessed March 20, 2014).

116 Julia Petrov, 'Exhibition Review: The Fashion Galleries (Room 40) at the V&A', *The Costume Society*, available online, http://costumesociety.org.uk/journal/exhibition-review-fashion-galleries-vanda (accessed January 24, 2014).

117 Agnes Rocamora, 'Personal Fashion Blogs: Screens and Mirrors in Digital Self-Portraits', *Fashion Theory: The Journal of Dress, Body and Culture* 15, no. 4 (2011), 408.

118 Ibid., 409.

119 Which, Rocamora cites as *nogoodforme*, on Rocamora, 'Personal Fashion Blogs', 409.

120 Sherry Turkle, *Life on the Screen: Identity in the Age of the Internet* (New York: Simon and Schuster, 1995), 180.

121 Chappell Ellison, 'The Shopping Haul Phenomenon', *The Etsy Blog,* 18 August 2011, available online, https://blog.etsy.com/en/2011/the-shopping-haul-phenomenon/ (accessed March 21, 2014).

122 Ari Seth Cohen, *Advanced Style* (Brooklyn, NY: PowerHouse Books, 2012).

123 Julia Twigg, *Fashion and Age: Dress, the Body and Later Life* (London and New York: Bloomsbury, 2013), 47.

124 'Brooklyn Style Watch', *Brooklyn Museum of Art,* December 5, 2013.

125 A. McRobbie, *British Fashion Design. Rag Trade or Image Industry?* (London, Routledge, 1998), 10–11.

126 Greg Seigworth and Michael E. Gardiner, 'Rethinking Everyday Life: And Then Nothing Turned Itself Inside Out', *Cultural Studies* 18, no. 2/3 (2004), 153.

127 Barry Sandywell, 'The Myth of Everyday Life: Toward a Heterology of the Ordinary', *Cultural Studies* 18, no. 2/3 (2004): 162.

128 Ibid.

129 Ibid., 161.

BIBLIOGRAPHY

Abel, R., Bertellini, G., and King, R. (eds), *Early Cinema and the 'National'*, Bloomington, IN: Indiana University Press, 2008.

Abelson, E.S., *When ladies Go A-Thieving: Middle-Class Shoplifters in the Victorian Department Store*, New York: Oxford University Press, 1989.

Abercrombie, N., and Longhurst, B.J., *Audiences*, London: Sage, 1998.

Adkins, L., and Skeggs, B. (eds), *Feminism After Bourdieu*, Oxford: Blackwell, 2004.

Agnew, J.-C., *Worlds Apart: The Market and the Theater in Anglo-American Thought 1550–1750*, Cambridge and New York: Cambridge University Press, 1986.

Alexander, S., *Becoming a Woman in London and Other Essays in 19th and 20th Century Feminist History*, London: Virago, 1994.

Apfel, B.I., *Dragon Threads: Court Costumes of the Celestial Kingdom: Chinese Textiles from the Iris Barrel Apfel and ATTATA Foundation Collections*, Newark, NJ: Newark Museum, 1992.

Arnold, P., and White, P., *Clothes and Cloth: America's Apparel Business*, New York: Holiday House, 1961.

Arnold, R., *The American Look: Fashion, Sportswear and the Image of Women in the 1930s and 1940s in New York*, London and New York: I.B. Tauris, 2009.

Ash, J., and Wilson, E. (eds), *Chic Thrills*, Oakland: University of California Press, 1992.

Ash, J. and Wright, L. (eds), *Components of Dress: Design, Manufacturing, and Image-Making in the Fashion Industry*, London and New York: Comedia (Routledge), 1988.

Attfield, J. (ed), *Utility Reassessed: The Role of Ethics in the Practice of Design*, Manchester: Manchester University Press, 1999.

Attfield, J., *Wild Things: The Material Culture of Everyday Life*, Oxford and New York: Berg, 2000.

Balzer, D., *Curationism: How Curation Took Over the Art World and Everything Else*, London: Pluto Press, 2015.

Banner, L.W., *American Beauty*, New York: Knopf, 1983.

Barnes, R., *Mods!* London: Plexus, 1979.

Basinger, J., *A Woman's View: How Hollywood Spoke to Women, 1930–1960*, Hanover, NH: Wesleyan University Press, 1993.

Baudelaire, C., *Baudelaire: Selected Writings on Art and Artists*, translated by P.S. Charvet, Cambridge, MA: Cambridge University Press, 1972.

Beckerman, I., *Love, Loss and What I Wore*, Chapel Hill, NC: Algonquin Books, 1995.

Beckett, J., and Cherry, D. (eds). *The Edwardian Era*, Oxford: Phaidon Press and the Barbican Art Gallery, 1987.

Beddoe, D., *Back to Home & Duty: Women between the Wars 1918–1939*, London: Pandora, 1989.

Belton, J., *Movies and Mass Culture*, New Brunswick, NJ: Rutgers University Press, 1996.

Bender, M., *The Beautiful People*, New York: Coward-McCann, 1967.

Benjamin, W., *The Arcades Project*, Cambridge, MA: Harvard University Press, 2002.

Benson, S.P., *Counter Cultures: Saleswomen, Managers and Customers in American Department Stores, 1890–1940*, Urbana and Chicago: University of Illinois Press, 1987.

Benstock, S., and Ferriss, S., (eds), *On Fashion*, New Brunswick, NJ: Rutgers University Press, 1994.

Berch, B., *Radical by Design: The Life and Style of Elizabeth Hawes, Fashion Designer, Union Organizer, Best-Selling Author*, New York: E.P. Dutton, 1988.

Berry, S., *Screen Styles: Fashion and Femininity in 1930s Hollywood*, Minneapolis: University of Minneapolis Press, 2000.

Birmingham, N.T., *Store: A Memoir of America's Great Department Stores*, New York: G.P. Putnam's Sons, 1978.

Bivins, J.L., and Adams, R.K., (eds), *Inspiring Beauty: 50 Years of Ebony Fashion Fair*, Chicago: Chicago History Museum, 2013.

Black, G., *Living up West: Jewish Life in London's West End*, London: London Museum of Jewish Life, 1994.

Blake, A.M., *How New York Became American, 1890–1924*, Baltimore: Johns Hopkins University Press, 2006.

Bliss, H.E., *Intimate Studies in the Lives of Fifty Working Girls*, New York: Columbia University, Archive.org and Project Gutenberg, 1915.

Blum, S.(ed). *Everyday Fashions of the Thirties: As Pictured in Sears Catalogs*, New York: Dover Publications, 1981.

Bolton, A., *The Supermodern Wardrobe*, London: V&A and New York: Harry Abrams, 2002.

Boorstin, D.J., *The Americans: The Democratic Experience*, New York: Random House, 1973.

Boorstin, D.J., *Portraits from the Americans – the Democratic Experience*: An Exhibition at the National Portrait Gallery, New York: Random House, 1975.

Booth, C., *Poverty, Vol. 4: The Trades of East London Connected with Poverty, Life and Labour of the People of London, 1st series*, London and New York: Macmillan & Co. Ltd., 1902.

Bowlby, R., *Just Looking: Consumer Culture in Dreiser, Gissing and Zola*, New York and London: Methuen, 1985.

Bowman, E., and Koda, H., *Rare Bird of Fashion: The Irreverent Iris Apfel*, New York: Thames and Hudson, 2007.

Boyer, M.C., *Manhattan Manners: Architecture and Style, 1850–1900*, New York: Rizzoli, 1985.

Breton, A., *What Is Surrealism?* London: Pluto Press, 1981.

Breward, C., *The Culture of Fashion*, Manchester: Manchester University Press, 1995.

Breward, C., *The Hidden Consumer: Masculinities, Fashion and City Life 1860–1914*, Manchester: Manchester University Press, 1999.

Breward, C., *Fashioning London: Clothing and the Modern Metropolis*, Oxford and New York: Berg, 2004.

Breward, C., Conekin, B., and Cox, C. (eds), *The Englishness of English Dress*, London: Penguin, 2002.

Breward, C., Ehrman, E., and Evans, C. (eds), *The London Look: Fashion from Street to Catwalk*, New Haven and London: Yale University Press with Museum of London, 2004.

Breward, C., and Evans, C., (eds), *Fashion and Modernity*, Oxford and New York: Berg, 2005.

Breward, C., and Gilbert, D., (eds), *Fashion's World Cities*, Oxford and New York: Berg, 2006.

Breward, C., Gilbert, D., and Lister, J. (eds), *Swinging Sixties: Fashion in London and beyond 1955–1970*, London: V&A Publications, 2006.

Briggs, Asa., *Go To It: Working for Victory on the Home Front, 1939–1945*, London: Imperial War Museum/Mitchell Beazley, 2000.

Brown, D.M., *Setting a Course: American Women in the 1920s*, Boston: Twayne Publishers, 1987.

Brown, J., *I Had a Pitch on the Stones*, London: Nicholson & Watson, 1946.

Brown, M.P., *Closet Space: Geographies of Metaphor from the Body to the Globe*, New York: Routledge, 2000.

Bruzzi, S., and Church Gibson, P. (eds), *Fashion Cultures: Theories, Explorations and Analysis*, London: Routledge, 2000.

Buckley, C., *Designing Modern Britain*, London: Reaktion Books, 2007.

Buckley, C., and Fawcett, H., *Fashioning the Feminine: Representation and Women's Fashion from the Fin de Siècle to the Present*, London: I.B.Tauris, 2002.

Burke, W., *London in My Time*, New York: Loring & Mussey, 1934.

Burman, B. (ed), *The Culture of Sewing: Gender, Consumption and Home Dressmaking*, New York and Oxford: Berg, 1999.

Burman Baines, B., *Fashion Revivals from the Elizabethan Age to the Present Day*, London: Batsford Ltd, 1981.

Butler, J., *Gender Trouble: Feminism and the Subversion of Identity*, New York: Routledge, 1990.

Cahan, A., *The Rise of David Levinsky*, 1917. Reprint, New York: Penguin, 1993.

Chang, J., *Can't Stop Won't Stop: A History of the Hip-Hop Generation*, New York: St. Martin's Press, 2006.

Chapman, R., and Rutherford, J. (eds), *Male Order: Unwrapping Masculinity*, London: Lawrence and Wishart, 1998.

Charney, L., and Schwartz, V. (eds), *Cinema and the Invention of Modern Life*, Berkeley, CA: University of California Press, 1995.

Church Gibson, P., *Fashion and Celebrity Culture*, London and New York: Berg, 2012.

Clark, H., and Brody, D. (eds), *Design Studies: A Reader*, Oxford and New York: Berg, 2009.

Cohan, S., *Masked Men: Masculinity and the Movies in the Fifties*, Bloomington, IN: University of Indiana Press, 1997.

Cohen, A.S., *Advanced Style*, Brooklyn, NY: PowerHouse Books, 2012.

Cole, S., *Now We Don Our Gay Apparel: Gay Men's Dress in the Twentieth Century*, Oxford and New York: Berg, 2000.

Cook, P., *Fashioning the Nation: Costume and Identity in British Cinema*, London: British Film Institute, 1996.

Craik, J., *The Face of Fashion: Cultural Studies in Fashion*, London: Routledge, 2004.

Crawford, M.de C., *The Ways of Fashion*, New York: Fairchild, 1948.

Cunningham, M., and Marberry, C., *Crowns: Portraits of Black Women in Church Hats*, New York: Doubleday, 2000.

Currid, E., *The Warhol Economy: How Fashion and Music Drive New York City*, Princeton: Princeton University Press, 2007.

Daves, J., *Ready-Made Miracle*, New York: G.P. Putnam's Sons, 1967.

Davis, C., *We Too Shall Wear a Crown: Honoring and Celebrating the Legacy and Tradition of African-American Women Who Wear Hats to Church*, Bloomington, IN: Authorhouse, 2005.

Davis, D.A., *History of Shopping*, London: Routledge & Keegan Paul, 1966.

De Beauvoir, S., *The Second Sex*, 1949. Reprinted, London: Penguin, 1981.

De Certeau, M., Giard, L., and Mayol, P., *The Practice of Everyday Life*, vol. 2, Minneapolis and London: University of Minnesota Press, 1988.

Douglas, A., *The Feminization of American Culture*, New York: Avon Books, 1978.

Dreiser, T., *Sister Carrie*, Clementine Classics, 1900. Reprint, New York: Black Balloon Publishing, 2013.

Dresser, D. and Jowett G.S., (eds), *Hollywood Goes Shopping*, Minneapolis: University of Minnesota Press, 2000.

Duberman, M., *Stonewall*, New York: Dutton, 1993.

Dunseath, K. and Atwood M., (eds), *A Second Skin: Women Write About Clothes*, London: Women's Press, 1998.

Dyhouse, C., *Glamour: Women, History and Feminism*, London and New York: Zed Books, 2011.

Edwards, T., *Men in the Mirror: Men's Fashion, Masculinity, and Consumer Society*, London: Cassell, 1997.

Edwards, T., *Cultures of Masculinity*, London: Routledge, 2006.

Eicher, J. (ed), *Encyclopedia of World Dress and Fashion*, New York: Oxford University Press, 2010.

Ellison, R., *The Invisible Man*, 1952. Reprinted, New York: Vintage Books, 1995.

Emery, J.S., *A History of the Paper Pattern Industry: The Home Dressmaking Fashion Revolution*, London: Bloomsbury, 2014.

Enstad, N., *Ladies of Labor, Girls of Adventure: Working Women, Popular Culture, and Labor Politics at the Turn of the Twentieth Century*, New York: Columbia University Press, 1999.

Entwistle, J., *The Fashioned Body: Fashion, Dress, and Modern Social Theory*, Cambridge, MA: Polity Press, 2000.

Entwistle, J., *The Aesthetic Economy of Fashion: Markets and Values in Clothing and Modelling*, Oxford and New York: Berg, 2009.

Erenberg, L., *Steppin' Out: New York Nightlife and the Transformation of American Culture, 1890–1930*, Westport: Greenwood Press, 1981.

Evans, C., *Fashion at the Edge: Spectacle, Modernity, and Deathliness*, New Haven, IL: Yale University Press, 2003.

Evans, C., and Thornton, M., *Women and Fashion: A New Look*, London and New York: Quartet Books, 1989.

Ewen, E., *Immigrant Women in the Land of Dollars: Life and Culture on the Lower East Side*, New York: Monthly Review Press, 1985.

Ewing, E., *History of 20th Century Fashion*, London: Batsford, 1989.

Farrell-Beck, J., and Parsons, J., *20th-Century Dress in the United States*, New York: Fairchild, 2007.

Ferguson, M., *Forever Feminine: Women's Magazines and the Cult of Femininity*, London: Heinemann, 1983.

Fine, B., and Leopold, E., *The World of Consumption*, London and New York: Routledge, 1993.

Fisher, R., *The Walls of Jericho*, 1928. Reprinted, Ann Arbor: Ann Arbor paperbacks, University of Michigan Press.

Fiske, J., *Understanding Popular Culture*, London and New York: Routledge, 1989.

Fogarty, A., *Wife Dressing: The Fine Art of Being a Well-Dressed Wife*, New York: Julian Messer, 1959.

Francis, M., *The Flyer: British Culture and the Royal Air Force, 1939–1945*, Oxford and New York: Oxford University Press, 2008.

Freidan, B., *The Feminine Mystique*, New York: Norton, 1963.

Friedberg, A., *Window Shopping: Cinema and the Postmodern*, Berkeley and Los Angeles: University of California Press, 1993.

Fuller, K.H., *At the Picture Show*, Washington, DC: Smithsonian Institution Press, 1996.

Gaines, J., and Herzog, C. (eds), *Fabrications: Costume and the Female Body*, London: Routledge,1990.

Gamber, W., *The Female Economy: The Millinery and Dressmaking Trades, 1860–1930*, Urbana: University of Illinois Press, 1997.

Geczy, A., and Karaminas, V., *Queer Style*, London, New Delhi, New York and Sydney: Bloomsbury, 2013.

Giddens, A., *Modernity and Self-Identity: Self and Society in the Late Modern Age*, Cambridge: Polity Press, 1991.

Gill, J., *Harlem: The Four Hundred Year History from Dutch Village to Capital of Black America*, New York: Grove Press, 2011.

Gilroy, P., *There Ain't No Black in the Union Jack. The Cultural Politics of Race and Nation*, London: Unwin Hyman, 1987.

Gilroy, P., *The Black Atlantic: Modernity and Double Consciousness*, London: Verso, 1993.

Gledhill, C. (ed), *Stardom: Industry of Desire*, London and New York: Routledge, 1991.

Glenn, S.A., *Daughters of the Shtetl: Life and Labor in the Immigrant Generation*, Ithaca, NY: Cornell University Press, 1990.

Goffman, E., *The Presentation of Self in Everyday Life*, London: Penguin, 1971.

Goldstein, G.M., and Greenberg E.E. (eds), *A Perfect Fit: The Garment Industry and American Jewry, 1860–1960*, Lubbock, TX: Texas Tech University Press, 2012.

Gough-Yates, A., *Understanding Women's Magazines: Publishing, Markets and Readership*, London: Routledge, 2003.

Gray, G.T., *Cinema: A Visual Anthropology*, Oxford and New York: Berg, 2010.

Green, J., *All Dressed Up: The Sixties and the Counterculture*, London: Pimlico, 1999.

Green, N.L., *Ready-to-Wear and Ready-to-Work: A Century of Industry and Immigrants in Paris and New York*, Durham: Duke University Press, 1997.

Greer, G., *The Female Eunuch*, London: Paladin, 1971.

Greif, M., Ross, K., and Tortorici, D. (eds), *What Was the Hipster: A Sociological Investigation*, New York: n+1 Foundation, 2010.

Grippo, R.M., *Macy's: The Store, The Star, The Story*, New York: Square One Publishers, 2009.

Grossberg, L., Nelson, C., Treichler, P.A. (eds), *Cultural Studies*, Florence, KY: Taylor & Francis, 1991.

Gudis, C., *Buyways: Billboards, Automobiles, and the American Landscape*, New York: Routledge, 2004.

Gunn, T., and Moloney, K., *Tim Gunn: A Guide to Quality, Taste & Style*, New York: Harry N. Abrams, Inc., 2007.

Habermas, J., *The Structural Transformation of the Public Sphere*, 1962. Reprinted, Cambridge: MIT Press, 1989.

Haley, A., and Malcolm X., *The Autobiography of Malcolm X*, New York: Ballantine Books, 1964.

Hall, S., and Jefferson, T. (eds), *Resistance through Rituals: Youth Subcultures in Post-War Britain*, New York: Routledge, 2005.

Harvey, J., *Men in Black*, London: Reaktion, 1995.

Haskins, J., *Black Dance in America: A History through Its People*, New York: Harper Collins, 1990.

Hawes, E., *Fashion Is Spinach*, New York: Random House, 1938.

Hawes, E., *It's Still Spinach*, Boston: Little Brown, 1954.

Hebdige, D., *Subculture: The Meaning of Style*, London: Methuen, 1979.

Heinze A.R., *Adapting to Abundance: Jewish Immigrants, Mass Consumption, and the Search*, New York: Columbia University Press, 1990.

Hendrickson, R., *The Grand Emporium: The Illustrated History of America's Great Department Stores*, New York: Stern & Day, 1979.

Hepburn, K., *Me: Stories of My Life*, New York: Ballantine Books, 1991.

Heron, L. (ed), *Truth, Dare or Promise: Girls Growing up in the 50s*, London: Virago, 1985.

Heti, S., Julavits, H., and Shapton, L., *Women in Clothes*, New York: Blue Rider Press/ Penguin, 2014.

Highmore, B., *Everyday Life and Cultural Theory: An Introduction*, Abingdon and New York: Routledge, 2002.

Highmore, B. (ed), *The Everyday Life Reader*, London and New York: Routledge, 2002.

Highmore, B., *Cityscapes: Cultural Readings in the Material Culture and Symbolic City*, London: Palgrave Macmillan, 2005.

Holtby, W., *Women and a Changing Civilization*, London: John Lane, 1934.

hooks, b., *Black Looks: Race and Representation*, Boston, MA: South End Press, 1992.

hooks, b., *Feminist Theory: From Margin to Center*, 1984. Reprinted, London: Pluto Press, 2000.

Hopkins, H., *The New Look: A Social History of the Forties and Fifties*, London: Secker & Warburg, 1964.

Howell, G., *Wartime Fashion: From Haute Couture to Home-made, 1939–1941*, London and New York: Berg, 2012.

Hower, R.M., *History of Macy's of New York, 1858–1919*, Cambridge, MA: Harvard University Press, 1943.

Hulanicki, B., *From A to Biba*, London: Hutchinson & Co, 1983.

Huyssen, A., *After the Great Divide: Modernism, Mass Culture, Postmodernism*, Bloomington and Indianapolis: Indiana University Press, 1987.

Jackson, K.T. (ed), *The Encyclopedia of New York City*, 2nd edn. New Haven and London: Yale University Press, 2010.

Jacobs, J., *The Death and Life of the Great American City*, New York: Vintage Books, 1961.

Jaffe, R., *The Best of Everything*, New York: Simon and Schuster, 1958.

Jephcott, P., *Girls Growing Up*, London: Faber and Faber Ltd, 1942.

Jephcott, P., *Rising Twenty: Notes on Some Ordinary Girls*, London: Faber & Faber, 1948.

Jobling, P., *Advertising Menswear. Masculinity and Fashion the British Media since 1945*. Bloomsbury: London and New York, 2014.

Johnson, J.W., *Black Manhattan*, 1930. Reprinted, New York: Arno Press, 1991.

Johnson, K., *Sisters in Sin: Brothel Drama in America, 1900–1920*, Vol. 24. Cambridge, Cambridge University Press, 2006.

Johnston, L., (ed), *The Fashion Year*, Volume III. London: Zomba Books, 1985.

Joselit, J.W., *A Perfect Fit: Clothes, Character, and the Promise of America*, New York: Metropolitan Books, 2001.

Kaiser, S., *Fashion and Cultural Studies*, London and New York: Berg, 2012.

Kazin, A., *A Walker in the City*, New York: Harcourt Inc., 1951.

Kelley, R.D.G., *Race Rebels: Culture, Politics, and the Black Working Class*, New York: Free Press, 1994.

Kelly, K., *The Wonderful World of Women's Wear Daily*, New York: Saturday Review Press, 1972.

Kershen, A.J., *Off the Peg: The Story of the Women's Wholesale Clothing Industry 1880 to the 1960s*, London: The Jewish Museum, 1988.

Kidwell, C.B., and Christman, M.C., *Suiting Everyone: The Democratization of Clothing in America*, Washington, DC: Smithsonian Institution Press, 1974.

Kirkham, P. (ed), *The Gendered Object*, Manchester: Manchester University Press, 1996.

Kisseloff, J., *You Must Remember This: An Oral History of Manhattan from the 1890s to World War II*, Baltimore, MD: Johns Hopkins University Press, 1989.

Kitch, C.L., *The Girl on the Magazine Cover: The Origins of Visual Stereotypes in American Mass Media*, Chapel Hill and London: University of North Carolina Press, 2001.

Knott, J.J., *Music for the People: Popular Music and Dance in Interwar Britain*, Oxford: Oxford University Press, 2002.

Kyvig, D.E., *Daily Life in the United States, 1920–1940: How Americans Lived through the 'Roaring Twenties' and the Great Depression*, Chicago: Ivan R. Dee, 2004.

Lancaster, B., *The Department Store: A Social History*, London and New York: Leicester University Press, 1995.

Langhammer, C., *Women's Leisure in England, 1920–60*, Manchester: Manchester University Press, 2000.

Lanham, R., *The Hipster Handbook*, New York: Anchor Books, 2002.

Lankevich, G.J. *American Metropolis: A History of New York City*, New York: New York University Press, 1998.

Latham, A.J., *Posing a Threat: Flappers, Chorus Girls and Other Brazen Performers of the American 1920s*, Hanover, NH and London: Wesleyan University Press of New England, 2000.

Leach, W.R., *Land of Desire: Merchants, Power and the Rise of the New American Culture*, New York: Pantheon, 1993.

Leese, E., *Costume Design in the Movies: An Illustrated Guide to the Work of 157 Great Designers*, 1976, Reprinted, New York: Dover Publications Inc, 1991.

Leland, J., *Hip: The History*, Pymble, NSW and New York: HarperCollins, 2008.

Lewis, D.L., *When Harlem Was in Vogue*, New York: Penguin, 1997.

Ley, S., *Fashion for Everyone: The Story of Ready-to-Wear, 1870s-1970s*, New York: Charles Scribner's, 1975.

Lieberson S., *A Matter of Taste: How Names, Fashions, and Culture Change*, New Haven: Yale University Press, 2000.

Light, A., *The Vibe History of Hip Hop*, London: Plexus, 1999.

Lipovetsky, G., *The Empire of Fashion: Dressing Modern Democracy*, Princeton: Princeton University Press, 1994.

Longstreth, R.W., *The American Department Store Transformed, 1920–1960*, New Haven: Yale University Press, 2010.

Maeder, E., Annas, A., Lavalley S., and Jenssen, E. (eds), *History and Hollywood: Costume Design in Film*, London: Thames and Hudson and Los Angeles: Los Angeles Museum of Art, 1987.

Majer, M., (ed) *Staging Fashion, 1880–1920: Jane Hading, Lily Elsie, Billie Burke*, New Haven and London: Yale University Press and Bard Graduate Center, 2012.

Malnig, J. (ed) *Ballroom, Boogie, Shimmy Sham, Shake: A Social and Popular Dance Reader*, Chicago: University of Illinois Press, 2009.

Manbeck, J.B. (ed), *The Neighborhoods of Brooklyn*, New Haven and London: Yale University Press, 1998.

Marchand, R., *Advertising the American Dream: Making Way for Modernity, 1920–1940*, Berkeley, CA: University of California Press, 1985.

Masotti, L.H., and Hadden, J.K. (eds), *Suburbia in Transition*, New York: New Viewpoints, 1974.

Massey, A., *Hollywood beyond the Screen: Design and Material Culture*, Oxford: Berg, 2000.

Mast, G., *The Movies in Our Midst: Documents in the Cultural History of Film in America*, Chicago: University of Chicago Press, 1982.

Maynard, M., *Dress and Gobalisation*, Manchester: Manchester University Press, 2004.

McCardell, C., *What Shall I Wear? The What, Where, When and How Much of Fashion*, New York: Simon and Schuster, 1956.

McCracken, G., *Culture and Consumption*, Indianapolis: Indiana University Press, 1988.

McDowell, C., *Forties Fashion and the New Look*, London: Bloomsbury, 1997.

McLinkoff, E., *What We Wore: An Offbeat Social History of Women's Clothing 1950–1980*, New York: Quill, 1984.

McNeil, P., and Karaminas, V. (eds), *The Men's Fashion Reader*, Berg: London and New York, 2009.

McRobbie, A. (ed), *Zoot Suits and Second-Hand Dresses: An Anthology of Fashion and Music*, London: Macmillan, 1989.

McRobbie, A. *British Fashion Design. Rag Trade or Image Industry?*, London: Routledge, 1998.

Mellon, T., *In My Shoes*, New York: Portfolio/Penguin, 2013.

Miller, N., and Jensen, E., *Swingin' at the Savoy: The Memoir of a Jazz Dancer*, Philadelphia: Temple University Press, 1996.

Millet, K., *Sexual Politics*, London: Abacus, 1972.

Mitchell, J., *Woman's Estate*, London: Penguin, 1971.

Montgomery, M.E., *Displaying Women: Spectacles of Leisure in Edith Wharton's New York*, New York: Routledge, 1998.

Mowat, C.L., *Britain between the Wars, 1918–1940*, Cambridge: Cambridge University Press, 1955.

Muller, P.O., *Contemporary Suburban America*, Englewood Hills, NJ: Prentice-Hall, 1981.

Nasaw, D., *Going Out: The Rise and Fall of Public Amusements*, Cambridge, MA: Harvard University Press, 1999.

Nead, L., *Victorian Babylon: People, Streets and Images in Nineteenth-Century London*, New Haven and London: Yale University Press, 2000.

Nelson, C., and Grossberg, L. (eds), *In Marxism and the Interpretation of Culture*, London: Macmillan, 1988.

Nelson, G., *Hip Hop America*, New York: Viking, 1998.

Nord, D.E., *Walking the Victorian Streets: Women, Representation and the City*, New York: Cornell University Press, 1995.

O'Bryne, R., *Style City: How London Became a Fashion Capital*, London: Francis Lincoln Limited, 2009.

Okonkwo, U., *Luxury Fashion Branding: Trends, Tactics, Techniques*, New York: Palgrave Macmillan, 2007.

O'Neill, A., *London: After a Fashion*, London: Reaktion, 2007.

Oppenheimer, J., *Front Row: Anna Wintour, the Cool Life and Hot Times of Vogue's Editor-in-Chief*, New York: St Martin's Press, 2005.

Orbis, S., *The Princess of Wales Fashion Handbook*, London: Orbis, 1984.

Osgerby, B., *Playboys in Paradise: Masculinity, Youth and Leisure-Style in Modern America*, New York: Berg, 2001.

O'Shea, A., and Nava, M., (eds), *Modern Times: Reflections on a Century of English Modernity*, London and New York: Routledge, 1996.

Palladino, G., *Teenagers: An American History*, New York: Basic Books Inc, 1996.

Palmer, A., and Clark, H. (eds), *Old Clothes, New Looks: Second Hand Fashion*, Oxford and New York: Berg, 2005.

Parsons, D.L., *Streetwalking the Metropolis: Women, the City and Modernity*, Oxford: Oxford University Press, 2000.

Pasdermadjian, H., *The Department Store: Its Origins, Evolution and Economics*, London: Newman Books, 1954.

Paulicelli, E., and Clark, H. (eds), *The Fabric of Cultures: Fashion, Identity, and Globalization*, London: Routledge, 2009.

Peiss, K.L., *Cheap Amusements: Working Women and Leisure in Turn-of-the-Century New York*, Philadelphia: Temple University Press, 1986.

Peiss, K.L., *Hope in a Jar: The Making of America's Beauty Culture*, New York: Metropolitan Books, 1998.

Peiss, K.L., *Zoot Suit: The Enigmatic Career of an Extreme Style*, Philadelphia: University of Pennsylvania Press, 2011.

Pelangi, D., *Hijab Street Style*, Jakarta: Penerbit, 2014.

Perez, G.M., Burgos, A., and Guridy, F., *Beyond El Barrio: Everyday Life in Latina/o America*, New York: New York University Press, 2010.

Pevsner, N., *The Buildings of England: London, Volume 1, The Cities of London and Westminster*, London: Penguin, 1957.

Pink, S., *Doing Visual Ethnograpy: Images, Media and Representation in Research*, London and Thousand Oaks, CA: Sage, 2007.

Plath, S., *The Bell Jar*, 1971. Reprinted, New York: Harper Perennial, 2005,

Polan, B. (ed), *The Fashion Year*, London: Zomba Books, 1983.

Polhemus, T., *Street Style*, London: Thames and Hudson, 1994.

Porter, R., *London: A Social History*, London: Penguin, 2000.

Prichard, P.S., *Film Costume: An Annotated Bibliography*, Metuchen, NJ: The Scarecrow Press, 1981.

Priestley, J.B., *An English Journey*, London: Heinemann/Gollancz, 1934.

Priestley, J.B., *Our Nation's Heritage*, London: JM Dent and Sons Ltd, 1939.

Prosser, J., *Image-Based Research: A Sourcebook for Qualitative Researchers*, London and Bristol, PA: Falmer Press, 1998.

Quant, M., *Quant By Quant*, London: Pan Books, 1966.

Rees, G., *St Michael: A History of Marks and Spencer*, London: Pan Books Ltd, 1973.

Rees, H., *British Youth Culture*, London: The Conran Foundation, 1986.

Rennolds Milbank, C., *New York Fashion: The Evolution of American Style*, New York: Harry Abrams Inc., 1989.

Richards, J., *The Age of the Dream Palace: Cinema and Society in Britain 1930–1939*, London: Routledge & Kegan Paul, 1984.

Richardson, B.J., *The Woman Who Spends: A Study of Her Economic Functions*, Boston: Witcomb and Barrows, 1904.

Roche, D., *The Culture of Clothing: Dress and Fashion in the Ancien Regime*, Cambridge, MA: Cambridge University Press, 1994.

Rooks, N.M., *Ladies' Pages: African American Women's Magazines and the Culture That Made Them*, New Brunswick, NJ: Rutgers University Press, 2004.

Rose, G., *Doing Family Photography: The Domestic, the Public, and the Politics of Sentiment*, Farnham: Ashgate, 2010.

Ross, C., *Biba: The Label, The Lifestyle, The Look*, Newcastle upon Tyne: Tyne and Wear Museums, 1993.

Ross, C., *Twenties London: A City in the Jazz Age*, London: Museum of London, 2003.

Roth, H., *Call It Sleep*, New York: Robert O. Ballou, 1934.

Rowbotham, S., *Hidden From History*, London: Pluto Press, 1973.

Rowbotham, S., *Promise of a Dream. Remembering the Sixties*, London: Penguin, 2000.

Rowbotham, S., Segal, L., and Wainwright, H., *Beyond the Fragments: Feminism and the Making of Socialism*, London: Merlin Press, 1979.

Ruiz, V.L., *From Out of the Shadows: Mexican Women in Twentieth-Century America*, Oxford and New York: Oxford University Press, 1998.

Rydell, R.W., *All the World's a Fair: Visions of Empire at American International Expositions, 1876–1916*, Chicago: University of Chicago Press, 1984.

Samuel, R., *Theatres of Memory: Past and Present in Contemporary Culture*, London and New York: Verso, 1994.

Sanchez, G.J., *Becoming Mexican American: Ethnicity, Culture, and Identity in Chicano Los Angeles, 1900–1945*, New York: Oxford University Press, 1993.

Scaduto, A., *Bob Dylan*, 1972. Reprinted, New York: Helter Skelter Publishing, 2001.

Schoener, A., *New York: An Illustrated History of the People*, New York: W.W. Norton & Co, 1998.

Schor, J., *The Overspent American: Upscaling, Downshifting and the New Consumer*, New York: Basic Books, 1998.

Schorman, R., *Selling Style: Clothing and Social Change at the Turn of the Century*, Philadelphia: University of Pennsylvania Press, 2003.

Schreier, B.A., *Becoming American Women: Clothing and the Jewish Immigrant Experience, 1880–1920*, Chicago: Chicago Historical Society, 1994.

Schreir, S., *Hollywood Dressed and Undressed*, New York: Rizzoli International Inc, 1998.

Schrum, K., *Some Wore Bobby Sox. The Emergence of Teenage Culture, 1920–1945*, New York: Palgrave Macmillan, 2004.

Schweitzer, M., *When Broadway Was the Runway: Theater, Fashion, and American Culture*, Philadelphia: University of Pennsylvania Press, 2009.

Segal, L., *Making Trouble*, London: Serpent's Tail, Profile Books, 2007.

Severa, J.L., *Dressed for the Photographer: Ordinary Americans and Fashion, 1840–1900*, Kent, OH: Kent State University Press, 1995.

Sheppard, F., *London: A History*, Oxford: Oxford University Press, 1998.

Sheringham, M., *Everyday Life: Theories and Practices from Surrealism to the Present*, Oxford and New York: Oxford University Press, 2006.

Shinkle, E., *Fashion as Photograph: Viewing and Reviewing Images of Fashion*, London: I.B. Tauris, 2008.

Silverman, D., *Selling Culture: Bloomingdale's, Diana Vreeland, and the New Aristocracy of Taste in Reagan's America*, New York: Pantheon Books, 1986.

Simmel, G., *On Individuality and Social Forms: Selected Writings*, edited by Donald N. Levine. Chicago, IL: Chicago University Press, 1971.

Simmel, G., *La tragédie de la culture*, Paris: Rivages, 1988.

Sorkin, M. (ed), *Variations on a Theme Park: The New American City and the End of Public Space*, New York: Hill and Wang, 1992.

Spivak, E., *Worn Stories*, New York: Princeton Architectural Press, 2014.

Stacey, J., *Star Gazing: Hollywood Cinema and Female Spectatorship*, London and New York: Routledge, 2004.

Stanfill, S., *New York Fashion*, London: V&A Publications, 2007.

Stanley, L., *The Auto/Biographical I: The Theory and Practice of Feminist Auto/Biography*, Manchester: Manchester University Press, 1998.

Stansell, C., *American Moderns: Bohemian New York and the Creation of a New Century*, New York: Metropolitan Books, 2000.

Stead, C., *A Little Tea, a Little Chat*, London: Virago, 1945.

Stearns, M., and Stearns, J., *Jazz Dance: The Story of American Vernacular Dance*, New York: Da Capo, 1994.

Steedman, C., *Landscape for a Good Woman: Two Women's Lives*, London: Virago, 1986.

Steele, V. (ed), *Encyclopedia of Clothing and Fashion*, Volume II, New York: Thomson Gale, 2005.

Steele, V., *Daphne Guinness*, New Haven: Yale University Press, 2011.

Stern, R.A.M, et al. *New York 1930*, New York: Rizzoli, 1987.

Stokes, M. and Maltby, R. (eds), *American Movie Audiences: From the Turn of the Century to the Early Sound Era*, London: BFI Publishing, 1991.

Summers, J., *Fashion on the Ration: Style in the Second World War*, London: Profile Books in partnership with the Imperial War Museum, 2015.

Swartz, J.M., and Ryan, J. (eds), *Picturing Place*, London: I.B. Tauris, 2002.

Taylor, A.J.P., *English History, 1914–1945*, London: Penguin, 1983.

Taylor, L., *Mourning Dress: A Costume and Social History*, London: Allen and Unwin, 1983.

Taylor, M.J., *The Downtown Book: The New York Art Scene 1974–1984*, Princeton and Oxford: Princeton University Press, 2009.

Taylor, W.R., *In Pursuit of Gotham: Culture and Commerce in New York*, New York and Oxford: Oxford University Press, 1992.

Tedlow, R.S., *New and Improved: The Story of Mass Marketing in America*, New York: Basic Books, 1990.

Thompson, E.P., *The Making of the English Working Class*, London: Pelican, 1963.

Thornton, S., *Club Cultures: Music, Media and Subcultural Capital*, Middletown, CN: Wesleyan University Press, 1996.

Thorpe, M.F., *America at the Movies*, 1939. Reprinted, New York: Arno Press Inc., 1970.

Tinkler, P., *Constructing Girlhood: Popular Magazines for Girls Growing up in England, 1920–1950*, Washington, DC: Taylor & Francis, 1995.

Trachtenberg, A., *The Incorporation of American Culture and Society in the Gilded Age*, New York: Hill & Wang, 1982.

Tulloch, C. (ed), *Black Style*, London: V&A Publishing, 1995.

Tulloch. C. *The Birth of Cool: Style Narratives of the African Diaspora*, London and New York: Bloombury, 2016.

Turkle, S., *Life on the Screen: Identity in the Age of the Internet*, New York: Simon and Schuster, 1995.

Twigg, J., *Fashion and Age: Dress, the Body and Later Life*, London and New York: Bloomsbury, 2013.

Veblen, T.B., *The Theory of the Leisure Class*, London: Macmillan, 1899.

Vinken, B., *Fashion Zeitgeist: Trends and Cycles in the Fashion System*, Oxford and New York: Berg, 2005.

Walker, N.A., *Shaping Our Mothers' World: American Women's Magazines*, Jackson, MN: University Press of Mississippi, 2000.

Walkowitz, J.R., *City of Dreadful Delight: Narratives of Sexual Danger in Late-Victorian London*, London: Virago, 1992.

Walkowitz, J.R., *Nights Out: Life in Cosmopolitan London*, New Haven and London: Yale University Press, 2012.

Wallace, M., and Spanner, C., *Chav! A User's Guide to Britain's New Ruling Class*, London: Bantam, 2004.

Watson, S., *The Harlem Renaissance: Hub of African American Culture, 1920–1930*, New York: Pantheon Book, 1995.

Welters, L., and Cunningham, P. (eds), *A Twentieth-Century American Fashion*, Oxford and New York: Berg, 2005.

Wendt, L., and Kogan, H., *Give the Lady What She Wants! The Story of Marshall Field and Company*, Chicago: Rand McNally, 1952.

Westwood, S., and Williams, J., *Imagining Cities: Scripts, Signs, Memories*, London and New York: Routledge, 1997.

Whitaker, J., *Service and Style: How the American Department Store Fashioned the Middle Class*, New York: St Martin's Press, 2006.

White, C., *Women's Magazines, 1693–1968*, London: Michael Joseph, 1970.

White, E. (ed), *The Fashion Year, Volume Two*, London: Zomba Books, 1984.

White, J., *London in the Twentieth Century: A City and Its People*, London: Random House, 2008.

White, S., and White, G., *Stylin': African American Expressive Culture from Its Beginnings to the Zoot Suit*, Ithaca, NY and London: Cornell University Press, 1998.

Wickstrom, M., *Performing Consumers: Global Capitalism and Its Theatrical Seductions*, New York: Routledge, 2006.

Wilson, E., *Women and the Welfare State*, London and New York: Tavistock, 1977.

Wilson, E., *Only Halfway to Paradise. Women in Postwar Britain: 1945–1968*, London and New York: Tavistock, 1980.

Wilson, E., *Adorned in Dreams: Fashion and Modernity*, London: Virago, 1985.

Wilson, E., *The Sphinx in the City: Urban Life, the Control of Disorder, and Women*, Berkeley and Los Angeles: The University of California Press, 1992.

Wilson, E., and Taylor, L., *Through the Looking Glass: A History of Dress from 1860 to the Present Day*, London: BBC Books, 1989.

Wilson, M.G., *The American Women in Transition: The Urban Influence, 1870–1920*, Westport, CT: Greenwood Press, 1979.

Winder, E., *Pain, Parties, Work: Sylvia Plath in New York, Summer 1953*, New York: Harper Collins, 2013.

Winship, J., *Inside Women's Magazines*, London: Pandora Press, 1987.

Wolfe, T., *The Bonfire of the Vanities*, New York: Farrar, Strauss and Giroux, 1987.

Woodward, S., *Why Women Wear What They Wear*, Oxford and New York: Berg, 2007.

Worth, R., *Fashion for the People: A History of Clothing at Marks and Spencer*, Oxford and New York: Berg, 2007.

Wray, Margaret. *The Women's Outerwear Industry*, London: G. Duckworth, 1957.

York, P., *The Sloane Ranger Handbook: The First Guide to What Really Matters in Life*, London: Ebury Press, 1982.

Young, W.H., and Young, N.K., *The 1930s*, Westport, CT: Greenwood Press, 2002.

Zola, E., *Au bonheur des dames (The Ladies' Delight),* Penguin Classics, 1883. Reprinted, London: Penguin Group, 2001.

Zukin, S., *The Culture of Cities*, Cambridge, MA and Oxford: Blackwell, 1995.

Zukin, S., *Point of Purchase: How Shopping Changed American Culture*, New York and London: Routledge, 2005.

INDEX

Note: The letter 'f' and 'n' following locators refers to figures and notes.